D1598418

JESUS OF NAZARETH

JESUS OF NAZARETH

MESSAGE AND HISTORY

JOACHIM GNILKA

English translation by Siegfried S. Schatzmann
© 1997 by Hendrickson Publishers, Inc.
P. O. Box 3473
Peabody, Massachusetts 01961–3473
All rights reserved
Printed in the United States of America

ISBN 1–56563–164–1

First Printing—November 1997

Original edition: *Jesus von Nazaret: Botschaft und Geschichte.* © Verlag Herder, Freiburg im Breisgau, 1993.

Library of Congress Cataloging-in-Publication Data

Gnilka, Joachim, 1928–
    [Jesus von Nazaret.   English]
    Jesus of Nazareth: message and history   /   Joachim Gnilka;
translated by Siegfried S. Schatzmann.—1st English ed.
    Includes bibliographical references and indexes.
    ISBN 1–56563–164–1 (cloth)
    1. Jesus Christ—Teachings.   2. Jesus Christ—Biography—
Public life.   I. Title.
BS2415.G63   1997
232.9—dc21
                                                            97–5408
                                                               CIP

To my Munich audience

Table of Contents

Preface

In recent years and decades the interest in Jesus of Nazareth has increased markedly. It extends to broad, not merely Christian, segments of the population. In this context it could be argued that the interest in Jesus of Nazareth is greater than the interest in his proclamation by the church, and the question of the underlying cause of this development is raised. This interest is also evident from the publication of numerous books on Jesus by non-Christians. Jews are discovering him to be their brother (S. Ben-Chorin), while philosophers declare him to be one of the epoch-making persons (K. Jaspers). It is important to remember here that the interest focuses on the historical Jesus, as he is called in the scholarly jargon, hence on the human Jesus—his life, his message, his history.

New Testament exegesis has been circumspect with regard to the inquiry into the historical Jesus and the reconstruction of his career—rightly so in view of the existing difficulties. Surely in German-speaking areas at least, exegesis in recent decades has been influenced by R. Bultmann, who wrote a brief book about Jesus but who considered the inquiry theologically irrelevant. This has changed. It is important to rediscover the continuity of the proclamation of the post-Easter church with the proclamation of Jesus, a continuity within discontinuity.

It is not possible, of course, to write a biography of Jesus. One may attempt to reconstruct his message and to elucidate his ministry from the political and intellectual-religious perspective of his time. The biblical depiction of his life takes on quasi-biographical traits only for the final hours, the hours of his passion, which we know were preserved, perhaps with theological reflection, in an early passion narrative. Therefore the reader should not expect this book to be a biography of Jesus but should read it as a pointer to the one who for us, as Christians, is simply decisive.

A separate comment needs to be directed to those who are conversant with the problem of the topic. They are familiar with the flood of literature, especially that pertaining to matters of detail. Certain limitations had to be accepted in order to make this book less cumbersome. Their understanding in this regard is appreciated.

Munich, July 1990
Joachim Gnilka

Preface to Special Edition

Herder Press is to be congratulated for making it possible for my book, *Jesus von Nazaret: Botschaft und Geschichte,* to be released in a special paperback edition and so to make it accessible to an even wider readership. This also fulfills the desire voiced repeatedly by a number of colleagues and students. The question of Jesus continues to be relevant. Objectively it has abiding relevance. The publication of numerous works on Jesus in recent years has indeed emphasized that relevance. In my previous preface I drew attention to the growing interest in the question of Jesus and in the person of Jesus, by the public as well as by the nontheological, scholarly world. In this context I pointed in particular to the works of two important contemporaries of ours, *Die massgebenden Menschen* by the philosopher Karl Jaspers and *Bruder Jesus* by the Jewish author Shalom Ben-Chorin. Both books are well worth reading and to be wrestled with. Jaspers places Jesus alongside Socrates, Confucius, and Buddha, whom he considers to be humankind's authoritative individuals. His delineations, though from a distanced observer, belong to the best of what has been said about Jesus in this century. Ben-Chorin's contribution, engaging and, by his own admission, inspired by intuition, bears witness that Jews are beginning to rediscover Jesus as one of their own people.

Meanwhile we have reached a stage in which Jesus is becoming a cheap fad. Of paramount importance here is not information but sensation. Unverified assumptions, suspicions, and opinionated reporting are being mixed into a Jesus-mush and then offered as the latest trend. Such developments may well be prompted by anti-Christian influences. In part, however, they are also linked with the realms of print and media in which sensational news is generally taken to be good news. Even the mothballed Srinagar story has been resurrected. There it is alleged that after his apparent death Jesus awoke again and went to Kashmir, where he died and was buried after a period of successful ministry. Why has nobody in recent times come up with the notion that in his youth Jesus made a pilgrimage to India and Tibet to become acquainted with Buddhism and then returned to his home to proclaim an adapted Buddhistic teaching by means of his Gospel?

There is a Jesus-portrait of faith. In this case it may perhaps be better to speak of a Christ-portrait. On the whole, this portrait deals with the exalted Christ. A glance over the history of Christian art demonstrates that this portrait could change, extending from the catacombs, via the various periods of art, into our own time. Christ was viewed differently, always through the eyes of the particular period. Perhaps it may even be said that every pious Christian has a personal portrait of Christ, shaped by his or her own experiences. Especially the portrait of the crucified Christ, encouraged by art, has left its imprint on the believer's mind. The most ancient depiction of Christ crucified is found on the wooden door of the church of Santa Sabina (ca. 430) on the Aventine in Rome. The human Jesus becomes the focal point in the events of particular periods of time, such as the Franciscan movement and the Crusades.

The scholarly-historical interest in the human Jesus arose in the Enlightenment. It drew from other kinds of sources and, to begin with, grew outside or at the periphery of the church. It penetrated the church only gradually and for a long time was viewed sceptically. It seemed important to me to account for these beginnings of the discussion of the question of Jesus in this book as well (cf. chapter 1). Here too it can be observed that the events of the time influenced the portrayal of Jesus. This could be demonstrated even more clearly if, in addition to the historical and exegetical literature, the sermons of the various churches were consulted as well. Jesus the author of order, the liberal Jesus, Jesus the social reformer—all these are aspects that were meaningful for a time. Apparently it was hardly possible to separate the subjective from the objective in this regard. A. Schweitzer once said that there is no more personal historical endeavor than to write a life of Jesus, and that one breathed into these books all of the hatred or love one was capable of mustering.

What is presented here is not a life of Jesus. The nature of the sources makes it impossible to write a life of Jesus. The focal point is the message and history of Jesus, with more emphasis on the message. In the Gospels, history is concentrated in his public ministry and becomes particularly concrete in his passion. The historical element finds expression even if the description of the contemporary intellectual-religious situation, as well as the social context are included in the discussion. Hence it is hoped that this book will assist the reader in gaining a portrait of the Jesus who was a turning point in history.

Munich, January 1993
Joachim Gnilka

1

The Question of Jesus

1. From Reimarus to the present

"The study of the Life of Jesus has had a curious history. It set out in quest of the historical Jesus, believing that when it had found Him, it could bring Him straight into our time as a Teacher and Saviour. It loosed the bands by which He had been riveted for centuries to the stony rocks of ecclesiastical doctrine, and rejoiced to see life and movement coming into the figure once more, and the historical Jesus advancing, as it seemed, to meet it. But He does not stay; He passes by our time and returns to His own. What surprised and dismayed the theology of the last forty years was that, despite all forced and arbitrary interpretations, it could not keep Him in our time, but had to let Him go. He returned to His own time, not owing to the application of any historical ingenuity, but by the same inevitable necessity by which the liberated pendulum returns to its original position." These are the classic words A. Schweitzer used in 1913 to describe the efforts of the so-called critical study of the life of Jesus, characteristic of the nineteenth century.[1] This description is at the same time an explanation of its failure. It had been initiated with the wrong presuppositions.

This was followed by a period of reflection upon the particular form of our Gospels, to which we are indebted for our knowledge of Jesus. Further inquiry concerning Jesus was postponed during this

---

[1] A. Schweitzer, *The Quest of the Historical Jesus* (ET; 2d ed.; London: A. & C. Black, 1926) 397. The words of this English title are commonly used to refer to the whole movement (German *Leben-Jesu-Forschung*).

period of time. Yet in the process of clarifying the particular form of the Gospels there emerged chances to pose the neglected question again. R. Bultmann, who began his scholarly work after the conclusion of the study of the life of Jesus described earlier, wrote a book about Jesus, although in the final analysis he was not seriously interested in the historical inquiry. Thus in the introduction to this book he describes the approach to his study by stating, "Whoever prefers to put the name of 'Jesus' always in quotation marks and let it stand as an abbreviation for the historical phenomenon with which we are concerned, is free to do so."[2] In other books the inquiry into Jesus is taken up decisively. In his research, for instance, M. Dibelius[3] tries to determine what we do know about the historical appearance of Jesus. H. Braun[4] introduces his discussion with the words " 'Who was Jesus of Nazareth?' That is the question this little book seeks to answer." It is in this arena that the inquiry currently is taking place, where accesses to the historical Jesus have been rediscovered, where the criteria to secure these accesses are worked out, and where the theological importance and theological ordering of the inquiry of Jesus are discussed as well. This general sketch of the situation must now be followed by more detail.

It began with the "quest of the historical Jesus," which was itself a child of the Enlightenment and was ill-fated from the start. It undertook the separation of Jesus and the Gospels, not out of the scholarly methodological understanding that the Gospels are faith-related writings and are to be read as such, but out of the suspicion that the Jesus described for us in the Gospels is not identical to the historical Jesus. The important task, therefore, was to rescue him from the clutches of dogmatism and to present him as he really was. A. Schweitzer remarked[5] that there is no historical endeavor more personal than to write a life of Jesus and that all of the hatred or all of the love capable of being expressed has been breathed into the books that have been written. Hence this era, which without a doubt also yielded productive insights, was characterized by aggression and apologetics, by an assault on the Gospels and defense of them. Rarely was the absence of presuppositions, so frequently claimed, more neglected than here. The Jesus-portraits that were presented, not least those of the "enlight-

---

[2] R. Bultmann, *Jesus and the Word* (ET; New York: Scribners, 1958).

[3] M. Dibelius, *Jesus* (ET; Philadelphia: Westminster, 1949).

[4] H. Braun, *Jesus of Nazareth: The Man and His Time* (ET; Philadephia: Fortress, 1979) 1.

[5] Schweitzer, *Quest,* 4.

ened," bear a high proportion of subjective features. In the would-be historical Jesus many rediscovered the portrait that they themselves had made of him. A brief overview of the development of the history of ideas featured in the quest of the historical Jesus, its tendencies and more direct intentions, will be instructive.

One of its primary characteristics appears already in H. S. Reimarus (d. 1768), the initiator of the quest of the historical Jesus, namely, the rationalistic explanation of miraculous and supernatural events reported in the Gospels. The rationalistic explanations extend from the miracle stories, through Jesus as the Son of God, to the resurrection account, from which Reimarus spins a detective novel–like episode, including the theft of a corpse and the disciples' deception of the people. Reimarus repeatedly turned to the representatives of a "religion of reason" or a "natural religion," intending to defend their rights against the ecclesiastical faith.[6] Rationalizations took on grotesque features. In the context of Jesus' baptism, for instance, K. A. Hase explains the description of the opening of heaven as the chance appearance of a meteor, and the account of the coin in the mouth of the fish (Matt. 17:24–27) he rationalized with the idea that they were able to sell the fish for a four-drachma coin.[7]

Although similar attempts continue, the quest of the historical Jesus attained a fundamentally new position in D. F. Strauss (d. 1874), probably its most important representative. He seeks to demonstrate that the Gospel stories are filled with material that has parallels in the OT and in the history of religions. The Jesus of the Gospels is held to be mythological. Strauss thus arrives at his conception of myth. At first one might have the impression that myth is synonymous with legend and used for the purpose of combatting the historical credibility of the Gospels, such as when Strauss argues concerning the star of the Magi that it is impossible "to conceive of such unnatural things as really having taken place" and that stories such as these have to be construed as invention.[8] But Strauss's interpretation of myth is more incisive. His so-called philosophical or evangelical myth represents an idea, couching a thought or philosophical notion in story form. This myth expresses a truth, though a truth not made concrete in the story but reflected in the idea. In the NT we encounter the idea of Jesus, the God-man, depicting the unity

---

[6] Cf. ibid., 13–26.
[7] Ibid., 59.
[8] D. F. Strauss, *A New Life of Jesus* (ET; London: Williams and Norgate, 1865) n.p.

of divine and human consciousness. While Jesus does not himself become an idea, mythical narratives attached themselves to him. What matters is that the language of myth penetrates to the language of thought. The individuality of the God-man was necessary for humanity to be brought to the consciousness of the noblest idea. Where this has been achieved, there is no longer any need for Jesus. This will be the case when the final dividing wall collapses, when the unity of self-consciousness is no longer merged with the absolute being of Jesus but is realized and enjoyed as something that transpires in all truly human thought and deed. The concept of the Gospel myth has its origin in a philosophy rather than in a consideration of the text. Strauss was not concerned with the evidence of a historical core in the individual Gospel narratives.[9]

Once Strauss had taken the path of disregarding Jesus, it almost inevitably had to lead to the denial of Jesus' historical existence.[10] This happened in the case of B. Bauer, in the Christ myth of A. Drews,[11] and with many others. Now the argument was turned on its head. If Strauss's Jesus was clothed in myth, in this new position it was the myth that brought Jesus to light. Drews further added bizarre astral mythological conceptions. In the denial of Jesus' existence these efforts, in some respects, reached a decisive conclusion, albeit one which also demonstrated the arrogance of numerous speculations. On this position it may suffice to cite the words of C. M. Wieland to Napoleon, who whispered to Wieland that it was indeed a major question whether Jesus Christ had ever lived: "I do indeed know, your Majesty, that there are some fools who doubted it. But I regard it just as foolish as doubting whether Julius Caesar ever lived or whether your Majesty is alive."[12]

Before this end point was reached, however, and alongside the line leading from Strauss to Drews, there was the endeavor in the

---

[9] D. F. Strauss, *The Life of Jesus Critically Examined* (ET; London: Chapman, Brothers, 1846) 39–40.; idem, *Die christliche Glaubenslehre in ihrer Entwicklung und im Kampfe mit der modernen Wissenschaft* (Tübingen: C. F. Osiander; Stuttgart: F. H. Kohler, 1840) 220; G. Backhaus, *Kerygma und Mythos bei David Friedrich Strauss und Rudolf Bultmann* (Hamburg-Bergstedt, 1956); E. Wolf, "Die Verlegenheit der Theologie: D. F. Strauss und die Bibelkritik," 219–39 in *Libertas Christiana* (FS F. Delekat; Munich, 1957); K. Barth, *D. Fr. Strauss als Theologe* (2d ed.; Zollikon: Verlag der Evangelischen Buchhandlung, 1948); W. G. Kümmel, *The New Testament: The History of the Investigation of its Problems* (ET; Nashville: Abingdon, 1972) 120–28.

[10] On this cf. the detailed discussion in Schweitzer, *Leben-Jesu-Forschung*, 444–564.

[11] The first edition of the book was published in Jena in 1909 and its third edition in 1910.

[12] In Schweitzer, *Leben-Jesu-Forschung*, 445f.

scholarly inquiry into the life of Jesus to construct the Gospel data biographically.[13] The use of imagination here was enormous, and thus the designation "Jesus-novels" is appropriate. They are voluminous: the *Natürliche Geschichte des grossen Propheten von Nazareth* (The Natural History of the Great Prophet of Nazareth) by K. H. Venturini comprised four volumes, totalling 2700 pages, while the biography of Jesus by K. F. Bahrdt reached a respectable 3000 pages. The former work was published in 1800–1802 and the latter in 1784–92. The noteworthy element in both authors is that, to my knowledge, they were the first to propose the Essene hypothesis, according to which Jesus was a member of the Essene sect and worked on their behalf to communicate a rationalistic religion. Josephus's description of the Essenes might have contributed to crediting this community with rationalistic purposes. From the Qumran scrolls found in 1947, however, we are very well informed about the Essenes' eschatological character. Perhaps Venturini was also the first to develop a fanciful romance between Jesus and Mary of Bethany. More recent depictions and films of this kind concentrate their efforts rather on Mary Magdalene.

E. Renan was presumably the most successful, albeit not the most intelligent, author of a Jesus-novel. He was a student of D. F. Strauss and a former Catholic who turned his back upon his church. With his book, which went through eight printings within three months, he introduced the new portrait of Jesus to the world of romance languages and Catholicism.[14] The mass of readers may have been impacted by his sentimental language, which indulges in colorful descriptions of the countryside along the lake, the villages and towns. Of particular interest is the attempt at dividing the ministry of Jesus, though it lasted a mere eighteen months, into several periods and thereby to trace an inner development. At the outset, for Renan, there is the gentle Jesus who in Galilee seeks to usher in the kingdom of God on earth. Not least as a result of his stay in Jerusalem, this Jesus developed into a revolutionary who then interpreted the kingdom of God apocalyptically and was prepared to die for his idea. Although critics charged Renan with offering "Christian art" at its cheapest and with having stolen his figures from the shop windows of the Christian art galleries at the Place St.-Sulpice, his book confronts us with the question of the kingdom of God in the

---

[13] Cf. ibid., 38–47.
[14] E. Renan, *La vie de Jésus* (Paris: Michel Lévy Frères, 1863).

life of Jesus and with the attempt to detect a turning point in the ministry of Jesus by means of the kingdom of God concept.

The kingdom of God denotes a key concept in the ministry of Jesus. For us it represents an issue that has spawned perhaps the most intense discussion, with the positive result that in Jesus the kingdom of God has to be viewed as something eschatological. Though this insight may be obvious today, it took time for it to prevail, for the common view of the kingdom of God was that it was present, had an institutional character, and hence was not infrequently viewed as synonymous with the church. Of particular interest in this regard is the book by J. Weiss, *Die Predigt Jesu vom Reiche Gottes*.[15] Just how sensational, indeed revolutionary, the awareness of the eschatological character of the kingdom of God was can be illustrated with a remark made by R. Bultmann in which he remembers a statement J. Kaftan made in a lecture during his student days: "If the kingdom of God is an eschatological entity, its concept is of no use to dogmatics." But more to the point than this reaction of shock is the observation that this new insight made a bourgeois understanding of Christianity painfully aware of how alien the NT proclamation was.[16]

This awareness of the eschatological quality of the kingdom of God was incorporated into a life of Jesus by A. Schweitzer, who developed the theory of thoroughgoing eschatology.[17] For Schweitzer, eschatology not merely is the basis for a biographical sketch of the ministry of Jesus but provides him with the possibility of distinguishing two epochs. The dividing point is marked by the sending out of the disciples. Jesus, aware that he was the Messiah and anticipating his inauguration as the Son of man, was captivated by an intense imminent expectation. The secret of the kingdom of God, referred to in Mark 4:11, is closely related to this imminence. It was his rejection at Nazareth that prompted Jesus to send out the disciples. Here and elsewhere Schweitzer takes the sequence of the pericopes of Mark 6:1–13 to be strictly historical. When Jesus had sent his disciples on the mission to Israel, the thought occurred to him that they would not return to him in this age. In this way Matt 10:23 takes on crucial

---

[15] The first edition was published in Göttingen in 1892, and the second, fully revised edition in 1900. The English translation, *Jesus' Proclamation of the Kingdom of God* (Philadelphia: Fortress, 1971), includes Bultmann's foreword to the 1964 German edition.

[16] Bultmann's remarks are printed as a foreword in the reprint of the second edition of the book by J. Weiss, published in Göttingen in 1964. On the discussion, see the chapter "Against Eschatology" in Schweitzer, *Quest*, 241–68.

[17] Cf. Schweitzer, *Quest*, 348–95.

significance: "for truly, I say to you, you will not have gone through all the towns of Israel before the Son of man comes."

This prediction, which for Schweitzer had clear limitations of time, was not fulfilled. The disciples did return to Jesus, and the appearance of the Son of man did not take place. The second phase began with disappointment, yet Jesus did not give up his work but, rather, understood it in terms of a new readiness to go to Jerusalem and to die there. Thus for Schweitzer the problem of the so-called delay of the Parousia is responsible for the entire development that follows.

The wide variety of results of the quest of the historical Jesus and its link with subjectivist points of departure can only be sketched briefly here. If labels are permitted, the portraits developed were those of a liberal Jesus (present kingdom, spiritualized messiahship, e.g., in H. J. Holtzmann, B. Weiss, W. Beyschlag, et al.), a Jewish Jesus (in De Jonge's Jesus as a disciple of Rabbi Hillel), a socialist Jesus (A. Kalthoff, K. J. Kautsky), and a Germanic (!) Jesus (O. Holtzmann). Psychiatric studies were made about him (E. Rasmussen, H. Schaefer, H. Werner); he was even labeled a pathological case.

The emphasis on Jesus the Jew did mark the discovery of an important factor. Though part of the initial period of the quest, it pointed to the scholars whose efforts continue to be significant today or at least triggered initiatives that have had further results. G. Dalman was concerned with the reconstruction of Jesus' native tongue and discovered that he must have spoken the Galilean dialect of the Aramaic language. A. Wünsche, H. L. Strack, and J. Klausner sought to link the life of Jesus with the Talmud and the midrash—a contribution that P. Billerbeck later was to bring to a provisional conclusion with his incisive commentary on the NT from Talmud and midrash. Furthermore, J. Klausner was a significant Jewish scholar who joined the quest of the historical Jesus. In the Catholic world there was no quest of the historical Jesus; exegesis began to unfold only in conjunction with the later Gospel studies.

The later Gospel studies are linked with the discovery of narrative rules and forms or genres that influenced the origin, shaping, and finalization of the Gospels, as well as the traditions they contain. More will be said in connection with this in the following section. This discovery has to do with the concepts of form, redaction, tradition, or historical criticism in the study of the Gospels, making possible a viable access to the Gospels, yet also making us aware of the difficulties encountered and the ways to be taken in order to penetrate to the historical Jesus. It can be said, therefore, that at the close of the quest of the historical Jesus, described above and essentially concluding with A. Schweitzer, and with the development of the new methods to be used in the scholarly inquiry, a new grasp of Jesus ensued, followed by a period of relative calm in this field of study. The new epoch began at the end of World War II. It would be completely impossible to introduce this literary body in detail, even in a cursory fashion.[18] But an overview of the literary output of this period leads to the observation that a number of authors substantiate their presentations methodologically in line with the new understanding, in a sense exposing their cards (e.g., H. D. Betz, G. Bornkamm, J. Blank, H. Braun, T. Holtz, E. Schweizer, W. Trilling), while others do not. Some, especially in the English-language literature, reject the form-critical analysis of the Gospels. Others enthusiastically pursue the old quest of the historical Jesus, including its common truncations, phantasies, and subjectivisms.

To provide the reader with a taste of this, at least a few of the wealth of impressions will be given here. There are a number of authors, as in the quest, who begin with the narrative framework of the Gospel of Mark, taken as historical. In this manner an overview of the ministry of Jesus is gained in which the ministry in Galilee, the retreat to the north, and the journey to Jerusalem lead up to the passion (V. Taylor). For R. H. Fuller, Simon Peter's confession of the Messiah is the turning point in the ministry of Jesus as presented in Mark. E. Barnikol attempts to establish the life of Jesus from his postulated Ur-Markan Gospel.

There is an increase in the presentations of the ministry of Jesus in which Jesus the Jew takes center stage. It is gratifying to see Jewish authors participate increasingly in this discussion. S. Ben-Chorin, for instance, has discovered Jesus to be a brother and has even been able to write a book on "Mary in Jewish perspective." Generally Jesus is depicted as a Jew who is faithful to the Torah, who never at any point violated the Mosaic and rabbinic law (P. E. Lapide). In the context of endeavors such as these, D. Flusser considers the plucking of wheat on the Sabbath (Mark 2:23ff.)—the only offense against the law in the synoptic tradition, in his view—as a later interpolation. Similarly G. Vermes, who holds Jesus to be a true charismatic and a holy worker of miracles, explains the elimination of distinctions between clean and unclean food (Mark 7:15), a teaching which was considerably different

---

[18] On this cf. W. G. Kümmel, *Dreissig Jahre Jesusforschung (1950–1980)* (BBB 60; Königstein: P. Hanstein, 1985).

from Judaism, as a misunderstanding of the tradition. The conflict leading to Jesus' death is interpreted by Lapide as connected with Jesus' alleged political and military intentions. Ben-Chorin projects the portrait of the eschatological enthusiast upon Jesus, borrowing rather obviously from Schweitzer's thoroughgoing eschatology.

Among the new works on Jesus there is also no dearth of the sociocritical and socialistic interpretations. The most impressive work in this context has probably been written by the Czech Marxist M. Machoveč. He focuses especially on the message of Jesus, the eschatological quality of which he accepts without strictures but which he interprets in terms of a lived future: Jesus brought the future down from the clouds of heaven and made it a matter of the tangible present and thus our business. In keeping with the author's presuppositions, the theocentric perspective is excluded from Jesus' radical effort on behalf of humanity and human dignity; he thereby offers a Jesus who is admittedly not unsympathetic to the atheist. In comparison with Machoveč the books on Jesus by A. Holl and M. Craveri, arguing the same viewpoint, are inferior. The latter moves largely along the lines of the old quest, whereas Holl offers a redrawn "Jesus in bad company." S. G. F. Brandon, on the other hand, whose book has caused quite a stir particularly in the English-language world, reintroduces the interpretation of Jesus as Zealot. None of the fundamental views of the Zealots were foreign to Jesus. His temple protest, accompanied by force and pillaging, has to be understood as a revolutionary act that triggered the intervention by the authorities. Jesus died the death of a Zealot. The only thing distinguishing him from the Zealots was that he turned his opposition primarily against the priestly aristocracy because he believed that they were the main obstacle to the removing of Roman rule. The price Brandon has to pay for his thesis is enormous. He must interpret the Gospel of Mark, his point of departure, as a work that was deliberately written to conceal the Zealot Jesus, as an apologetic for the Roman Christians under the pressure of Titus' victory over the Jews.

In the earlier period J. Weiss was instrumental in the success of the view that the kingdom of God was of a future, eschatological nature, and just as there were numerous opponents to this view then, so the denial of the future quality of the kingdom gained a new formidable representative in the second period, namely, C. H. Dodd. According to his conception of "realized eschatology," all of the kingdom of God sayings and parables must be related to the present and interpreted symbolically. The language of apocalyptic images was not characteristic for Jesus; his sayings about the future are to be understood as symbols for the kingdom of God beyond history. The statements about the coming of the Son of man have to be understood as a "vision of the final victory of God's cause over all powers in the universe."[19] Even the psychological interpretation of Jesus experienced a revival in the present period. To be sure, there was no more interest in penetrating into the personal psyche of Jesus. K. Niederwimmer considers this impossible from the available sources, and inquires rather into the psychological relevance of the movement instigated by Jesus. The crucial aspects of Jesus' fate are given archetypal character. The proclamation of the nearness of the kingdom of God means to indicate that the unconscious is awaiting an imminent transformation, and Jesus' passion becomes the symbol for human existence, which is defeated in the struggle for the attainment of meaning.

To conclude, there is another group of scholars to be mentioned who explore Jesus' relationship to the contemporary Jewish religious parties and so attempt to shed light on his work. For instance, K. Schubert notes that Jesus' position relative to the law involved him in polemical disagreement with the Pharisees, while his confrontation with the Sadducean temple aristocracy belongs to the passion narrative. He himself was closer to the apocalyptic groups, though he rejected their separatist attitude. While G. Baumbach takes a similar view on Jesus' attitude to the Pharisees and Sadducees, for W. E. Phipps it is a foregone conclusion that Jesus is to be seen as a Pharisaic Jew. The primary difference between him and the Pharisees is that he accepted women, Gentiles, and the common people in his circle. Thus he showed that he was a prophet and as such was bold enough to overturn traditional societal structures and conceptions. According to H. Leroy, too, Jesus is to be associated with the Pharisaism represented by Rabbi Hillel, a contemporary and eminent leader of a school.

This brief presentation of various books on Jesus that have been published in recent years indicates that many questions remain unresolved and the information given varies widely. To be sure, many of these positions are highly subjective, as, for instance, Brandon's concerning the Zealot Jesus who has been stripped of his Zealotism by the Gospel of Mark. Certainly many of the viewpoints are unten-

---

[19] C. H. Dodd, *The Founder of Christianity* (London: Collins, 1971) 126.

able, based on the general scholarly consensus, such as Dodd's view of a realized eschatology in the preaching of Jesus. But the intention here has been to sketch differing and, on the whole, unsatisfactory presentations of Jesus, in order to show the necessity of constructing as reliable a path as possible, given the complexity of the problem. This cannot be achieved effortlessly. This path has to be pursued in the direction indicated by those scholars mentioned above who both clarified their methodological approach and sought to communicate a comprehensive portrait of Jesus.

First, however, something needs to be said concerning the reasonableness, indeed the necessity, for the inquiry into the historical Jesus. It is essential for theological reasons. In the Bultmannian school the discussion of this question was such that it struck the observer on the outside, especially the Catholic observer, as somewhat esoteric. Bultmann objected to the theological reasonableness of the quest and decided on the hardly comprehensible formulation that the thatness of his coming, ultimately articulated in the cross, was sufficient for him. He differentiated between objective and historical continuity and explained that the former is sufficient in order to gain the continuity that consists of giving and appropriating a new self-understanding, brought about by accepting the kerygma of Christ by faith. E. Käsemann strongly objected to the distinction between objective and historical continuity and correctly observed that it is impossible to have the one without the other.[20] Thus he supported the theological necessity of research on Jesus. Even though we essentially concur with the heart of his concerns, it is not possible to agree with the radical criticism that he (and the Bultmannian school and their descendants in general) represents regarding the possibilities of the quest of the historical Jesus.

This leads us to an explanation of how research on the historical Jesus, which we are to undertake in what follows, is to be ordered. While this inquiry is to be viewed and acknowledged as theologically meaningful and necessary, its results are surely not accorded any dogmatic ranking. The exegete cannot cull out content that is normative for faith by means of his historical work. His results may indeed be well founded, but ultimately they are hypothetical. This can already be seen in the many diverse results in

[20] On this discussion cf. E. Käsemann, "Blind Alleys in the 'Jesus of History' Controversy," *New Testament Questions of Today* (Philadelphia: Fortress, 1969) 23–65; idem, "The Problem of the Historical Jesus," *Essays on New Testament Themes* (SBT 41; Naperville, Ill.: Allenson, 1964) 15–47.

historical scholarship. Our faith focuses on the NT witness of faith. The aim of the historical work is to investigate the relationship between Jesus and the NT witness of faith, between his proclamation and that of the post-Easter community, as presented in the NT and especially in the Gospels. To attain in this manner a demonstrable continuity with its antecedent developments, unfoldings, and tensions, it may be best to do two things: first to portray Jesus in his life, words, and deeds and then, beyond that, at least to describe initial directions that were carried further through his words and deeds, that is, initial interpretations linked with his person and message.

Select bibliography: E. Barnikol, *Das Leben Jesu der Heilsgeschichte* (Halle: Max Niemeyer, 1958); G. Baumbach, *Jesus von Nazareth im Lichte der jüdischen Gruppenbildung* (AVTRW 54; Berlin: Evangelische Verlagsanstalt, 1971); S. Ben-Chorin, *Bruder Jesus: Der Nazarener in jüdischer Sicht* (Munich: Deutscher Taschenbuch Verlag, 1967); O. Betz, *Was wissen wir von Jesus?* (Stuttgart: Kreuz, 1965); J. Blank, *Jesus von Nazareth* (Theologisches Seminar; Freiburg: Herder 1972); S. G. F. Brandon, *Jesus and the Zealots* (Manchester: Manchester University Press, 1967); H. Braun, *Jesus of Nazareth: The Man and His Time* (ET; Philadelphia: Fortress, 1979); M. Craveri, *The Life of Jesus* (ET; New York: Grove Press, 1967); C. H. Dodd, *The Founder of Christianity* (London: Collins, 1971); D. Flusser, *Jesus in Selbstzeugnissen und Bilddokumenten* (RoMo; Hamburg: Rowolt, 1968); R. H. Fuller, *The Mission and Achievement of Jesus* (2d ed.; SBT 12; London, SCM, 1956); G. Ghiberti, "Überlegungen zum Stand der Leben-Jesu-Forschung," *MThZ* 33 (1982) 99–115; W. Grundmann, *Die Geschichte Jesu Christi* (Berlin: Evangelische Verlagsanstalt, 1956); A. Holl, *Jesus in schlechter Gesellschaft* (Stuttgart: Deutsche Verlagsansalt, 1971); T. Holtz, *Jesus von Nazareth* (2d ed.; Berlin: Union Verlag, 1979); W. G. Kümmel, "Jesusforschung seit 1965, Nachträge," *ThR* 46 (1981) 317–64; ibid., 47 (1982) 136–65, 348–83; idem, *The New Testament: The History of the Investigation of Its Problems* (ET; Nashville: Abingdon, 1972); P. E. Lapide, *Der Rabbi von Nazareth* (Trier: Spee Verlag, 1974); H. Leroy, *Jesus: Überlieferung und Deutung* (Darmstadt: Wissenschaftliche Buchgesellschaft, 1978); M. Machoveč, *Jesus für Atheisten* (Stuttgart: n.p., 1972); K. Niederwimmer, *Jesus* (Göttingen: Vandenhoeck & Ruprecht, 1968); W. E. Phipps, "Jesus, the Prophetic Pharisee," *JES* 14 (1977) 17–31; E. Schillebeeckx, *Jesus: An Experiment in Christology* (ET; New York: Seabury, 1979); K. Schubert, *Jesus im Lichte der Religionsgeschichte des Judentums* (Vienna/Munich: Herold, 1973); A. Schweitzer, *The Quest of the Historical Jesus* (2d ed.; ET; London: A. & C. Black, 1926); E. Schweizer, *Jesus* (ET; London: SCM, 1971); E. Stauffer, *Jesus and His Story* (ET; New York: Knopf, 1960); V. Taylor, *The Life and Ministry of Jesus* (London, Macmillan, 1955); E. Trocmé, *Jesus as Seen by His Contemporaries* (ET; Philadelphia: Westminster, 1973); G. Vermes, *Jesus the Jew* (London: Collins, 1973).

2. Matters of methodology

(a) The first thing to be addressed is the distinctiveness of our Gospels. In this context we shall focus on the Synoptic Gospels, Matthew, Mark, and Luke. There is no doubt at all that these Gospels have historical interests. This is also true of the Gospel of John, but while it is in some respects dependent upon the Synoptics or the synoptic tradition, it is clearly different. For this reason we intend to appeal to the Fourth Gospel only with reference to specific questions. Even a cursory comparison with the NT letters, such as the letters of Paul, indicates clearly the historical interests of the synoptic writers. In the former, apart from a few exceptions, statements by and about the human Jesus remain unimportant. This is not to argue that the apostle Paul did not know the synoptic tradition. That issue may remain open at this point. What is clear is that, whatever he may have known, he made almost no use of it.

But the historical interest of the Synoptics has limitations that need to be taken seriously. The distinctiveness of their historical interest is apparent, for instance, from the observation that they do not provide a coherent description of the life of Jesus from birth to death. Their attention is focused on his public ministry from the baptism by John to the cross. This limitation is evident in Mark, and in Acts 1:21f. it is associated with the essential witness for this period of time. If Matthew and Luke preface their Gospels with infancy narratives and thus show a certain biographical concern, the focus is on the birth and the story is permeated considerably with biblical-theological motifs. We learn nothing about Jesus' childhood, upbringing, youth, vocational training, and early adulthood. Though it would be very relevant to someone with biographical interests, we do not hear anything about what Jesus looked like, what color hair or eyes he had, what his physical stature was, or what type of clothes he wore. Later on, especially in the apocryphal gospels, this information is supplied profusely, just as such gospels are also primarily occupied with Jesus' childhood.[21] This information, of course, has no historical value.

An important element in understanding the Synoptic Gospels is that they are composed of individual traditions or pericopes. In these pericopes, which at one time existed separately and were passed on

---

[21] Cf. W. Bauer, *Das Leben Jesu im Zeitalter der neutestamentlichen Apokryphen,* (1909; reprint, Darmstadt: Wissenschaftliche Buchgesellschaft, 1967) 311–41. This book deals with external aspects of Jesus—his occupation, dress, meal traditions. The information about the external aspects of Jesus appeals to OT references. Following Isa 53:2f., the assertion is made, for instance, that his appearance was inconspicuous, indeed repulsive. Based on Exod 2:2 (Moses typology), it is said that he was a handsome person, and some of the apocryphal Acts of the Apostles frequently call him the beautiful one (*Acts of John* 73f.). It was not only the desire on the part of Christians to invent stories that produced such statements but also the aggressiveness on the part of opponents. Origen, *Contra Celsum* 6.75, argues with Celsus about Christ's outward appearance.

in the tradition, Jesus is presented in the beam of a searchlight, as it were, in a particular and specific type of ministry, such as his activity as a healer, his disputation with various groups of Jews, or his association with his disciples. The linking of these pericopes in the Gospels was frequently prompted by subject matter or theological concerns, not by chronological concerns, so their sequence does not allow for conclusions concerning the sequence of events in Jesus' ministry. The itinerary of his activity in the land of Israel, which was of no interest to the community that passed on the tradition, has been lost to us.[22] While many pericopes do provide topographical references (at the Sea of Galilee, in Capernaum, etc.), the majority of them are vague or not localized at all. The only thing that can be ascertained is that most of the ministry was in Galilee, in the lake country. According to the Synoptics, Jesus visits Jerusalem only once during his public ministry, at the time of his passion. This too may be an artificial framework. In John's Gospel we see Jesus traveling to Jerusalem several times. Yet even here the motivating factor is not to provide a better itinerary; rather, considerations of subject matter and theological reflection are decisive, as the placing of the temple cleansing at the beginning may indicate (John 2:13ff.). The discourses of Jesus, as presented by the Synoptics, are compositions of speeches. They are constructed from individual sayings and groups of logia and are frequently ordered according to considerations of content, thus making their use in preaching and catechesis easier. The passion narrative is a notable exception in this regard. It is not only distinct because of specific names of people (Caiaphas, Pilate, Simon of Cyrene, Joseph of Arimathea, the names of the women at the cross) and topographical references (Gethsemane, The Pavement, Golgotha); it also preserves a genuine sequence of events, from Jesus' Last Supper with his disciples, the arrest, the trial, and the death to the discovery of the opened sepulcher.

With regard to the quantity and scope of Jesus materials, one notes a development from an initial selection process to an assiduous endeavor at collecting them. There was a time, to be sure, when there was a wealth of recollections of Jesus, both personal and general. Much of this was not passed on or recorded. Of course this also has to do primarily with the abilities and limitations of human memory. People's memory at that time surely was better than it is with today's flood of stimuli. They also made skillful use of particular techniques in

---

[22] Cf. K. L. Schmidt, *Der Rahmen der Geschichte Jesu* (Berlin: Karl Ludwig, 1919) 317.

orally transmitting large segments of tradition. One of these is the association of catchwords, which can still be recognized in many synoptic contexts.[23] What was important and essential was selected and passed on, especially in the early stage of the transmission. This is true of the phase of the oral transmission. The concluding remark after the parables of Mark 4 points to a selection of this kind: "With many such parables he spoke the word to them, as they were able to hear it" (v. 33). Likewise John 20:30f., though formulated in a certain abundance of language, may well have preserved a reminiscence of such beginnings. Even the evangelist Mark, who wrote the earliest Gospel around 70 CE, is selective. He has little to offer concerning the sayings material. Conversely the transmitters and authors of the sayings source, which was inserted into the Gospels of Matthew and Luke as a presynoptic source, on the whole bypassed the narrative material. Thus a trend can be observed in Matthew and Luke, especially in the latter, to collect Jesus material that otherwise might be lost. He refers to this in his prologue when he says that he "followed all things closely for some time past" (Luke 1:3). We may infer, then, that the aspects of Jesus' deeds and words that are decisive and significant for our faith have been preserved in the Gospels for us.

The fact of lost Jesus materials is shown by the existence of some traditions, albeit not many, outside the Gospels. These are referred to as agrapha, unwritten traditions.[24] Perhaps the best-known example is found in Acts 20:35, in Paul's address to the Ephesian elders, where he cites a saying of Jesus not found in the Gospels: "It is more blessed to give than to receive." Some minor collections of sayings of Jesus can be traced in the apostolic fathers, which one may assume were not cited from one of the Gospels but still circulated as minor independent traditions.[25] Later, however, there were distorted developments, which arose in part from narrative imagination and in part from heresy and which led to the formation of the apocryphal gospels. The Gnostic *Gospel of Thomas,* discovered in upper Egypt in 1947, is a particularly good example of this.

Other elements represent secondary additions to the text of the canonical Gospels. This is true of the valuable pericope of Jesus' encounter with the adulteress, which is to be viewed as a synoptic

---

[23] For instance, the group of three seed parables in Mark 4.

[24] J. Jeremias, *Unknown Sayings of Jesus* (ET; London: SPCK, 1957), has collected a number of such materials.

[25] On this cf. H. Koester, *Synoptische Überlieferung bei den Apostolischen Vätern* (TU 65; Berlin: Akademie-Verlag, 1957).

tradition and has been secondarily incorporated in John 8:1–11.[26]
This also applies to the brief pericope of the man who worked on the
Sabbath, which is only found in Codex D in place of Luke 6:5: "On
the same day he saw a man working on the Sabbath. He said to him,
'Blessed are you, fellow, if you know what you are doing. But if you
do not know, you are cursed and a transgressor of the law.' "

Probably the most influential factor in the shaping of the
Gospels is the faith in Jesus' resurrection from the dead. However,
the shaping of the tradition did not begin merely with the Easter
event. We may assume that the formation of the tradition already
began with the pre-Easter Jesus, that Jesus impressed his teaching,
or substantial elements of it, upon his disciples; this may best be
understood in the context of their mission.[27] The Christian proclamation did not originate until after Easter, however, namely, the
passing on of the teaching of Jesus, which now developed by incor-
porating Jesus himself in his proclamation, and thus the significant
transition from the proclaimer to the one proclaimed came about.
This transition meant that the earthly Jesus was seen in the light of
Easter, that powerful features of the exalted Lord were transferred
to Jesus of Nazareth. Probably the most vivid illustration of this
perspective can be seen in the conception and manner of presentation in the Gospel of John. But it also left a significant imprint on
the shaping of the Synoptic Gospels. Many of the miracle stories are
shaped in such a way that Jesus' lordship becomes apparent in them.
In the case of many stories related to the life of the earthly Jesus,
such as the transfiguration on the mountain or the walking on the
lake, the question has been raised whether or not they are Easter
stories. Even if this idea is to be rejected, these stories are nevertheless inconceivable apart from the perspective of Easter. Whether or
not some stories are to be understood as pre- or post-Easter remains
uncertain on account of their divergent order, as in the case of the
account of the plentiful catch of fish, which is given as a commissioning narrative in Luke 5:1ff., while John 21:1ff. presents it as an
Easter narrative. By immersing the earthly Christ in the splendor of
the exalted Christ, the faith undergirding the community affirms
that the crucified Christ has been raised and is alive. For this reason
the Gospels are not merely reminiscences of what has been but also

---

[26] Cf. U. Becker, *Jesus und die Ehebrecherin* (Berlin: A. Töpelmann, 1963).

[27] Cf. Schürmann, "Die vorderösterlichen Antänge der Logiatradition," in *Der historiche und der kerygmatische Christus: Beiträge zum Christusverständnis in Forschung und Verkundigung* (ed. H. Ristow and K. Mattihae; Berlin: Evangelische Verlagsanstalt, 1961).

a witness to the living Christ; they are report and kerygma at the same time, the story of one who is alive.[28]

If by hearing the words of Jesus one hears the word of the exalted Christ who dwells with God and attends the community, the subsequent process, meaningful for the understanding of the Gospels as well, becomes comprehensible. Reference was made back to Jesus' message to get counsel for new questions and problems arising in the concrete life of the post-Easter community. Although these problems were new, the desire was to follow Jesus' instructions, so the latter were interpreted in the context of the newly arisen questions. There are numerous examples to demonstrate this process. Perhaps the most obvious are those instances where the new interpretation was placed alongside the old tradition. This is true of parables that were given their own interpretation, such as the parables of the sower, the tares among the wheat, the fishing net (Matt 13:18–23 par., 36–43, 49f.). But this process also directly affects the reshaping of Jesus' words. Awareness of this process ought to make us more careful in classifying Jesus' words with such labels as authentic and inauthentic.[29] Apart from the fact that the written word of Scripture is the normative word for us, it would be important to retrace the process indicated in a historical reconstruction. The church's current practice of preaching is a similar process, though different from the use of the words of Jesus in primitive Christianity that can be discerned in the Gospels. The sermon is prefaced by a word of Jesus and then interprets it. The Gospels likewise give us a glimpse into the sermon, catechesis, and apologetic of primitive Christianity.

Especially with regard to the narrative parts of the Gospels, constituting the bulk of the tradition apart from the sayings of Jesus, it is important to consider that the Christians who passed along these materials made use of certain narrative forms, genres, that were already available in their milieu, especially in the OT and in the Jewish world. Hence the new content could be poured into old narrative structures. The form-critical investigation of the Gospels has studied these structures and has taught us their rules. There are narrative units characterized by a memorable saying (apophthegm);[30] there are disputes and

---

[28] This concept is taken from E. Schillebeeckx.

[29] Cf. Hahn, "Methodologische Überlegungen zur Rückfrage nach Jesus," 23–26, in Kertelge, ed., *Rückfrage nach Jesus: zur Methodik und Bedeutung der Frage nach dem historischen Jesus* (Freiburg: Herder, 1974).

[30] An apophthegmatic story is narrated with the focus directed to the climactic saying; e.g., the story of the plucking of grain (Mark 2:23–27) focuses on the sentence "The sabbath was made for man, not man for the sabbath."

didactic dialogues, just as they also exist structurally in Judaism, and many other structures. To this must be added the miracle stories. They are told similarly to how miracles were narrated already in the OT, except that now they refer to Jesus and are filled with the new content, especially with the motif of faith. In many instances OT miracle stories may have affected the synoptic ones, especially those originating from the Elijah-Elisha tradition. A comparison of the Jairus story in Mark 5:21–43 par. with 2 Kgs 4:25–37, 1 Kgs 17:17–24, or of the feeding of the multitudes in Mark 6:30–44 with 2 Kgs 4:42–44, brings out the similarities and differences more clearly. The transmission of the sayings likewise can be structured in terms of genres (Beatitude, woe, wisdom saying, etc.). In this case it is to be understood, of course, that Jesus himself had already made use of such forms in expressing his sayings. The result is seen in the notable distinction between the transmission of deeds and that of sayings: in the former others tell about Jesus, while in the latter the core and the bulk of material around it are traced back to him.

To conclude the characterization of the Gospels, two difficulties need to be considered. The first of these is the language. Jesus spoke Aramaic, or, more precisely, the Galilean dialect of Aramaic, as G. Dalman has taught us. In Jerusalem, Galileans could be recognized because of their dialect, as the incident with Peter shows (Matt 26:73). In particular this dialect was distinctive because of its imprecise articulation of the gutteral sounds. Especially the ayin was interchanged with the aleph.[31] The Gospels, however, were written in Greek. We do not have a single Aramaic saying of Jesus.

Prior to the Gospels' composition Jesus' sayings were translated into Greek. Yet since Greek, too, was spoken in Galilee, the question may be asked seriously whether Jesus did not also use the Greek language occasionally. M. Hengel[32] has shown the extent to which Judaism was already hellenized at the time of Jesus. Surely occasionally there were Gentiles in Jesus' audience. Among the Twelve there were two with Greek names: Andrew, the brother of Simon Peter, and Philip.[33] This

---

[31] Cf. P. Billerbeck and H. Strack, *Kommentar zum Neuen Testament aus Talmud und Midrasch* (Munich: Beck, 1926–61) 1.157.

[32] M. Hengel, *Judaism and Hellenism* (ET; Philadelphia: Fortress, 1974) esp. 107–15 (on the problem of language); also E. Schürer, *History of the Jewish People in the Period of Jesus Christ* (ET; 4 vols.; Edinburgh: T. & T. Clark, 1973–86) 2.1–28.

[33] It is noteworthy that Andrew and Philip are prominent in John's Gospel, particularly in conjunction with the Greeks who come to Jesus: 1:40, 43–48; 6:5–8; 12:21f.; 14:8f.

question deserves to be explored thoroughly, but this cannot be undertaken here.

The second difficulty concerns the written form of the sayings of Jesus. Apart from the parables we only have logia from him, that is, individual sayings in sentence form. Even a number of the parables seem to be extremely compressed; for instance, the parable of the leaven consists of a single sentence (Matt 13:33 par.), and the parable of the treasure in the field, of two sentences (Matt 13:44). It may be plausible to assume that in the course of passing on what is memorable and then committing it to writing, his sayings were compressed and thus perhaps they frequently are merely the summation or the conclusion of a speech given by Jesus himself. It has already been mentioned that the speeches offered in the Synoptic Gospels are compositions, pieced together from independent single logia or from minor groups of sayings.

(b) How, then, can a portrait of the historical Jesus be reconstructed positively? Scholarly research of the last forty years has wrestled with criteria and characteristics that are to assist us in this endeavor. What is important here is to arrange the achievements in an overall picture. If it is not possible to derive a life of Jesus, there are within his ministry and preaching certain attitudes and concerns of a general nature that can be accentuated to clarify insights and make possible an outline. Thus it may undoubtedly be assumed that the center of his proclamation was the kingdom of God. The latter has to be grasped in the form in which Jesus proclaimed it. His ethical demands and working of miracles belong to this realm. Jesus gathered a group of disciples around him. Linked with the understanding of being a follower is discipleship, and so is the question of whether there was an inner circle of the Twelve among the disciples and what the relationship and mission of Jesus was with regard to the people of God. Soon he was also embroiled in a conflict. It is in this context that his relationship with the various Jewish groups needs to be explored and the causes to be sought for this conflict that eventually lead to his violent death. To be sure, the importance of the trial and his death is such that they call for a detailed investigation. Finally, attention has to be given, as the overarching issue, to his claim of mission, by asking the theologically formulated question whether there are any points of reference in his ministry—and if so, what they were—that might serve as premise for the post-Easter christological development. These, then, are the major complex issues by means of which we shall endeavor to construct a portrait of

Jesus: kingdom of God, discipleship, conflict, death, authority in mission. Within these major complex issues there certainly are a number of partial aspects that will require our attention.[34]

We shall now introduce the individual criteria, established by scholarship, by means of which the study of Jesus is to be advanced. These criteria are to be understood as functional rules in evaluating the synoptic material. It is apparent that almost all of these rules use matters of content as their standard.

aa. The "criterion of dissimilarity" holds that we are dealing with a tradition originating in Jesus if the tradition can neither be derived from Judaism nor attributed to the early church. E. Käsemann has called for renewed attention to this criterion; this had already been observed in P. W. Schmiedel, E. Hirsch, and W. Heitmüller. Käsemann wants this to be the only criterion.[35] It is apparent that what matters here is absolute originality. Only what was truly new and distinct from what was already known can be regarded as valid. The presuppositions implied in this criterion may be based, consciously or not, on a particular christological concept. While its usefulness has been acknowledged, some have argued against this criterion that it could contain an anti-Jewish bias[36] and that its orientation is not form critical but the history of religions.[37] This criterion is a helpful but sharp sword. What is certain is that, if it is applied radically, a lot of Jesus material would be severed from him. Had Jesus always been original, he would resemble a missionary to China who refuses to speak Chinese. This criterion does, however, deserve our attention as a point of departure.

bb. The "criterion of coherence" refers to the agreement of Jesus' word and deed. If his word is congruent with his action, if both are coherent—that is, if there are sayings traditions, especially those making claims, which are in agreement with behavior reported about him and possibly typical of him—then we are on a reliable track. In this connection E. Fuchs pointed out that the distinctive-

---

[34] Hahn, "Überlegungen," 40–51, stresses the necessity of these partial aspects. Comparable ideas are also found in J. Roloff, "Auf der Suche nach einem neuen Jesusbild," *TLZ* 98 (1973) 561–72. M. Lehmann, *Synoptische Quellenanalyse und die Frage nach dem historischen Jesus* (BZNW 38; Berlin: de Gruyter, 1970) 195–99, shows that gaining a general setting has long been recognized as important in scholarship.

[35] On the discussion, cf. Lehmann, *Quellenanalyse,* 174–86.

[36] F. Mussner et al., "Methodologie der Frage nach dem historischen Jesus," 132, in Kertelge, ed., *Rückfrage nach Jesus.*

[37] D. Lührmann, "Die Frage nach Kriterien für ursprüngliche Jesusworte," 64 in *Jésus aux origines de la christologie* (ed. J. Dupont; BETL 40; Louvain: Leuven University Press, 1975) 64.

ness of Jesus' didactic proclamation is to be found in the fact that he made his obedience the standard for his disciples and that we find in Jesus' word and deed the same orientation.[38] His relations with publicans and sinners may serve as an example.

cc. The "criterion of multiple attestation" is similar to the criterion of coherence, and certainly comparable with it, but is more formal and broader.[39] It takes into account the content-related traditions dealing with a particular type of action on the part of Jesus, a type attested in various strands and in different forms (such as the apophthegm, the dispute, and the parable). Here support from different forms is crucial. Frequency of occurrence alone would be inadequate, since the Synoptics' interdependence automatically led to the repetition of numerous traditions.

dd. Traditions that were corrected because they were hard or offensive, or that receded into the background, are regarded as traditions that lead us to the original saying of Jesus. This criterion concerns the sayings traditions. We could cite Mark 2:27 as an example: "The sabbath was made for man, not man for the sabbath," a logion that Matthew and Luke no longer used, presumably on account of its offensiveness. We might also refer to Jesus' position on marriage being unending or to his prohibition of taking an oath, both of which presented problems.

ee. N. A. Dahl has suggested an independent approach.[40] He begins with Jesus' death on the cross as the most certain fact of Jesus' life, though the death itself requires interpretation, to be sure. A historical understanding of Jesus' proclamation can be achieved only in conjunction with his execution on the cross: "The end of Jesus' life serves the purpose of focusing on the provocative claim of authority which he must have used in public."[41] Consequently Dahl detects and analyzes this claim of authority in the parables and in the Sermon on the Mount.

ff. A final criterion is that one should preferably turn to the oldest layers of the synoptic tradition. This criterion, already important

---

[38] Cf. E. Fuchs, *Hermeneutik* (2d ed.; Bad Cannstatt: R. Mullerschon, 1958) 228; idem, *Studies of the Historical Jesus* (ET; London: SCM, 1964) 21.

[39] Mussner, "Methodologie," 127, refers to evidence in terms of a cross section. It is better to replace this concept with that of the "criterion of multiple attestation."

[40] N. A. Dahl, "Der historische Jesus als geschichtswissenschaftliches und theologisches Problem," *KD* (1, 1955) 104–32; idem, "Der gekreuzigte Messias," 149–69 in *Der historische Jesus und der kerygmatische Christus* (ed. H. Ristow and K. Matthiae; Berlin: Evangelische Verlagsanstalt, 1960).

[41] Dahl, "Der historische Jesus," 121f.

in the old life-of-Jesus quest and different from those mentioned thus far because it addresses a general tradition-critical consideration, certainly requires more precise explanation. The quest of the historical Jesus frequently began with the Gospel of Mark or, where more careful work was done in terms of literary criticism, with an alleged Ur-Mark. We have now learned to differentiate the synoptic layers of tradition more precisely. Among the oldest, we consider an ancient account of the passion and the source of the logia. Yet even in the identification of these, however decisive their consideration may be, it is essential to apply these criteria.

Surveying the list of criteria, which vary considerably in their usefulness and application, we may surely find that they yield results if they are used together. Yet the methodological equipment can be expanded further. We have already mentioned that the criteria—from first to last—are determined by content, that is to say, their standards are derived from the content of a tradition. Behind this is the realization that the evaluation of a narrative form must in no wise be carried out in such a way that its content is essentially seen only as a reflection of the history of the early church. It was handled in this way by a particular form critical approach to the Gospels. The content does precede the form, and this can also mean, of course, that the content is earlier in time.[42] Thus it is quite feasible for an apophthegm-like story to reflect a historical reminiscence of Jesus' ministry, and it should not be classified as community reflection simply because it is an apophthegm-like story.

Along with the criteria governing the assessment of the Jesus tradition, some achievements have been made concerning the characteristics of his language. In this connection reference is made primarily to the parables of Jesus. While they share the imagery with the Jewish parabolic tradition, they contrast sharply in their freshness, urgency, and compelling kind of proclamation. In this sense it can be said that they have neither forerunners nor successors, for even the early Christian community could no longer rise to the uniqueness of this pictorial language. If in the Jewish world parables are largely the means of memorizing erudition that has been handed down, in the mouth of Jesus they become the message that captivates his listeners. To be sure, most of the parables were produced in the context of their tradition, and many of them were raised to a new

---

[42] This is emphasized in T. Holtz, "Kenntnis von Jesus und Kenntnis Jesu," *TLZ* 104 (1979) 1–12.

level of understanding by allegorizing them. Nevertheless, strictly speaking, it is always possible to recover their basic form. The reason for this lies in the independence of every single parabolic story, as well as in their aesthetic and balanced character. If the modern language of literary science describes parables as aesthetic objects, the point is precisely this: that each and every one of them represents a small world. For this reason it will be important for us to return to the parables of Jesus.

The more detailed forms of speech[43] that Jesus preferred are paradox, antithetical parallelism, the divine passive, and certain rhythmic structures that emerge if one attempts to translate the Greek text back into Aramaic. These may be used as additional support. Two Aramaic expressions that remained untranslated in Greek were characteristic for him; one of them is significant on account of its position. This is the phrase "Amen, I tell you," in which the front position of the amen is conspicuous because (liturgically) the term generally functions as a confirmation. The second is the term "Abba," the address in prayer (Mark 14:36) that is without parallel in the world around it. In addition, a particular two-part structure has been discovered in various sayings of Jesus, by means of which the present and the (eschatological) future can be juxtaposed in such a way that the determination of the present by this future is made compellingly prominent. Luke 12:8 may be cited as an example: "Every one who acknowledges me before men, the Son of man also will acknowledge before the angels of God" (cf. Matt 23:12; Mark 10:31; Luke 6:20f.).[44]

Detailed features of Jesus' language that are more strongly shaped by content are the sayings denouncing human self-righteousness, which is offended by God's mercy. More negatively,[45] F. Mussner draws attention to sayings with an open, indirect, vague Christology or soteriology in which the absence of the influence of post-Easter confessions gives evidence of their great antiquity.[46] R. Riesner, who addressed this problem in depth but who may have missed the mark in many instances, searches for reference points in Jesus' preaching for the formation of tradition, or at least reference points that make

---

[43] Cf. J. Jeremias, *New Testament Theology I: The Proclamation of Jesus* (ET; New York: Scribners, 1971) 8–37; Hahn, "Überlegungen," 35f.; Lehmann, *Quellenanalyse,* 189–95.

[44] Cf. J. M. Robinson, *Kerygma und historischer Jesus* (Zurich, 1960) 228–31.

[45] Cf. Farmer, "A Historical Essay on the Humanity of Jesus Christ," in *Christian History and Interpretation: Studies Presented to J. Knox* (Cambridge: Cambridge University Press, 1967) 124f.

[46] Mussner, "Methodologie," 133.

it comprehensible that his words were impressed upon the memory of the hearers. He draws attention to the authority with which Jesus spoke, to his timely calls to careful hearing ("He who has ears to hear, let him hear"), to enigmatic or prophetic sayings that called for thought, to formulations chosen for the purpose of memorization, and to the fact that Jesus himself provided tersely formulated summaries of his teaching.[47]

In contrast to the past era of Bultmann, the confidence of scholarship in the reliability of the Jesus tradition has increased markedly. The methodological instrument at our disposal offers criteria and characteristics that promise success if used together. What has to be rejected primarily, however, is the critical bias which argues that the burden of proof rests on those who seek to show the authenticity of a tradition.[48] Of course, this means starting with inauthenticity as a principle. Quite apart from the fact that the concept of "proof" is untenable in the context of historical research, this school of thought thereby handles its case too easily. Because we know, as delineated above, that the Jesus traditions were carried further and interpreted, and because this further formation too calls for plausibility, both have to be examined to the best of our ability, that which pertains to Jesus, his very own word, his very own deed, as well as the new interpretation and reshaping by the post-Easter community. The assessment of the tradition is factual and meaningful only in this overall context. Many interpreters have contributed to the shaping of criteria by means of which, it is argued, a tradition can be recognized as being formed by a community.[49] For W. G. Kümmel this is associated with the tendencies that typify the early Christian development of faith and hence must have made changes in the Jesus tradition.[50]

We shall also attempt to do justice to this last aspect and to show, at least in a cursory fashion, the directions these post-Easter reshapings and new interpretations took. By extrapolating them, the portrait of Jesus may be seen more clearly. In addition we intend, to

---

[47] R. Riesner, *Jesus als Lehrer* (2d ed.; WUNT II/7; Tübingen, 1984) 423.

[48] This has been reiterated frequently since Bultmann, as in Hahn, "Überlegungen," 27f., though he does so with restrictions.

[49] Cf. O. Cullmann, "Unzeitgemässe Bemerkungen zum 'historischen Jesus' der Bultmannschule," 141–58, here 154–57 in *Vorträge und Aufsätze 1925–1962* (Tübingen: Mohr, 1966).

[50] W. G. Kümmel, "Der persönliche Anspruch Jesu und der Christusglaube der Urgemeinde," 429–38, here 432, in *Heilsgeschehen und Geschichte* (MThSt 3; Marburg: N. G. Elwert, 1965).

the extent that it is profitable and capable of shedding light on the background of the ministry of Jesus, to make frequent use of contemporary extrabiblical sources. For this reason we begin with two chapters dedicated to the description of the political, spiritual, and social milieu in Israel at the time of Jesus.

Select bibliography: J. Blank, "Lernprozesse im Jüngerkreis Jesu," *TQ* 158 (1978) 163–77; N. A. Dahl, "Der gekreuzigte Messias," 149–69 in *Der historische Jesus und der kerygmatische Christus* (ed. H. Ristow and K. Matthiae; Berlin: Evangelische Verlagsanstalt, 1960); N. A. Dahl, "Der historische Jesus als geschichtswissenschaftliches und theologisches Problem," *KD* (1, 1955) 104–32; W. R. Farmer, "A Historical Essay on the Humanity of Jesus Christ," 101–26 in *Christian History and Interpretation: Studies Presented to J. Knox* (ed. W. R. Farmer and C. F. D. Moule; Cambridge: Cambridge University Press, 1967); R. and W. Feneberg, *Das Leben Jesu im Evangelium* (QD 88; Freiburg: Verlag Herder, 1980); J. A. Fitzmyer, *Die Wahrheit der Evangelien* (SBS 1; Stuttgart: Verlag Katholisches Bibelwerk, 1965); M. Hengel, "Kerygma oder Geschichte?" *TQ* 151 (1971) 323–36; T. Holtz, "Kenntnis von Jesus und Kenntnis Jesu," *TLZ* 104 (1979) 1–12; K. Kertelge, ed., *Rückfrage nach Jesus* (QD 63; Freiburg: Herder, 1974), with the following contributions among others: F. Hahn, "Methodologische Überlegungen zur Rückfrage nach Jesus," 11–77; F. Lentzen-Deis, "Kriterien für die historische Beurteilung der Jesusüberlieferung in den Evangelien," 78–117; F. Mussner, "Methodologie der Frage nach dem historischen Jesus," 118–47. H. Koester, "The Historical Jesus," 123–36 in *Christology and a Modern Pilgrimage: A Discussion with Norman Perrin* (ed. H. D. Betz; Claremont, Calif.: NT Colloquium, 1971); R. Latourelle, *Finding Jesus Through the Gospels* (ET; New York: Alba House, 1979); D. Lührmann, "Die Frage nach Kriterien für ursprüngliche Jesusworte," 59–72 in *Jésus aux origines de la Christologie* (ed. J. Dupont; BETL 40; Louvain: Louvain University, 1975); J. Roloff, "Auf der Suche nach einem neuen Jesusbild," *TLZ* 98 (1973) 561–72; E. P. Sanders, *Jesus and Judaism* (London, 1985); G. Schille, "Prolegomena zur Jesusfrage," *TLZ* 93 (1968) 481–88; S. Schulz, "Die neue Frage nach dem historischen Jesus," 33–42, in *NT und Geschichte* (FS O. Cullmann; Tübingen: Mohr, 1972); G. Strecker, "Die historische und theologische Problematik der Jesusfrage," *EvT* 29 (1969) 453–76; U. Wilckens, "Jesusüberlieferung und Christuskerygma," *ThViat* 10 (1966) 310–30.

2

Israel's Political Situation in the Time of Jesus

1. The Roman emperors Augustus and Tiberius

From the standpoint of the center of Roman politics, the lifetime of Jesus is located in the time of the reigns of two emperors, Octavian Augustus (27 BCE–14 CE) and Tiberius (14–37). Neither of the two ever came to the eastern regions of the empire; neither ever stepped on Syrian or Palestinian soil. Yet the extended period of their reigns secured peace and prosperity for the political commonwealth. The name of Augustus, who was able to conclude the civil wars successfully and whose prudent reign benefited from a time of bliss, is linked with the memory of the Pax Romana Augusta. Poets and priests applauded. In his fourth *Eclogue* Virgil announces the golden era. Horace, the writer of the *Carmen saeculare*, elsewhere lauds Augustus as the greatest of rulers.[1] Though he rejected it in Rome itself, the emperor allowed those in the eastern part of the empire to venerate him as a deity, especially when this cult was linked with the goddess Roma. The striking evidence for this is the temple in Ancyra (today's Ankara), dedicated to him and to the *dea Roma,* on the walls of which the extensive Latin and Greek inscription of the *Res gestae divi Augusti* was discovered as early as the sixteenth century. There, at the age of seventy-six (about one year before his death), in the emperor's own list of his accomplishments, he remarks in conclu-

---

[1] *Carmina* 4.14.6 (9th ed., ed. H. Färber; Munich, 1982) 212.

sion with particular satisfaction that the Senate, the nobility, and the population of Rome as a whole had granted to him the name "father of the fatherland" (*pater patriae*).[2] Although Palestine never personally concerned Augustus, his might was present in the country, represented by King Herod and then by Herod's sons and by the Roman procurators in Judea.

Similar things can be said about Tiberius, who was supposedly shy and, as he aged, increasingly retreated to Campania and to the island of Capri. Sejanus, the prefect of the guard, whose influence upon the emperor began to rise around 20 CE,[3] became virtually all-powerful in the emperor's absence from Rome. It was to Sejanus, an enemy of the Jews, to whom Pontius Pilate was indebted for his appointment as procurator of Judea. In the fifteenth year of the reign of the emperor Tiberius there appeared John the Baptist (Luke 3:1). The appointment of L. Vitellius as the governor of Syria in 35 CE is attributed to Tiberius; the name of Vitellius is linked with the removal of Pilate from his post.[4]

2. Herod the Great

Jesus was born during the reign of Herod, who was thus his first sovereign. Because he came from a wealthy Idumean family— Antipater was his father and his mother, Kypros, was a Nabataean— the Jewish people regarded him an intruder and foreign usurper. His government is charged with the altercation, understandable as far as power politics are concerned but nevertheless bloody, with the members of the Hasmonean royal house, which preceded him in power. Even the Hasmonean princess Mariamne, his second wife, became the victim of political power. Herod succeeded in forging a domain that encompassed Idumea, Judea, Samaria, Galilee, Perea, and extensive areas of northeastern Palestine, and in controlling it peaceably for almost thirty years. Toward the end of 40 BCE, by decree of the Roman Senate and with the urging of the triumvirs Anthony and Octavian, later to become Augustus, Herod was declared king of Judea. The Roman regents viewed Herod as the ideal man to pacify the unruly Jewish people, settled at the empire's periphery, and to subordinate them to the power of Rome. To argue that he acted merely on the basis of selfish ambitions of power is to insinuate too

---

[2] *Res gestae Augusti* 35 (3d ed.; ed. E. Weber; Munich: Heimeran, 1975).
[3] Cf. Tacitus, *Ann.* 1.24; 3.29.4.
[4] Sejanus, who later instigated a conspiracy, was executed in 31 CE.

base an attitude on the part of Herod. He was much more convinced
of the political mission of Rome, into which he endeavored to fit,
and especially of the ecumenical task on the part of Augustus, who
graciously received Herod after conquering Mark Anthony, though
Herod had previously supported Anthony.

Herod's political position in the power structure of the Roman
Empire is designated by the title "associated king and friend of the
people of Rome" (*rex socius et amicus populi Romani*). As Rome's extended arm for his country, his use of power internally was not
restricted, though he was not allowed to engage in foreign policy. His
internal authority encompassed the entire practice, public as well as
private, of civil and criminal law, the public and financial administration, and the right to maintain an army. The fact that he was restricted
in terms of foreign policy can be illustrated by an event in 9 BCE.
Augustus had heard that Herod had undertaken a campaign against the
Arabs without seeking prior permission from Rome. As a result, the
emperor wrote to him in no uncertain terms that hitherto he had
treated him as a friend but from now on he would regard him as a
subject.[5] Nevertheless, the king was accorded extraordinary powers for
internal affairs *ad personam*. This meant, among other things, that he
was not readily able to let his sons inherit these powers; and to be
legally binding, his will required the emperor's sanction.

Herod applied the power vested in him with the skill of a states-
man and with consistency, but at times also with hardness and
brutality. In their practice the courts of law that he established
resembled the Hellenistic Roman interpretation of law. The details
of the individual taxes he levied can be ascertained only with difficulty. There is some evidence, however, that for his own affairs he levied
a head tax that exceeded the one used during the Hasmonean period
and that he also had to raise a tribute to be passed on to the emperor.
In addition there were various kinds of taxes: head tax, census levy,
income and property tax, salt tax, and others.[6] He reorganized the tax
system in a way that outlasted his own lifetime. The areas of authority of the Sanhedrin, the highest Jewish judicial body, were very
restricted. They certainly did not possess the *potestas gladii*, that is, the
authority to execute a person. Schalit suspects that they were even
deprived of the right to function as an advisory body.[7] While the

---

[5] Cf. Josephus, *Ant.* 16.290; A. Schalit, *König Herodes* (SJ 4; Berlin: de Gruyter, 1969) 166.
[6] Cf. Schalit, *Herodes,* 262–98.
[7] Ibid., 302.

Hasmoneans had combined royalty with the high-priestly office, Herod had to be satisfied with the former. As a foreigner from Idumea, he could not afford to grasp for the high-priestly office as well. This much is clear. Yet the high-priestly office functioning alongside him was curtailed considerably. Its hereditariness, according to which the high-priestly honor was passed from the father to the son, was abolished, as was the right of the officiating high priest to remain in office for life. Now the high priest was but a cultic official who depended on the will of Herod.

Nevertheless, Herod endeavored to lift his kingdom beyond being a mere political power and to give it a religious flair. This, of course, he did in such a way that every pious Jew deemed it offensive and was stirred with abhorrence. In one instance the king was willing to oblige Jewish sensitivities. He refurbished the Jerusalem temple with new splendor, thus raising the city's prestige within the country as well as outside it. But then he enlarged his realm to an extent reminiscent of the kingdom of David. David, however, was the prototype of the Messiah. It must be said, however, that for Herod it was not Israel and the expected Messiah who were the guarantors of peace, prosperity, and redemption, but Rome and the universal emperor, especially Augustus. As a king by the grace of Rome, he claimed to represent Rome's splendor. For his own part, he was prepared to participate in the imperial cult when it began to spread in the provinces. It is instructive that he named the newly established capital of Samaria "Sebaste," which (as a Greek equivalent of *augustus*) has connotations of a dedication to the divine emperor. In the final analysis, because by his attitude Herod questioned Israel's distinctiveness and election as God's people, his Roman imperial messianism must have appeared suspicious to the people and led to the further deepening of the chasm between king and people.

3. The sons of Herod

Herod had to change his will. To begin with, he accorded primacy to Antipater, the son from his first marriage to Doris, the Jerusalemite. Herod intended for him to be king over the entire state, while Alexander and Aristobulus, the sons from his marriage to Mariamne, the Hasmonean, were only to be given the status of king over a specific territory. Incredible intrigues, however, especially on the part of Antipater against his two half brothers, resulted in their execution. But even Antipater himself, having instigated a conspiracy, fell victim to the violence shortly before his father's death. Five days before Herod's death, around the end of March or beginning of April in 4 BCE, Herod mustered his remaining strength and made provision in his will for Archelaus to be declared king, that is, governor of the entire country. Antipas and Philip were to be tetrarchs, one over Galilee, Perea, and Transjordan, the other over Gaulanitis, Trachonitis, Batanea up to the town of Panea, and all of the northeastern territories. Archelaus and Antipas were Herod's sons from his fourth marriage, to Malthace, a Samaritan, and hence full brothers, while Philip, the son from his fifth marriage, to Cleopatra of Jerusalem, was their half brother.[8] Herod also ordered Archelaus to bring his signet ring and the sealed governmental documents to Augustus in Rome, for he had the final decision on all matters decreed by the king.[9]

Following Herod's death, however, turmoil began to break out in various parts of the country. Before Archelaus could leave for Rome, he had to crush an uprising in Jerusalem. Until the succession to the throne was settled, Augustus provisionally sent a procurator, Sabinus, to Israel to see to peace and quiet. But Sabinus was reckless in his behavior and provoked the people. There were squabbles about the succession among the heirs. Antipater accompanied Archelaus on the journey to the emperor because he felt he had been treated badly. Other relatives of the Herodian house were also present in Rome. Meanwhile a certain Judas gathered a group of rebels around him in Galilee, near Sepphoris, and made the region insecure. The same was done in Perea by a certain Simon, one of Herod's former slaves. The Roman legate Varus intervened against the troublemakers with an army from Syrian Antioch, advancing almost to Jerusalem, and en route burned down Sepphoris. In this connection it is good to realize that Sepphoris was only two and one-half miles from Nazareth, where the child Jesus was growing up with his family at the time.

In Rome, Emperor Augustus summoned the various representatives in the feud over Herod's succession to the temple of Apollo, where he heard their case. Broadly speaking, his decision confirmed Herod's will. Perhaps the most important change was that he refused to give Archelaus the royal title; instead he was declared

---

[8] Herod the Great had ten marriages: with Doris of Jerusalem, Mariamne the Hasmonean, Mariamne the daughter of a priest, Malthace the Samaritan, Cleopatra of Jerusalem, Pallas, Phaidra, Elpis, and two whose names are unknown.

[9] Cf. Josephus, *War* 11.668f.; *Ant.* 17.188f.

ethnarch of Judea, Samaria, and Idumea. Antipas and Philip were accorded the title of tetrarch. Archelaus had to relinquish the towns of Gaza, Gadara, and Hippos to the province of Syria. Nevertheless he gained by far the best deal, as indicated by the tribute the rulers collected from their possessions. For Archelaus this amounted to six hundred talents annually, for Antipas only two hundred, and for Philip one hundred.[10]

For the life of Jesus, the most important of Herod's sons was without a doubt his sovereign, Herod Antipas (4 BCE–39 CE). He began his reign at the age of sixteen, was famed as ambitious, smart, and loving splendor, but was less energetic than his father. He rebuilt Sepphoris, which Varus had destroyed, built walls around it, and made it his residence. The construction of an open amphitheater attests to the tetrarch's Hellenistic-Roman mindset, which was further demonstrated by his naming of Betharamphtha, which he fortified, after Livia, the emperor's wife, later Julia. The most significant town he established was Tiberias, on the western shore of the Lake of Gennesaret; he named it in honor of the emperor Tiberius and moved his residence there. It is not possible to indicate the precise date of the founding of the town; in all likelihood it could not have been before 20 CE. At the time of Jesus' ministry the town was already established.[11] The construction of the town caused quite a stir, for to make room for the new town, a large number of gravestones had to be removed. Since this rendered the town unclean according to Levitical law, pious Jews refused to settle in Tiberias despite enticing offers. Antipas was forced to attract all kinds of migrant people, partly by force.[12] The fact that Tiberias is not mentioned anywhere in the Gospels as a place of his ministry probably sheds a distinctive light on Jesus as a Jew.[13] Presumably he did not enter the town either. In his country Antipas exercised absolute judicial authority. It was he who had John the Baptist captured and executed. This information we gain

---

[10] Cf. Josephus, *Ant.* 17.318–320.

[11] Ibid., 18.35f., does not mention the founding of Tiberias until after Pilate's inauguration in office, which could be a chronological link.

[12] Cf. ibid., 18.36–38.

[13] Tiberias is mentioned three times in John's Gospel. John 21:1 mentions the "Sea of Tiberias," as Lake Gennesaret was called. In 6:1 one finds the awkward phrase "Sea of Galilee of Tiberias." In 6:23, an obscure text content-wise, reference is made, after the feeding of the multitudes, to boats having come from Tiberias. On this cf. R. Schnackenburg, *The Gospel according to John* (ET; New York: Crossroad, 1990) 2.32–35. In any case, Jesus is not directly associated with Tiberias. In the Synoptics the place is not mentioned at all.

both from the Synoptic Gospels and from Josephus. Nevertheless, there are divergences regarding the motive for the tetrarch's intervention and regarding the circumstantial details of the execution. Mark 6:17–29 par. Matt 14:3–12 narrate the well-known account of the vengeful Herodias, who was out to kill the Baptist because he castigated her relationship with Antipas following the dissolution of her marriage with one of Antipas's stepbrothers,[14] and who achieved her goal with the help of her dancing daughter at the occasion of the tetrarch's birthday. According to Josephus (Ant. 18.116–119), however, Antipas's action had political reasons. He was afraid that John might incite the people to rebellion through his popularity and eloquence. Because of his suspicion, he had the Baptist chained, moved to the Machaerus fortress on the eastern shore of the Dead Sea, and there had him executed. The true motive is preserved in Josephus. The synoptic tradition is shaped according to the model of the prophet Elijah, who was persecuted by Jezebel, the wife of King Ahab of Samaria (1 Kgs 19:1–3).[15] The Baptist's martyrdom should be dated to the end of the twenties.[16]

For Jesus, too, Antipas was dangerous. According to Luke 13:31 he was warned about the ruler and told to leave the region because he intended to have Jesus killed. The assessment of the incident in the passion narrative, found only in Luke 23:6–12, in which after the arrest of Jesus Pilate had presented him to Antipas, will be made later. In any case, in Jerusalem the tetrarch had no legal authority whatsoever.

It is on account of the ambitions of his wife Herodias that Antipas lost his country.[17] Because of her constant insistence he went to Rome to ask Caligula to bestow on him the title of king, which the emperor had given to Agrippa, the heir of Philip, in 7 CE. Agrippa,

---

[14] According to Josephus, Ant. 18.109, the stepbrother was named after his father Herod and was the offspring of his marriage to Mariamne the priest's daughter. Philip, mentioned in Mark 6:17 par., was married not to Herodias but to her daughter Salome.

[15] In Josephus, Ant. 18.109–115, the marital affairs of Antipas play a part in the history of the Baptist as well, though only indirectly. According to Josephus the tetrarch had disowned his first wife, a daughter of the Nabatean king Aretas IV, in order to marry Herodias. Consequently Aretas moved into battle against Antipas and inflicted a major defeat upon him. The people interpreted this event as God's punishment of Antipas because of his execution of the Baptist. On the event as a whole, cf. J. Gnilka, "Das Martyrium Johannes des Täufers," 78–92 in Orientierung an Jesus (FS J. Schmid; Freiburg: Herder, 1973).

[16] W. Schenk, "Gefangenschaft und Tod des Täufers," ZNW 29 (1983) 453–83, has argued for the time between the end of 34 and 36.

[17] Cf. Josephus, Ant. 18.245–256.

however, made accusations (some false) against Antipas; so Antipas was instead deposed and exiled to Lugdunum (Lyons) in Gaul, where he died. His proud wife Herodias followed him into exile.

Along with Antipas, Philip, the tetrarch of the northeastern regions (4 BCE–34 CE), is mentioned in the Gospel as well. This is the case in the major synchronism of Luke 3:1, where he is introduced as the tetrarch of Iturea and Trachonitis. His is said to have been a benevolent, just, and peaceful reign. From Josephus we learn that he was always eager to grant legal assistance to everyone seeking it.[18] He was the only ruler of a territory with a Jewish population to mint coins with the portrait of Augustus and Tiberius. The population of his territory was mixed, however, with the Greco-Syrian element even exceeding the Jewish one. Philip further demonstrated his devotion to the imperial house by giving the new name Caesarea, in honor of the emperor, to Paneas, a place he enlarged at the source of the Jordan river, and by giving the name Julia, in honor of Augustus's daughter, to Bethsaida, not far from where the Jordan issues into Lake Gennesaret—a small place that he elevated to the status of a town and expanded. In the Gospels Caesarea, in the area of which Simon Peter's messianic confession occurred, is called Caesarea Philippi (Mark 8:27 par.), thus also preserving the tetrarch's name. Julia, however, the home of the apostles Simon Peter, Andrew, and Philip, is consistently referred to as Bethsaida (John 1:44; 12:21; Mark 6:45; 8:22; Matt 11:21 par.; Luke 9:10). Jesus himself entered the territory of Philip and ministered in Bethsaida. This is supported not only by the disciples who came from there but also by the rebuke of Bethsaida in the woes against the Galilean towns (Matt 11:21 par.). It is also possible that he occasionally visited the region in an attempt to escape being apprehended by Antipas. Philip the tetrarch resided in Bethsaida and died there in the twentieth year of the reign of the emperor Tiberius (33/34 CE) and was interred in a magnificent burial place which he had built during his lifetime.

Archelaus (4 BCE–6 CE), who had been favored in his father's will as well as by Augustus, proved to be the least worthy son of Herod. He was a tyrannical and capricious ruler of his people. Soon after his induction as ethnarch of Judea and Idumea he replaced the officiating high priest, Joazar, with his brother Eleazar. In turn Eleazar himself had to give way soon to a certain Joshua Ben Sie. The people were particularly offended by his second marriage, to Glaphyra, the wife of

---

[18] Cf. ibid., 18.106–108.

his half brother Alexander. In the tenth year of his reign a delegation of noble Jews and Samaritans went to Rome to lodge a complaint with Augustus against Archelaus's cruelty and tyranny.

The allegations must have been extremely serious, for Augustus's reaction was unusually severe. He did not even respect Archelaus enough to send him a letter but ordered him to Rome by means of a delegate. There he was removed from office by the court of law and was punished by being stripped of his estate and banned to exile in Vienna, in Gaul.[19] The only direct mention of Archelaus in the Gospel confirms his bad reputation (Matt 2:22). The Lukan version of the parable of the ten minas may contain an allusion to Archelaus. It is assumed that the episode of the heir to the throne who traveled to a distant country to be confirmed as the new king, of the endeavors of the inhabitants of that country to prevent this from happening, and of the cruel vengeance by the new king upon his return (Luke 19:12–27) contains a reminiscence of the events surrounding Archelaus's induction as ethnarch in 4 BCE.[20]

4. The Roman procurators in Judea

The territory that had been governed by Archelaus was placed directly under the auspices of the Roman administration in 6 CE. Within the territories of Judea, Samaria, and Idumea it encompassed the cities of Jerusalem, Caesarea Maritima, Samaria/Sebaste, and Joppa. A procurator of equestrian rank was appointed over the country. The few Roman provinces governed by procurators were subject to continuing unrest; hence Rome was of the opinion that they needed a firm hand. The title of the procurator is given various renditions in contemporary literature. The dominant term in the NT is ἡγεμών, while Josephus prefers ἐπίτροπος. In the Latin inscription of Caesarea, Pilate is called *praefectus Judaeae*.[21] The title *praefectus* was probably chosen by Augustus.[22] The procurator was loosely subordinated to the governor of Syria, especially in cases of emergency. In conjunction with establishing the Roman administration, P. Sulpicius Quirinius, the governor of Syria, and Coponius, the first procurator of Judea, conducted a census of the people for taxation purposes. Although Herod and his

---

[19] Cf. ibid., 17.337–344.

[20] J. Jeremias, *The Parables of Jesus* (ET; 2d rev. ed., London: SCM, 1972) 59.

[21] Cf. Y. Israeli, *Highlights of Archaeology: The Israel Museum, Jerusalem* (Jerusalem: Israel Museum, 1984) 92f.

[22] Cf. Schürer, *History*, 1.358.

sons had maintained some sort of mindfulness of Jewish sensibilities, it became clear quite quickly that the Roman yoke was even more oppressive and ignominious. The founding of the anti-Roman party of the Zealots is related to this census.

The procurators of Judea resided in Caesarea Maritima. But for special occasions, especially during major Jewish festivals when the population swelled, they used to relocate to Jerusalem. At their disposal was an army composed not of soldiers who were Roman citizens, as was the case in the Roman legions, but of soldiers who were drafted from the population of the country. Thus these were auxiliary troops. Since the Jewish population was exempted from military service, the troops may have been made up primarily of Samaritans and Arabs. The Romans may well have made use of their opposition to the Jews, as indicated in the extant examples of anti-Semitism among the soldiers.[23] The taxes raised by the procurator went directly to the imperial treasury, rather than to the state treasury. The organization of Judea into eleven toparchies was most probably for the purpose of a smoother process of taxation.

The temple of Jerusalem was under government protection. The generous scope of this protection can be seen in the death penalty associated with the prohibition against non-Jews entering the sacred area behind the temple gates. The Romans had posted relevant warnings in Greek and Latin.[24] They respected Jewish convictions inasmuch as they avoided carrying standards depicting the emperor when they entered Jerusalem. Yet they kept the magnificent robe of the high priest under tight security in the Antonia fortress. Twice a day a sacrifice had to be offered in the temple for the emperor and the Roman people. The procurator probably exercised some sort of supervision over the financial administration of the temple. Likewise the appointment of the high priest was made by the Romans, either by the Syrian governor or by the procurator of Judea. In any case, this was true from 6 to 41 CE.

Five Roman procurators held office during the time of Jesus. Their terms of office can be indicated roughly as follows: 1. Coponius, 6–9 CE; 2. Marcus Ambibulus, 9–12; 3. Annius Rufus, 12–15; 4. Valerius Gratus, 15–26; 5. Pontius Pilate, 26–36. The census took place during the term of Coponius. We have virtually no information

---

[23] When Agrippa died in 44 CE the soldiers expressed their joy over the demise of this pro-Jewish king in an inappropriate manner. Cf. Josephus, *Ant.* 19.354–366.

[24] Text in Dittenberger, OGJS II, no. 598.

about the second and third procurators. During his tenure of eleven years Valerius Gratus appointed four high priests, all but one of whom officiated only one year each. The last of them was Joseph Caiaphas.[25] Valerius Gratus was appointed by Tiberius, whose policy it was to grant the procurators as long a term of office as possible. This is the reason for the eleven and ten years of office by the two procurators of Judea mentioned last. What is significant, however, is the reason for this policy. Tiberius was of the opinion that procurators were like flies on the body of an injured person; once they have absorbed enough blood, they become more moderate in their extortions.[26]

The most important procurator for us, of course, is Pilate, from the equestrian Pontii family. He became famous throughout the world and for all times because of his decisive collaboration in the crucifixion of Jesus of Nazareth. Another member of this family, L. Pontius Aquilius, is remembered in history for his part in the murder of Julius Caesar. The name of Pilate's wife is Procula Claudia, according to tradition. It is reasonable to expect that she resided in Judea as well (cf. Matt 27:19). Caesar Augustus had previously rescinded the order that Roman wives were not allowed to accompany their husbands to their procuratorial posts. Philo of Alexandria describes Pilate as by nature unbending, stubborn, and intransigent and charges him with corruptibility, brutality, robberies, cruelties, libel, ongoing executions without legal proceedings, and continuous and unbearable atrocities. Even if this assessment is exaggerated, the impression remains of an unpredictable, cruel individual. Several events from his tenure that have been handed down highlight his conduct in office and the tense relationship between him and the Jewish people. In this connection Philo reports that the Roman had ordered gold-plated votive shields be brought to Jerusalem. The people's indignation did not achieve anything until a complaint was lodged before Caesar himself.[27] Josephus tells of an even more dramatic incident: This time Pilate had ordered ensigns bearing the portrait of the emperor brought into the city, although the Jewish law forbade all images. After several petitions presented to him in vain, Pilate assembled the people in the arena in Caesarea, had his soldiers encircle them, and then threatened them with immediate massacre. When the Jews cast themselves to the ground and bared their necks, declaring that they would rather die

[25] Cf. Josephus, *Ant.* 18.29–35.
[26] Cf. Schürer, *History,* 1.383.
[27] Philo, *On the Embassy to Gaius* 299–305.

than permit what the law forbids, he had to concede defeat and order the images be removed from Jerusalem. Josephus also reports an uprising that resulted when Pilate built a water conduit in Jerusalem with funds from the temple. The uprising was crushed with considerable bloodshed.[28] According to Luke 13:1 the procurator had some Galileans massacred in the temple precinct while they were offering their sacrifices. Josephus does not mention this incident.

Against this backdrop it is even more surprising that not a single new high priest was appointed during Pilate's ten years of procuratorship. The high priest Joseph Caiaphas, appointed by Valerius Gratus, did not lose his office until the year when Pilate was deposed and Vitellius, the Syrian governor, declared Jonathan ben Ananos to be the high priest. This lengthy joint tenure of Pilate and Caiaphas and their simultaneous loss of office in 36 CE lead to the conclusion that Caiaphas was prepared to cooperate with the Roman to a considerable extent. This is probably also significant with regard to the execution of Jesus. The reason for Pilate's dismissal from office was a massacre of Samaritans for which he was responsible in the village of Tirathaba. They were about to ascend to their holy mount Gerizim, and because they carried weapons, Pilate felt he had to intervene. Vitellius, to whom the Samaritans brought their complaint, ordered Pilate to leave for Rome to answer to the emperor. But before he reached Rome, Tiberius died.[29] At this point Pilate vanishes from the stage of history. Reports that arose later about his suicide or his execution by emperor Nero are to be attributed to Christian legend.[30]

5. The high priests and the Sanhedrin

When Jesus was born, it probably still was Simon ben Boethos (ca. 24–5 BCE) who officiated as the high priest in Jerusalem; he originated from an Alexandrian family and a lower priestly house. His installation as high priest by Herod the Great sheds significant light on the political conditions and the status of the second in command after the king in the Jewish state. Simon had a daughter, Mariamne, who was deemed the most beautiful woman of her time. Herod, desiring her to be his wife, removed the obstacle of social distance by promoting her father to the high priesthood.[31] We have previously met the son

---

[28] Josephus, *Ant.* 18.55–62.
[29] Cf. ibid., 18.85–89.
[30] Cf. Schürer, *History*, 1.389 n. 151.
[31] Cf. Josephus, *Ant.* 15.320–322.

Mariamne bore, also named Herod. He was married to Herodias, whom Antipas later stole from him—the event against which John the Baptist protested. But ultimately Simon the high priest fell out of favor with Herod the Great in connection with the conspiracy of Antipater. The king dismissed him on the spot, and his place was taken by Matthias ben Theophilos, a citizen of Jerusalem.[32]

Matthias held office for only one year. He lost the high-priestly honor when offerings brought by Herod were destroyed during disturbances in the temple.[33] We barely know more than the names of the high priests that followed. Among them were Joseph ben Ellem, Joazor ben Boethos, and Eleazar ben Boethos. It is apparent that Herod favored the Boethos family. Eleazar was indeed appointed as high priest by Archelaus, in 4 BCE.[34] Later on Archelaus reappointed to the high-priestly office Joazor ben Boethos, who had held the office previously and had supported the Roman census. In 6 CE, however, Quirinius divested him because he was caught in a quarrel with the people.[35] The office was given to Annas ben Sethi. With him one of the most important high priests enters the stage, and his traces are also found in the NT. He is mentioned in the Lukan and Johannine traditions only, but quite prominently. According to John 18:13f., 19–24, Jesus is examined by him during the trial. In this connection it is important to consider that the Fourth Gospel does not mention the trial before the Sanhedrin. According to Luke 3:2, Annas and Caiaphas held the high-priestly office jointly during the time of John the Baptist's ministry. Acts 4:6 even conveys the idea that Annas alone was the high priest who questioned Peter shortly after Jesus' death. In reality Joseph Caiaphas was in office at that time. Annas officiated from 6 to 15 CE but was quite influential even in subsequent years. Must Luke have been mindful of that, or did he have the impression of two functioning high priests? According to Josephus,[36] Annas was considered most fortunate because five of his sons were reported to have served the Lord as high priests—an unprecedented situation. Elsewhere he parenthetically mentions the tomb of Annas, situated south of the city.[37]

---

[32] Cf. ibid., 17.78. Mariamne was disowned and Herod's son eliminated from the will.

[33] Cf. ibid., 17.155–167. It happened during the term of Matthias that a high priest had to be appointed for a single festival day because Matthias declined to exercise his ministry on account of a dream. The substitute was Joseph ben Ellem. Cf. ibid., 17.164–167.

[34] Cf. ibid., 17.339–341.

[35] Cf. ibid., 18.3; 18.26.

[36] Ibid., 20.198.

[37] Josephus, War 5.506.

Between the tenures of Annas and Caiaphas there were three high priests, each of whom officiated only one year. Annas, removed from office by the procurator Valerius Gratus, was replaced by Ishmael ben Phiabi. The latter was followed in office by Ishmael ben Annas,[38] then by Simon ben Camithi, and finally by Joseph from the house of Caiaph (hence the epithet Caiaphas), 18–36 CE. According to John 18:13 he was the son-in-law of Annas, who for his part was able thereby to secure the political power for his house. In the Synoptic Gospels Caiaphas enters the spotlight of history in the context of the passion narrative. Here he emerges as the leader in the endeavor to remove Jesus. This applies to the account of the investigation in Mark 14:53–65 par. and John 11:47–51. Josephus[39] provides a very brief reference to his demotion by Vitellius. In the same connection reference is made to returning the high-priestly vestments to the Jews. Despite the deals he made with Pilate, Caiaphas apparently was unable to achieve this goal. In retrospect this scene sheds further light on Pilate, who was not ready for this gesture, given his disposition to the Jews, which was distanced and full of hatred.

The high-priestly clan, purchasing the office and determined to maintain it as its own, was unpopular, held in low regard, and hated among the people. A folk song handed down in the Talmud, a popular melody of sorts, expresses aptly the resentment over the wheelings and dealings of the priestly aristocracy:

Woe is me in front of the house of Boethos: woe is me because of their clubs!

Woe is me in front of the house of Annas: woe is me because of their denunciations! . . .

For they are high priests, and their sons are treasurers, and their sons-in-law are administrators, and their servants beat the people with canes.[40]

In order to get a better overview, the following provides a listing of the governing authorities in Palestine at the time of Jesus:

---

[38] Cf. Josephus, *Ant.* 18.34f. Annas's remaining four sons, who became high priests in the period after Caiaphas, were Jonathan, Theophilos, Matthias, and Annas. Annas ben Annas was in office for only three months. At the beginning of the Jewish War he was murdered by the mob.

[39] Ibid., 18.90–95. In rabbinic literature Caiaphas is mentioned only once and only parenthetically, as the father of the high priest Elionaios. To be accurate, he was the grandfather. Cf. Str-B, *Kommentar* 1.985 (on Matt 26:3). Caiaphas is also cited in Acts 4:6.

[40] *B. Pes.* 57a; see also Klausner, *Jesus of Nazareth* (ET; New York: Macmillan, 1929) 467f.

The Herodians

Herod the Great (37–4 BCE)

Antipas (4 BCE–39 CE: Galilee/Perea); Philip (4 BCE–34 CE: Gaulonitis, Trachonitis, Batanea); Archelaus (4 BCE–6 CE: Judea, Samaria, Idumea)

Procurators in Judea, Samaria, and Idumea

Coponius (6–9 CE)
Marcus Ambibulus (ca. 9–12)
Annius Rufus (ca. 12–15)
Valerius Gratus (15–26)
Pontius Pilate (26–36)

High Priests in Jerusalem

Simon ben Boethos (24–5 BCE)
Matthias ben Theophilos (5–4)
Joseph ben Ellem (officiated for one festival only)
Joazor ben Boethos (4)
Eleazar ben Boethos (4–?)
Joshua ben Sie (term unknown)
Joazor ben Boethos (second term in office, from ? to 6 CE)
Annas ben Sethi (6–15)
Ishmael ben Phiabi (ca. 15–16)
Eleazar ben Annas (ca. 16–17)
Simon ben Camithi (ca. 17–18)
Joseph Caiaphas (ca. 18–36)

The Sanhedrin, the highest Jewish administrative and legal authority, was closely linked with the high priest, since the officiating high priest always presided over this body of seventy-one men. Arising from a gathering composed of representatives of the priestly and landed gentry, it had originated in all likelihood during the Persian period and is mentioned for the first time in an edict of the Syrian king Antiochus III (223–187 BCE), under the term γερουσία (council of elders). Scribes may have been members of the council from the beginning, albeit in smaller numbers.[41] Their influence did not increase until the reign of Queen Alexandra (76–67 BCE), at which time scribes of the Pharisaic persuasion may have gained

---

[41] Cf. Hengel, *Judaism and Hellenism*, 1.27.

power as a faction of the council.[42] Herod the Great began his reign with a demonstrative act of power against the Sanhedrin. He had a large number of its members executed because the council had dared to summon him before the court.[43] In their place he appointed people who were submissive to him. All the same, the Sanhedrin—this designation now also appears—was more or less insignificant during the many years of his reign. The same is true for the time of Herod's son Archelaus, in which the council's jurisdiction was restricted to Judea, in keeping with the division of the country.

Only in the period of the Roman procurators would the Sanhedrin resume its former rights, though these rights remained restricted to Judea, to be sure. It was able again to act as a legal court in civil and penal matters. This was in conformity with the policies of the Romans in the conquered provinces. The Sanhedrin's most severe restriction, of course, came from Rome's occupation force reserving the right to intervene by its own initiative and to act independently. In connection with the trial of Jesus it is of particular interest to ask whether the Jewish council had the power of the *potestas gladii,* the authority to pronounce and execute the death sentence, or whether this remained the procurator's prerogative. We shall discuss this problem in more detail below in the treatment of the trial of Jesus.

Select bibliography: S. R. de Franch, *Etudes sur le droit palestinien à l'époque évangélique* (AJSUF; Fribourg: Library of the University, 1946); R. Heinze, *Die augusteische Kultur* (3d ed.; Darmstadt: Wissenschaftliche Buchgesellschaft, 1960); S. B. Hoenig, *The Great Sanhedrin* (New York: Bloch Publishing, 1953); H. Mantel, *Studies in the History of the Sanhedrin* (HSS 17; Cambridge, Mass.: Harvard University Press, 1961); A. Schalit, *König Herodes* (SJ 4; Berlin: de Gruyter, 1969); A. Schlatter, *Geschichte Israels von Alexander dem Grossen bis Hadrian* (3d ed.; Stuttgart: Calwer Verlag, 1925).

---

[42] Cf. E. Lohse, "συνάδριον," *TDNT* 7.862f.

[43] Cf. Josephus, *Ant.* 14.168–176. Josephus indicates that Herod had all of the members of the Sanhedrin executed. In *Ant.* 15.6 the number of those massacred is said to have been forty-five. This may be a correction and thus indicate that not all of them fell victim to the massacre.

3

Israel's Intellectual-Religious and Social Setting in the Time of Jesus

1. The intellectual-religious setting

Just as Israel had lost its political unity at the time of Jesus, so the people were divided intellectually and religiously. The major unifying factors, which will be addressed in what follows, were indeed still at work. In the life of Jesus, too, they still played a significant part. A closer examination indicates, however, that these factors were no longer able to unify the people.

"Israel" was the designation for God's people. To be called an Israelite, to bear this hallowed name, meant to belong to this chosen people. Yet there emerged certain groupings that separated from the bulk of the people and claimed to be the true Israel, the Israel within Israel. Israel was no longer the all-encompassing social entity but became the decisive nucleus of the continuity of the history of salvation, resulting in the exclusion of opposing groups and persons.[1]

Jerusalem, the holy city, emerged as the intellectual and religious center of international Judaism, not least because of the politics of Herod the Great, as well as of the Hasmoneans before him. The boundaries with the extensive Diaspora were fluid. During the Hellenistic and Roman era the city, to an extent, had taken on an international character.[2]

---

[1] Cf. Maier, "Antikes Judentum," 167 in *NT–Antikes Judentum* (ed. G. Strecker and J. Maier; Stuttgart: W. Kohlhammer, 1989); Hengel, *Judaism and Hellenism,* 1.311f.

[2] Hengel, *Judaism and Hellenism,* 313f.

Yet this is where the temple was. It was the only place in the world where legitimate sacrifices were offered to Yahweh, the God of Israel. Apart from the Essenes, everyone respected the Jerusalem sanctuary as the place of the cult of Yahweh. But even the Essenes' separation from the temple was only temporary. Indeed, they longed for the temple to be restored to its original holiness. For the great majority of the people the sanctuary remained the place of atonement, the place where the cult effected purity and holiness for the priests, people, families, the individual, and the country. This common attitude toward the temple reinforced the authority of the priests who carried out the cultic ministry.

The temple was the place where festivals were held, the order of which was regulated by the liturgical calendar. The new year's festival observed in the fall is no longer clearly comprehensible in terms of its theological intent. Was it connected with Yahweh's kingship, with the idea of his ascent to the throne, of his royal entry, as many of the Psalms seem to suggest, or was it the idea of judgment that was prominent, as later assertions seem to suggest? According to *Pesiqta* 189, on new year's day God sits in judgment of all who would enter this world. Ten days after new year's day, intended to be a time of return, Yom Kippur, the day of Atonement, was observed, when the high priest, dressed in white garments, entered the holy of holies of the temple. On this day only, he alone was allowed to enter this room at the back of the temple building, situated behind the second curtain, in order there to atone for his sins, as well as those of the priests and the people, by means of the blood of animals. This was also the day for the ritual of the Azazel, or scapegoat, that was sent into the desert and pushed off a precipice, thus taking away the people's sins. On the sixth day after the great Yom Kippur, which was a festival more for the priests, Israel celebrated the Feast of Tabernacles. Because of its popularity it was occasionally simply called "the Festival" and lasted about seven days. Originally this was the festival of the wine harvest and as such was probably celebrated in the vineyards. This in turn gave rise to dwelling in huts covered with foliage and to the numerous expressions of festal joy. In the course of time it became identified with the remembrance of the time of Moses' generation in the desert and of the conquest of the land. A relatively recent festival, however, was the Feast of Dedication, celebrated in commemoration of the rededication of the temple by Judas Maccabaeus, after its desecration by King Antiochus IV Epiphanes. The national character of this festival can be seen in the fact that it was celebrated on 25th of Kisler (November/December), the day of the temple's desecration and desolation. Judas Maccabaeus had established the rededication in this manner. Josephus calls it the festival of lights, "because this liberty beyond our hopes appeared to us."[3] Finally there was the Passover with the unleavened bread, celebrated in the spring (15th of Nisan), the great pilgrims' festival that brought thousands of Jews to Jerusalem from all parts of the empire.[4] They came in order to commemorate Israel's deliverance from Egyptian slavery, a remembrance which at the same time served to reinforce the idea of national liberation. The Feast of Weeks (Pentecost), celebrated fifty days after the Passover, was the festival at the conclusion of the grain harvest. Later it was linked with the notion of the giving of the law at Sinai.

Sacrifices were offered daily in the temple; they expressed objectively the people's will for unity. In the morning, soon after sunrise, it was the morning sacrifice, followed by the evening sacrifice in the early afternoon. These were interspersed with times of prayer. While the cultic ministry was focused in the temple of Jerusalem, the faithful, scattered across the whole country, gathered, especially on the Sabbath, in the synagogues to observe the weekly day of rest with prayer, hearing the Scriptures, and the sermon. This noncultic service would certainly have contributed to internalizing and personalizing the individual's piety. The preachers associated with the synagogues had a profound influence on the people's consciousness and mentality. Jewish religion was firmly anchored in home and family, where domestic feasts and especially the Sabbath were celebrated. The observance of the Sabbath was in no wise limited to attending the synagogue service but was prepared and continued at home. Whereas in Jerusalem the beginning of the Sabbath evening was announced by the blowing of a trumpet and in the countryside by proclamation, in the home it was ushered in by lighting the Sabbath lamp, exchanging everyday apparel for a more formal piece of clothing, and sitting at a table to eat the evening meal at the outset of the Sabbath. The Sabbath was a sign of Israel's election and hence also a meaningful token of its unity. It was observed with joy. Any kind of work was frowned upon and prohibited. One emulated the Sabbath rest of the Creator, who rested on

---

[3] Josephus, *Ant.* 7.325.
[4] J. Jeremias, *The Eucharistic Words of Jesus* (ET; Philadelphia: Fortress, 1977) 42, indicates that we can reckon on a figure of 85,000–125,000 pilgrims to the Passover.

the same day, at the conclusion of his work of creation. At the meal
one should be mindful of the needy, the tired traveler, the beggar,
and invite him to the meal. After stringent instructions regarding the
Sabbath rest, the *Book of Jubilees* has the following challenge: "Keep
Sabbath . . . and bless the Lord your God who has given you a festal
day and a holy day; and this day shall be a day of the holy kingdom
for all Israel among their days forever" (50.9).

The Bible, in which the law of Moses had taken on particular
prominence, was Israel's common possession. Yet the interpretation
of the law represented the fiercest religious problem. Which interpretation was correct? Did one require additional insights to comprehend its true meaning? Was there a need for further interpretative
stipulations in order to conform to Yahweh's will? Since the law
pointed the way to salvation, these questions were very important.

This brings us to the factions and splits among the people. A
detailed tracing of the developmental history of the various parties is
not required here. It is more important to point out the distinctives,
though these are not entirely comprehensible if history is dispensed
with entirely. The paralysis of Israel[5] has its source in the political
upheaval precipitated by the reign of the Seleucids in Syria and Palestine. The Maccabees successfully combated this rule by foreigners.
Subsequently the Hasmonean dynasty established itself but dared to
unite the royal and high-priestly office in one person. This era gave
rise to the movement of the Hasidim, the pious ones. It is important to
recognize from the beginning that the divisions arose out of the
endeavor to preserve or restore the purity and holiness of God's people
in a time of Israel's humiliation and thus to measure up to his calling.
Thus the majority of the Hasidim, who had supported the Maccabean
resistance, resisted the Hasmonean usurpation. In it they saw a be-
trayal of God's cause, for they expected the ultimate salvation not from
practical political measures but from an ultimate intervention by God.

The political changes took place alongside a fundamental
change in the conception of the fulfillment of salvation. This change
is linked with the concept of apocalyptic, which has to be viewed in
conjunction with the Hasidim. Apocalyptic writings, among which
the books of Daniel and Enoch are to be reckoned, provide us with
certain insights. Whereas God's work in judgment and salvation
until then had been viewed as an altogether intraworldly event, now

---

[5] K. Müller, "Die jüdische Apokalyptik," *TRE* 1.222, refers to a paralysis of the
concept of "Israel."

the focus rests on the end of history. In the end God will reveal himself, the dead will be called out of the graves and be raised to new life, and an individual judgment will be held in accordance with one's works. Regardless of the conception of this resurrection of the dead, which developed from a resurrection of the righteous to one of all the dead and became more and more pervasive, what is significant is that this view, going beyond this world into the other, new world to come, provided an entirely different historical and eschatological position. This change, inconceivable without external—likely Iranian—influence and probably supported by the hitherto unresolved problem of theodicy faced with glaring, unjust earthly conditions,[6] made possible a comprehensive view of past historical events from the perspective of the end, as presented, for instance, in the vision of the four empires in Daniel 7. The customary biblical theological view is maintained to the extent that God's sovereignty is prominent, indeed that everything depends on God's ultimate intervention, in the final analysis, so that there is no transition between history and salvation. This intervention of God was expected in the near future because, according to this viewpoint, the escalating wickedness in the world called for God's act of judgment. The time delay could become a problem, though, ultimately, depending upon the sovereignty of God, who alone orders everything, assisted in overcoming chronological problems. According to this theocentric view the coming figure of redemption or judgment is the Son of man, a heavenly being who awaits his revelation as the hidden one and who cannot diminish God's salvific initiative, which determines everything. According to Dan 7:13 the one like a son of man is brought before the Ancient of Days (i.e., God), whereas in 2 Esd 13:3 (a later writing) he is brought up out of the heart of the sea by a wind.

The apocalyptic view encompassing history is linked with a universal perspective encompassing the nations, thus causing Israel to be pushed into the background. Yet this development unfolds—paradoxically, one might say—in such a way that a remnant in Israel perceives itself as the bearer of revelations that effect salvation. This group claims to possess special knowledge and insights relative to the *eschaton,* the heavenly world, as well as the creation and its structure, having obtained them through visions and dreams. Part of

---

[6] Cf. Grundmann, "Das palästinische Judentum im Zeitraum zwischen der Erhebung der Makkabäer und dem Ende des jüdischen Krieges," in *Umwelt des Urchristentums* (ed. J. Leipoldt and W. Grundmann; Berlin: Evangelische Verlagsanstalt, 1965–67) 1.222.

its peculiarity is also its use of a special calendar, namely, the solar calendar (*1 Enoch* 72–82). Humans are accorded freedom, responsibility, and capacity to obey the law (*1 Enoch* 98.4); at the same time, however, they are understood to be bound up in a disaster precipitated by evil powers.[7]

The Hasidic mentality continued to ferment. At the time of Jesus there were no longer any communities or conventicles of a Hasidic-apocalyptic type.[8] Nevertheless, their movement proved to be a melting pot from which emerged most of the religious groups that were active during his time and most of which are mentioned in the Gospels. These groups will now be briefly described.

a) The one best known to us today is the monastic community of Qumran at the Dead Sea; their writings became known through the sensational discovery in 1947. Generally we refer to the Essenes. There should not be any major distinction made between the Qumran community and the Essenes. The writings, in any case, are Essene. Yet we have to assume that apart from the Qumran community there were Essene communities scattered around the country. The difference was that the former practiced a more rigorous, monastically organized life. The *Manual of Discipline* (1QS) depicts a different type of life from the *Damascus Document* (CD).

> The founding of the Dead Sea community is attributed to the "Teacher of Righteousness," an honorific name given to him in the scrolls. His actual name can no longer be ascertained. He was a priest associated with the temple of Jerusalem who indignantly turned away from the temple and called for an exodus into the desert, in accordance with the Isaianic declaration "make straight in the desert a highway for our God" (Isa 40:3). In his opinion the temple cult lost its worthiness under the priesthood of the Hasmonean era. The exodus may have occurred around 150 BCE. The goal of the separation was to maintain and restore the people's holiness in a restricted area. The community learned to perceive itself as the holy remnant of Israel, as the true people of God among the people, upon whom God acted redemptively again. God hid his face from Israel and his sanctuary on account of their unfaithfulness, because they forsook him, and handed them over to the sword. "But remembering the Covenant of the forefathers, he left a remnant to Israel and did not deliver it up to be destroyed" (CD 1:3–5). God had entered into a new covenant with them (CD 8:21; 19:34; 20:12).

> The concrete goal of the separation was to preclude any pollution caused by contact with the rest of the people. There are a number of regulations to insure this. Business contact and table fellowship with outsiders are not permitted, nor is one allowed to accept gifts. If community property is practiced at Qumran and the individual member of the order renounces

---

[7] Cf. Müller, "Apokalyptik," 1.202–51.
[8] Cf. Maier, "Judentum," 165.

personal possessions, it is not in the first place for the purpose of realizing a poverty-related ideal but, rather, cultic holiness. New members are subjected to stringent tests; for two years they are considered novices before being allowed to be accepted into full membership. The community is structured hierarchically. Priests and Levites occupy prominent functions. Yet alongside them there also is the council of twelve, which may have to be construed as a committee of laymen, whereas the leadership was likely composed of three priests. The *Damascus Document* tells us of a community leader *(mebaqqer)*, whose official tasks are reminiscent of those of a Christian bishop.

Separated from the Jerusalem temple, the Qumran community developed a self-understanding that enabled it theologically to carry through this turning away from the sanctuary. It perceived itself as a spiritual temple, temporarily representing the perfect replacement for the unworthy temple ministry of Jerusalem. Incidentally, this notion of a "spiritualization of the temple" is later also encountered in the Pauline corpus (cf. 1 Cor 3:16; Eph 2:21f.), the difference being that Qumran anticipated the eschatological restoration of the temple. In the *Manual of Discipline* we read, "The men of the community shall be set apart as a house of holiness for Aaron for the union of supreme holiness" (1QS 9:5f.). The temple cult is replaced with a spiritual service—with the "oblation of the lips" as a genuine aroma of appeasement and with "perfect conduct" as a free-will, pleasing gift—"to atone for guilty rebellion and for sins of unfaithfulness that they may obtain loving-kindness for the land without the flesh of burned offerings and the fat of sacrifice" (1QS 9:4f.).

In terms of external rituals they observed daily washings; the baths, accessible by stairs leading down to them, as well as cisterns and a sewage system in the ruins of Qumran still attest to them. After the washings, having put on the white priestly garment, they gathered for a meal of bread and drink. Concerning this meal Josephus says: "Nor is there ever any clamor or disturbance to pollute their house, but they give every one leave to speak in their turn; which silence thus kept in their house, appears to foreigners like some tremendous mystery."[9] Although the meal, as far as its substance (i.e., bread and wine) is concerned, is reminiscent of the eucharistic meal of the Christian community, it had an entirely different meaning. It did not have the characteristic of remembrance; rather, together with the ablutions, it continued the priestly meals and washings in the temple, both of which became more important in their practice in isolation, to be sure. A certain messianic significance may well have been attributed to the meals, for a prophetic preview of the messianic era depicted the Messiah, i.e., the two Messiahs, as participating in this meal (1QSa 2:17–20). Participation in the common meal, as well as in the baths, called for repentance and living in the community in the spirit of repentance. Otherwise this ministry would be for naught: "He shall not be purified by

[9] Cf. Josephus, *War* 2.129–133. Josephus may intend a parallel between the celebration and the Greek mysteries.

atonement, nor cleansed by purifying waters, nor sanctified by seas and rivers, nor washed clean with any ablution. Unclean, unclean shall he be. For as long as he despises the precepts of God he shall receive no instruction in the community of His counsel" (1QS 3:4–6).

Serving God thus becomes the obvious expression of the holiness of the community as the spiritual temple indwelt by God, or in which God's Spirit is present, and becomes the expression of the "purity of the many," as the scrolls often express it. This purity is also guarded by means of a detailed penal code to facilitate a temporary or permanent exclusion from the community for members who did wrong and committed criminal offences. One of the highlights was the annual celebration of the "covenant renewal festival," in which the community was inspected like an army and gave an account of itself. Everyone had to submit to the judgment of the "many," the plenary assembly of the community, and was then allowed to hear the priestly blessings that were pronounced over the "sons of light," as well as all of the curses that the Levites leveled at the "sons of darkness."

Part of the community's own possession was a special revelatory knowledge that was guarded as something esoteric and was not to be divulged to any outsider. This knowledge was obtained through intensive study of the Mosaic law and of the Prophets. In this context, too, the Teacher of Righteousness led the way, for he used the Scriptures to initiate this special activity of unveiling mysteries. Some of the community's interpretations of Scripture are preserved for us, so that we are informed about their procedure. Among these, particular mention is to be made of the commentary on the prophet Habakkuk, also called *Pesher on Habakkuk,* in keeping with the method of interpretation used. In this explanation each verse is applied to the present in such a way that the events of the present (and future) are seen proleptically in the prophet. Thus Habakkuk already prophesied about the Teacher of Righteousness, as well as about the persecution he and his community were to experience. This view of Scripture arose from the conviction that the prophet wrote for the end time in which they lived.

In this matter, too, the Essene community came in contact with early Christianity. Part of the consequences of this interpretation of Scripture relative to the Mosaic law was, for instance, the interpretations of the commandment of the Sabbath, which seem to be particulary stringent. Thus it was prohibited to assist cattle in giving birth on a Sabbath, or to rescue them when they had fallen into a pit (CD 11:13f.). Furthermore, in contrast to the temple of Jerusalem, their calendar was not lunar but solar, as we have already observed it in the book of Enoch. The Jerusalem priests were particulary offended by this separate calendar. Presumably this was the reason for the rebuke of the Teacher of Righteousness by the officiating high priest. In any case, the way to salvation was through the law, despite the fact that its proper, redemptive understanding called for a special, revealed interpretation.

> The human being is seen as weak, made of dust, existing in the domain of sinfulness. Against this backdrop the work of God's grace can be experienced all the more profoundly. We have some impressive expressions of this, especially in the *Hodayot,* psalms that originated in the community and that, at least in part, reflect the Teacher's personal experiences. Many of these psalms are indeed attributed to him. Yet the human being does not stand alone over against God. He is incorporated into a cosmic order ruled by two supernatural powers, the spirit of light and the spirit of darkness. This dualism does not, however, rend the world into metaphysically good and bad parts. God's sovereignty is maintained, for "from the God of knowledge comes all that is and shall be. Before ever they existed He established their whole design" (1QS 3:15–4:6). He brings his community's history to a redemptive goal.

More than anything else, the Essenes were focused on the impending end of this world and expected it to happen imminently. In this eschatological orientation especially, they were the spiritual descendants of Hasidic apocalyptic. But they differed from the latter in one important area—their messianism. In apocalyptic it was the Son of man who was to appear. While the Essenes perpetuated the apocalyptic conceptions—apocalyptic writings have been found in Qumran—they did expect the advent of the Messiah, or, more accurately, three Messiahs to come: "until there shall come the Prophet and the Messiahs of Aaron and Israel" (1QS 9:11). Hence the royal Messiah is joined by the priestly one. In fact the latter is accorded a superior role, as also assumed in the description of the celebration of the common meal in the messianic era (1QS 2:19f.). The *Testament of Judah,* under Essene influence, contains the following declaration, which Judah pronounces upon himself and Levi: "For the Lord gave me the kingdom and him the priesthood; and he made the kingdom inferior to the priesthood" (21:2). This careful distinction and the preference for the messianic high priest from the house of Aaron may also reflect a reaction to the Hasmonean usurpation of the priesthood. The prophet, according to Deut 18:18f. the eschatological prophet like Moses, may later have been identified with the Teacher of Righteousness. In their messianic eschatological expectation the community also prepared for the end-time battle of the sons of light against the sons of darkness, in which all evil powers are to be destroyed with the assistance of the heavenly hosts and thus God's rule may finally be established. One of the scrolls deals with the topic of this eschatological battle (1QM). The final days also expect a new gathering of the entire community of Israel, from which all those are to be removed, of course, who have become cultically unfit because of physical ailments (1QSa 1:1, 3–11). Eschatologically the concept of purity and holiness likewise is maintained consistently.

b) While the Gospels do not mention the Essenes at all—an issue to which we will have to return later—they familiarize us with the Pharisees. Yet if one wants to get to know the Pharisees from their own sources, considerable difficulties are encountered. These are associated especially with the problem of dating the traditions handed down in the rabbinic literature.[10] Nevertheless, the following may be ascertained: The Pharisees too evolved from the Hasidim movement. They too disagreed with the Hasmonean usurpation of royalty and priesthood. *Psalm of Solomon* 17, Pharisaically oriented and alluding to the Hasmoneans, refers to those who put the kingship in the place of their exalted rank (i.e., the high priesthood) and destroyed the throne of David in the arrogance of this change (vv. 4–6).[11] Their name, Pharisees, derived from *perushim* (i.e., the separated ones), may be associated with their physical separation from another group—at that time the Hasidim—or more likely with inward separation from the rest of the people. The disrespectful identification of the people as *am-ha-arez* (people of the land, common people) may have originated in their circles. Still, they did not push separation to the exent the Essenes did. They remained in the towns and villages; they remained with the temple.

Nevertheless, the sanctification and purity of the people were their pressing concern as well. According to J. Neusner[12] the primary characteristic of Pharisaism was the observance of purity laws associated with cultic ritual, even outside the temple. The cult became the central metaphor. This means that priestly purification regulations were also observed in everyday life. Everyday life was ritualized and thus sanctified. This kind of worship, linked with numerous restrictions and compulsory exercises, attests to sincerity and dignity. With regard to the practice of the temple cult, the law moved center stage. The significance of the law as the way of salvation was heightened

---

[10] A very skeptical assessment is provided by K. Müller, "Zur Datierung rabbinischer Aussagen," *Neues Testament und Ethik* (FS R. Schnackenburg; Freiburg: Herder, 1989) 551–87.

[11] K. G. Kuhn, *Die älteste Textgestalt der Psalmen Salomos* (BWANT 73; Giessen, 1937) 64f.

[12] Maier, "Judentum," 43–66.

probably by attributing cosmic significance to it, by regarding it as God's creative tool that secured the world's order.[13] Alongside the law they placed the tradition. In their concern for the law the Pharisees created interpretative regulations, traditions of interpretation, later called the tradition of the elders, which were to assist in adhering concretely to the Mosaic law in everyday life. The number of these interpretations was not insignificant. In the first place, they were considered as binding as the directive of the law. There were numerous Sabbath regulations, for instance, such as the number of steps one was allowed to take on the Sabbath without violating the commandment of the Sabbath rest, i.e., the Sabbath-day's journey (cf. Acts 1:12).

Within Pharisaism there were indeed various groups or schools that even opposed one another and represented differing viewpoints in matters of interpretation of the law. Hillel and Shammai were the best-known heads of schools at the time. The former was viewed as lax, the latter as rigorous. K. Schubert refers to a democratic principle in the Pharisaic interpretation of the law.[14] Whether at the time of Jesus the Pharisees still lived in organized brotherhoods is questionable. In all likelihood this was no longer the case.[15]

In his descriptions of the Pharisees, Josephus ably addresses their conceptions of the relationship between human freedom and divine predestination. In this regard he seems to have been influenced by the interests of his Hellenistic readers. He attributes a mediating position to the Pharisees: In their opinion it pleased God to allow the power of fate and human reason to cooperate with one another. He also attests to their belief in the individual's life after death.[16] According to the reliable witness of Acts 23:8, they believed in the resurrection of the dead. In their eschatological expectation they pinned their hope on the advent of the royal Messiah from the house of David. Through him Israel will be liberated from every tribulation and oppression. *Psalm of Solomon* 17:21 confirms this: "Behold, O Lord, and raise up for them their king, the son of David, for the time which thou didst foresee, O God, that he may reign over Israel thy servant."

---

[13] Cf. K. Schubert, "Die jüdischen Religionsparteien im Zeitalter Jesu," 66–69 in *Der historische Jesus und der Christus unseres Glaubens* (ed. K. Schubert; Vienna: Herder, 1962).
[14] Ibid., 62.
[15] Cf. R. Meyer, "φαρισαῖος," *TDNT* 9.16–20; Schubert, "Religionsparteien," 62.
[16] Josephus, *Ant.* 18.11–15; 13.171–173; *War* 2.162–165. One gets the impression that Josephus has the Pharisees represent a theory of reincarnation.

As far as the imminent expectation of the messianic age of salvation is concerned, shared by apocalyptic and the Essenes, the Pharisees were reticent, even sceptical, in view of the disappointments that those circles already had to accept. This aspect may also have caused them to be cautious with regard to the Jesus movement as an eschatological movement. All the same, they considered themselves open to an end-time advent of the kingdom of God. In this regard they were "sceptics without resignation."[17] With regard to the individual human being, they reckoned on an individual reward, in accordance with one's works, in the final judgment. In this context they developed the conception of a heavenly treasure in which works of love and good deeds could be deposited, as it were. We also encounter this conception in the Gospels (Matt 6:20f.; 19:21 par.; Luke 12:33f.). We may assume that their inner disposition with regard to the expectation of the judgment had been shaped both by trust in their own "righteousness" and by dependence upon God's mercy.

Because of their religious sincerity, their striving for holiness, because they did not live in separation from the public, they enjoyed the respect of broad segments of the population. Josephus remarks that their influence on the people was such that all of the worship-related tasks, prayers as well as offerings, were carried out in line with their instructions.[18] Furthermore, as a lay movement, they were open to everyone. In this respect they must have been particularly attractive. They were not unanimous in their political disposition. Here the old Hasidic differences of opinion continued to be effective. On the one hand, it was argued that a political regime, even a foreign power, could be tolerated as long as it did not interfere with religious concerns. On the other hand, the supremacy of God could become so prominent that any collaboration with a foreign power had to be deemed reprehensible. The Shammaites should be reckoned among the left wing of the Pharisees.

The portrait of the Pharisees would be incomplete without mentioning the scribes. In the Gospels they appear bearing differing names: experts in the law (νομικοί, e.g., Luke 7:30), teachers of the law (Luke 5:17), scribes (γραμματεῖς, the most frequent designation). They represent a profession whose task it was, in keeping with the twofold function of the Bible as a book of law and religion, to provide theological teaching and to administer justice. They established

---

[17] Schubert, "Religionsparteien," 69.
[18] Josephus, *Ant.* 18.15.

theological schools in which they trained students after their own kind. They were the best-equipped synagogue preachers on the Sabbath. Frequently they may have practiced their profession alongside a trade (such as the apostle Paul's), or they were wealthy enough to devote themselves completely to teaching. Only a few may have been able to afford that, however. Sirach 38:24–39:11 warns the teachers of wisdom against maintaining two professions. Hence many may have been dependent upon support and donations. Most of the scribes at the time of Jesus belonged to the Pharisaic party. On the whole, this may well have increased the Pharisees' influence and significance even more. Yet there were also scribes in the ranks of the Sadducees.

In the time of the Roman procurators the political influence of the Pharisees was less than that of the Sadducees. Yet since the time of Queen Salome Alexandra, who died in 67 BCE, there were Pharisees in the *gerousia* (Sanhedrin). Though the Sadducees were the most powerful political group, they had to consider the Pharisees because of their respect among the people. While this says something about the relationship between the Pharisees and the Sadducees, the Essenes' relationship with the Pharisees was hostile. The Qumran writings offer representative expressions. To them the Pharisees were people who watered down the law and dissolved it, who emanated deception, lies, misdirection, and error.[19] There was a different relationship, however, between the Pharisees and the Zealots.

c) As an independent party the Zealots emerged from the Pharisees, especially from their left wing, the Shammaites. Josephus points out concerning the Zealots that they agree with the Pharisees in all aspects other than that they cling to liberty with great tenacity and acknowledge God alone as their Lord and king.[20] Their appearance is associated with a particular political event, the census the Romans took in Judea, levied by Coponius the first procurator and the Syrian legate Quirinius. Judas, a man from Gaulanitis, and Sadduk, a Pharisee, called for resistance against these measures and hence for the organization of a new faction. If the former was also called Judas the Galilean, it shows that Galilee was particularly responsive to this concern. Judas also may well have been a Pharisee and scribe.[21]

---

[19] Documentation in Meyer, "φαρισαῖος," *TDNT* 9.29–30.
[20] Josephus, *Ant.* 18.23.
[21] Josephus, *War* 2.118, calls him σοφιστής. This may indicate that he was a scribe.

Their rebellion was theologically motivated; they too were concerned with Israel's holiness. Their supreme motto was Yahweh's sovereignty, which did not allow for Israel to be subjected to a pagan power. They interpreted the first commandment of the Decalogue in this manner and thereby also provided a concrete interpretation to the prayer "Hear, O Israel: The LORD our God is one LORD" (Deut 6:4), which every Israelite had to pray daily. The figure of Phinehas (Num 25) from the generation of the wilderness became their example, for he too acted spontaneously for God's glory with holy zeal and force. Their probably self-given name, Zealots, i.e., zealous ones, characterizes their mindset and also explains their action, because the zeal for God and the law that distinguished them had long been an honorable designation. Their mindset and behavior can be understood only if it is understood that God and the people, Yahweh's honor and the people's liberty, were deemed inseparable and hence the humiliation of the people included the humiliation of Yahweh.

What made them conspicuous immediately was their use of force, which they believed necessary to pave the way for the kingdom of God. Though they were convinced that ultimately God alone was able to procure salvation, by means of some sort of a synergistic model God became dependent upon human cooperation. This was closely linked with a heightened practice of the Torah, with readiness for martyrdom, which to them signaled the imminence of the kingdom of God, and with the conception of a holy war.[22] In addition, their movement had a sociorevolutionary feature. Through the advent of the kingdom of God they promised the poor and oppressed the reinstatement of their rights and God's inauguration of a new order. When necessary, their Torah-related rigor was coupled with the renunciation of possessions.[23]

They gained increasing sympathy among the people, considering the pervasive social deprivation of the rural population. Ultimately, however, they led the people into war with Rome, which began thirty-five years after Jesus' death and was catastrophic for Israel.[24] The notion of a holy eschatological war linked the Zealots with the Essenes. But only during the time of the war did an alliance

---

[22] Cf. M. Hengel, *The Zealots* (ET; Edinburgh: T. & T. Clark, 1989) 146–228.

[23] Ibid., 306–12.

[24] According to Josephus the name "Sicarii" designates the group of Menahem's adherents who fled to Masada after his murder. Originally this name (= wielders of swords) was given by the Romans to insurrectionists because of their peculiar method of combat at the time of the procurator Felix. Cf. Hengel, *Zealots,* 76.

become evident. Masada, situated in the vicinity of Qumran, is a symbol of conspiracy and downfall. As a group, the Zealots are not mentioned in the Gospels either, though their influence extended to the circle of Jesus' disciples, among whom there was a certain Simon the Zealot (Luke 6:15; Acts 1:13).

d) A fourth group stands out in particular from the parties mentioned so far: the Sadducees. From the Gospels we are acquainted with them. Although they are occasionally cited in the same breath with the Pharisees (Matt 3:7; 16:1, 6, 11f.; 22:34), it is important to note that we are dealing with a quite different kind of people. Even during the time of the Hasmoneans their disposition was different. They proved to be adherents of the Hasmoneans, in contrast to the Hasidim, Essenes, and Pharisees. Among them were the noble and the rich, the members of the high-priestly families and the aristocracy, even though they were not necessarily homogeneous among themselves. During the final seventy years of the Jewish state the officiating high priest, the highest Jewish representative of authority, regularly came from their ranks. Their position of power, still curtailed during the time of Herod the Great because they rejected his Roman universal politics, was solidified under the Roman procurators with whom they were prepared to cooperate. For them, too, Israel was a holy entity. They saw Israel's holiness as guaranteed by the temple, in which the legitimate sacrifice was presented that atoned for people and country. For them the fulfillment of the salvific eschatological expectation was a national, distinct temple-state with the boundaries of the realm that king David once possessed.[25]

Thus in their theological thought they proved to be conservative in the sense that they rejected any reform and possibly acknowledged only the Pentateuch as normative.[26] They did not accept the Pharisaic traditions of interpretation, the traditions of the elders. They did not share the apocalyptic-eschatological hopes. For them there was neither life after death nor a resurrection of the dead. Salvation is realized within history itself. They also rejected the existence of angels. In this regard they were in full agreement with the "Old Testament" in its ancient form.

Concerning the Sadducees, Josephus reports that they deemed human destiny to be solely dependent upon one's own will and hence

---

[25] Cf. Meyer, "φαρισσαῖος," *TDNT* 9.45.
[26] Cf. Schürer, *History,* 2.481.

not determined by God.[27] One gets the impression that he presents
them to his Hellenistic readers as a group comparable to the Epicure-
ans. In their work they were political realists; as far as their mindset
was concerned, the pious may have perceived them as "progressive."
In terms of criminal justice they pursued a more stringent jurisprudence. Their relationship to the Essenes was clear, given the fact that
the latter separated from the temple and hence from the Sadducees in
spectacular fashion. At Qumran they were reckoned among the blinded
"sons of darkness." Their relationship to the Pharisees is difficult to
describe. The two parties, Pharisees and Sadducees, were frequently
forced to get along with one another. The Sadducees had the official
power, while the Pharisees exerted influence upon the people. Thus
the Pharisees had to show consideration to the Sadducees. The name
Sadducees is derived from Zadok, one of the influential priests of
David's time (cf., e.g., 1 Sam 15:24), from whom the high-priestly clan
of the Zadokites originated.[28] This name was possibly not self-given
but imposed upon them with a polemical motive.[29]

Select bibliography: E. Bammel, "Sadduzäer und Sadokiden," *ETL* 55 (1979)
107–15; H. Bardtke, *Qumran-Probleme* (Berlin: Akademie-Verlag, 1963); G. Baumbach, "Das Sadduzäerverständnis bei Josephus Flavius und im NT," *Kairos* 13 (1971)
17–37; J. M. Baumgarten, "The Phaisaic-Sadducean Controversy about Purity," *JJS*
31 (1980) 157–70; J. Becker, *Das Heil Gottes* (SUNT 3; Göttingen: Vandenhoeck &
Ruprecht, 1964); F. M. Cross, *The Ancient Library of Qumran and Modern Biblical
Studies* (New York: Doubleday, 1958); A. Finkel, *The Pharisees and the Teacher of
Nazareth* (AGSU 4; Leiden: E. J. Brill, 1964); W. Grundmann, "Das palästinische
Judentum im Zeitraum zwischen der Erhebung der Makkabäer und dem Ende des
Jüdischen Krieges," 143–291 in *Umwelt des Urchristentums* (J. Leipoldt and W. Grund-
mann, eds.; 3 vols.; Berlin: Evangelische Verlagsanstalt, 1967); M. Hengel, *The
Zealots* (ET; Edinburgh: T. & T. Clark, 1989); G. Jeremias, *Der Lehrer der Gerechtigkeit*
(SUNT 2; Göttingen: Vandenhoeck & Ruprecht, 1963); J. Le Moyne, *Les Sadducéens*
(Paris: Lecoffre, 1972); H. Lichtenberger, *Studien zum Menschenbild in Texten der
Qumrangemeinde* (SUNT 15; Göttingen: Vandenhoeck & Ruprecht, 1980); J. Maier,
"Antikes Judentum," 137–84 in *NT-Antikes Judentum* (G. Strecker and J. Maier,
eds.; Stuttgart: W. Kohlhammer, 1989); R. Marcus, "The Pharisees in the Light
of Modern Scholarship," *JR* 32 (1952) 153–64; J. Neusner, *Das pharisäische und
das talmudische Judentum* (Tübingen: J. C. B. Mohr, 1974); idem, *The Rabbinic
Traditions about the Pharisees before 70* (3 vols.; Leiden: Brill, 1971); P. von der
Osten-Sacken, *Gott und Belial* (SUNT 6; Göttingen: Vandenhoeck & Ruprecht,
1969); K. Schubert, "Die jüdischen Religionsparteien im Zeitalter Jesu," 15–101 in
idem, ed., *Der historische Jesus und der Christus unseres Glaubens* (Vienna: Herder, 1962);
M. Weise, *Kultzeiten und kultischer Bundesschluss in der "Ordensregel" vom Toten Meer*
(SPB 3, Leiden: Brill, 1961).

---

[27] Josephus, *War* 2.164ff.; *Ant.* 13.173.
[28] There is a later rabbinic tradition associating the name "Sadducee" with Zadok, a
disciple of Antigonus of Soko (beginning of the 2d cent. BCE). Cf. Str-B, *Kommentar*, 4.343f.
[29] Cf. Meyer, "φαρισαῖος," *TDNT* 9.43.

2. The social setting

> The country also that lies over against this lake hath the same name of
> Gennesareth; its nature is wonderful as well as its beauty; its soil is so fruitful
> that all sorts of trees can grow upon it, and the inhabitants accordingly plant all
> sorts of trees there; for the temper of the air is so well mixed, that it agrees
> very well with those several sorts, particularly walnuts, which require the
> coldest air, flourish there in vast plenty; there are palm trees also and olives
> grown near them, which yet require an air that is more temperate. One may
> call this place the ambition of nature, where it forces those plants that are
> naturally enemies to one another to agree together; it is a happy contention of
> the seasons as if every one of them laid claim to this country; for it not only
> nourishes different sorts of autumnal fruit beyond men's expectation, but
> preserves them a great while; it supplies men with the principal fruits, with
> grapes and figs continually during ten months of the year, and the rest of the
> fruit as they become ripe together, through the whole year; for besides the
> good temperature of the air, it is also watered from a most fertile fountain.
> The people of the country call it Capharnaum.[30] . . . The length of this
> country extends itself along the banks of this lake that bears the same name,
> for thirty furlongs, and is in breadth twenty.[31]

In these almost effusive terms Josephus describes the region
between Capernaum and Magdala, the plain of Gennesaret, Galilee's
fertile heartland. Yet the social and economic conditions were different for most of the people.

To get a glimpse of these conditions among the total population
of Palestine of about one million, one needs to distinguish between
Galilee (and Samaria) on the one hand and Judea and Jerusalem on
the other. Economically the country was characterized by agriculture
(raising crops and cattle), the work of artisans, and trade. To be sure,
in Galilee agriculture, including fishing along the lake, was dominant, while to the south and in Jerusalem trade and the work of
artisans were prominent. Yet even in Judea there was pasture, farming,
and gardening, just as certain artisans were indispensible in Galilee.
Among such artisans there were tailors, sandal makers, builders—as
a τέκτων (Matt 13:55), Joseph of Nazareth belonged to them—
butchers, tanners (cf. Mark 9:3), bakers, smiths, potters. In Jerusalem
there were artistic weavers. The cheese-making valley west of the
temple area of Jerusalem points to that trade. Beyond that we have to
reckon with a significant number of unemployed people, but it is
altogether impossible to provide precise numbers here.

---

[30] The region of Capernaum is rich in springs. Josephus, *Life,* 403, narrates that
he got caught in a marsh not far from this place and was thrown from his horse.

[31] Josephus, *War* 3.516–521. The furlong—its precise measurement ranges between 177 and 185 meters—represents a distance covered in two minutes. Cf. O. W.
Reinmuth, *Der kleine Pauly* (Stuttgart: Druckenmüller, 1964–75) 5.336f.

The social stratification of the population showed great differences. On top was a small number of big landowners who could afford to live in an apartment in Jerusalem. At the bottom there was the mass of smallhold farmers and day laborers. The latter were the worst off, living from hand to mouth, generally finding work only for a short time or for a day and thus waiting day after day for someone to find and hire them. Just as described in the parable of the laborers in the vineyard, they stood around idle in the marketplace, waiting for things to happen (cf. Matt 20:1–16). They could be hired for agricultural jobs, as well as for fishing and other trades. Concerning Zebedee, the father of James and John, we learn that he employed day laborers for fishing (Mark 1:20). A day's wage generally amounted to one denarius.

Nevertheless, there also was a middle class. Among them were the craftsmen and small traders, as well as the regular priests (and Levites), of whom there were reputed to be seven thousand.[32] They were engaged in the weekly ministry. Given their large number, they were rarely called upon, so that it was impossible for them to make a living from temple service and instead they were forced to practice other trades. Most of them could not afford to live in the capital. Jericho was known as the city of priests. This social middle class may well have represented a stabilizing factor in the societal structure.

Just as in the ancient world as a whole, so there were slaves in Israel as well. It is important to grasp the conditions of the slave status in all its severity. To be a slave meant to be someone else's property. The existence of slaves in Israel once again is confirmed indirectly in the parables of the Synoptic Gospels. Whenever possible, the relevant Greek term δοῦλος should be translated as "slave," rather than as "servant," so as not to project later social conditions inadvertently on the time of Jesus. To be sure, the situation for slaves in Jewish households was not as hard as in Greek or Roman ones, at least not for Jewish slaves. Countrywide their number may not have been very high compared with Greece or indeed Rome. The Jewish slave knew he was under the protection of the law and had to be treated like a day laborer who sold his labor. In this way he was able to obtain some meager possessions. Most important, he was to be released in the Sabbath year. This feature exhibits a most humane trait of the law. Pagan slaves, however, faced a different plight. They

---

[32] Cf. W. Foerster, *Palestinian Judaism* (ET; Philadelphia: Fortress, 1964) 96f.

did not enjoy the Jewish privileges. Hence they frequently endeavored to be accepted as proselytes in the synagogue.

The contrasts in the social conditions were intensified through a most disparate distribution of the possession of land, the bulk of which was concentrated in the hands of a few. During the time of Herod the Great the king himself was the biggest landowner. But things were no different under his sons. Presumably they secured for themselves the most fertile areas. We know of Herod Antipas that he exacted two hundred talents annually from Galilee and Perea.[33] After his exile Archelaus's property was sold. While we know nothing of the buyers, they had to have been financially strong.[34] It could happen—already in the Seleucid period, incidentally—that the king donated estates as fiefs to outstanding people in his area (such as government ministers and military).

The Zenon papyri provide an interesting glimpse into the running of these estates. Zenon was a representative of Apollonius, who was the minister of finance for the king of Egypt. Apollonius owned an estate in Beth-Anath in Galilee, which Zenon went to see, together with a considerable entourage of Greeks in 260–259 BCE. He took care of several other items of business at the same time.[35] A delivery list has been preserved for us, referring to waxed barrels and pitched jugs with wine. We may assume that Apollonius leased his estate to Galilean farmers and had them tend it. A papyrus reports on the representative's efforts of conciliation when farmers caused difficulties during the delivery of goods.[36] This yields a picture that largely agrees with the conditions presumed in the parable of the tenants (Mark 12:1–9 par.). Here too we have a vineyard that a foreign owner leased to Galilean tenants who posed problems when they had to deliver the rent. Two types of leasehold contracts can be ascertained. In the case of a partial lease the property owner leased the field or vineyard and had his representative supervise the harvest. The rent consisted of delivering a determined share of the harvest, which differed from year to year, of course. For this reason the owner had to be present at the harvest or have it monitored, as was

---

[33] Josephus, *Ant.* 17.318ff.

[34] Cf. G. Theissen, *Studien zur Soziologie des Urchristentums* (WUNT 19; Tübingen: Mohr, 1979) 137.

[35] M. Rostovtzeff, *The Social and Economic History of the Hellenistic World* (3 vols.; Oxford: Clarendon, 1953) 1.265ff.

[36] Cf. M. Hengel, "Das Gleichnis von den Weingärtnern Mc 12:1–12 im Lichte der Zenonpapyri und der rabbinischen Gleichnisse," *ZNW* 59 (1968) 1–39, esp. 12–14.

the case in the parable mentioned. In the second type the rent for a piece of land is fixed from the start. There also was the household economy. In this case an administrator acts on behalf of the absentee landlord. He is responsible for the laborers and slaves and is accountable to his master, of course.[37] The household economy, too, is reflected in many parables (Luke 12:42f.; 16:1–8; Mark 13:34f.).

The expansion of big land ownership also brought increased export,[38] consisting largely of natural produce, such as oil, wine, olives, and grain. Supported by the Romans, the network of roads was relatively well developed. Thus there was a road from Caesarea Maritima through Galilee (the Via Maris) to Damascus. Jerusalem had a road connection with the port city as well. The increase in trade can also be seen in the fact that Herod the Great had expanded Caesarea, formerly called Straton's Tower. The new city was founded in 10 BCE. The big landowners enjoyed favorable foreign relations. International trade was boosted by the Imperium Romanum and the Pax Romana. Acts 12:20 makes a passing reference to the royal export business that Herod Agrippa maintained with the coastal cities of Tyre and Sidon, which obtained food from his country. There were regular markets in Jerusalem for such goods as grain, livestock, fruit, and timber. There also was an auction block where male and female slaves were exhibited and offered for sale. Well known in the Gospels is the market in the outer temple precinct, associated with the Passover, which began about three weeks prior to the festival. The gains made from the export trade certainly benefited the proprietors. For them the saying proved to be true: "For to him who has will more be given, and he will have abundance" (Matt 13:12).

Yet the continuation of this saying, "but from him who has not, even what he has will be taken away," was reality as well, especially for the smallholding farmers and day laborers. The smallholding farmers, together with their families, worked the sparse land they owned. They were most affected by irregularities in the economic supply, caused by political and other external circumstances. In the famine of 25 BCE Herod was able to prevent the worst by selling part

---

[37] Cf. H. G. Kippenberg, *Religion und Klassenbildung im antiken Judäa* (2d ed.; SUNT 14; Göttingen: Vandenhoeck & Ruprecht, 1982) 146–52. Kippenberg reckons on a conflict between the old established aristocracy, which was represented in the *gerousia* or in the Sanhedrin, and the aristocrats engaged in government lease-holding, as the latter appeared to be favored. They also represented the newly rich, moneyed nobility, which had to be deemed suspect to the hereditary nobility (133f.).

[38] Cf. Theissen, *Studien,* 137; J. Herz, "Grossgrundbesitz in Palästina im Zeitalter Jesu," *PJ* 24 (1928) 98–113.

of his own fortune.[39] In later times we no longer hear of comparable relief efforts by the state. Only rarely did these people know moments of joy in their dismal life. It was the religious festivals, the weddings celebrated over several days, and mutually expressed hospitality that allowed some light to brighten their somber life. The inheritance laws contributed to the worsening of the situation for the next generation, for it always was only the eldest son who inherited house and home, which remained undivided. The other sons had to be satisfied with a part of the movable possessions. This in turn explains the extensive Jewish Diaspora, for many preferred to leave the meager home province and to move to another country. The Gospels confirm that there were not a few beggars. Among these there were especially the ill and those unable to work, such as the blind and paralytics. Along the highways used by pilgrims and in Jerusalem there were preferred spots for begging, for instance at the temple doors (Acts 3:2). In Jericho the blind beggar Bartimaeus is sitting by the roadside used by pilgrims (Mark 10:46). Among these wretched people Jesus should have found attentive hearers.

Incidentally, the construction of the Jerusalem temple, carried out on the orders of Herod and spread over decades, offered a livelihood to many people.[40] Here stone masons, carpenters, and craftsmen found their occupation. Eighteen thousand laborers are said to have been involved in its construction, for we are told that upon completion of the work between 62 and 64 CE, eighteen thousand laborers were unemployed. At that time Agrippa II had Jerusalem paved with white stone, for social reasons and under pressure from the people to provide work for them. To pay for it, he withdrew the money from the temple treasury, of which he was in charge.[41] In the course of time the temple treasury had amassed enormous amounts of money.

The numerous taxes were perceived to be particularly burdensome. The tax of two drachmas to be paid to the temple may have been rendered as a matter of course by the pious, especially since the Jewish tax collectors volunteering their services regarded such service meritorious (Matt 17:24–27). The dues the tax collectors gathered were irregular, indirect levies, especially taxes on goods transported from one country to another, but also levies such as

---

[39] Cf. Josephus, *Ant.* 15.299–316.
[40] Cf. J. Jeremias, *Jerusalem in the Time of Jesus* (ET; Philadelphia: Fortress, 1969) 21–27.
[41] Cf. Josephus, *Ant.* 20:9.

market dues and road tolls. Tax collectors leased toll booths and thus were able to pad their own pockets by increasing the amounts demanded. Hence they were unpopular and equated with publicans and sinners.

The regular taxes were the most burdensome. The Romans regarded conquered provinces as Rome's property.[42] For this reason the provincial population, which enjoyed property rights only, had to render taxes. These essentially were a land and poll tax *(tributum agri et capitis)*. How much they were cannot be established with certainty. In Sicily the land tax amounted to one-tenth of the agricultural yield. The poll tax depended upon the social status. To determine the latter, a census was carried out when the province of Judea was established. At the time of Jesus the direct taxes were not leased out. The procurator presumably delegated the collection of taxes to a financial officer.[43] It seems that the Romans raised taxes in comparison with what had to be paid previously.[44] Galilee was under a different tax system.[45] Herod Antipas, the ethnarch of Galilee, had his own financial and tax administration through which he collected the taxes. He used the lease system. Publicans who leased the office collected taxes on his behalf. Hence the τελῶναι in Galilee were more than tax officials; they were tax collectors.[46] The τελώνιον ("tax office") where Levi sat (Mark 2:14) may be construed as simply an exchange table at which payments were made and receipted.

The people's living conditions are also instructive for the social context. Rural houses often consisted of only one room in which the whole family lived and slept. Various parables provide insights into this type of house. A lamp placed on a stand was sufficient to light up the whole house (Matt 5:15). If a woman lost a coin, she lit this lamp and scoured the whole house to find what she had lost (Luke 15:8). Very telling is the parable of the entreating friend, which recounts

---

[42] Cf. T. Pekáry, KP 5.952–54.

[43] Philo, *Legat.* 199, tells of a Roman finance procurator in Judea called Capito. O. Michel, "τελώνης," *TDNT* 8.97ff., assumes that it was the Sanhedrin's task to collect the taxes under the procurator's supervision.

[44] Tacitus, *Annales* 2.42, reports that Judea petitioned the emperor Tiberius to lower the tax. We do not know whether he granted their request.

[45] Cf. O. Michel, "τελώνης," *TDNT,* 8.97.

[46] Cf. Rostovtzeff, *Social and Economic History,* 1.265ff., who apparently argues that the taxation of Judea was leased out as well. Only the indirect levies were leased, however, such as the *portorium,* a levy on all sales and leases. It was mostly the natives who functioned as lessees, such as the chief tax collector Zachaeus in Jericho (Luke 19:1f.). Cf. Schürer, *History* 1.374ff.; O. Michel, "τελώνης," *TDNT* 8.97f.

the story of a man who, together with his children, has already gone to bed and locked the door and hence does not want to be disturbed any more (Luke 11:5–7). If there was some livestock, it too might find shelter in the house. In this case the living area for the people was built at a slightly higher elevation. The roofing consisted of reed, hay, and branches, so that the roof could be broken open (Mark 2:4: ἐξορύξαντες). The outside walls should be thought of as constructed of clay or brushwood.[47] By contrast, urban houses in Jerusalem were two-level dwellings. Above was a single upper room (ὑπερῷον), encompassing the whole area of the house, that was accessible from the outside by a staircase. According to Acts 1:13 the apostles gathered in a room such as this, as did perhaps Jesus to celebrate the Last Supper with the Twelve (Mark 14:14). Palatial houses had a considerable courtyard with a gateway (Matt 14:68).

What was life like indoors? The societal structure was patriarchal. The husband was the master and owner of the house. In terms of rights, the wife in many respects was disadvantaged. She was considered the husband's property. This husband-wife relationship, based on property rights, is expressed in the Decalogue, where these two prohibitions are found side by side: "You shall not covet your neighbor's house; you shall not covet your neighbor's wife, or his manservant, or his maidservant, or his ox, or his ass, or anything that is your neighbor's" (Exod 20:17). Nothing had changed in this understanding. On the contrary, in the context of marriage laws it led to the viewpoint that a husband could only violate by adultery someone else's marriage, never his own. But a wife was considered an adulteress even if she got involved with an unmarried man. Divorce was relatively simple. In practice, it always meant the husband's dismissal of his wife from the marriage. It was not possible for the wife to sever the marriage.

How extensively divorce was practiced at the time of Jesus is very difficult to say. The Pharisees permitted it. Yet within the different schools the legal standards varied in stringency. The Hillelites were said to permit divorce if the wife burned the soup. The Essenes frowned on divorce. As far as the wife's position in society was concerned, her place was in the house. The husband appreciated a good housewife. Her praise is found in the wisdom literature: "A good wife who can find? She is far more precious than rubies. The heart of

---

[47] According to Matt 24:43 a thief could break through the wall of a house (with a knife).

her husband trusts in her, and he will have no lack of gain. She does him good, and not harm, all the days of her life. She seeks wool and flax. . . . She reaches out her hands to the needy. She has no fear of snow for her household; for all her household are clothed in scarlet," etc. (Prov 31:10–31). Since the daughter's marriage was the father's business, one may ask whether marriage for love could ever happen. At any rate, we do have the biblical Song of Solomon, in which love between two young people is lauded in the loftiest language.

In matters of education, too, the girls were disadvantaged. Learning the Torah was a matter for the boys. Apart from infancy, education was the father's responsibility. Women were not entitled to inherit, nor were they admitted as witnesses in a court of law. When guests were invited to festive meals, women were not admitted. Only at the Sabbath and Passover meals were they allowed to appear. For men the appearance of women at a meal was unusual and conspicuous (cf. Mark 14:3 par.; Luke 7:36–50). It was for the prostitutes to entertain the men with dancing at such meals (cf. Mark 7:22 par.).

Societal stratification relative to reputation and popularity also arose from association with certain professions. It almost goes without saying that the publicans and tax collectors were not particularly popular. Other professions were despised because their work was associated with filth and stench, such as tanners. Others had the reputation of being dishonest, such as shepherds and wagon drivers.[48] A further criterion was the ethnic origin of Israel. The genealogies in the books of Ezra, Nehemiah, and Chronicles may indicate the value attributed to belonging to Israel by blood. For the priests, knowing their genealogy was important. Preferential treatment was given to Israelites of pure descent in the selection for certain honorary offices, such as alderman, relief administrator, member of the Sanhedrin. The evangelists Matthew and Luke try to construct Jesus' genealogy.

Select bibliography: S. Applebaum, "Economic Life in Palestine," 2.631–700 in *The Jewish People in the First Century* (ed. S. Safrai et al.; Assen: Van Gorcum, 1976); S. W. Baron, *A Social and Religious History of the Jews* (New York: Columbia University Press, 1952); W. Foerster, *Neutestamentliche Zeitgeschichte* (2 vols.; Hamburg: Furcheverlag, 1968); idem, *From Exile to Christ* (ET; Philadelphia: Fortress, 1964); F. C. Grant, *The Economic Background of the Gospels* (London: Oxford University Press, 1926); J. Herz, "Grossgrundbesitz in Palästina im Zeitalter Jesu," *PJ* 24 (1928)

---

[48] The lists of despised trades cited in Jeremias, *Jerusalem,* 303–12, are quite excessive. According to Acts 10:6, Peter, in Joppa, dwells with Simon the tanner.

98–113; H. G. Kippenberg, *Religion und Klassenbildung im antiken Judäa* (2d ed.; SUNT 14; Göttingen: Vandenhoeck & Ruprecht, 1982); H. Kreissig, "Die landwirtschaftliche Situation in Palästina vor dem jüdischen Krieg," *Acta Antiqua* 17 (1969) 223–54; idem, *Die sozialen Zusammenhänge des jüdischen Krieges* (Berlin: Akademie-Verlag, 1970); B. O. Long, "The Social World of Ancient Israel," *Int* 36 (1982) 243–55; M. Rostovtzeff, *The Social and Economic History of the Hellenistic World* (3 vols.; Oxford: Clarendon, 1953).

4

Jesus in the Period before His Public Ministry

1. Jesus in Nazareth

Jesus spent by far the longest time of his life in Nazareth.[1] Something needs to be said briefly about Nazareth, from which he obtained the appellation "of Nazareth" (Mark 1:24 et al.).[2] The location itself is not mentioned in the OT at all, nor by Josephus. This can only be attributed to its negligible importance. All the same, Nazareth had to have existed at least as early as the Hellenistic era, as the rock sepulchres demonstrate. According to the burial gifts, one of these more than twenty graves can be dated around 200 BCE.[3] A. Alt assumes that Nazareth was established from Japha, located merely three kilometers (two miles) to the southwest,[4] a town that

---

[1] On Jesus' birth in Bethlehem, cf. H. Schürmann, *Das Lukasevangelium* (2d ed.; HTKNT; Freiburg: Herder, 1982) 1.103; on the theological and historical evaluation of the virgin birth, see J. Gnilka, *Das Matthäusevangelium* (2d ed.; HTKNT; Freiburg: Herder, 1992) 1.28–32.

[2] The other Greek word translated "Nazarene" (e.g., Matt 2:23) also refers to Nazareth but may have messianic implications as well. It is derived from the (messianic) term "shoot" *(neser),* which the prophet had announced. Cf. Gnilka, *Matthäusevangelium,* 1.55–57.

[3] Eighteen of these tombs belong to the *kokim* type. Two of the tombs were still untouched, while four were sealed with a rolling stone. Since in the Jewish domain the latter was not used widely until the Roman era, it may be assumed that Nazareth was somewhat more densely populated at this time. This statement is to be taken in relative terms, of course. Cf. C. Kopp, *Die heiligen Stätten der Evangelien* (Regensburg: F. Pustet, 1959) 87.

[4] A. Alt, *Kleine Schriften zur Geschichte des Volkes Israel* (3 vols. Munich: Beck 1953) 2.443. In agreement with F. M. Abel, *Géographie de la Palestine* (3d ed.; Ebib; Paris:

occurs in the list of locations associated with the tribe of Zebulun (Josh 19:10–16). Nazareth also is situated in the territory of Zebulun. It is surrounded by hills; to the north is the Nebi Sa'in, where the still existing spring may indicate the proximity of the ancient settlement. To the southwest a gorge-like wadi descends rapidly to Lake Gennesaret, which lies 550 meters lower, if we may assume that the town was situated about 340 meters above sea level. For the inhabitants of the town this was an arduous access to the world, because about ten kilometers (six miles) to the east was the Via Maris, which linked Damascus with the south of Israel and with Egypt.

In the Gospels Nazareth is identified as a town (Matt 2:23; Luke 1:26; et al.). This has no implications for its size, for the Greek Bible (LXX) also translates the Hebrew '*ir,* which designates every autonomous community, regardless of size, as πόλις. Based on the evidence of Mark 6:1f. par., Nazareth had a synagogue. At least ten men were required to establish a synagogal community, but that was sufficient. In this small town Jesus lived with his family. He was the firstborn son (Luke 2:7).

If we may presuppose a *communiter contingentia,* the general custom, his mother Mary would have been about fifteen to seventeen years older than he, and Joseph about twenty-five years older. The assumption that Joseph, who is only mentioned in the infancy narratives of the Gospels, died early has much to commend itself. In this case Mary and her son might have been accepted into the wider kinship group. The names of the Lord's brothers, James, Joseph, Jude, and Simon (Mark 6:3), all of them names of Jewish patriarchs, point to a family rooted in the Jewish faith.[5] We have no information about the names of the Lord's sisters. His name, incidently, was Jeshuah, and his mother's Miriam. The names Jesus and Mary are their later, Greek equivalents, just as in Mark 6:3 the Lord's brother Joseph is introduced by the Greek name Joses (cf. Matt 13:55). In the remote town of Nazareth there was probably not much to be felt of the Hellenistic influence of the world as a whole. But Sepphoris was situated four kilometers (2.5 miles) north of Nazareth; it was the residence of Herod Antipas, lover of splendor, who dwelt there until about 20 CE and was receptive to Hellenistic influence. The amphi-

---

J. Gabalda et Cie, 1967) 1.395, the alternative name Ναζαρά (Luke 4:16; Matt 4:13) is to be taken as a Hellenistic form. In his Latin translation of the *Onomastikon* of Eusebius, Jerome likewise has the name Nazara (GCS 11/1,; ed. E. Klostermann) 141.

[5] On the question of the Lord's brothers, cf. J. Gnilka, *Das Evangelium nach Markus* (3d ed.; EKK; Zurich: Benzinger; Neukirchen-Vluyn: Neukirchener, 1978–79) 1.234f.

theater he built attests to that. We may assume that the people of
Sepphoris were Hellenistic in their orientation as well, for during
the subsequent Jewish War they went out to meet the Roman troops
and surrender.[6] The inhabitants of Nazareth did not follow suit.
Most of them may have been killed in the war.[7]

We have no details concerning Jesus' lengthy period of time in
Nazareth. The Gospels are silent about it. In his infancy he may have
been raised by Mary, then by Joseph, who was responsible for intro-
ducing him to the Torah. In the synagogue he heard the reading of
the Scriptures and their interpretation in the sermon. In everyday
life he practiced a trade. The same word, τέκτων, customarily translated as "carpenter," is used for his own trade as well as for Joseph's.
The Gospel mentions both in the same reference to Jesus' appearance in his home synagogue in Nazareth. The townspeople take
offence and, according to Mark 6:3, say: "Is not this the carpenter?"
and following Matthew 13:55: "Is not this the carpenter's son?" Luke
4:22 avoids identifying the trade. Here Mark offers the earliest form,
for the tendency is obviously to remove the trade identification from
Jesus. Yet we may assume that both practiced the trade of a τέκτων,
that Jesus learned this trade from Joseph, since it can be documented
in later rabbinic Judaism that it was the father's obligation to teach
his son a trade. A rabbinic saying states: "Whoever does not teach
him a trade, teaches him robbery" (*b. Qidd.* 30b).[8]

Describing the activity of a τέκτων as carpentry is to view it too
narrowly, however. It applied to the working not only of lumber but
also of stones, hence it also denoted stonemasonry (cf. 2 Kgs 5:11
LXX). In the Greek papyri the τέκτονες have the following activities:
sluice construction, waterwheel maintenance, construction of doors
and houses, saddle repairs, etc.[9] Therefore their range of activity is
multifaceted. Incidently, this is already attested in Homer's *Iliad,*
which refers to a τέκτων "whose hands formed all kinds of works of
art" (5.60f.). Despite his versatility, it may be appropriate to ask

---

[6] Josephus, *War* 3.29–31, mentions Sepphoris as the only peace-loving town in
this region.

[7] According to ibid., 3.289–292, Japha vehemently resisted the Romans. It may
well be that the inhabitants of Nazareth sought refuge in this fortified town and after
the conquest of Sepphoris perished, to a large extent, together with the inhabitants of
Japha. Nevertheless, relatives of the family of Jesus survived. Eusebius, *Hist. eccl.* 3.20,
refers to the emperor Domitian issuing a summons to relatives of Jesus.

[8] Cf. Riesner, *Lehrer,* 116–18.

[9] F. Preisigke and E. Kiessling, *Wörterbuch der griechischen Papyruskunde* (vols. 1–3,
Berlin: self-published, 1925–31; vol. 4, Amsterdam: A. K. Hakkert, 1969) 2.585.

whether a τέκτων had sufficient work in Nazareth. A. Schlatter[10] reckoned with the possibility that Joseph participated in the rebuilding of Sepphoris, which Varus had destroyed in 4 BCE. Since the reconstruction took years, could it be that Jesus was involved in these jobs as well? Yet we cannot go beyond making suppositions.

Why did Jesus stay in Nazareth for so long? How many years did he live there? And what finally did prompt him to leave his hometown? The external cause was John the Baptist's appearance in Judea. The news of the great preacher of repentance in the southern Jordan region had reached as far as Nazareth. And Jesus went from Nazareth in Galilee to the Jordan to be baptized by John (cf. Mark 1:9). With this he enters into public life. First, however, we want to ask how long he stayed at home. At the same time, this question concerns his age.

The Gospels offer us two points of reference. While one of them is rather vague, the other seems to be quite precise. According to Luke 1:5 and Matthew 2, Jesus' birth (as well as that of John the Baptist) coincides with the time of King Herod's reign. According to Luke 3:1, John the Baptist's public appearance was in the fifteenth year of the reign of the emperor Tiberius.[11] We further learn from Luke 3:23 that Jesus was about thirty years old when he began his ministry. The latter reference is also theologically motivated, since it may refer to 2 Sam 5:4: David, the Messiah's prototype, was thirty years old as well when he became king. Nevertheless, the relative age reference of "about thirty years" indicates Luke's chronological-historical interest. This interest does in fact also vouch for the accuracy of the general reference "in the days of Herod" as the time of Jesus' birth.

Yet Herod died in 4 BCE. Dionysius Exiguus, a monk who in 525 determined the date of Easter on orders of Pope John I and was the first to calculate the years since Christ, miscalculated.[12] The fifteenth year of Tiberius's reign ran from October 1, 27 CE, to October 1, 28. This assumes the Syrian system of counting, which is to be favored for Luke. According to this reckoning the time from Tiberius's accession to the throne (August 19, 14 CE) to the beginning to the new civic year (October 1, 14 CE), though it encompassed

---

[10] A. Schlatter, *Der Evangelist Matthäus* (Stuttgart: Calwer, 1929) 455.

[11] The remaining references to Pontius Pilate, Herod Antipas, Philip, Lysanias, Annas, and Caiaphas in Luke 3:1f. are not of much help since they do not indicate the years within their respective tenures.

[12] Cf. J. Lenzenweger, *LTK* (2d ed.; Freiburg: Herder, 1993) 3.406.

merely six weeks, counts as the first year of his reign.[13] There are incalculabilities that remain, to be sure. If the death of Herod the Great is the final possible point in time for Jesus' birth, the possibility of an earlier time remains open. Jesus may have been in his early thirties when he came to John at the Jordan.

In terms of further chronological calculations it is necessary to consider that the fifteenth year of Tiberius's reign (Luke 3:1) refers to the beginning of John the Baptist's ministry, not to that of Jesus' ministry.[14]

2. John the Baptist and Jesus

Whom did Jesus meet when he encountered John the Baptist? John cannot be categorized in any one of the Jewish religious parties described earlier. He was neither Pharisee, nor Zealot, nor Essene. Time and again he has been moved into the spiritual proximity of Qumran, near whose location he ministered and with whose existence he must have been acquainted. Occasionally it has even been argued that he was educated in Qumran. Yet he was distinct from Qumran precisely because of the public nature of his ministry, which addressed all Israelites. Only vaguely can he be linked with baptist movements that may have existed at that time.[15] What characterizes him is relentless proclamation of judgment, which he combined with the offer of baptism. He is a figure of significance and stature reminiscent of the old prophets, the contours of which have to be drawn from what has been handed down to us. Unfortunately there is but little of that.[16]

---

[13] As in C. Cichorius, "Chronologisches zum Leben Jesu," *ZNW* 22 (1923) 18f. In a different approach, also mentioned by Schürmann, *Lukasevangelium,* 1.150, Tiberius' first regnal year ran from August 19, 14 CE, to August 18, 15 CE, and the fifteenth year from August 19, 28 CE, to August 18, 29 CE. This would be the literal reckoning. Compared with the Syrian method of counting, the difference is ten and one-half months.

[14] Cf. E. Meyer, *Ursprung und Anfänge des Urchristentum* (3d ed.; Stuttgart: J. G. Cotta, 1921) 1.50, who points out that John the Baptist is also referred to in the Jewish tradition, as Josephus indicates.

[15] Cf. J. Thomas, *Le mouvement baptiste en Palestine et Syrie* (Gembloux: J. Duculot, 1935).

[16] Josephus' terse account (*Ant.* 18.117–119) depicts John as a philosophical educator of his people. While he mentions baptism, he totally ignores the decidedly eschatological components. His interest is focused on the Baptist's death and its more immediate circumstances. Cf. R. Schütz, *Johannes der Täufer* (ATANT 50; Zurich: Zwingli, 1967) 13–27.

Central to John's proclamation of judgment is the expected end of history. His anticipation of the end as near was so pressing and relentless that comparable eschatological tendencies in apocalyptic and among the Essenes are eclipsed and it can be characterized as an expectation of the imminent. The impending judgment is inexorable and is vividly presented as such: "Even now the axe is laid to the root of the trees; every tree therefore that does not bear good fruit is cut down and thrown into the fire" (Matt 3:10 par.). As the woodcutter bares the root of a tree before applying the final blows to fell the tree, so the hearers' situation has become critical. The expected judge already has in his hand the winnowing fork with which he will clear his threshing floor (Matt 3:12 par.). Nothing further is to be expected from history, which moves toward its goal. Speculations about the end, such as those commonly practiced in apocalyptic, seem superfluous. The anticipated future is exclusively God's work, setting limits for everything present.

The anticipated end will mean the unleashing of the divine wrath upon God's people. No one can expect to escape the coming wrath (Matt 3:7 par.). The fire to which the unfruitful tree falls victim expresses the unyielding wrath of God (see Amos 7:4; Zeph 3:8; Jer 21:12; Ezek 22:31; Ps 89:47; et al.). Yet in the saying about the baptism of fire, the fire becomes real, destroying what is there, an unquenchable fire to which the chaff, that is, the persons who were unable to bear fruit, are to be delivered (Matt 3:11f.). Lastly, it also denotes the fire of Gehenna that will break open on this day (cf. Job 20:26: Isa 34:10; 66:24; Dan 12:2).[17] There is no escape, for God's wrath is just. John views Israel as having reached the end. Belonging to the people of Israel no longer has any meaning. It is of no avail to be a descendant of Abraham. This is made clear almost sarcastically in the reference to the stones scattered in the desert. God is able to raise up from them children for Abraham (Matt 3:9). In this devastating assessment the Baptist agrees with the Teacher of Righteousness of Qumran. He does not attempt, however, to gather a community around himself as a holy remnant of Israel. It is already too late for that. He only receives disciples as his followers (cf. Mark 2:18 par.).

In view of the approaching judgment John demands that everyone repent. He further calls for submission to his baptism in

---

[17] J. Becker, *Johannes der Täufer und Jesus von Nazaret* (BibS[N] 63; Neukirchen: Neukirchener, 1972) 28f., assumes that the fire was purely a fire of destruction, cleansing the earth from sinners.

Jordan's running water. This rite of baptism was the new thing that characterized his ministry and earned him the nickname Baptist. In his presence the ones being baptized confessed their sins; this probably was a general type of confession, comparable to the confession of sins on the Jewish day of Atonement or at the covenant renewal festival at Qumran (Mark 1:5; cf. 1QS 1:22–2:1). The baptism he offered could be received only once, because the last hour had come. Its uniqueness expresses its obligating character. In Mark 1:4 it is called a baptism of repentance for the forgiveness of sins. The promised forgiveness of sins presupposes genuine willingness to repent. This means that baptism alone does not guarantee the forgiveness of sins but, as it were, the seal on the declaration of willingness to repent. Nevertheless, it is important to see that, as the provider of baptism, John is involved in the process of the person's acceptance. The turning that takes place is toward God. Here we may assume, though this is not explicitly stated, that it implied the turning to the will of God decreed in the law. The sermon offered in Luke 3:10–14, likely the work of the Lukan redaction, cannot inform us about the Baptist's unique intentions. The reference to the fruit worthy of repentance (Matt 3:8)[18] seems to leave it to the individual to make concrete his readiness to repent in his practical life. Should there be no fruit, however, the baptism would also lose its meaning. This brings to full prominence the individualized character of the call to repentance, calling the individual to accountability.

But the baptism offered in the Jordan points beyond itself. In its eschatological context it points to the baptism offered in view of the day of judgment in the immediate future to which everyone will have to submit. What is disputed, however, is whether John announced this baptism as the baptism with the Holy Spirit and with fire (so Matt 3:11; Luke 3:16=Q) or only with the Holy Spirit (so Mark 1:8) or only with fire. Often the reference to the Holy Spirit is taken to be a Christian interpolation in the Baptist's sermon, pointing to the later experience of the Spirit by the Christian community. Yet they were successful in not allowing the Baptist to announce the baptism of fire only. They branded him as a thoroughgoing prophet of doom. It should further be considered that in this manner he could be attributed greater signficance in mediating salvation than

---

[18] Luke 3:8 speaks of fruit in the plural and thus focuses more on the individual deeds to be expected.

the one he awaited.[19] When he announced the baptism with the Spirit and with fire, therefore, one may want to remember that this parallelism is also encountered in the community rules of Qumran where the future purification through the Holy Spirit is announced alongside the destruction in the fire of gloom (1QS 4:13, 21; cf. Joel 3:1-3). Clearly the baptism with the Spirit and fire refers to different groups: while some are to receive destruction by fire, others are to receive the cleansing through the Holy Spirit.[20]

Still greater difficulties are encountered in the attempt to answer the question of the identity of the one who the Baptist said would baptize with the Holy Spirit and with fire, that is, whose "forerunner" John understood himself to be. In any case, John was not a disciple of Jesus. However obscure the coming baptizer with the Spirit and with fire may seem to be in John's preaching, it may be correct to say that for him the baptism with the Spirit and with fire was more prominent than the idea of who was to provide it. Thus it can be recognized that in his conception the awaited one, who is to appear on the day of judgment, is a being that belongs to the heavenly realm. The baptism with the Spirit and with fire are eschatological functions, which can no longer be attributed to a human being. For this reason only two possibilities deserve serious consideration: God himself or the Son of man. The Son of man denotes the judging and saving figure known from apocalyptic, who is hidden in heaven and awaits the end in order to reveal himself. Moving the Baptist nearer the Son of man Christology does not mean to declare him to be an apocalyptist. And given the widespread influence of apocalyptic, it should not surprise to find current apocalyptic elements in his preaching.

It is difficult to decide between God and the Son of man. In favor of the Son of man it could be argued that the expectation of him continued in Jesus' preaching and hence that this represents an element that Jesus adopted from the Baptist's preaching, not without altering it, to be sure. The most important objection against a connection between the baptizer with the Spirit and with fire and the Son of man is that the eschatological baptism with the Spirit is always uttered by God. But against this it can be said that in the eschatological expectation of contemporary Judaism there were no-

---

[19] Cf. Schürmann, *Lukasevangelium* 1.176.

[20] There is also the solution of understanding πνεῦμα in terms of "storm" to accompany the fire, hence fiery breath; so R. Pesch, *Das Markusevangelium* (2 vols.; HTKNT; Freiburg: Herder, 1976–77) 1.85. This is possible linguistically but may amount to a stopgap measure objectively.

tions according to which God and the eschatological bearer of salvation work together very closely, where their respective work in fact
merges.[21] *First Enoch* 49 states concerning the Son of man that he has
the fullness of the gifts of the Spirit, and wisdom is poured out
before him like water.[22]

Mark 1:7 par. contains the statement about his great humility:
"After me comes he who is mightier than I, the thong of whose
sandals I am not worthy to stoop down and untie." Matthew 3:11
varies: " . . . whose sandals I am not worthy to carry." This statement
allows for no other connection than with the Son of man or the
Messiah. Who would ever speak about God's thongs?[23] Presumably
this saying arose later,[24] for even applied to the Son of man construed
as a heavenly being, it presents difficulties. It arose at a time when
John was retrospectively recognized as Jesus' forerunner and was
claimed as such.

The Baptist's outward lifestyle agreed with his proclamation of
judgment. As the locus for his activity he chose the wilderness, since
it was understood to be the place of the new eschatological beginning. It is doubtful that he appealed to Isa 40:3: "In the wilderness
prepare the way of the LORD, make straight in the wilderness a
highway for our God" (cf. Mark 1:3). It is true that the Qumran
community also based its desert existence on Isa 40:3 (cf. 1QS
8:13f.), but there is no evidence for this scribal reflection on the part
of the Baptist.

He wore a garment made of camel hair and a leather belt
around his waist. For food he ate grasshoppers and wild honey. The
description of his clothing does not warrant the assumption that he
viewed himself as Elijah redivivus, or that he patterned his ministry
after that of the ancient prophet. The garment made of camel's hair
is the clothing of the desert dweller. It can also be understood as an
expression of great poverty. The leather belt is part of the normal
garb of peasants and Bedouins. The interpretation of the Baptist as the
second Elijah emerged only in the Christian community. Wild honey
and grasshoppers were the scant nourishment that the wilderness

---

[21] Cf. P. Volz, *Die Eschatologie der jüdischen Gemeinde im neutestamentlichen Zeitalter*
(2d ed.; Tübingen: Mohr, 1934) 224f.

[22] *T. Jud.* 24:3 says concerning the Messiah that he will pour out the Spirit. The
reference is suspected to be a Christian interpolation. Cf. also J. Becker, *Untersuchungen
zur Entstehungsgeschichte der Testamente der zwölf Patriarchen* (AGAJU 8; Leiden: Brill,
1970) 320–23.

[23] Cf. Becker, *Johannes*, 34.

[24] Cf. Gnilka, *Markus*, 1.41.

yielded. Grasshoppers were boiled in salt water and roasted over coal. Wild honey is honey from wild bees, hardly fruit syrup, as in an assertion that can be traced all the way back to the Ebionite Gospel. Since no other foods are mentioned, the description is that of the Baptist's strict ascetic lifestyle.

Jesus joined the crowd of people and was baptized by John. He recognized the Baptist's ministry. At a later stage he was to verbalize this recognition and to speak of John's unique significance: "What did you go out into the wilderness to behold? A reed shaken by the wind? Why then did you go out? To see a man clothed in soft raiment? Behold, those who wear soft raiment are in kings' houses. Why then did you go out? To see a prophet? Yes, I tell you, and more than a prophet. . . . Truly, I say to you, among those born of women there has risen no one greater than John the Baptist" (Matt 11:7b–9, 11a). These words elevate John above the prophets, though they avoid a messianic title. Jesus also rejects a disassociation from the Baptist.[25]

That Jesus received John's baptism cannot be contested seriously. This fact evidently posed difficulties for the Christian community. Matthew 3:14f. narrates a dialogue, taking place at the baptism, which has the inappropriateness of baptism for Jesus as its background. Luke 3:21 only makes inferential mention of Jesus' baptism, in a subordinate clause, and John 1:29–34 no longer even mentions it. More recently W. Haenchen[26] has cast doubt upon Jesus' baptism, especially arguing that the proclamation of Jesus is predicated upon a different portrait of God than that of the Baptist. While Jesus speaks of judgment as well, God's offer of grace becomes powerfully prominent in his preaching. The Baptist did not talk about the kingdom of God, which is the central concern of Jesus' proclamation,[27] nor do we hear anything about miracles he worked or about healing the sick. Nevertheless, these relevant observations cannot call into question the historicity of Jesus' baptism.

In a secondary context, however, they need to be taken seriously. It is argued that for a time Jesus belonged to the circle of the

---

[25] Disassociations in the text cited are made via insertion of the logion "he who is least in the kingdom of heaven is greater than he" (Matt 11:11b) and the so-called violence saying (11:12; par. Luke 10:16), which in its original form may have said the following: "The law and the prophets (extend) to John. From that point on the kingdom of God suffers violence and men of violence take it by force." Cf. Gnilka, *Matthäusevangelium,* 1.412f.

[26] W. Haenchen, *Der Weg Jesu* (STö.H 6; Berlin: Töpelmann, 1966) 58–63.

[27] Matt 3:2 is a secondary adaptation of Matt 4:17 and is the work of the evangelist's redaction.

Baptist's disciples.[28] John 1:35–51 confirms at least that some of his later disciples had previously been disciples of John. Among these was Andrew the brother of Simon Peter, and the latter presumably as well. In support of Jesus' discipleship, appeal is made to the logion already mentioned, "After me comes he who is mightier than I . . ." (Mark 1:7 par.).[29] "To follow after someone" does indeed express discipleship. Jesus uses the same term, for instance, in Mark 8:34, "If any man would come after me (ὀπίσω μου ἀκολουθεῖν), let him deny himself . . ." Yet it can also be understood in a temporal sense.[30] In this case it expresses nothing more than that the stronger one will appear after the Baptist.

Jesus' discipleship of John could be corroborated by two references in the Gospel of John, according to which Jesus also baptized. Thus the proponents of Johannine discipleship argue that as a disciple of the Baptist, it was the baptism of John that Jesus administered. In John 3:22f. we read: "After this Jesus and his disciples went into the land of Judea; there he remained with them and baptized. John also was baptizing at Aenon near Salim." This statement is corrected in 4:1–3: "Now when the Lord knew that the Pharisees had heard that Jesus was making and baptizing more disciples than John (although Jesus himself did not baptize, but only his disciples), he left Judea and departed again to Galilee." The parenthetical correction may be a remark from the later redaction.[31] It is feasible that the Fourth Gospel preserved an ancient historical reminiscence for us.[32] It does not say, of course, that Jesus baptized as a disciple of John, but that he already had his own disciples. If he himself baptized as well, his baptism is by no means to be equated with John's baptism. It is not clear what meaning Jesus associated with baptism; no special significance is attributed to it. Did it have preparatory character, in the sense of readiness to hear his call?[33]

The assumption that Jesus, for a time, was a disciple of John, encounters a fortiori the problem already mentioned above, that his

---

[28] For instance Becker, *Johannes,* 12–15.
[29] Cf. P. Hoffmann, *Studien zur Theologie der Logienquelle* (3d ed.; NTA 8; Münster: Aschendorff, 1982) 24.
[30] Examples in F. Passow, *Handwörterbuch der griechischen Sprache* (5th ed.; Leipzig: Darmstadt, 1970) 1.497.
[31] In 4:2 the rare καίτοιγε and the absence of the article with the name of Jesus are conspicuous. Cf. Schnackenburg, *Gospel of John,* 1.422 n. 4.
[32] R. Bultmann, *The Gospel according to John* (ET; Philadelphia: Fortress, 1971) 167f., is inclined to see John 3:22 as the evangelist's construction.
[33] So Schnackenburg, *John,* 1.411.

subsequent ministry is substantially different from that of the Baptist. This would mean that he severed his ties with John or that he had a special experience, a divine commissioning or call.[34] There is no hint for either, however. Even Mark 1:10f. cannot be adduced in support of the latter. Certainly Jesus announced the judgment as well.[35] But his proclamation of judgment has its own connotations and cannot be separated from his proclamation of the kingdom of God, especially not in the sense that the former preceded the latter in time. Hence we reach the conclusion that Jesus accepted the Baptist's movement, joined it, was baptized by John, but did not become his disciple.

Afterward Jesus returned to Galilee, not to Nazareth but to the region around the western and northern shore of Lake Gennesaret, in order to begin his own ministry. He did not choose the wilderness but rather the pleasant and fertile land of the peasants and fishermen. Should he previously have ministered in John's circle and there gained his first disciples, this would have to be understood as a type of prelude.

Overview

If we pursue the history of the traditions on the Baptist in the Gospels, one orientation is dominant: to characterize John as Jesus' forerunner. This lent precision to what was uncertain in the announcement of the one who was to come. In the light of faith in Christ, the Baptist was to predate and be subordinate to Jesus. We recognize the decisive step in the logia source, in which the proclamation of the Baptist was incorporated and placed before Jesus' proclamation. Something similar is found in Mark, the earliest evangelist, who begins his Gospel with a description of the Baptist's activity and thus becomes the model for the other evangelists. In the logia source the Baptist may well be seen even more emphatically as the forerunner of Jesus, the Son of man who comes to bring judgment, thereby achieving a link to the Baptist's proclamation, which was replete with intensive, imminent expectation. Yet John's inquiry from prison represents the seam of a patch in terms of the clarifying

[34] U. Wilckens reckons on an experience of this kind, "Das Offenbarungsverständnis in der Geschichte des Urchristentums," 52–54 in *Offenbarung als Geschichte* (ed. W. Pannenberg; Göttingen: Vandenhoeck & Ruprecht, 1961).

[35] Cf. Becker, *Johannes,* 86–104, who wants to move Jesus closer to the Baptist via his proclamation of judgment.

development: "Are you he who is to come, or shall we look for another?" (Matt 11:3 par.). The response to the question is affirmative, of course. The disassociation of the Baptist from Jesus, in terms of being the forerunner, takes on increasingly more precise contours until the temporal separation; hence Jesus is to begin his public ministry after John's incarceration (cf. Mark 1:14).

Select bibliography: F. J. Andersen, "The Diet of John the Baptist," *AbrN* 3 (1961) 60–74; C. Cichorius, "Chronologisches zum Leben Jesu," *ZNW* 22 (1923) 16–20; M. S. Enslin, "John and Jesus," *ZNW* 66 (1975) 1–18; J. Gnilka, "Die essenischen Tauchbäder und die Johannestaufe," *RevQ* 3 (1961) 185–207; G. Lindeskog, "Johannes der Täufer," *ASTI* 12 (1983) 55–83; H. Merklein, "Die Umkehrpredigt bei Johannes dem Täufer und Jesus von Nazaret," *BZ* 25 (1981) 29–46; J. Pryke, "John the Baptist and the Qumran Community," *RevQ* 4 (1964) 483–96; R. Schütz, *Johannes der Täufer* (ATANT 50; Zurich: Zwingli, 1967); P. Vielhauer, "Tracht und Speise Johannes' des Täufers," 47–54 in idem, *Aufsätze zum NT* (TB 31; Munich: Kaiser, 1965); W. Wink, *John the Baptist and the Gospel Tradition* (SNTSMS 7; London: Cambridge University Press, 1968).

5

The Message of the Reign of God

The center of Jesus' proclamation was indisputably the reign of God (βασιλεία τοῦ θεοῦ). Time and again he spoke about it and explained it in parables. The reign of God can be taken literally as the center of his work. Everything else can be ordered around this central issue, not only his message but also his ministry in healing and miracles, as well as his ethical imperative. And though we will have to inquire into his claim to have a mission, this message can be used as the reference point.

The link of the proclamation of the reign of God to the person of Jesus is apparent from its predominance in the Synoptic Gospels. In the Gospel of John it is almost entirely missing (except in John 3:3, 5). Relatively speaking, its continuation is strongest in Acts. Here the term βασιλεία τοῦ θεοῦ still occurs six times (1:3; 8:12; 14:22; 19:8; 28:23, 31). The explanation for this lies in the overall plan of the two Lukan works. In the Pauline corpus it is found ten times (Rom 14:17; 1 Cor 4:20; Col 4:11; 2 Thess 1:5; et al.). Within the remaining NT writings we also encounter it in the Apocalypse (12:10). These findings are instructive because they indicate the differing theological languages within the various writings of the NT, as well as the Synoptics' link to Jesus.

As far as the terminology is concerned, it should be noted that Matthew speaks of the kingdom of heaven (βασιλεία τῶν οὐρανῶν) rather than of the reign of God. In some passages, however, the concept "reign of God" is evident as well (Matt 12:28; 19:24;[1] 21:31,

---

[1] Some text witnesses have "kingdom of heaven" here.

43). The question arises as to the language Jesus used, what formulation he preferred. The term "kingdom of heaven" has a more Jewish ring to it. "Heaven" is to be construed as a substitute term for the name of God. We also encounter the term "kingdom of heaven" in the rabbinic literature,[2] as well as the term "reign of God," of course. There is a tendency in the rabbinic literature to circumscribe the divine name so as not to desecrate it by excessive use.[3] Although part of the rabbinic evidence may be late, the Matthean tradition here links up with a Jewish custom. But the first evangelist did not introduce the term "kingdom of heaven" in his Gospel for fear of the divine name, because four times he left the ancient form unchanged. He did it for theological reasons. "Kingdom of heaven," to him, seemed to be a suitable term to circumscribe the universality and global power of the anticipated revelation of the reign of God.[4] Despite its Jewish flair, therefore, we consider the reference to the kingdom of heaven to be secondary. Jesus spoke of the reign of God.

There are various options in rendering the term βασιλεία τοῦ θεοῦ in English: reign, realm, kingdom of God. The rendering of "reign of God" is to be preferred and appropriate in all the relevant references. In the "entrance sayings," which deal with entering the *basileia,* and other pictorial descriptions, it may be preferable to use the translation "kingdom of God."[5] Today the term "reign" may be discredited because of human abuse. With reference to God it retains its validity. God's reign is different from that exercised by humans. When Jesus moved the reign of God to center stage in his proclamation, he ultimately declared that for him God was the center. In what follows, the reign of God in Jesus' proclamation will be presented in its various dimensions.

Select bibliography: J. A. Baird, *Rediscovering the Power of the Gospels* (Wooster, Ohio: Iona, 1982); J. Bonsirven, *Le règne de Dieu* (Aubier: Editions Montaigne, 1957); M. Buber, *Königtum Gottes* (3d ed.; Heidelberg: L. Schneider, 1956); O. Cullmann, *Königsherrschaft Christi und Kirche im NT* (2d ed.; Zollikon-Zurich: Evangelischer, 1946); G. Gloege, *Reich Gottes und Kirche im NT* (Gütersloh: C. Bertelsmann, 1929); J. Gray, *The Biblical Doctrine of the Reign of God* (Edinburgh: T. & T. Clark, 1979); J. Héring, *Le royaume de Dieu et sa venue* (Paris: F. Alcan, 1937); A. M. Hunter, *Christ and the Kingdom* (Edinburgh: Saint Andrew, 1980); A. Kretzer, *Die Herrschaft der*

[2] Documentation in Str-B, *Kommentar,* 1.172–84.
[3] Thus one also spoke of the name of heaven, the fruit of heaven, being occupied with the heavens, etc. "Heaven" is used in place of "God."
[4] Cf. A. Kretzer, *Die Herrschaft der Himmel und die Söhne des Reiches* (SBM 10; Stuttgart, 1971) 24f.
[5] Cf. R. Schnackenburg, *Gottes Herrschaft und Reich* (3d ed.; Freiburg: Herder, 1963) 247.

Himmel und die Söhne des Reiches (SBM 10; Stuttgart: Echter, 1971); R. Morgenthaler, *Kommendes Reich* (Zurich, 1952); N. Perrin, *Jesus and the Language of the Kingdom* (London: SCM, 1976); J. Schlosser, "Le règne de Dieu dans les dits de Jésus," *RevScRel* 53 (1979) 164–76.

1. Jesus' discourse in parables

Jesus proclaimed the reign of God. Time and again he spoke of it in parables. The son of Galilee dressed his thoughts "in his native clothes and with a firm hand led his disciples from the known to the unknown, from the sensory realm to the kingdom of heaven."[6] By describing the known, indeed the ordinary, the parables allow our mind's eye to see the life of ordinary people of his time, such as the farmer who scatters seed on his field, the fisherman with his net in tow, but also the city-dweller of Jerusalem hosting guests at a meal or visiting the temple to pray. Yet the vivid story that grabs the hearer, the picture that still today is able to grab the receptive reader, points beyond itself to the reign of God, making it intelligible and its presence known.

In recent decades research has dealt intensively with the parables of Jesus. Since Jesus the narrator is almost invariably taken into account in this research, albeit with varying importance, and since the parables were taken seriously as his message, we want to utilize them in the endeavor to focus on the question of interest to us. For this reason we intend to present, though selectively and in condensed fashion, various approaches to interpreting the parables which, in line with our interests, we might understand as differing ways of accessing Jesus' message. In order to make the access easier for the reader, we shall demonstrate the methods of interpretation by using a single parable as example. Various authors' approaches to interpretation will be described, as well as their concrete interpretations of the chosen parable. Thus the concrete interpretation should clarify the interpretative approach. The example we have chosen is the parable of the laborers in the vineyard (Matt 20:1–16). The text is as follows:

"For the kingdom of heaven is like a householder who went out early in the morning to hire laborers for his vineyard. ²After agreeing with the laborers for a denarius a day, he sent them into his vineyard. ³And going out about the third hour he saw others standing idle in the market place; ⁴and to them he said, 'You go into the vineyard too, and whatever is right I will give you.' So they went. ⁵Going out again about the sixth hour and the ninth hour, he did the same. ⁶And about the eleventh hour

---

[6] A. Jülicher, *Die Gleichnisreden Jesu* (2d ed.; Tübingen: Mohr, 1910) 1.145.

he went out and found others standing; and he said to them, 'Why do you stand here idle all day?' ⁷They said to him, 'Because no one has hired us.' He said to them, 'You go into the vineyard too.' ⁸And when evening came, the owner of the vineyard said to his steward, 'Call the laborers and pay them their wages, beginning with the last, up to the first.' ⁹And when those hired about the eleventh hour came, each of them received a denarius. ¹⁰Now when the first came, they thought they would receive more; but each of them also received a denarius. ¹¹And on receiving it they grumbled at the householder, ¹²saying, 'These last worked only one hour, and you have made them equal to us who have borne the burden of the day and the scorching heat.' ¹³But he replied to one of them, 'Friend, I am doing you no wrong; did you not agree with me for a denarius? ¹⁴Take what belongs to you, and go; I choose to give to this last as I give to you. ¹⁵Am I not allowed to do what I choose with what belongs to me? Or do you begrudge my generosity?' ¹⁶So the last will be first, and the first last."

a) How did A. Jülicher, the founder of modern parable research, understand the parables as Jesus' message, and how did he interpret the above parable as Jesus' message? Jülicher is aware of the distance between the Gospels and Jesus. The meaning that the evangelist derives from the parable is not the same as the one Jesus had in mind. The evangelists were no longer aware of when and to what audience Jesus told a given parable. For this reason we find the parables placed in different contexts in the Gospels. It is still possible to rediscover the original meaning of the parable. The crucial insight for Jülicher is that the evangelists viewed the parables as obscure speech and difficult to understand, hence requiring interpretation. In this pursuit they adopted an understanding of parables that was already present in Hellenistic Judaism. The parable becomes the twin of the riddle, containing a complete idea, being a comparative form of speech and disguising a deeper meaning. For Jülicher the parables' mysteriousness, which for the evangelists was a given, is seen in the allegories that have penetrated the tradition. Allegory caused parabolic speech to become figurative, thus needing interpretation, as it were.[7]

If one is to find the original meaning of the parable, the allegories that have intruded must be removed, according to Jülicher's rule of thumb in reconstruction. In doing so Jülicher is directed by Aristotle's conception of parable. This makes Jesus' parable a sort of argumentative speech and construes it as evidence. It is to be understood, of course, as a readily intelligible form of speech that is lucid in and of itself. By means of the parable the thread of the speech is

---

[7] Ibid., 1.1f., 39–42, 49.

doubled, as it were. Alongside the issue itself there is the picture. Jesus uses the picture, readily affirmed by the audience, to motivate them also to affirm the issue itself, to which they might have some objection. The parable is evidence of what is conceded, in contrast to what is similar but not conceded as yet. In picture form truth is more powerful than in abstraction. The parable has been fully grasped as evidence if the point of comparison between picture and issue has been discovered. In contrast to the many layers of an allegory, the clarity of parabolic speech is found in this focus on the *one* point of comparison.[8]

The clarity or paucity of interpretative rules can be seen again in the interpretation of the parable cited above. In the picture part it narrates that the owner of the vineyard pays everyone the same wage, to those who arrived first as well as to those who entered work in the final hour. Some receive what is just, while others experience the master's goodness. What is good takes its rightful place alongside what is just, for it is not proper to demand gifts. Hence there is to be no complaining on the part of those who received their due, though they did not receive any gifts. Goodness is reproached only by envy, not by a self-centered sense of justice. The point of comparison here is the identical wage for different labor. And this is what Jülicher names the parable. The issue at stake is the kingdom of God, whose doors are open to all, to the just as well as to sinners. What the righteous receive as obligatory wage for their piety, God freely grants the repentant sinner by grace. Jesus wanted the parable understood in this way. Jülicher cautiously points to a possible audience by referring to Jewish eloquence, Pharisaic arrogance of merit, those to whom Jesus' offer of the kingdom of God for all was considered to be πρῶτον ψεῦδος (the "foremost lie").[9]

The reconstruction of the original parable and its meaning is not considered difficult for Jülicher because the evangelist Matthew or the tradition shaped it only in two ways, by putting it in its context and by adding the saying in verse 16: "So the last will be first, and the first last" (in reverse order in 19:30).[10] By means of this minor reworking, the meaning of the parable has been changed dramatically. Now the payment of wages becomes an allegory of the final judgment. Paying the wages to the last one first, which formerly

---

[8] Ibid., 1.69–72.

[9] Ibid., 2.465–67.

[10] In addition Jülicher reckons that originally v. 8 said: "Pay them the *same* wage," ibid., 2.463.

expressed the master's goodness, now loses its significance in favor of the notion of a reversal of values. The challenge "Take what belongs to you, and go" takes on a dimension of threat. At the same time, the owner of the vineyard becomes a metaphor for God, the vineyard for Israel or the church. The advancing allegorization in the church tradition, prefigured in Matthew, is indicated from this point on. In the different hours when laborers were hired, one now sees reflected the entire history of humanity, from Adam to Christ; the wage of a denarius represents being a child of God, and the householder represents Christ; etc.[11]

In critique of Jülicher's attempt at interpretation it is to be said that his fundamental error was his reliance upon Aristotle. His achievements in the investigation of the parables are uncontested. Jesus, however, is removed from Aristotle by a considerable distance. It is highly questionable that Jesus' parables are a construct of two particular statements that are similar in terms of logical correlations of judgment. The metaphor requires space.[12] Jesus does not argue against doubt, nor does he primarily intend to enrich the understanding of his hearers by means of his parables.[13] He has greater concerns.

b) Another interpretative orientation, building upon Jülicher's work and characterized by such names as J. Jeremias and E. Linnemann, endeavors to find its own access to the Jesus of the parables. The shaping of this orientation is strictly historical. The original meaning of the parable can be ascertained only if the historical situation in which the parable was originally told is reconstructed successfully. The individual parable is completely situational, arising out of the hour for the hour. Linnemann agrees with Jeremias[14] in describing the task at hand as the reclamation of the historical locus of the parable in the life of Jesus. The interpreter has to reflect the original context without detaching from it the abiding meaning of the parable as eternal truth. If one wants to know how to undertake this task, Linnemann has somewhat more to offer. This ingenious author is not only of the opinion that Jesus' parables were addressed predominantly to his opponents; she also considers them as evidence—a Jülicher legacy. She concurs with the separation between picture and issue,

---

[11] Ibid., 2.468–71.

[12] Cf. H. J. Klauck, *Allegorie und Allegorese in synoptischen Gleichnissen* (2d ed.; NTA 13, Münster: Aschendorff, 1986) 4–12.

[13] Cf. E. Jüngel, *Paulus und Jesus* (2d ed.; HUT 2; Tübingen: Mohr, 1964) 95f.

[14] Jeremias, *Parables,* 18.

though she argues against construing the picture as such as incomplete. Rather, in Jesus' situation the narration of the parable was his complete message, without needing interpretation, because it could be understood directly from the situation. The meaning of the parable, that is, the issue itself, is added as a second aspect to the narration of the parable only for the later reader and interpreter, who is no longer conversant with this situation. The reconstruction of the situation is undertaken by means of the interlinking model, according to which the hearer's (mostly conflicting) opinion is inserted into the successful narration of the parable. In this manner the hearer indirectly gets a chance to speak in the parable. Hence in the parable the narrator's verdict concerning the situation in question interlinks with that of the hearer. The narrator accomplishes this by conceding several aspects to the hearer while maintaining the upper hand by means of his verdict. Only by paying attention to the interlinking does one arrive at what Jesus had in fact said. For this reason an interpretation whose focus is on a singular point of comparison is inadequate.[15]

In their interpretation of the parable of Matt 20:1–16 Jeremias[16] and Linnemann[17] agree that it must be read against the backdrop of Jesus' table fellowship with tax collectors and sinners, against whom the scribes and Pharisees protested. While Jeremias is content to assert that in this parable Jesus wanted to justify the good news to its critics, Linnemann probes deeper. In the narration of the parable she observes Jesus' counterimage, juxtaposed against his opponents' established portrait of justice and order in God's world. They have the impression that the order they represent, determined, even in the religious realm, by effort and reward, is being attacked most severely by his behavior. The parable makes clear that the sort of conduct that to them seems like a violation of the law is in truth the emergence of goodness and love, against which there is no objection. For Linnemann the interlinking of the verdicts of the opponents and of Jesus comes to prominence especially in the scandalous statement "you have made them equal to us" and in the response, "do you begrudge my generosity?" She further recognizes the christological relevance of the story that gave impetus to the realization that God's goodness was manifested in Jesus' love of sinners, which was intended to motivate the hearers to appropriate understanding and conduct.

[15] E. Linnemann, *Jesus of the Parables* (ET; New York: Harper & Row, 1966) 27–41.
[16] Jeremias, *Parables,* 33–35.
[17] Linnemann, *Parables,* 86–88.

This interpretative orientation also doubtless furthered the understanding of parables. Nevertheless, one may want to pose the critical question whether it is appropriate to burden the historical reconstruction of the narrative situation of a parable with this significance. H. Schürmann observed that the parables of Jesus are misjudged if one inquires into their concrete situations in his life.[18] Elsewhere Linnemann also moves the significance of the parables into what she calls the language event, following M. Heidegger, whom she also cites: "Language speaks. Language? And not man? . . . Man speaks in so far as he conforms to language. The conforming is listening."[19] This provides the transition to what follows.

c) For D. O. Via the key to the parables is to view them as aesthetic objects. This is to say that the parables, like other literary works, ought to be understood as autonomous, self-existent entities. Their independence, their inward orientation can be seen in the pattern of connection between the individual narratival elements. The meaning of form and content are contained in the unity of shape. More specifically within their pattern of connection as a whole, the parable's many elements contain an existential understanding that needs to be communicated. The mythical hypostatizing of language ("language speaks") seems to be taken seriously. In its aesthetic power the parable is able to grasp the hearers' attention so as to direct it fully to the schema of the existential understanding produced in history, and it calls for a decision. The focus of the interpretation on the point of comparison is rejected, as is that of the interlinking of the verdicts of the one telling the parable and of the hearers in a reconstructed situation in the life of Jesus, which was Linnemann's concern. In fact there is the statement that the literary work, as an autonomous one, is independent of its author, that although there are links with his life, the work itself cannot be traced back to his biography or his milieu. Against Linnemann he argues that she moved the hearer's attention from the realization of a historical situation to the parable, instead of from the parable to a new understanding of the self, to a new existence to be gained.[20]

---

[18] On the pre-Easter beginnings of the logia tradition, cf. Ristow and Matthiae, *Der historische Jesus und der kerygmatische Christus,* 342–70, esp. 352.

[19] Linnemann, *Parables,* 32. Cf. M. Heidegger, *Unterwegs zur Sprache* (Pfullingen: Neske, 1959) 33.

[20] D. O. Via, *The Parables: Their Literary and Existential Dimensions* (Philadelphia: Fortress, 1967) 33f., 58f., 77–80.

There is no need to pursue further these remarkable hermeneutical explanations, whose goal is the communication of the message of the parable. From what has been said, it might appear that Via is not interested at all in the determination of the function of the parables in the ministry of the historical Jesus.

This is not the case, however. He asserts, for instance, that in the parables *Jesus* brought together the presence of God and the context of daily life.[21] Elsewhere he explains that by means of his parables Jesus focused his hearers' attention and that correlations of admonitions with aspects of his life were of less significance. More constructive for the further discussion is the observation that the parables need to be correlated with Jesus' situation as a whole.[22]

What this means is explained in a section concerning the parables and Jesus' self-understanding.[23] It means that the new existential understanding, which in his parables he offers his hearers in the crisis of their life, is the one for which he had already decided for himself. He brought to reality the existence that his tragic parabolic figures fail to attain and that the prodigal son brings about only in part through his way from death to life. He took the decisive risk of renouncing both passivity aimed at self-protection and self-authenticating action. He rejected every self-designed self-conservation and became fully dependent upon the sustaining power of the gracious, though hidden, God, etc. Thus, for Via, the parables become the key to Jesus' self-understanding, the expression of an implied Christology. The correlation of the parables with Jesus is essential, because salvation can take place and authenticity for us can be truly possible only if authentic existence happened and was fully realized, and not if it was merely described. Since the parables declare God's intervention, especially in their surprising and improbable features, Jesus claimed for himself that his conduct was the work of God. In this manner the advent of the reign of God occurs in anticipation of the possibility of the advent of faith for humans. Thus Jesus became the model of faith.

If this understanding is applied to the parable of the laborers in the vineyard, the divine dimension can be perceived especially in the master's surprising behavior at the payment of the wages. If the

---

[21] Ibid., 56.

[22] Ibid., 88 and 31. In the latter statement Via echoes one of C. H. Dodd's viewpoints.

[23] Ibid., 189–95.

divine dimension crosses our daily reality, it can conjur up a crisis of ultimate significance in the midst of the normal. Our existence depends upon our acceptance of God's gracious deeds, dashing our calculations on how the things of the world ought to be ordered. God gives gifts to people who have no place. The one who does not accept God's gracious acts as the meaning of life may lose himself or, as Via says, may suffer the tragic loss of his existence. It is to be noted that he understands v. 14, "Take what belongs to you, and go," as exclusion from God's goodness. Beyond the framework of interpreting the parable as an autonomous language event, Via establishes correlations with Jesus, though these are subordinate in the interpretative context. Perhaps Jesus addressed the parable to his opponents in order to defend his fellowship with sinners.

The parable itself contains an allegorical tendency in the person of the owner of the vineyard, who, though the main character, is not taken into the constant shift in the narratival sequence. This might point to Jesus and his work.[24]

The important issue for our concern is that this interpretation of the parable maintains the link between message and messenger, between the parable and Jesus. Critically one might ask whether the parables' significance as mediating an existential understanding and hence as identifying faith in terms of gaining this new existential understanding is at the heart of the issue. Exegetically Via's interpretation of v. 14 is questionable, but it too is associated with the reliance upon a contemporary philosophy.

d) For W. Harnisch the message of the parable is even more emphatically autonomous and further removed from the person of Jesus.[25] The parable as a poetic and imaginary form of speech is indeed considered significant for the preaching of Jesus, and if one inquires into the relationship between message and messenger, the answer provided is that the eschatological message of Jesus renders the messenger himself the unique eschatological person.[26] Nevertheless, the only interpretation appropriate for the parables is to take them seriously as autonomous entities. Jesus' parables allow God to be heard. They do this by speaking the language of love. The kingdom of God occurs if the hearer allows this love to encounter him and allows it to take shape in his life. When Harnisch calls for

---

[24] Ibid., 140–46.

[25] W. Harnisch, *Gleichniserzählungen Jesu* (UTB 1343; Göttingen: Vandenhoeck & Ruprecht, 1985) 305–12.

[26] Ibid., 309. The latter is Jüngel's formulation, cf. *Paulus und Jesus*, 190.

taking the message contained in the parables in its totality and construing it as a kind of musical harmony in which the individual narratives are mutually supported, the idea may be akin to the one already mentioned above, that the parables are to be placed in correlation with Jesus' situation as a whole.

Helpful for our concerns is the observation that in the context of the Gospels the parables undergo a shift in meaning, a considerable change in their linguistic characteristics. Previously they brought to light a new dimension of being; they spoke the language that was capable of transforming everything that is real. Embedded in the Gospels, they fulfill an argumentative purpose, they intend to communicate a certain understanding, they diminish into the level of an incident's evidential value. This change of the parable is necessary because what is at stake in the gospel is the persuasive power of the message. This observation helps us to realize that it is possible to ascertain a parabolic meaning antedating the Gospels.

What has been said here can be clarified by means of the parable of the laborers in the vineyard.[27] Against Via, Harnisch does not understand v. 14 as promoting exclusion but instead as the opening up of the possibility of a new point of view. The incredible provocation, namely, the violation of the factual norm, that is, the effort-oriented mindset, in the end is turned in a subversive direction to the extent that it directs its focus on generosity alone: "Or do you begrudge my generosity?" (v. 15). The conclusion solicits the approval of those who are playing the role of those first, angry workers. A world such as this, changed in the light of love, can be expected by the hearer as an abiding and compelling possibility.

In Matthew the parable is reshaped into an explanation of the kingdom of heaven. For the evangelist the transposition of the places of the first and the last, originally a minor feature, becomes the pivotal point and an opportunity to describe the final judgment. In addition he comes out against discriminating against the "lowly" in the community.

Harnisch, too, by no means obstructed the way to Jesus for us. Even though for him Jesus' parabolic message may be detached from the original context for the sake of contemporaneous mediation, it remains Jesus' message. There would be reason for concern if the hypostatized autonomy of the message were understood in such a way that the new existence of love that has been given birth might be

---

[27] Harnisch, *Gleichniserzählungen,* 177–200.

construed as separate and separable from the love of Jesus. In my view, however, there is no such separation to be found in Harnisch, since he emphasizes the cross as the locus of God's love. The message of the love of God that transforms existence, offered in the parables, can ultimately be understood, become effective and convincing, only in the context of Jesus' life, in which he brought this love to reality. If the kingdom of God ever occurred, it was he who made it an event.

2. The offer of salvation

a) The parable of the laborers in the vineyard addresses a fundamental concern of Jesus' proclamation, namely, mediating the incomprehensible goodness of God. Since God's goodness is not something arbitrary but the power whereby a person is capable of coping with life and death and of ordering them meaningfully, it addresses ultimate issues. Goodness has to do with the reign of God, quite independent of whether or not the parable's introductory formula, referring to the kingdom of heaven, is original. (In all likelihood it was formed by Matthew himself.) What is more important is recognizing the content-related correlation to the reign of God.

We may assume confidently that this parable had been told by Jesus. We are led to his intentions if we remove it from its Matthean framework. Yet even Matthew is still aware that it deals with God's transforming action, despite the fact that he transfers this action to the eschatological judgment and causes God's goodness to recede in comparison with his judgment, by highlighting the reversal of values taking place in the judgment. For Jesus the parable ended with the reference to goodness: "Or do you begrudge my generosity?"

It is advisable and, in the framework of the recent investigation of parables, even imperative first of all to allow the parable to speak for itself. It is a self-contained text, a world of its own, an aesthetic object. Thus we come to realize that the world of the parable derives its life from two actants in particular. One is the owner of the vineyard, who, as sovereign, sets the action as a whole in motion and determines it to its very end, beginning with the hiring of the laborers at various hours of the day, up until and including the payment of their wages. The other actant is the workers called upon in the morning, who were paid last and witnessed the pay that all the others received. In this context the juxtaposition of the first and the last is important. The payment scene intensifies the dramaturgy, culminating in this confrontation. It is to be noted further that the only important matter here is the relationship that the first are to gain with the last. The relationship of the last to the first is irrelevant.

This means that the initiatory action of the one acting sovereignly establishes a new order. There is nothing to argue, as it were, about this order. The grumbling of those who were dissatisfied is directed against the payment already made. The owner of the vineyard does not negotiate with them. He had agreed with them for a denarius. He only solicits their agreement with his action. His arguments are those of his inviolate justice—"did you not agree with me for a denarius?"—and his goodness. In this context justice is clearly subordinated to goodness, for goodness is foundational for the new order and hence also for a new mindset of justice. In plain theological terms this means that all people are dependent upon God's goodness or, more accurately—since the issue here is not only instruction but also bestowal—that all people receive God's goodness. This results in a new relationship among people. Those who are aware of being recipients of God's goodness can no longer judge others before God.

The newness of this new righteousness is still beautifully illustrated in a rabbinic parable that, though from a later period, may serve as a parallel. Here too differing lengths of time of labor are paid the same wage. Yet the one who had worked for only two hours receives the full pay because he accomplished more in two hours than the others in a whole day.[28] The mentality of those who were dissatisfied matches what happens commonly in daily life. It is precisely in his confrontation with the common mentality, described in bold relief, that the new order of goodness emerges in broad daylight in the case of Jesus.

The affirmation of the new order obtains its authenticity from the fact that it is Jesus who affirms it. If the message is separated from his person, the parable from his ministry, by rendering it autonomous as an "absolute" entity, it becomes a meaningless metaphor. The correlation with his person does not inevitably result in the individual features of the parable attaining a metaphorical meaning, whereby the first represent the Pharisees, for instance, and the last the country's indigent. Yet the narrative's overall structure agrees with an experience that reaches back into the life of Jesus. Indeed,

---

[28] In rabbinic literature the parable is found in various places: *j. Ber.* 2.3c; *Qoh. Rab.* 5.11; *Cant. Rab.* 6.2. Detailed documentation is given by Jeremias, *Parables,* 138f.

the mentality of the protagonists who oppose goodness is virtually timeless. But the generosity announced in his message could be experienced in his ministry. This does not render the message a mere illustration of his ministry, however. Yet the message would lose its abiding salvific power if it were not backed up by him. In his message and ministry salvation becomes a present event. It is the ultimate order that he wants to establish. It is the ultimate salvation that he affirms.

Time and again it is the parables in which the salvation mediated by Jesus is depicted for us. It appears from a somewhat different perspective in the parable of the unmerciful servant (Matt 18:23–35). Here too the account has first of all to be freed from its interweaving with the Matthean context. Similarly to the parable of the laborers in the vineyard, Matthew here accentuated the notion of judgment and thus of punishment. This point may be disputed, but what is broadly undisputed is that in Matthew the parable as a whole is addressed to the disciples and, through the disciples, to the post-Easter church. The evangelist achieved this reorientation by creating an appropriate framework. The parable is preceded by a dialogue between Peter and Jesus, introduced by the disciple's question: "Lord, how often shall my brother sin against me, and I forgive him?" (18:21f.).[29] In this framework the narrative is summarized at the conclusion as follows: "So also my heavenly Father will do to every one of you, if you do not forgive your brother from your heart" (18:35). This framework aside, the parable regains its original public audience. Yet even v. 34 may not be considered an original component of the narrative, for it deals with the surrender of the culprit to the torturers until he has repaid the entire debt. This verse was retained as a pointer to the tragic existence with which the narrator is concerned, along these lines: Those who forfeit forgiveness lose their existence.[30] The original conclusion is to be found in v. 33. Like many of Jesus' figures of argumentation, the conclusion is an open question: "should you not have had mercy on your fellow servant, as I had mercy on you?" We shall see that v. 34 virtually turns the argument on its head. In it the prospect of the judgment becomes the decisive motif.

Perhaps Matthew also introduced the huge sum of ten thousand talents. The parable of the entrusted talents (Matt 25:14–30; Luke

---

[29] The dialogue is based upon the dominical saying from Q: "and if he repents, forgive him; and if he sins against you seven times in the day, and turns to you seven times, and says, 'I repent,' you must forgive him."

[30] Cf. Via, *Parables*, 138–44.

19:12–27) demonstrates that he is capable of doing this. It is possible that the parable of the unmerciful servant previously did mention an enormous amount that can no longer be defined.[31] Jesus' audience was primarily the poor, whose milieu he reflected in his preaching. We surmise that the narrative had the following basic shape:

> "A king wished to settle accounts with his servants. [24]When he began the reckoning, one was brought to him who owed him (a large amount); [25]and as he could not pay, his lord ordered him to be sold with his wife and children and all that he had, and payment to be made. [26]So the servant fell on his knees, imploring him, 'Lord, have patience with me, and I will pay you everything.' [27]And out of pity for him the lord of that servant released him and forgave him the debt. [28]But that same servant, as he went out, came upon one of his fellow servants who owed him a hundred denarii; and seizing him by the throat he said, 'Pay what you owe.' [29]So his fellow servant fell down and besought him, 'Have patience with me, and I will pay you.' [30]He refused and went and put him in prison till he should pay the debt. [31]When his fellow servants saw what had taken place, they were greatly distressed, and they went and reported to their lord all that had taken place. [32]Then his lord summoned him and said to him, 'You wicked servant! I forgave you all that debt because you besought me; [33]and should not you have had mercy on your fellow servant, as I had mercy on you?' "

It is to be noted first of all that structurally the story has resemblances with the parable of the laborers in the vineyard. Here too the lord is the one acting sovereignly who has the reins in his hands from beginning to end, though it may seem that he is about to lose them in the middle part. The role of the protagonist is likewise accentuated by a reversal of the situation. If he seems to be a wretched debtor in the first part, he is allowed to appear as a power-wielding creditor in the second part. The finesse of the narrative is shown in the verbal repetition of the scene following the role reversal. Each time, the debtor falls on his knees before the creditor when called to account and implores him to postpone the repayment and the impending imprisonment until the debt is paid, with the assurance that everything is going to be repaid. On account of the minor amount, however, the promise is considerably more credible in the second instance than in the first one, in which the size of the debt seems to render any future settlement hopeless.

Hence in the two parts the story deals with a remission of debt granted and refused. Yet its strategy is secured by linking both parts

---

[31] The mention of the ten thousand talents also introduces the king into the story, which formerly probably dealt with a master (cf. 18:27, 31f.) and his slave. προσεκύνει in v. 26 is likely secondary as well and may have replaced παρεκάλει (cf. v. 29).

by means of the figure of the debtor-turned-creditor. It is advisable to approach it from both sides. Considering the second scene first, it presents a very routine process. A creditor calls his debtor to account, demands the repayment of the loan, and threatens him in case of his inability to repay. In a world shaped by money there is hardly anything more understandable than his insistence on his financial rights. The possible consequences for the debtor are not taken into consideration at all. But this scene is presented in a totally different light because it is preceded by the incredibly generous remission of debt. The creditor-debtor was granted more than he requested. He asked for the due date to be postponed and, against all expectations, received the remission of all claims. On account of this prehistory his treatment of his debtor, which would be deemed common under normal circumstances, became an outrageous brutality. The fellow slaves, who are brought into the narrative as extras and report the event to their master, articulate the general verdict.

If one undertakes the analysis of the story beginning with the second part, an incredible unscrupulousness becomes apparent. If one stays with the first part to begin with, however, and one is not irritated yet by the conclusion, the narrative deals with an incomprehensible, limitless goodness that defies all categories of normal human behavior. This goodness is giving without being ordered to give. In contrast to the parable of the laborers in the vineyard, goodness is found at the beginning. While generosity is the principle determining the action in the other parable also, it is goodness at work in secret and not revealed until the end. For this reason the parable of the unmerciful servant demonstrates even more compellingly that this goodness is meant to change people. Yet this goodness is not merely narrated, cleverly invented goodness to be taken lightly; it was an event in Jesus' ministry. In him salvation became present reality; in him the reign of God took place.

It should be noted here that the parable of the unmerciful servant is remotely related to the parable of the two debtors (Luke 7:41f.), which is inserted into the pericope of the sinful woman and presumably to be construed as an integral component.[32] Even if the latter is merely a comparison, rather than a fully developed parable, what is conspicuous here is that the money lender also, indeed twice, cancels debts in generous fashion. The role reversal from debtor to creditor, which is distinctive in the parable of the unmerciful servant, is lacking, but both agree in the subject matter of the loan.[33] Whatever might have been the case regarding a possible dependence of the brief narra-

---

[32] So Schürmann, *Lukasevangelium,* 1.434.
[33] Luke 7:41—δανιστῇ; Matt 18:27—δάνειον.

tive upon the longer one—the issue cannot be pursued further here—we are
citing the parable of the two debtors because its context provides us with an
example of where Jesus' unlimited goodness could be experienced: in the
acceptance of sinners. We shall come back to this.

But there is still a third elaborate parabolic story to be addressed
in the context of the topic of "the offer of salvation." There is no
consensus about its name. Recently it has been labeled the parable of
the gracious father or the parable of the two sons (Luke 15:11–32).
Yet it is advisable to adhere to the old designation "the prodigal son,"
for the structure of the parable is analogous to that of the two already
discussed. Just as the one acting sovereignly in the former is the
owner of the vineyard and the lord of the servants, so in the latter it
is the father. The protagonist is the younger son, introduced first. To
a certain degree the older son, introduced later, shares in his condition. Just as the other two parables are named after their protagonists
(the laborers in the vineyard, the unmerciful servants) and not after
the one acting sovereignly, the same ought to be true here.

It has occasionally been disputed that the parable of the prodigal
son came from Jesus. Its unity has also been questioned. These assumptions need to be addressed briefly. The parable has been treated
as the product of the evangelist Luke on account of its complete
agreement with his conception of salvation. It is known that the
understanding of Jesus' death as vicarious is diminished significantly
in the Lukan writings. Perhaps the most obvious example is the
omission of the ransom logion (Mark 10:45). According to Luke, Jesus
dies as the suffering righteous one who serves as the community's
example and whom God rewards by glorifying him. In the parable we
encounter the forgiving love of God as father, which is not yet over-
shadowed by Jesus' sacrificial death. Those who have not yet recognized this have not yet entered into the full meaning of the parable.[34]
Yet by picking up this parable Luke continues Jesus' understanding of
salvation. The authenticity of the tradition is reinforced by its essential
agreement with the two parables discussed earlier. More will be said
later about Jesus' understanding of salvation.

One of the common views held is that the second part, which
deals with the older son, is secondary. Accordingly, Jesus' parable
would have concluded with the return of the prodigal son at v. 24.

---

[34] Cf. J. Kögel, *Das Gleichnis vom verlorenen Sohn* (BZSF 5/9; Berlin: Edwin Runge,
1909) 4; K. Bornhäuser, *Studien zum Sondergut des Lukas* (Gütersloh: Bertelsmann,
1934) 103–37; L. Schottroff, "Das Gleichnis vom verlorenen Sohn," ZTK 68 (1971)
27–52.

This theory is based on such arguments as pointing to an alleged style difference or postulating that the second part shifts the meaning of the parable, so that allegorically the target is the Pharisee, whose features can be recognized in the portrayal of the older son.[35] This assumption, however, must be rejected as arbitrary as well. The parallels, especially in the father's encounters with his sons, link both parts. Parallel settings are typical of parables. The triangular relationship among the father and his two sons again corresponds with the two parables already discussed. Here the role of the second protagonist is played by the older son, while in the earlier parables it is those hired to work in the vineyard in the first hour and the debtor of the debtor-turned-creditor. We shall see later that the appearance of the older son does not shift the meaning of the parable at all.

In the Lukan context the parable is placed following the narratives of the lost sheep and of the lost coin, linked by means of the term "lost." In this context the return of the prodigal son is set in the context of the sinner who repents. There is repetitive mention of the sinner at the end of the two preceding parables (15:7 and 10). Luke stresses the individual's participation in the act of repentance and hence the parenetic concern. Yet the parable derives its superior strength from the father's mercy. Many interpreters would like to view the justifying statement at the conclusion of both parts, vv. 24 and 32 (introduced by ὅτι), as a Lukan redaction.[36] This is not compelling, however. The statements of justification do not detract from the father's initiative. It is also important to note the impressive relational shift: "this my son" (v. 24), "this your brother" (v. 32). For this reason we may assume that Luke left the parable essentially unchanged:

"There was a man who had two sons; [12]*and the younger of them said to his father, 'Father, give me the share of property that falls to me.' And he divided his living*

---

[35] A. Loisy, *L'évangile selon Luc* (Paris, 1924) ad loc., goes beyond this by turning the assumed addition of the second part of the parable into an allegory of the relationship between Gentiles and Jews. In addition, see J. Wellhausen, *Das Evangelium Lucae* (Berlin, 1904) ad loc.; Schweizer, "Analyse," 469–71. J. Kremer, *Lukasevangelium* (Neue Echter-Bibel 3, Würzburg, 1988) 160, is also sympathetic toward this view.

[36] Harnisch, *Gleichniserzählungen*, 200; F. Bovon, *La parabole de l'enfant prodigue: Exegesis* (ed. F. Bovon et al.; Neuchâtel-Paris, 1975) 48. H. Weder, *Die Gleichnisse Jesu als Metaphern* (FRLANT 120; Göttingen: Vandenhoeck & Ruprecht, 1978) 252, n. 22, leaves the question open. In addition to v. 32, B. Heininger, *Metaphorik, Erzählstruktur und szenisch- dramaturgische Gestaltung in den Sondergutgleichnissen bei Lukas* (NTA 24; Münster: Aschendorff, 1991) 152, also wants to attribute vv. 18f., 21, 24a, b to the Lukan redaction. The direct-address elements emphasize the notion of repentance.

between them. [13]Not many days later, the younger son gathered all he had and took his journey into a far country, and there he squandered his property in loose living. [14]And when he had spent everything, a great famine arose in that country, and he began to be in want. [15]So he went and joined himself to one of the citizens of that country, who sent him into his fields to feed swine. [16]And he would gladly have fed on the pods that the swine ate; and no one gave him anything. [17]But when he came to himself he said, 'How many of my father's hired servants have bread enough and to spare, but I perish here with hunger! [18]I will arise and go to my father, and I will say to him, "Father, I have sinned against heaven and before you; [19]I am no longer worthy to be called your son; treat me as one of your hired servants." ' [20]And he arose and came to his father. But while he was yet at a distance, his father saw him and had compassion, and ran and embraced him and kissed him. [21]And the son said to him, 'Father, I have sinned against heaven and before you; I am no longer worthy to be called your son.' [22]But the father said to his servants, 'Bring quickly the best robe, and put it on him; and put a ring on his hand, and shoes on his feet; [23]and bring the fatted calf and kill it, and let us eat and make merry; [24]for this my son was dead, and is alive again; he was lost, and is found.' And they began to make merry.

[25]"Now his elder son was in the field; and as he came and drew near to the house, he heard music and dancing. [26]And he called one of the servants and asked what this meant. [27]And he said to him, 'Your brother has come, and your father has killed the fatted calf, because he has received him safe and sound.' [28]But he was angry and refused to go in. His father came out and entreated him, [29]but he answered his father, 'Lo, these many years I have served you, and I never disobeyed your command; yet you never gave me a kid, that I might make merry with my friends. [30]But when this son of yours came, who has devoured your living with harlots, you killed for him the fatted calf!' [31]And he said to him, 'Son, you are always with me, and all that is mine is yours. [32]It was fitting to make merry and be glad, for this your brother was dead, and is alive; he was lost, and is found.' "

The triangular relationship of father–younger son–older son has its main axis in the relationship between the first two figures. The older son joins as contrasting figure.[37] He cannot be detached from the main axis because his function is to evaluate his father's relationship to his brother, to articulate the world's verdict. His verdict stands in stark contrast to the father's love. That his role becomes problematic can be seen in the apparent sensibleness of his judgment, if one considers further that the older son is the principal heir of the father's estate. But since the only thing he has to utter is the verdict—which is indeed essential for the story as a whole to make its point—that is, the verdict in keeping with the old order, the order of the world, the emphasis clearly rests on the first part. We

---

[37] Harnisch, *Gleichniserzählungen*, 216.

should not speak of a twin-peaked parable, let alone attribute greater importance to the second part.[38]

There has been substantial effort to determine the estate laws regarding the behavior of the younger son. These are certainly relevant because they show up in bold relief his involvement in debts—especially for the original audience—and because it may be assumed that what is presented is not contradicting legal convention at all. The legal realm, however, is only the framework, which should not conceal the core, which is formed through personal relationships. The most convincing solution has been suggested by W. Pöhlmann.[39] The father who, upon the younger son's request, hands him the share of the property of the inheritance to which he is entitled depicts the judicial figure of social stratification, according to Pöhlmann. The action denotes the minor becoming independent with regard to property rights when he leaves home in order to establish his own household. The important factor is that this happens during the lifetime of the testator, and the departing son thereby forfeits any further future claims.[40] When the younger son takes his share of the property, turned into cash, with him into the foreign country, his action is certainly legally proper. It may be appropriate here to point out that at that time many young people preferred emigration to staying within the country because they hoped for something better. The older son remains under the *potestas* of the father.[41]

The younger son gets into debt because he starts to lead a dissipated life and apparently in no time uses up his money, the amount of which may not be underestimated. He completely ruined the trust that others had in him. Ζῶν ἀσώτως ("in loose living,"

---

[38] Cf. Jeremias, *Parables,* 131.

[39] W. Pöhlmann, "Die Abschichtung des Verlorenen Sohnes," *ZNW* 70 (1979) 194–213, following D. Daube, "Inheritance in Two Lukan Pericopes," *ZSRG* 72 (1955) 326–34.

[40] Pöhlmann, 198–201, documents the social stratification in Judaism. Perhaps the oldest evidence is Sir 33:20–24, where the stratification is warned against. Pöhlmann's solution is more convincing than that suggested by K. H. Rengstorf, "Die Re-investitur des Verlorenen Sohnes in der Gleichniserzählung Jesu, Lk 15:11–32," *Arbeitsgemeinschaft für Forschung des Landes Nordrhein-Westfalen, Geisteswissenschaften,* 137 (1967), who appeals to the institution of the Jewish *qeshasha* for support, i.e., that the younger son had been expelled from the family.

[41] Verse 12b does not mean that the older son had been handed his share as well; it only means that his share had been determined at that point, too. Verse 29 confirms that he remained under the father's *potestas.* Otherwise the father would have been legally required to get his consent for the reinstatement of his brother.

v. 13) is an extremely sharp formulation denouncing his debauched lifestyle.[42]

The older son's judgment of his brother—here too the choice of words is not tentative—is not fabricated: He has "devoured" (v. 30) his living with prostitutes.[43] His plunge into misery is preparatory for the return and is not to be construed as punishment. In this context it is important to observe that the description of his desperate situation is perceived as thoroughly Jewish. Having to tend pigs renders him unclean and an outcast. The desire to fill his belly with pig feed on account of his hunger is a serious reversal of fortune. The precise description of the pig feed, the pods of the carob tree (v. 16: ἐκ τῶν κερατίων), has prompted a number of interpreters to cite the rabbinic proverb "If the Israelites are humiliated to the point of eating the pods of the carob tree they will repent."[44] In our case the resolve of the son, who has been driven into the worst of predicaments, to return to the father does not really arise from a repentant attitude but primarily from the quite sober realization that this is the only way for him to survive. He knows that he has nothing left to claim in his father's house. The status of a day laborer seems to him to be the only compromise possible.

The intent of this description is to direct the attention solely to the behavior of the father, who makes possible his son's return and ultimately also his repentance. The narrative lingers on his conduct: He is the first to see his son arrive, runs toward him, embraces him, orders a feast to be prepared, and reinstates the status of sonship. This is the intent of giving him the best robe, the ring, and the sandals. The father's behavior, which far exceeds all of the son's expectations, brings about something like a transformation of the son. He could only see his father as alienated. By being granted complete forgiveness and renewed acceptance, he experiences his father's presence. A new beginning is opened up for his life that had been forfeited. The solution offered by the narrative, which, in P. Ricoeur's terms, can be described as extravagant, is at the limit of what in real human life can still be viewed as possible. In order for it

---

[42] Passow, *Handwörterbuch*, 1.429, notes the following meanings for the adverb: desperate, hopelessly lost, esp. engrossed in lust, extremely dissipated, etc.

[43] Harnisch, *Gleichniserzählungen*, 207, wrongly considers this to be a misrepresentation.

[44] Via, *Parables*, 165. The carob tree pods were virtually inedible. G. Dalman, *Arbeit und Sitte in Palästina* (2d ed.; Hildesheim: G. Olms, 1987) 1.58 notes the Arabic saying "He is like a carob tree pod; he can neither be bitten nor chewed."

not to become an incredible fairy tale, the life-changing goodness that it proclaims calls for a corresponding experience. When we say that this was indeed the case in the ministry of Jesus, we do not change the parable into an allegory but attempt to describe correctly its relationship to the reign of God. The goodness that is depicted could be experienced in his ministry because the reign of God had already occurred in him. The reign of God releases the new order.

In the world, however, this new order is accepted only with difficulty and only by overcoming major obstacles. In the appearance of the older son, in the second part of the parable, the old order asks to speak. It refuses to participate in the celebration of the sinner's acceptance because its standard is that of an apparent justice and it perceives goodness as unfair. The meaning of the epilogue is to be found in the contrast between the new and the old order. To be sure, the younger son likewise gauged his situation in the foreign country by the old order. But he allowed the father's goodness to transform him. The father also attempts the transformation of the older brother by encouraging him to agree with the goodness. It is not as if he had not had any experience in life, as if he had not received any goodness from his father. He could have become aware that his former obedience to his father was based on misunderstanding; but because he ignored the goodness, he is not yet able to offer goodness.

Overview. Since it has already been delineated above, it may suffice here to reiterate the most important intentions with which the parables discussed in the Gospels are furnished. These can essentially be reduced to two. First there is the embedding in the communal, ecclesiastical situation after Easter. The message acquires a new audience, which was not present before Easter in the present arrangement. This was particularly vivid in the parable of the unforgiving servant, which Matthew develops into an urgent appeal for reconciliation in the community, for reconciliation with one's brother. Further, linked with the first, there also is the parenetic concern. Ultimately out of parenetic interest Matthew highlights the judgment motif in the parable of the laborers in the vineyard (Matt 20:1–15). Something similar can be said about Luke when he directs the attention to the individual's readiness to return in the parable of the prodigal son. The event-like aspect in the message that may be assumed in the case of Jesus' proclamation recedes when the message is textualized, thus making room for an argumentative style.

b) The parables we discussed verbalize paradigms of an incredible goodness. They derive the power of their seemingly utopian character from an experience that became evident in Jesus' ministry. We shall formulate this experience in theological language and call it forgiveness of sins. But the delineation of what Jesus understands sin to be will not be developed until later. It is appropriate to address it when we know what conception of God he communicated. To be sure, certain features of his portrait of God have already been sketched in the parables, and we sense that his God is filled with boundless goodness. Yet if we began with an abstract definition of what sin is, we would obstruct the access to his interpretation of sin in its particular nuancing and vitality.

It is informative that according to the Synoptic Gospels Jesus said little about sin. It is probably even more significant that he always speaks of forgiveness when he refers to sin: at the healing of the paralytic (Mark 2:5–10 par.), at the appearance of the sinful woman in the house of Simon the Pharisee (Luke 7:47–49), in the Lord's Prayer and its postscript (Matt 6:12, 14f.; Luke 11:4; Mark 11:25).[45] Yet precisely in conjunction with the concrete granting of forgiveness in these pericopes, one is to reckon with the influence of the community's theology.[46] In keeping with their experience with Jesus, the community practiced the granting of forgiveness. The term "sinner" occurs more frequently in the Gospels than elsewhere in the NT, especially in Luke.[47]

In the ministry of Jesus, this boundless goodness could be experienced in his dealings with people, in his relationship with sinners. In a religiously shaped society, characteristic of Judaism of that time, the sinner's role as an outsider is a given. It has to be regarded as a significant characteristic of Jesus' activity that he was concerned particularly with those people who were considered notorious sinners by their society and neighborhood. This can be shown by way of his relationship with the tax collectors.

In antiquity the tax collector was generally rated very low. To begin with, there were some very human reasons. Who likes to pay taxes and financial levies, collected by the tax collectors on behalf of the government? The tax lease system further gave them—often not without reason, to be sure—a reputation as cheaters. Aristophanes, the writer of comedy, calls the tax collector a maw, a Charybdis that swallows everything yet never has enough (*Equities* 248). Plutarch calls

---

[45] In Luke 24:47 the risen Christ proclaims the forgiveness of sins. Various terms are used in the Greek text: ἁμαρτία, παράπτωμα, ὀφείλημα.

[46] On this, see pp. 109–11 below.

[47] In Luke eighteen times; Mark six times; Matt five times.

him a sleep, robbing half of life.[48] Dio Chrysostom places the tax collector on the same level as the keeper of a brothel (*Orationes* 14.14). In Judaism labels to the same effect are associated with a religious judgment, which penetrates deeper. The tax collectors are considered unclean. They are regarded on the same level as pagans. Associating with them renders one unclean. It is noteworthy that in Matthew's Gospel the Jewish view of the tax collectors continues: "let him be to you as a Gentile and a tax collector" (18:17); "Do not even the tax collectors do the same? . . . Do not even the Gentiles do the same?" (5:46, 47).[49] In the parable, the tax collector's consciousness of being an outsider is sketched with psychological sensitivity. Standing before God, he does not dare to lift up his eyes and beats his breast (Luke 18:13). Here we are shown a person despairing of himself.

Jesus' conduct in relation to the tax collectors, which is in complete contrast to the general sentiment and which must even have been deemed scandalous, is conspicuous. He goes to tax collectors and he talks about them. Both aspects converge. The parable of the Pharisee and the tax collector (Luke 18:9–14) has just been mentioned, in which the tax collector as the one justified is juxtaposed with the Pharisee as the one not justified. In Jericho, according to Luke 19:1–10, Jesus enters the house of Zacchaeus, the chief tax collector. Of particular interest to us, however, is the table fellowship he practiced with the tax collectors.

This table fellowship is documented in two passages, the pericope of the meal with the tax collectors (Mark 2:13–17 par.) and a Son of man logion (Matt 11:19 par.). Both texts pose exegetical problems that need to be addressed. We turn to the meal with the tax collectors, which is available to us in its earliest form in Mark. Yet it too is already edited. The meal with the tax collectors is preceded by the call of Levi, the tax collector, the son of Alphaeus, who sits at his tax office, giving the impression that Levi is the host. Jesus is accompanied by his disciples. The "scribes of the Pharisees" are offended. Jesus defends his fellowship with two sayings: "Those who are well have no need of a physician, but those who are sick," and "I came not to call the righteous, but sinners." In order to determine the correlations between Levi's call and the meal in the history of traditions, the starting point may be that the two traditions were

---

[48] Plutarch, *Aquane an ignis utilior* 12. Documentation in O. Michel, "τελώνης," *TDNT* 8.100–101.

[49] These seemingly Jewish sentences are reshaped in Luke 6:32–34.

independent initially and were joined together by Mark.[50] Hence we cannot state with certainty whether or not the meal took place in Levi's house. While the scene of the call focuses upon a concrete individual event, the account of the meal is to be ranked as typical. This impression is underscored further because the discussion is about tax collectors *and sinners* with whom Jesus and the disciples are reclining at table (2:15). Therefore it is intended to describe something characteristic of Jesus' ministry rather than a specific meal. The justification of his conduct is of fundamental importance as well. This is even truer of the second justifying saying. Exegetically formulated, this is an "I-have-come saying," of which there are several in the Synoptics and whose consistent intent is to summarize Jesus' overall activity in terms of a particular aspect. The older of the sayings is that of the physician.[51] It expresses his total attention to the needy and despised. Here it is important to observe that those who are sick are the subject of the sentence (not Jesus); the emphasis is upon them. In this case the sick are the sinners who receive help and salvation from Jesus as the physician of their souls.

Jesus' acceptance of a despised tax collector into the ranks of his disciples expresses his mercy, which is not closed to anyone.[52] In Matt 11:19 par. his table fellowship with tax collectors is expressed once again in general terms: "the Son of man came eating and drinking, and they say, 'Behold, a glutton and a drunkard.' " The saying is found after the brief parable of the squabbling children who at play are willing neither to dance nor to mourn. The parable is applied to John the Baptist as the one who mourned and to Jesus as the merry one, the one who dances. They can be placed in parallel in the sense that both were rejected by "this generation." Even in its opacity this saying has preserved an insult of Jesus by his opponents, who were provoked by his table fellowship with the common, despised people, the Am-ha-arez, as they called them.

---

[50] This is argued against two interpretative directions. The one is represented by M. Dibelius, *From Tradition to Gospel* (ET; New York: Scribners, 1934) 64, n. 1, for whom the meal with the tax collectors arises from the call of Levi, the other by R. Pesch, "Das Zöllnergastmahl," in *Mélanges bibliques* (FS B. Rigaux; Gembloux: Duculot, 1970) 63–87, esp. 71, who construes Levi's call to have arisen from the meal with the tax collectors.

[51] On this cf. Gnilka, *Markus,* 1.104f.

[52] The parallel of Matt 9:9 exchanges the name Levi with that of Matthew, whom he knew to be a tax collector (10:3). It may not be appropriate to identify Levi with Matthew. There are intra-Matthean reasons for the name change. Cf. Gnilka, *Matthäusevangelium,* 1.330f.

The historical reliability of the tradition that Jesus sat at table and ate with tax collectors and sinners can be assured. This conduct tears down the order that has been the norm thus far and that makes value judgments in distinguishing between strata of society. Even the Jewish-Christian community of a later period finds it difficult to have a common table, as the so-called Antiochian incident illustrates (cf. Gal 2:11–14). Likewise in the Corinthian community there were inconsiderateness and difficulties with the common meal (cf. 1 Cor 11:17–22). The common table also fits well into Jesus' lifestyle. During his ministry he was an unsettled itinerant—perhaps in the home of Simon Peter's family in Capernaum he may have had a temporary abode—and stopped over in people's homes.

If one inquires into the meaning that Jesus attributed to the table fellowship he granted, surely it transcends the societal recognition of a despised group. The saying about the physician is instructive. It signals salvation. But since those whom Jesus accepted were flagrant sinners, or were viewed as such, the table fellowship may, in the framework of his total ministry, only be understood as a symbolic expression, as a prophetic sign, as it were, of the forgiveness of sins granted by him. The forgiveness takes place less by means of the message than by the manifest personal acceptance, the effective restitution and granting of a new beginning in the context of fellowship. In this connection it is true of Jesus' conduct as well as of the parables that forgiveness releases the new beginning, that is to say, repentance, because it makes these possible. It is forgiveness, the offer of salvation, that is prominent, not the demand for changing one's ways. Only in this sense does repentance become feasible for Jesus. It has frequently been pointed out that on this issue Jesus differs widely from John the Baptist. For John the call for repentance is the beginning point.[53] According to him repentance saves from the judgment. Jesus also called for repentance, of course, but it is ordered differently and for intrinsic and positive reasons.

Furthermore, the significance of table fellowship in ancient Judaism was different from that of our fast-paced world. The common table did indeed offer fellowship, truly uniting those who gathered to share a meal together. Beyond that we may expect an eschatological dimension of understanding as well. In Judaism, as well as in Jesus' parables (cf. Luke 14:16–24), eschatological salvation

---

[53] Cf. G. Bornkamm, *Jesus of Nazareth* (ET; 3d ed.; London: Hodder & Stoughton, 1969) 82–84.

could be compared with a festive meal. In this case Jesus' table fellowship would become an anticipatory reflection of the eschatological table in the kingdom of God.

One of the concrete examples of forgiveness of sins in Jesus' ministry is linked with a pericope that has its own story. Originally it was passed on separately. At the time of its incorporation into the Gospel it was placed at different points of the text. Today we customarily find it in the Gospel of John, as 7:53–8:11, though it clearly does not represent a Johannine but, rather, a synoptic text, mostly akin to the Lukan tradition. The pericope narrates Jesus' encounter with an adulteress who was caught in the act and led to Jesus by "the scribes and Pharisees" in order for him to pass judgment on her. More specifically, he is questioned about his opinion on the penal code of the law, which orders the punishment of stoning for an adulteress. While at first he creates the impression of not wanting to be entangled in this case—"he wrote with his finger on the ground"—he finally changes the scene with a sovereign response whereby the accusers become the accused. They are unable to meet the challenge of the one without sin casting the first stone. When everyone has walked away, the woman, who alone has remained, is not condemned by Jesus either but is released with the command not to sin again.

Is it possible to use this story in support of the historical portrait of Jesus? Its text has been transmitted quite freely. It was embellished with secondary paraphrases, though at the core the same essential structure can generally be recognized.[54] The narrative reflecting a locus in the temple district proves to be a Jewish-Christian tradition.[55] Text critics tend to argue that it had already found its way into the Gospel in the second century, although its reception was linked with substantial difficulties.[56] Those who oppose its authen-

---

[54] The following paraphrastic embellishments are worth noting: Mention is made that with his finger Jesus wrote "the sins of everyone of them" in the sand (vv. 6, 8). Verse 9 contains the addition that they went away, one after the other, *convicted by their conscience*. According to some text witnesses Jesus, in v. 10, asks the woman: "Where are your accusers?" On the text transmission, cf. K. Aland, "Glosse, Interpolation, Redaktion und Komposition in der Sicht der neutestamentlichen Textkritik," in *Studien zur Überlieferung des Neuen Testament und seines Textes* (ANTT 2; Berlin: de Gruyter, 1967) 35–57, esp. 39–46; U. Becker, *Jesus und die Ehebrecherin* (BZNW 28; Berlin: Töpelmann 1963) 8–43.

[55] Cf. Schnackenburg, *John,* 2.170.

[56] Cf. Aland, "Glosse," 40. Becker, *Ehebrecherin,* 38f., dates the adoption of the pericope into the Greek text a century later. He also demonstrates that the Syrian *Didaskalia* is familiar with it (124–45), and entertains the possibility that it was known by the *Protevangelium of James* and Origen (117–24).

ticity locate its origin in the community debates concerning the forgivability of heinous sins, such as adultery here.[57] This is unconvincing, however. The pericope is not characterized by a fundamental decision. The condemnation of the accusers further militates against a construal such as this. In terms of genre it is not to be categorized as a controversy dialogue but rather as a biographical apophthegm.[58] Positively, its content supports the observation that the pericope preserves a reminiscence of Jesus' ministry. The conduct of Jesus reflected in it agrees with the insights gained thus far. In a concrete incident Jesus stands up for a rejected sinner with boundless mercy and thereby snubs the guardians of the old order. His position is not primarily directed against the law, and even less is it his intention to cancel the law; rather, it is entirely motivated by feeling for the person who is to receive salvation. The disregard for a particular regulation in this context is one of the consequences arising from the incident. Ultimately the fate of the pericope must also be determined from its quality as a historical reminiscence. Indeed it never was an original component of a Gospel and was never removed from it, yet it is to be regarded as a noncanonical Jesus tradition. The resistance against it, which can be observed and which rendered its acceptance problematic, has to do with its goal. For many it appeared to be offensive. Jesus' goodness toward a sinful woman was perceived to be scandalous. It is difficult to come up with a different explanation of the data. For critical studies, resistance against a tradition is also relevant as a criterion of historical reliability.

Several things may now be said about the relevant specifics of the tradition. Since from the Jewish legal perspective the woman pledged to be married was already considered the wife of her betrothed, except that she had not yet been taken home (cf. Deut 22:23f.), the question arose whether or not the woman confronted with Jesus is to be regarded as an unfaithful fiancée or as a wife. J. Blinzler[59] has demonstrated convincingly that only the latter can be assumed. According to Lev 20:10 and Deut 22:22 adultery incurred the death penalty. When the story of the adulteress presupposes stoning as the specific type of

---

[57] So for instance H. Köster, "Die ausserkanonischen Herrenworte," *ZNW* 48 (1957) 220–37, esp. 233.

[58] In agreement with Schnackenburg, *John,* 2.169.

[59] J. Blinzler, "Die Strafe für Ehebruch in Bibel und Halacha: Zur Auslegung von Joh. 8:5," *NTS* 4 (1957/58) 32–47, esp. 34–38, e.g., by referring to the terms γυνή and μοιχευομένη in the pericope. The alternate view was argued by Str-B, *Kommentar,* 2.520; J. Jeremias, "Zur Geschichtlichkeit des Verhörs Jesu vor dem Höhen Rat," *ZNW* 43 (1950/51) 145–50, esp. 148f.

execution—"in the law Moses commanded us to stone such" (v. 5)—
we may surmise that the form of execution prescribed by the law was
generally interpreted to mean stoning.[60] The question whether the
woman was in the process of being taken to court or was on the way to
be stoned as one who was already convicted can no longer be answered
adequately. The uncertainty is there because the tradition does not
consider it important to relate this detail, which is of interest to us. In
favor of the viewpoint that the woman was already convicted by the
Jewish court and was being led to her execution, it has been pointed
out especially that only in this way would Jesus really have been
embarrassed and tested. If he affirmed the verdict, he would be
recognized as a revolutionary, because capital punishment was a Roman prerogative at that time. If he negated it, he would become
unpopular.[61] Yet the woman's observation, in response to Jesus' question, that no one had condemned her may be taken as evidence that
the condemnation had not yet been handed down. Even so, the
predicament is there for Jesus. Executions carried out by Jews did
occur at that time, despite the fact that the right to execute was the
prerogative of the occupying power.[62]

Attention is probably also to be given to the circumstance that
only the woman appears in the story, not the man who committed
adultery with her. This may be seen as an indication that in that rigidly
patriarchally structured society, even in this respect the woman was at a
disadvantage, and one was inclined to apprehend her first. The formulations in Ezek 16:38–41; 23:45–48 and Jub. 30.8f. indicate something
similar. This background would become particularly ominous if the
sin recalled by the accusers, beginning with the eldest, is of the same
level as the woman's sin. This is not certain, however.[63] In any case, by
his reaction Jesus turns the situation inside out. The verdict solicited
from him, which turns out altogether different from what was expected, affects both the accusers and the woman. The accusers have
their conscience pricked. The verdict on the woman, the weakest part
in the play, is tantamount to an acquittal, not in the sense that it put

---

[60] Cf. Ezek 16:38–41; 23:45–48; Jub. 30.8f. Blinzler, "Strafe," 42, correctly considers Lev 20:27, which speaks explicitly of stoning, as a more detailed reference to the
type of execution, thus explaining the general "he/she is to be put to death."
[61] So Jeremias, "Geschichtlichkeit."
[62] Cf. the stoning of Stephen. Among the Romans, Augustus's lex Julia de adulteriis
rescinded the old right of the offended husband to kill the adulterer and replaced it
with banishment and collecting a share of his estate. Later, however, they reverted to
the death penalty.
[63] Schnackenburg, John 2.166, has in mind sin in general and cites Matt 7:1.

her guilt in question but that she is granted a new beginning. Here as well the factually granted forgiveness is linked with making repentance and turning away from sin possible. The concrete person is encountered in the situation of failure, and in the enormous humiliation caused by the failure, and is placed on a new path. Here Jesus seems unconcerned about the risk of whether or not this path was indeed going to be taken, but rather is confident that the forgiveness granted so effectively will open up the freedom of renewed behavior.

An analogous story, comparable to Jesus' confrontation with the adulteress, is concealed behind Luke 7:36–50. At a meal in the home of a Pharisee called Simon, a woman appears unexpectedly. In town she is known as a sinner and hence is to be regarded as a prostitute, rather than as the wife of a man involved in a dishonorable occupation. She voices her gratitude with expressions of deep embarrassment, with the genuineness of an oriental temperament, by standing behind him and wetting his feet with her tears, then drying them with her hair and kissing his feet.

The reconstruction of this event has its difficulties because in its transmission the pericope was embellished, particularly with narrative features. Especially the anointing is an irritating feature here, for in the parallel references the story of an anointing of Jesus is firmly anchored in the passion account (Mark 14:3–9 par.). In John 12:3–8 the woman who anoints is identified as Mary, the sister of Lazarus. It is viable to assume that originally independent traditions that appear to be related could become more alike through narration. Thus the anointing motif in Luke 7:36–50 may well be secondary.[64] It may be assumed that the appearance of the woman was originally reported as described above. The story does not directly indicate a motive for the woman hurrying to Jesus, who was reclining at table in the house of the Pharisee. Yet the inserted parable of the two debtors, dealing with profound forgiveness, may point to the motive (7:41f.). As far as the logic of the story is concerned, the forgiveness of sins that Jesus pronounces at the end (v. 48) comes too late. At this particular locus it fulfils another function. It is directed to the community, which, by means of this (later) explicit pronouncement

---

[64] This is the assumption of Schürmann, *Lukasevangelium,* 1.441. The host's name, Simon, might have been added secondarily as well. According to Mark 14:3–9 the meal is held in the house of Simon the leper, in Bethany near Jerusalem. In the post-NT traditions the paralleling is carried further. The woman who anoints is equated with Mary of Magdala, and hence the latter with the sinful woman. This error has been particularly persistent.

of forgiveness, wants it understood that by appealing to Jesus' authority it practiced forgiving sins—most likely in the gathered community. The plausible motive for the woman is the forgiveness and acceptance experienced through Jesus, which presumably were expressed once again by means of his personal conduct, by being accepted into his fellowship or something similar.

Can it be demonstrated or is it to be assumed that Jesus himself explicitly forgave sinners as well? Since Luke 7:48 has been identified as a postscript, the pericope remaining to show this possibility is that of the healing of a paralytic (Mark 2:1–12 par.). This passage too has been used by the community for its practice of forgiving sins in the manner indicated above. The story has taken on the form of an apophthegm, that is to say, it climaxed in a saying of Jesus (= apophthegm) that was stamped upon it, in order to make it applicable to the community. This apophthegm says, "But that you may know that the Son of man has authority on earth to forgive sins . . . " (v. 10). The miracle of healing turns into the argument for the authority to forgive sins that continues to be effective in the community. It is to be noted, however, that Jesus forgave the paralytic his sins beforehand, in a manner quite distinct from the apophthegmatic statement. The paralytic, lying on a pallet in front of Jesus, is given this declaration: "My son, your sins are forgiven" (v. 5). The passive formulation is a circumlocution for the work of God. The forgiveness that God grants is mediated by Jesus. It is very plausible that Jesus said these words. The historical credibility of this tradition commends itself further through a circumstance that deserves attention because in its incomprehensibility it has preserved something of the vividness of the incident. The invalid is brought to Jesus by four men. But Jesus is in the house—in Simon Peter's in Capernaum?—and the house is besieged by many people. They climb up on the roof, dig through it, and let the invalid, including the pallet, down (v. 4). The digging through the roof is a rudimentary feature, pointing to the Palestinian house, which was covered with reeds, hay, and twigs, woven between the beams and then coated with a layer of clay. Luke 5:19 did not adopt this feature and instead adapted it to reflect the Greek house with which his readers were more familiar. These houses were covered with roof tiles: "[They] let him [the paralytic] down with his bed through the tiles."[65]

---

[65] The opening up of the roof presumably served an apotropaic purpose originally. The demon of sickness was to be deceived. If the ordinary entrance to the house was hidden from the demon, its return was made more difficult.

Jesus made salvation something to be experienced by devoting himself to people, accepting them, receiving them into fellowship with him, and granting them forgiveness of sins. The power of his affirmation is to be found in his attention to the concrete individual, in particular to the despised, the abused, the sinner, but also in involving himself with people in a very personal way, in a manner that can hardly be imitated, in giving himself away to them.

Overview

Involvement with sinners was continued by appealing to the authority and example of Jesus. In the organized community, however, this pronouncement and remission of sins (necessarily) assumed different forms and was firmly anchored, institutionalized, and ritualized in the fellowship of the community. More specific knowledge eludes us, even though the necessity of revitalizing Jesus' actions becomes particularly intense at this point.

Select bibliography: U. Becker, *Jesus und die Ehebrecherin* (BZNW 28; Berlin: Töpelmann, 1963); F. Bovon, *La parabole de l'enfant prodigue: Exegesis* (ed. F. Bovon et al.; Neuchâtel-Paris, 1975) 36–51, 291–306; I. Broer, "Die Parabel vom Verzicht auf das Prinzip von Leistung und Gegenleistung," 145–64 in *A cause de l'évangile* (FS J. Dupont; Paris: Cerf, 1985); H. von Campenhausen, "Zur Perikope von der Ehebrecherin," *ZNW* 68 (1977) 164–75; T. Deidun, "The Parable of the Unmerciful Servant," *BTB* 6 (1976) 203–24; C. Dietzfelbinger, "Das Gleichnis von den Arbeitern im Weinberg als Jesuswort," *EvT* 43 (1983) 126–37; idem, "Das Gleichnis von der erlassenen Schuld," *EvT* 32 (1972) 437–51; J. Dupont, "La parabole des ouvriers de la vigne," *NRT* 89 (1957) 785–97; A. Feuillet, "Les ouvriers envoyés à la vigne," *RevThom* 79 (1979) 5–24; P. Grelog, "Le père et ses deux fils," *RB* 84 (1977) 321–48, 538–65; B. M. F. van Iersel, *La vocation de Lévi: De Jésus aux Evangiles: Tradition dans les évangiles synoptique* (BETL 25; Gembloux: J. Duculot, 1967); 212–32; J. Kögel, *Das Gleichnis vom verlorenen Sohn* (BZSF 5/9; Berlin: Edwin Runge, 1909); P. Lamarche, "L'appel de Lévi," *Christus* 23 (1976) 106–18; D. Patte, "Structural Analysis of the Parable of the Prodigal Son," *Semiology and Parables* (ed. D. Patte; Pittsburgh: Pickwick, 1976) 71–149; R. Pesch, "Das Zöllnergastmahl," *Mélanges bibliques* (FS B. Rigaux; Gembloux: Duculot, 1970) 63–87; idem, "Zur Exegese Gottes durch Jesus von Nazaret," *Jesus. Ort der Erfahrung Gottes* (FS B. Welte; 2d ed.; Freiburg: Herder, 1977) 140–89; W. Pöhlmann, "Die Abschichtung des Verlorenen Sohnes," *ZNW* 70 (1979) 194–213; F. Rousseau, "La femme adultère," *Bib* 59 (1978) 463–80; F. Schnider, *Die verlorenen Söhne* (OBO 17; Freiburg/Schweiz: Universitätsverlag; Göttingen: Vandenhoeck & Ruprecht, 1977); idem, "Von der Gerechtigkeit Gottes," *Kairos* 23 (1981) 88–95; L. Schottroff, "Das Gleichnis vom verlorenen Sohn," *ZTK* 68 (1971) 27–52; E. Schweizer, "Zur Frage der Lukasquellen. Analyse von Lk 15,11–32," *TZ* 4 (1948) 469–71; H. Thyen, *Studien zur Sündenvergebung* (FRLANT 96; Göttingen: Vandenhoeck & Ruprecht, 1970).

3. Healings and miracles

Jesus did not limit himself to the proclamation of the message alone. His help and healing are placed alongside his preaching, his offer of forgiveness, his liberating fellowship with humans. We are talking about miracles. This element of his public ministry cannot be left aside, but much depends on correctly evaluating and classifying his help and healing. This is not an easy task. In numerous books on Jesus this element is omitted.[66]

The omission of Jesus' healing ministry has to be ruled out simply because of the extent of the relevant material. In the Gospel of Mark miracles represent a relatively large amount. As far as John's Gospel is concerned, it is frequently assumed that the evangelist had available a written source that contained predominantly miracles, known as the "semeia source." It is much more feasible to work out the interpretation of miracles in the individual Gospels than it is to penetrate to the understanding that Jesus himself was said to have attributed to his activity. In Mark's Gospel the miracles are set in the context of a battle that Jesus, the Messiah and Son of God, initiates and fights against Satan and the powers of evil. Within this my-thologically shaped historical portrait it is no surprise if Jesus' exor-cistic ministry becomes very prominent. In Matthew's Gospel the message of Jesus is dominant, as are the composed discourses, begin-ning with the Sermon on the Mount. The miracles are placed alongside and subordinated, in keeping with the summarizing observation "And he went about all Galilee, teaching in their synagogues and preaching the gospel of the kingdom and healing every disease and every infirmity among the people" (4:23; cf. 9:35). In the Gospel of Luke, by his helping and healing Jesus reveals himself as the great benefactor and eschatologi-cal prophet of his people, as Acts 10:38 states in summary: "he went about doing good [εὐεργετῶν] and healing all that were oppressed by the devil." For the Gospel of John it is important to understand Jesus' miracles as signs and by faith to receive them as signposts pointing to Christ as God's revelation. Hence the decisive reproach that says: "you seek me, not because you saw signs, but because you ate your fill of the loaves" (6:26). This also brings into play the criticism regarding the miraculous: "Unless you see signs and wonders you will not believe" (4:48). It is further noteworthy that the stories of exorcism are completely missing from the Fourth Gospel. Con-

---

[66] This applies to books on Jesus by Braun and Bultmann, though not to Dibelius; see "The Signs of the Kingdom," in Dibelius, *Jesus,* 70–81.

versely, however, it is precisely here that we learn of miracles of astounding power.

In order to get to the historical Jesus on this issue, it may be advisable to distinguish between miracle accounts and interpretative logia. The former represent accounts by third parties, telling about Jesus' healing ministry. The logia make it possible to know about his intentions. The logia—many of them—are without a doubt older. This insight is strengthened by the fact that the sayings source, as far as it can be reconstructed, contains only one detailed account of a healing, the story of the healing of the servant of the centurion from Capernaum (Matt 8:5–13 par.). Add to this the terse account of a miracle granted to a deaf-mute (Luke 11:14 par.).[67] We shall nevertheless leave the discussion of the interpretative sayings for section b and begin with the discussion of the miracle stories. In doing so we intend to discover specific traces of Jesus.

a) Since this kind of subject matter does not easily provide us with access to understanding it, it is necessary to delve further. To begin with, it may be advisable to become aware of the altogether different disposition of Jesus' Galilean audience regarding miracles. M. Dibelius aptly described the difference from the people of today in this regard:

> But Jesus' hearers, none of whom had been seriously influenced by the critical philosophy of the Greeks, supposed that God's working was to be seen precisely in the inexplicable. If something inexplicable should happen in our world and before our eyes, if someone should cause a person who was lying dead suddenly to get up perfectly well . . . , the stouthearted would regard the event as a subject for investigation, the timorous would draw away from it, those who disapproved would call in the police, while the enthusiastic would give the news to the press—but nobody, we can be sure, would fall on his knees in prayer! But this is just what seemed to Jesus' hearers the most natural thing to do when confronted by the marvellous. To them, anything that was not instantly explicable was miraculous. They did not reckon with laws of nature or trouble themselves with attempts at explanation, for it was the supernatural that they sensed at once in the unexplained. It was a case for either adoration or condemnation, for seeing either God's hand at work or the devil's—there was no other alternative, for them. We, however, insist on first having the unusual explained before we pass judgment.[68]

Furthermore it is to be remembered that the synoptic miracle stories fit in with their time. Those who at that time heard of Jesus'

---

[67] According to the parallel of Matt 12:22 the sufferer is dumb and blind. Matthew favors healings of the blind. Cf. Gnilka, *Matthäusevangelium,* 1.457.

[68] Dibelius, *Jesus,* 74.

miracles also knew of thaumaturges elsewhere to whom healings and sensational deeds were attributed. The first Christian century was an epoch in which the activities of charismatic miracle workers and healers increased. This meant a revitalization of experiences and abilities that had been forgotten or were pushed into the background for about three hundred years. G. Theissen speaks frankly of a "renaissance of belief in the miraculous."[69] In Hellenism it was associated with Pythagoras, who was credited with miracles. This is especially true of Apollonius of Tyana (ca. 3–97 CE), who traveled through the country as a charismatic miracle worker. In Judaism it was the prophets Elijah and Elisha whom the people remembered as powerful thaumaturges. We also know of Iarchas, an Indian sage whom Apollonius met on his travels,[70] and Simon Magus of Samaria. In Israel Hanina ben Dosa (ca. 70–100 CE) and Eliezer ben Hyrcanus (ca. 90–130 CE), two respected rabbis, were credited with miracles. Epidaurus represents a healing cult that lasted for centuries; here an institutionalized priesthood was charged with making experiences of healing possible in the temple of the god Asclepius. Though charismatically produced healings may have to be distinguished from those carried out in a temple cult, we are here interested in the accounts about them that are available to us. There are scarcely reasons for the reawakening of a heightened interest in miraculous healing. Perhaps an escalating destitution in general may have contributed to it. At the time of Jesus, Israel was politically subjugated.[71] It also needs to be remembered that the Essenes practiced a kind of "book medicine." Josephus reports that the Essenes examined ancient writings to inquire after medicinal roots and the characteristics of stones to cure diseases.[72] Similar features may apply to apocalyptic communities (cf. *1 Enoch* 7.1; 8.3; *Jub.* 10.12f.).

In the Gospels themselves we encounter roughly twenty stories of healing and exorcism.[73] In the case of healings of the blind it may

---

[69] G. Theissen, *Miracle Stories in the Early Christian Tradition* (ET; Edinburgh: T. & T. Clark, 1983) 265–76, esp. 274.

[70] Cf. Philostratus, *Vita Apollonii* 3.40 and elsewhere.

[71] On these contexts, cf. Theissen, *Miracle Stories,* 274.

[72] Josephus, *War* 2.136. O. Michel and O. Bauernfeind, eds., *Flavius Josephus: De bello Judaico* (2d ed.; Munich: Kösel, 1959) 1.434, n. 57, point out the attempt to derive the name "Essene" from the Aramaic *ʾasiāʾ*, "physician."

[73] Cf. Mark 1:23–28 par.; 1:29–31 par.; 1:40–45 par.; 2:1–12 par.; 3:1–6 par.; Matt 8:5–13 par.; Mark 5:1–20 par.; 5:25–34 par.; John 5:1–9; Matt 9:27–31; 9:32–34 par.; Mark 7:24–30 par.; 7:31–37 par.; 8:22–26; 9:14–29 par.; Luke 13:10–17; 14:1–6; 17:11–19; John 9:1–12; 11:38–44; Mark 10:46–52 par.; Luke 22:51.

be necessary to reckon on duplications (cf. especially Matt 9:27–32 and 20:29–34), but even apart from these there may have been occasional instances of varying and embellished repetitions.[74] This number does not include the "summary accounts," in which Jesus' healing ministry is summarized so as to create the impression of mass healings (e.g., Mark 1:32–34 par.; 3:7–12 par.; 6:53–56 par.). Again, likewise the tendency to expand is confirmed in the observation itself that Jesus did many (miraculous) signs in the presence of his disciples which had not been recorded (John 20:30; cf. 21:25). On account of this it is not possible to gain a precise picture of the scope of his miraculous healings. There are also observations indicating his fame as a miracle worker among the people (e.g., Mark 6:2; Luke 4:23). With regard to what really happened, it may nevertheless be necessary to take into account an apparent redundancy. In any case, for Jesus charismatic healing in no wise became an institutionalized matter, as it were, in which one could count on a miraculous healing at any time. The charismatic orientation and thus the element of surprise were always maintained.

The evaluation of Jesus' miracles is made particularly difficult because they were passed on in keeping with popular rules of the art of narration. The narrative had to adhere to certain rules, including the narration of miracle stories. In keeping with these rules the stories were set in a given schematic and filled in with recurring motifs, which could vary. G. Theissen has pinpointed thirty-three different motifs in the miracle stories of the Gospels. These range from the appearance of the distressed person, a representative, or an embassy, through description of a miracle by means of a command, a touch, or therapeutic treatment, to the demonstration of the accomplished healing.[75] These narratives, often appearing pale and stylized in terms of details, occasionally receive their color from the characterization of the crisis (the woman with the issue of blood had already consulted many physicians and spent all of her means [Mark 5:26]) or the motif of the obstacle impeding the one seeking help (the blind man crying out for mercy and thereby evoking the indignation of the masses [Mark 10:48]). The schematic and stereotypical miracle stories provide us with less insight into concretely described, individual events than into the general knowledge of

---

[74] What is the relationship of John 5:1–9 to Mark 2:1–12, for instance, in terms of the history of tradition? This question can only be posed here.

[75] Theissen, *Miracle Stories,* 47–80. Cf. R. Bultmann, *History of the Synoptic Tradition* (ET; 1963; reprint, Peabody, Mass.: Hendrickson, 1992) 221–28.

Jesus the miracle worker. It is not correct to say that these stories about his ministry were added subsequently. In general they maintain an important feature of his work, which, in order to describe it concretely, required examination of individual miracle stories, especially of those promising success.

As far as our modern conceptions are concerned, the references to the various diseases being healed are imprecise and vague. We shall briefly examine a few examples. According to Luke 14:2–4 Jesus heals one who suffered from dropsy (ὑδρωπικός). Since this "medical" term occurs only in the Third Gospel in the NT, it was at times viewed as proof that Luke was a physician. The fact that Pliny (*Nat. hist.* 28.232) also uses this designation *(hydropicus)* indicates that it was taken seriously in antiquity. Luke does indeed not suggest a symptom or a specific condition. If we consider the occurrence of this designation of sickness in ancient literature, what emerges is a uniform picture. Symptoms of dropsy seem to include an excessive need for drink (Polybius 13.2)[76] and physical trembling (Aristotle, *Problemata* 3.5); H. Pinkhof[77] has in mind a blood disease, and F. Fenner[78] a trophic neurosis that would cause contusions in the blood membranes of the joints. It is no longer possible to provide a precise diagnostic description of dropsy; it is a summary term encompassing numerous diseases.[79]

The term "paralytic" (παραλυτικός) has to be understood similarly. In the description of the healing of a paralytic in Mark 2:1–12 par. (Luke 5:18 describes him as παραλελυμένος)[80] it is evident that he is not able to walk at all. He is carried on a mat by four men. According to Matt 8:6 the centurion's servant is a paralytic, too.[81]

---

[76] According to Philostratus, *Vita Apollonii* 1.9, Apollonius heals one who has dropsy by drying him out. In rabbinic conceptions the disease is caused by a disorder in the distribution of fluid. Cf. Str-B, *Kommentar,* 2.203.

[77] In H. van der Loos, *The Miracles of Jesus* (NTS 8; Leiden, 1965) 506, n. 5.

[78] F. Fenner, *Die Krankheit im NT* (UNT 18; Leipzig: J. C. Hinrichs, 1930) 66. H. J. Cadbury, "Lexical Notes on Luke-Acts," *JBL* 52 (1933) 62f., likens dropsy to dysentery.

[79] If one examines the death registers of the sixteenth or seventeenth century in a vicarage, one notices that even at that time death was attributed to only a few causes of disease and decline. Herod's death, described by Josephus, *Ant.* 17.168–172, can hardly be linked with dropsy, as was occasionally claimed. The king probably died of the consequences of a venereal disease.

[80] Luke endeavors to be somewhat more precise medically. Does he have in mind the paralysis of one side of the body, caused by stroke or gout? Cf. Pape-Sengebusch, s.v. παραλύω.

[81] Here likewise Luke 7:2 avoids the term παραλυτικός. He simply refers to him being very ill and at the point of death.

The reference to "terrible distress" does not add anything to a more accurate identification of the disease. It may not be appropriate to restrict paralysis, which is mentioned in ancient literature as well,[82] to a particular case of paralysis in a medical-clinical sense; it should be expanded to include every kind of serious disorder in motor functions. Likewise the healing of the man with the lifeless (literally, withered) hand presupposes a partial paralysis (Mark 3:1–6 par.). We are also told of a withered hand in Kings (cf. LXX 3 Kgs 13:4). Repeated attempts have been made to construe it as a psychically caused physical disorder,[83] but the narrative is too sketchy to allow for any conclusions.

The leper (λεπρός), of whom Mark 1:40–45 par. informs us,[84] had a disease about which much is said in the OT and Judaism. Leviticus 13–14 deals with leprosy. What is prescribed here is addressed further in the Mishnah tractate *Nega'im.* The descriptions of the disease are extensive, referring to swellings, scabs, or spots appearing on the skin and developing into a mark of leprosy, to growths that form and heal up again and are replaced by a white swelling or a light-red spot, or to a burn whose growth develops into such a spot, etc. (Lev 13:2, 18f., 24, 29f.). The Mishnah distinguishes twenty-four kinds of leprosy. They knew of particularly dangerous forms, the description of which, however, is again too unprecise for us.[85] Philo places leprosy alongside malignant eczema and warts or refers to pluriform leprosy.[86] Though it has occasionally been argued that the leprosy of ancient times is to be identified as the current disease by that name,[87] there can be little doubt that it also represents a general term. It hardly refers to the incurable kind of leprosy, since in Lev 13–14 the possibility of healing exists and precisely the symptoms descriptive of an advanced stage of actual leprosy are not mentioned. Apparently there are different malignant and nonmalignant skin

---

[82] Cf. Pliny, *Nat. hist.* 28.127. The term is also used by the physicians Moschion and Dioscorides. Cf. H. J. Cadbury, "Lexical Notes on Luke-Acts," *JBL* 45 (1926) 204f. and n. 45.

[83] Cf. H. Seng, *Die Heilungen Jesu in medizinischer Sicht* (2d ed.; Arzt und Seelsorger 4; Königsfeld, 1926) 17; W. Ebstein, *Die Medizin im Neuen Testament und im Talmud* (Stuttgart: F. Enke, 1903) 101.

[84] Cf. Luke 17:11–19; 4:27. In Bethany Jesus is the guest of Simon the leper (Mark 14:3 par.), but we have no details about him. It is not stated that he was present at the meal. Speculation about whether or not he was healed by Jesus is unnecessary.

[85] Cf. Str-B, *Kommentar,* 4.745f.

[86] Philo, *On the Special Laws* 1.80; *On the Posterity and Exile of Cain* 47. Cf. Pliny, *Nat. hist.* 28.127.

[87] Cf. the detailed bibliography in W. Michaelis, "λέπρα, λεπρός," *TDNT* 4.233, n. 3.

diseases in view, whereby the person became cultically unclean, and though they need to be defined more accurately in our medical language, the available data are insufficient.[88]

Relatively speaking, Mark 9:14–27 par. comes closest to a more precise determination of a disease. The evangelist describes in detail the disease of a boy who is led to Jesus. Time and again the boy falls to the ground, foams at the mouth, gnashes his teeth, and becomes rigid. Matthew 17:15 summarizes the portrait of the patient by stating that the boy often falls into the fire or into the water. But he contributes his own diagnosis: the sufferer was an epileptic (σεληνιάζεται).[89] The most characteristic features of epilepsy were the fits that are so aptly described by Mark. The disease, whose manifestation could be frightening, had various names. It was associated with witchcraft and magic, and was called the holy disease. For the Romans the fit of an epileptic was deemed a bad omen.[90] In particular a magic link between the disease and the moon was established, which Galen explained in natural physical terms. If the disease is occasionally termed παίδειον πάθος, it attests to its frequent occurrence in childhood years. It was considered particularly grave and, in its advanced stages, incurable.

What particularly obstruct our access to Jesus' activity as a healer are the anthropological and cosmological conceptions of that time. Accordingly, demons dominate people as evil oppressors and cause physical and psychological harm. To a large extent the Synoptic Gospels share the ancient world's belief in the demonic. Yet compared with the OT, its prominence in these Gospels is conspicuous.[91] This might have something to do with Galilee, whose population was steeped in fear of demons at the time.[92] The nomenclature is fairly consistent. Apart from the terms "demon" (δαιμόνιον, δαίμων)[93] and "demonic" (δαιμονιζόμενος, especially in Matt/Mark), we frequently encounter the term "unclean spirit," which vividly articulates popular belief. Less frequently reference is made to evil spirits (Luke 7:21; 8:2).

---

[88] Cf. M. Noth, *Leviticus* (OTL; London: SCM, 1965) 105–6.

[89] In this instance Luke 9:39 does not offer more extensive details. Cf. E. Lesky and A. Waszink, *RAC* 5.819–31.

[90] Pliny, *Nat. hist.* 28.35, remarks that one would spit in view of epileptics so as to repel the contagion.

[91] In the OT, demons are pagan gods devalued by belief in Yahweh. Cf. G. Gloege, *RGG*³ II:2.

[92] The diminished mention of demons in John's Gospel is surely linked with the circle of the recipients as well.

[93] In the NT the term δαίμων occurs only in Matt 8:31.

The following distinctions are to be observed in order to understand the issue at hand. To begin with, we note the extreme view that one or more demons could take up residence in, inhabit, and take complete charge of a person. Thus the one demonized is no longer in control but seems to be a tool of the dominating spirit, virtually without a will of his own. The exorcism stories, culminating in the command to depart, narrate the deliverance of the demon-possessed person from the demon. Apart from the summary accounts, in the Gospels we encounter essentially two exorcism stories (Mark 1:23–28 par.; 5:1–20 par.); the second of these takes on grotesque vividness in the demons' temporary entry into a herd of pigs. Besides exorcisms, it is also important to note that diseases also were claimed to be caused by demons. This explains the frequent occurrence of exorcistic features in healing narratives. In the case of the "dumb demoniac" (Matt 9:32) or of the crippled woman who had a spirit of infirmity (Luke 13:11), the idea is of diseases caused by demons (cf. Mark 7:24–30 par.; 9:17 par.). The healer's authority over demons of disease is indicated in many ways, a fact easily overlooked in reading such accounts. When the Gentile centurion speaks of the authority he exercises as a soldier and to which he is subject as well (Matt 8:9), he alludes to Jesus' authority over demons of sickness that have to obey him unconditionally. The same conception underlies the occasion when Jesus *rebukes* the fever, according to Luke 4:39. Finally, it also deserves noting that in the understanding of the Synoptic Gospels the activity of demons is not associated with sin. Demons damage the health and psyche of humans.[94] Since we distinguish between exorcism and therapy with exorcistic features by considering the peculiarity of the synoptic material, the following observation can be made: The therapist deals with the effects of the demonic, whereas the exorcist deals with its presence.[95]

Jesus' healings are not completely dealt with by appealing to an outdated worldview in which the world is occupied by demons. The healing narratives of the Gospels are completely adapted to their addressees' scope of understanding. Jesus' exorcisms are more diffi-

---

[94] This, for instance, has led to the following misunderstanding: The reference in Luke 8:2 to Jesus having cast out seven demons from Mary of Magdala gave rise to the viewpoint that this woman had been a gross sinner. But her "possession" has nothing to do with sin; instead it expresses a serious disease. On the multifaceted belief in demons in antiquity, cf. K. Thraede, *RAC* 7.44–117; O. Böcher, *Dämonenfurcht und Dämonenabwehr* (BWANT V/10; Stuttgart: Kohlhammer, 1970). According to a Babylonian text, demons cover the earth like grass.

[95] Cf. Theissen, *Miracle Stories,* 86.

cult to evaluate. It is hardly a matter of debate that he was also active as an exorcist, regardless of how alien and inappropriate it might appear to us. There are relevant logia of Jesus at our disposal, such as the opponents' charge that he was casting out demons by Beelzebul, the ruler of demons (Matt 12:24; cf. 9:34). In this connection mention is made of other exorcists, apart from Jesus: "And if I cast out demons by Beelzebul, by whom do your sons cast them out?" (12:27). Apparently the people were familiar with the work of exorcists.

Can this kind of activity, which still exists among "primitive" peoples today, be made more relevant to us? Demonic possession has been associated with conspicuous and repulsive anomalies, especially with those suffering from nervous and mental illnesses, acute neurotics, and neurasthenics, as well as with the phenomenon of loss of identity.[96] It has been suggested that wars, oppression, and misery can escalate and trigger the fear of the demonic among simple people. In this case belief in demons becomes comprehensible as expressed in feelings of fear and loneliness, of subjection and terror caused by dreams, events in nature, diseases, insanity, and ecstasy. Demons become the objectivized projections of terrible experiences such as these.[97] The view of existence and life established thereby finds persons in an extremely depressive situation, from which they are scarcely able to free themselves. Jesus did not create this situation but found it. His exorcistic ministry deals in a liberating manner with persons in this predicament.

Worldview, diagnosis, and schematization in the narrative motivation link the miracle stories of the Gospels with extrabiblical miracle stories that are similar in milieu. By comparing them, it is perhaps possible to discover elements that typify the miracle stories of the Gospels. We are choosing the healing of the servant of the centurion of Capernaum as such a link. The story is part of the tradition of the logia source (Matt 8:5–13/Luke 7:1–10). It has a late witness in John 4:46b–54, which typically smooths out concrete features and is not relevant for the reconstruction of the earliest form of the text, which might be construed roughly as follows:

---

[96] Cf. O. Böcher, *Christus Exorcista* (BWANT 96, Stuttgart: Kohlhammer, 1972) 166; Klausner, *Jesus,* 363; T. K. Oesterreich, *Possession and Exorcism* (ET; New York: Causeway Books, 1974) 19; van der Loos, *Miracles of Jesus,* 374. The latter mentions the case of the "dédoublement de la personnalité."

[97] Cf. G. van der Leeuw, *Religion in Essence and Manifestation* (London: Allen & Unwin, 1938) 134–40.

As he entered Capernaum, a centurion came forward to him, beseeching him and saying, "Lord, my servant is lying paralyzed at home, in terrible distress." And he said, "Shall I come and heal him?" And the centurion answered and said, "Lord, I am not worthy to have you come under my roof, but only say the word, and my servant will be healed. For I too am a man under authority. I have soldiers under me, and I say to one, 'Go,' and he goes, and to another, 'Come,' and he comes, and to my slave, 'Do this,' and he does it." When Jesus heard this, he marveled, and said to those who followed him, "Truly, I say to you, with no one in Israel have I found such faith." And when the centurion returned to his home he found the servant in health.[98]

The story focuses on the personalized encounter of the centurion with Jesus. The servant for whom the centurion entreats is not brought in. The faith demonstrated by the centurion is fundamental; Jesus lauds it and is prompted by it to come to his aid. Though the healing that is granted is to be expected in a miracle story, it gains or retains the quality of a surprise gift on account of this faith.

A talmudic miracle story, associated with the name of Hanina ben Dosa, comes astoundingly close to the Gospel tradition, especially to its Johannine version:

Once the son of R. Gamaliel fell ill. He sent two scholars to R. Hanina b. Dosa to ask him to pray for him. When he saw them he went up to an upper chamber and prayed for him. When he came down he said to them: Go, the fever has left him. They said to him: Are you a prophet? He replied: I am neither a prophet nor the son of a prophet, but I learned this from experience. If my prayer is fluent in my mouth, I know that he is accepted: but if not, I know that he is rejected. They sat down and made a note of the exact moment. When they came to R. Gamaliel, he said to them: By the temple service! You have not been a moment too soon or too late, but so it happened: at that very moment the fever left him and he asked for water to drink (b. Ber. 34b).

As in the Gospel tradition, this represents a "long-distance healing." It shares with the Lukan version the delegation motif and

---

[98] On the reconstruction: The description of the disease in Luke 7:2, that he was sick and at the point of death (cf. John 4:47), is surely secondary. Likewise the two delegations, first elders of the Jews and then friends, have to be viewed as Lukan. In the final analysis the expression of humility, here brought by the friends, is appropriate only if voiced by the centurion. The mediating delegation of the Jews can be reconciled well with Luke's "salvation-history perspective." Conversely the logion of the coming of the many from east and west (Matt 8:11f.) is inserted into the pericope by Matthew. Luke 13:28f. has this saying in an entirely different locus. The original conclusion can no longer be reconstructed adequately. Matt 8:13 is shaped by Matthew, as the agreement with 15:28b suggests. Perhaps there was a sentence such as "And he said to the centurion, 'Your servant is healed.' " Verse 7 is to be read interrogatively. Cf. Gnilka, *Matthäusevangelium*, 1.299f.; Theissen, *Miracle Stories*, 182f.; U. Busse, *Die Wunder des Propheten Jesus* (2d ed.; FB 24; Stuttgart: Katholisches Bibelwerk, 1979) 1.141–60.

with the Johannine version the recognition of the moment, the father-son relationship between petitioner and patient, and the diagnosis of fever (cf. Luke 7:3–6; John 4:46, 52). The agreements with John 4 are so extensive that P. Fiebig raised the possibility of literary dependence.[99] While he correctly dismisses this possibility, the impression of a schematic narration remains nevertheless. In any case there are two noteworthy points of difference: First, in one instance the healing comes about through Hanina's prayer and in the other through Jesus' authority, which the centurion had described vividly in the imagery of the authoritative command. Second, the faith motif, which is decisive for the Gospel narrative, is not present in the rabbinic story.

A third example takes us into the Greco-Roman world. Tacitus, *Hist.* 4.81, has two accounts of healings that the emperor Vespasian accomplished in Egypt.

Among the lower classes at Alexandria was a blind man whom everybody knew as such. One day this fellow threw himself at Vespasian's feet, imploring him with groans to heal his blindness. He had been told to make this request by Serapis, the favourite god of a nation much addicted to strange beliefs. He asked that it might please the emperor to anoint his cheeks and eyeballs with water of his mouth. A second petitioner, who suffered from a withered hand, pleaded his case too, also on the advice of Serapis: would Caesar tread upon him with the imperial foot? At first Vespasian laughed at them and refused. When the two insisted, he hesitated. . . . Finally he asked the doctors for an opinion. . . . The doctors were eloquent on the various possibilities. The blind man's vision was not completely destroyed, and if certain impediments were removed his sight would return. The other victim's limb had been dislocated, but could be put right by correct treatment. Perhaps this was the will of the gods, they added; perhaps the emperor had been chosen to perform a miracle. Anyhow, if a cure were effected, the credit would go to the ruler; if it failed, the poor wretches would have to bear the ridicule. So Vespasian felt that his destiny gave him the key to every door and that nothing now defied belief. With a smiling expression and surrounded by an expectant crowd of bystanders, he did what was asked. Instantly the cripple recovered the use of his hand and the light of day dawned again upon his blind companion. Both these incidents are still vouched for by eye-witnesses, though there is now nothing to be gained by lying.[100]

The different shape of this miracle story is evident. There can be no doubt that it has a religious component as well but as such is

[99] P. Fiebig, *Wundergeschichten des neutestamentlichen Zeitalters* (Tübingen: J. C. B. Mohr, 1911) 21f.

[100] English translation by K. Wellesley, *Tacitus: The Histories* (Baltimore: Penguin, 1964).

restricted to the petitioners. Prompted by the god Serapis, they turn to the emperor, who, after overcoming considerable doubts, is virtually pushed into the role of being the deity's tool. The action results in a public spectacle. The story is told *ad gloriam Caesaris.*

Faith may be considered one of the unique features of the miracle stories of the Gospels. In most instances it is explicitly stated: "And when Jesus saw their faith" (Mark 2:5); "not even in Israel have I found such faith" (Matt 8:10); "your faith has made you well" (Mark 5:34; 10:52); "great is your faith" (Matt 15:28); and negatively, "O faithless generation, how long am I to be with you?" (Mark 9:19). In this connection the following statements may well be taken as expressions of faith: "If you will, you can make me clean" (Mark 1:40) or the cry for mercy (Matt 9:27, cf. v. 28). The theme of faith continues in the miracle stories of the Gospel of John, though in this case it has undergone further theological editing (John 9:35–38) or is being confronted by unbelief (5:10ff., 24). When the issue of faith arises in extrabiblical, Hellenistic miracle stories, its orientation is different.[101]

If faith is characteristic of the Gospels' miracle stories, one may attempt to trace the issue further. How does this relate to Jesus? That the granting of healings in the ministry of the historical Jesus was closely related to faith is supported by two traditions that are yet to be examined; both of them tell of the miraculous being refused on account of flagrant unbelief.

In Mark 6:1–6a we are told of Jesus' unsuccessful appearance in his hometown, Nazareth. When Jesus was teaching in the synagogue, his fellow countrymen took offense at him because to them his descent from a petty bourgeois family that they knew and his many years of working among them as a craftsman were irreconcilably contradictory to his wisdom and miraculous power. This failed appearance in his hometown cannot have taken place at the beginning of his activity. When Luke, in 4:14–30, has Jesus begin in Nazareth and preach, as it were, his induction sermon, which he

---

[101] The association of miracle and faith is found frequently in Lucian, *Pseudologista* 13, 15, 28f. Faith, however, has no theological quality here. It focuses on the possibility of these wondrous things, the broad usefulness of magic spells, the existence of demons and spirits. Theissen, *Miracle Stories,* 129–34, has shown that in this case, as well as in Iamblichus, Plutarch, and Strabo, "faith" follows the miracle. Where "faith" precedes the miracle—the evidence is scant and limited to Epidaurus—πίστις is not used. Perhaps Aischines, *Anthologia Palatina* 6.330, comes closest: "When the means of mortals failed, he put all his hope in the divine." The text is also found in O. Weinreich, *Antike Heilungswunder* (1909; reprint, RVV VIII/1, Giessen: Töpelmann, 1969) 195.

arranges dramatically, he has his own theological reasons for it. In his hometown they have already heard about Jesus' miracles. It is natural that they entertained appropriate expectations from the now adult hometown son. The proverbial logion of the prophet who is not without honor except in his own country, which is adduced to explain the incomprehensible rejection, in no wise exhausts the situation and presumably was not linked with the pericope until later. The original reactions are to be found in the statements "they took offense at him," referring to the people of Nazareth, and "he marveled because of their unbelief," referring to Jesus.[102] The remark that Jesus could not do any miracles there (v. 5a) is stinging and for this reason belongs to the early tradition. Mark attempts to alleviate this sting (v. 5b, likewise par. Matt 13:58; Luke 4:23 reinforces it). From a historical perspective this permits the conclusion that Jesus withheld miracles from his own people because he found no faith in Nazareth at all.

The relationship between the refusal to perform miracles and unbelief is brought to bear no less drastically in an incident mentioned at various places in the Gospels. Some people—according to Mark 8:11 they are Pharisees, according to Matt 12:38 some are scribes and Pharisees; according to Matt 16:1 Pharisees and Sadducees, Luke 11:16 speaks vaguely of others—demand a sign from Jesus. The scene in question was passed down both by Mark and by the sayings source. This explains why it occurs twice in Matthew.[103] They want to know about his legitimation and expect him to authenticate himself, just as miracles of authentication by the prophets are handed down (1 Sam 10:1ff.; 1 Kgs 13:3; 2 Kgs 19:29; critically Deut 13:1ff.). They want to see a sign from heaven. In terms of the synoptic use of language, signs are distinct from "mighty works" (δυνάμεις)—this is the term for Jesus' miracles (Matt 11:20f., 23; 14:2; etc.)—miracles that rule out any doubt. The expectation for the

---

[102] On the reconstruction, cf. Gnilka, *Markus,* 1.227–29. The following are among the earliest components of the pericope: an introduction which is difficult to reconstruct with certainty, narrating Jesus' appearance in the synagogue of Nazareth, plus vv. 2b, 3, 5a, 6a. Alternate analyses can be found in Bultmann, *History,* 31f.; D.-A. Koch, *Die Bedeutung der Wundererzählungen für die Christologie des Markusevangeliums* (BZNW 42; Berlin: de Gruyter, 1975) 147–53; E. Grässer, "Jesus in Nazareth," in E. Grässer, et al., *Jesus in Nazareth* (BZNW 40; Berlin: de Gruyter, 1972) 13.

[103] John 2:18 and 6:30 place the demand for a sign into concrete situations. By means of a sign Jesus is to demonstrate that he is authorized to clear out the temple market. He is further to authenticate himself in the manner of Moses, who provided the people with manna in the wilderness.

sign to remove any doubt is heightened in that the sign is to be from heaven, that is, wrought by God himself, in order to authenticate him. The brusque rejection of this inappropriate request has to do with the issue of faith. According to Mark 8:12f., Jesus left those demanding a sign. His rejection makes use of an incantation formula which, in its full form, would say, "If this generation is to be given a sign, may I be damned."[104] Demanding a sign, for Jesus, expresses obstinate unbelief. He discloses himself only to faith. Faith alone is given access to his salvation.

Nevertheless, it may be reasonable to suggest that he promised a sign to those seeking a sign, without changing his position. He called it "the sign of Jonah" (Luke 11:29). Its interpretation varies in the Gospels. In Matt 12:40 it refers to Jesus' resurrection. This interpretation is clearly secondary. Luke 11:30 may proffer the interpretation already found in the sayings source: "For as Jonah became a sign to the men of Nineveh, so will the Son of man be to this generation." Most probably the idea here is that of the Parousia of the Son of man, which was of particular interest for the logia source. The omission of Jesus' mention of the sign of Jonah in Mark 8:12 is not to be viewed as the oldest version but rather indicates that Mark no longer knew precisely what the sign of Jonah encompassed or that he wanted to formulate Jesus' response as brusquely as possible. The difficulties they had with the saying about the sign of Jonah may be seen as evidence for its authenticity. Presumably Jesus alluded to his preaching on repentance, whereby he perceived himself to be linked with Jonah. There is no need to pursue the issue further. The important thing is that a sign promised in this manner insists upon the demand of faith and perhaps also takes into account the possibility of a "too late."[105]

The involvement of faith in Jesus' healings shows us the way of understanding them. Faith is not to be restricted to the possibility of healing. Trust placed in Jesus transcends the help that has been granted concretely and sees in him the bringer of salvation who is able to save. The relationship between miracle and word, with which we will be dealing in more detail shortly, may also be indicated in the Gospel presentation of Jesus granting help primarily by his word. We

---

[104] On Mark 8:12, cf. BDF §372 (4); J. Doudna, *The Greek of the Gospel of Mark* (JBLMS 12; Philadelphia: Society of Biblical Literature and Exegesis, 1961) 110f.

[105] G. Schmitt, "Die Zeichen des Jona," *ZNW* 69 (1978) 123–29, assumes that the sign of Jonah announces the destruction of Jerusalem and appeals to the *vita prophetarum* for support. This, too, renders the suggestion suspect.

do indeed hear of touching (Matt 8:3, 15; 9:29; 20:34; etc.), as well as of healing manipulation (saliva: Mark 7:33; 8:23) and other things (John 9:6f.) that show him as the great miracle worker. This may be attributed to later Hellenistic influence.[106] The original focus on the spoken word establishes the link with the word of the proclamation of the kingdom of God and subordinates the miracle to such proclamation. Healings are assessed correctly only if they are seen in the context of the proclamation of the kingdom of God.

Since the historical concern is of interest to us, an overview will be provided of some particulars in the healing narratives that may have preserved concrete reminiscences. Indications of the latter could be seen in the combining of the reference to the place of action with the name, such as the blind beggar Bartimaeus of Jericho (Mark 10:46) and Simon Peter's mother-in-law in his house in Capernaum (Mark 1:29f.). In the case of the centurion from Capernaum there is the additional rudimentary feature that Jesus initially rejects the notion of entering the house of a Gentile (Matt 8:7 as an interrogative statement). In the healing of the paralytic we construed the opening up of the roof to have been an old reminiscence (Mark 2:4).

In retrospect, the rejection of the demand for a sign from heaven shows us the kind of miracles Jesus granted. They were no overwhelming miracles in the literal sense; to the unbelievers they did not suffice. As mighty works (δυνάμεις) they became real only to those who in faith opened themselves to Jesus. Hence the rejection of the demand for a sign takes on a critical function in the overall evaluation of his miracles.

b) The number of sayings of Jesus relevant to the interpretation of his work as a miraculous healer is remarkably scant. This may also serve as a corrective in classifying this area of his ministry. Let us begin with the topic of faith! If faith can be argued to be Jesus' characteristic requirement in this realm, it may be assumed that a relevant saying can be found.

There is a saying about faith which is confident that it can do anything. Its slightly reproachful tone may indicate that it was originally addressed to the disciples. This is further confirmed by its use in the Gospels, even though we encounter it in different settings: Mark 11:23 par. Matt 21:21 adduce it as instruction for the disciples following the cursing of the fig tree. In Matt 17:20 it is cited once more,

---

[106] Cf. Dibelius, *Jesus*, 77.

again in the context of a terse lesson for the disciples, following the healing of the epileptic boy whom the disciples were unable to heal on account of their unbelief. Only in Luke 17:6 is it a detached directive addressed to the apostles. We may assume that its insertion in the contexts of Matthew and Mark was secondary. The logion is an ancient one, to be sure, of which there are essentially two variants (Mark 11:23 par. Matt 17:20 for one; Luke 17:6 for another). For the purpose of reconstruction we refer to Matt 17:20 and Luke 17:6:

"For truly, I say to you, if you have faith as a grain of mustard seed, you will say to this mountain, 'Move hence to yonder place,' and it will move."

"If you had faith as a grain of mustard seed, you could say to this sycamine tree, 'Be rooted up, and be planted in the sea,' and it would obey you."

The only thing relevant to us here is the central question of whether it is the mountain or the sycamine tree that offers the original image. The tree is the preferred option. Probably this depiction was originally spoken in view of a sycamine tree at Lake Gennesaret. In the attempt to trace back the original image to the mountain-moving faith, the use of a proverb is plausible (cf. 1 Cor 13:2; *Gos. Thom.* 48).[107]

The instruction which the logion provides is characterized by an impressive contrast, the antithesis of small and large. The mustard seed represented the smallest visible thing. The sycamine tree was reputed to have powerful roots.[108] Hence there is great effectiveness arising from what is least. The picture is not to be taken literally, as if it were a case of moving a tree into the lake by magic, nor is faith to be measured. True faith has great effectiveness, but it is given only if a person is open to God by faith and thus is put at God's disposal. God is then able to work through the person. A similar connection has already been noted in the pericope of Jesus' appearance in Nazareth, where it was evident that the people's unbelief impaired

---

[107] This is understood differently by F. Hahn, "Jesu Wort vom bergeversetzenden Glauben," *ZNW* 76 (1985) 156–58, for whom the image is determined by the mountain and the lake. This is the case in Mark 11:23; this saying may have been inserted by Mark, however. The striking feature in the Markan logia tradition is that it often seems to be fragmented. Matt 21:21 is dependent upon Mark. Matthew has the logion twice because he found it in both Q and Mark. On this discussion, cf. Gnilka, *Matthäusevangelium*, 2.105f., 110; idem, *Markus*, 2.133. The saying of the mountain-moving faith is also extant in the rabbinic literature. Cf. Str-B, *Kommentar*, 1.759.

[108] The text uses συκάμινος for mulberry tree, not συκομορέα (Luke 19:4); cf. V. Reichmann, *RAC* 7.683–88.

God's power. The logion elucidates the converse, positive situation, namely, that the person's faith is God's power to the extent that God is given a chance to do his work. While the work God intends to accomplish is manifold, in this context it also has to be linked with healings and miracles. As a saying of Jesus, this can hardly be interpreted other than as an expression of his own faith.

This leads us to the realization that not only the faith of the one who was helped was important in the miraculous healings but also Jesus' faith. In turn this is correlated with the kingdom of God.[109] In his unique openness to God, Jesus demonstrated unique faith.[110] This faith that makes all things possible is further reflected in another instance. When Jesus tells the father of the epileptic boy, following Mark 9:23, "All things are possible to him who believes," this denotes an invitation to share in his faith. Mark has perceived the matter quite correctly by describing the reaction to such a challenge as the father's realization of his own unbelief.

The direct association of miracles with the reign of God is provided in a saying that was found already in the sayings source in the context of the opponents' reproach, according to which Jesus cast out demons through Beelzebul, the prince of demons. We assume that in an older tradition the response to this reproach was as follows: "if I cast out demons by Beelzebul, by whom do your sons cast them out? Therefore they shall be your judges" (Matt 12:24, 27 par. Luke 11:15, 19).[111] The logion we are now considering is not polemical and was handed down as an isolated one. When we compare Matthew and Luke, there is only one difference: "if it is by the finger [Matt: Spirit] of God that I cast out demons, then the kingdom of God has come upon you." Here the Lukan "finger of God" is certainly preferable. It represents the more original version and brings us closer to understanding it. If in his mighty works Jesus uses the finger of God—perhaps it would even be plausible to say, "is the finger of God"—then God is working through him. The idea of God working with his finger was a familiar one already in the OT; he

---

[109] Hahn, "Jesu Worte," 156–58, noted the eschatological orientation of the logion.

[110] On this issue, cf. G. Ebeling, "Jesus und Glaube," *ZTK* 55 (1958) 64–110.

[111] Cf. Gnilka, *Matthäusevangelium,* 1.461. The view taken by D. Lührmann, *Die Redaktion der Logienquelle* (WMANT 33; Neukirchen: Neukirchener Verlag, 1969) 33, and adopted by H. Merklein, *Die Gottesherrschaft als Handlungsprinzip* (2d ed.; FB 34; Würzburg: Echter Verlag, 1981) 158, that Luke 11:19 is to be attributed to the redaction of Q, is not convincing.

wrote the tablets of the law with his finger (LXX Exod 31:18; Deut 9:10), and the heavens are the work of his fingers (Ps 8:4).

The power of God manifested in Jesus' exorcisms is evidence that the kingdom of God has already come to humans. The verb ἔφθασεν used in the Greek text can be understood properly only in the sense of the presence of the kingdom.[112] What is noteworthy and hence deserves to be highlighted is the link between the kingdom of God as the eschatological salvation and the person of Jesus. From the Qumran writings we know that this Jewish community also was familiar with the conception of salvation as present. But at Qumran salvation is not linked with a mediating person but rather with entry into the community of God. Further, the idea of the reign of God is not found in the sayings about the presence of salvation.[113] For Jesus the reign of God can be experienced as eschatological salvation in his mighty works, though not yet in its finality. Since the kingdom is linked with his person in its present experience, he remains the guarantor for its final, perfected manifestation.

It would be inadequate to construe his mighty works merely as signs of the coming kingdom.[114] Its salvific power is already genuinely at work in them. Hence this has been referred to as dynamic presence.[115] Perhaps this formulation is particularly appropriate. It is important to take into account that the logion has to be accorded essential significance. Jesus understood his exorcisms and miraculous healings, framed in an exorcistic context of that time, as anticipatory revelation of the reign of God taking place in his ministry, and thus interpreted the kingdom by it. The newness of this understanding vouches for the authenticity of its interpretation.

A very similar situation is illustrated in the brief parable of the strong man to be overcome. The Markan rendition is clearly the earlier one of the two: "But no one can enter a strong man's house and plunder his goods, unless he first binds the strong man; then indeed he may plunder his house" (Mark 3:27; cf. Matt 12:27). This saying, spoken in the context of exorcisms, likewise has to do with

---

[112] A thorough discussion on this can be found in W. G. Kümmel, *Promise and Fulfilment* (SBT 23; ET; London: SCM, 1957) 105–9; H.-W. Kuhn, *Enderwartung und gegenwärtiges Heil* (SUNT 4; Göttingen: Vandenhoeck & Ruprecht, 1966) 191–93.

[113] Cf. Kuhn, *Enderwartung*. In Qumran the presence of salvation is construed as fellowship with angels, new creation, proleptic transposition into heaven, protection from Sheol. The community's self-understanding as a spiritual temple played a significant part in the development of this conception.

[114] So, e.g., Dibelius, *Jesus*, 69.

[115] Schnackenburg, *Herrschaft*, 87.

the reign of God and has far-reaching significance.[116] The parable is full of intent to overcome a strong man. The characteristic battle motif, which also denotes the new concept in comparison with the saying on exorcism discussed above, picks up on Satan's kingdom, which is construed as a structured realm, populated with destructive demons. The material of this image is already found in Isaiah 49:24f.: "Can the prey be taken from the mighty, or captives of a tyrant rescued? Surely, thus says the LORD: 'Even the captives of the mighty shall be taken, and the prey of the tyrant be rescued, for I will contend with those who contend with you, and I will save your children.' "

Any direct dependence, of course, is a matter of uncertainty. The defeat of Satan's kingdom, that is, overcoming physical and psychological human misery, construed as caused by demons, advances God's reign. The dualistic form of the reigns of Satan and of God being in conflict with one another represents a closed conceptual model. In the end the battle has been decided, for the strong man is already bound. To this extent the saying is optimistic and certain of victory. It also solidifies the significant insight that the reign of God, which is becoming effective, intends the person's total salvation and total deliverance and cannot be restricted to the inner, mental spheres. The logion's authenticity is further underscored in the post-Easter texts, especially in hymns used in the context of worship, because they link the victory over the "powers" with the cross, resurrection, and ascension of Jesus, whereas here it is connected with his earthly ministry.

The parallel text of Luke 11:21f. allegorizes the parable, referring to the strong man as one who is fully armed, who is assailed by one who is stronger, who takes away his armor (τὴν πανοπλίαν) in which he trusted and divides the spoil. It may be assumed that the strong man and the one who is stronger refer directly to Satan and Jesus, while the πανοπλία points to the realm of the demonic, and the spoil to people who have been liberated.[117] An allusion to Isa 53:12 is by no means certain.[118]

The statement "I saw Satan fall like lightning from heaven" (Luke 10:18) fits in well with the point under discussion. Luke attached it to the return of the seventy disciples, who joyfully report

---

[116] Jeremias, Parables, 122f., argues that the saying refers to Jesus' temptation (Matt 4:1–11), where the strong one was overcome. There is no support for this correlation.

[117] Cf. Jülicher, Gleichnisreden, 2.226–28.

[118] So Jeremias, Parables, 122f.; Merklein, Gottesherrschaft, 161, n. 563.

on their successful exorcisms. It may have to be taken as an isolated saying, or as one whose original context has been lost. To be sure, the context can have been none other than Jesus' exorcistic ministry. Whether there is an allusion here to a visionary experience of Jesus or the language is figurative has to remain open.[119] Nevertheless, it points up the certainty of the final defeat of evil. Satan's fall means that the collapse of his kingdom has begun. God is the one causing the fall; he announces to Jesus the victory of his reign, in which Jesus plays an active part. Jülicher[120] pointed to the linguistic association of Satan's fall from heaven with the sign from heaven that the opponents demanded. There is no direct correlation, to be sure. If the comparison is accepted, however, it follows that God is the one granting Jesus the assurance.

When John the Baptist inquired from prison whether Jesus was the one to come, Jesus answered by alluding to various passages in Isaiah (35:5f.; 26:19; 61:1), thereby pointing to his healing of the blind, the lame, the lepers, the deaf, to his raising of the dead, and to his proclamation of the Gospel to the poor (Matt 11:2–6 par.). To the extent that the sequencing of these acts of Jesus describes an ascending line and culminates in proclamation, this interpretation of his ministry fully agrees with his intentions. The miracles point to the message; only via his proclamation can they be accepted in the appropriate manner. Nevertheless, it is advisable to attribute this text, which radiates scribal reflection, to a later context.[121]

If we summarize the insights resulting from the attempt to reconstruct the significance of Jesus' miraculous healings, the following can be said: The miraculous healings are part of the proclamation of

---

[119] For Bultmann (*History*, 161), Luke 10:18 appears to be a fragment. The saying belongs to Jesus' exorcisms, to be sure, rather than to the disciples'. Only on the basis of Job 1:6–12; 2:1–7 is it possible to project the end of Satan's role as accuser in heaven. So W. Foerster, "σατανᾶς," *TDNT* 7.157. On Satan's fall as an eschatological motif, see P. von der Osten-Sacken, *Gott und Belial* (SUNT 6; Göttingen: Vandenhoeck & Ruprecht, 1969) 210f. M. van Rhijn, *Een blik in het onderwijs van Jezus* (2d ed.; Amsterdam: H. J. Paris, 1927), took the logion to be ironic (according to Jeremias, *Parables*, 122, n. 6). There is no hint of irony here. U. B. Müller, "Erwägungen zur prophetischen Struktur der Verkündigung Jesu," *ZTK* 74 (1974) 416–48, wants to relate the logion to a vision of Jesus with sweeping consequences. On account of the logion's uniqueness, however, it seems prudent to be cautious.

[120] Jülicher, *Gleichnisreden*, 2.216.

[121] Contra Kuhn, *Enderwartung*, 195–97. On this discussion, cf. Gnilka, *Matthäusevangelium*, 1.405–10; A. Vögtle, "Wunder und Wort in urchristlicher Glaubenswerbung (Matt 11:2–5 par. Lk 7:18–23)," 219–42 in *Das Evangelium und die Evangelien* (Düsseldorf: Patmos, 1971); W. G. Kümmel, *Jesu Antwort an Johannes den Täufer* (Wiesbaden: Steiner, 1974).

God's reign and in this context are subordinated to and aligned with the message. They signal the eschatological change and allow the dynamic presence of God's reign to be experienced in its healing, helping, and saving power. Incorporated in the process of the proleptic revelation of the kingdom, they share in particular in the struggle against wickedness and evil, which, though already overcome in principle, continue to be effective in the world. In a dualistic worldview in which the reigns of God and of Satan are juxtaposed, it is possible to be assured of God's cause. Ultimately, however, miraculous healings can be experienced only by faith. Such faith characterizes Jesus' existence; for those receiving his help he is the access to these miraculous healings. Jesus' faith is unique, to be sure. When people are invited to participate in his faith, they gain access to God's work as encountered in him, to the kingdom present in his ministry. For this reason faith is more than trusting in his healing power. It is the "yes" to his word, which brings eschatological salvation. We saw this perspective confirmed in the focus of the healings upon the message. Finally, in their performance miracles usually are charismatic events, depicting what is surprising and surprisingly new in the reign of God. They serve to hold in check the voice of human despair, to expose before God the one who is cultically impure, and to restore human dignity. Jesus' exorcisms are a protest against demonic fears and are intended to assist in overcoming them. As experiences of the future reign of God, they illustrate God's will focused upon the salvation of the whole person.

Overview

The miracle traditions in particular were caught in the current of Easter; that is to say, they were given a new reading and were developed further in light of the Easter faith in Jesus' resurrection from the dead, and also new stories came about. Precisely the miracle stories were intended to communicate that the exalted Christ who remains present in the community devotes his support to his own and answers their petitions. Most of these newly emerging stories, of course, are bound up with the Easter faith in such a way that it is neither possible nor meaningful to reconstruct them. The fundamental truth they convey is that the earthly Jesus is now the exalted one. The question to be asked is not what he formerly did and was but rather what he continues to do and be for us.

Given these qualifications, it is necessary to comment briefly on particular traditions. The narratives of the calming of the storm (Mark 4:35–41 par.), of Jesus walking on the water (Mark 6:45–52 par.), and of his transfiguration (Mark 9:2–10 par.) allow his sovereignty to be made apparent; they are epiphany miracles. The sea stories contain elements of a miracle of rescue, especially that of the calming of the storm. The epiphany miracles have affinities with the appearances of the resurrected Christ. The discussion frequently revolves around the question whether the epiphany miracles did not originally tell of Easter epiphanies and were then projected back secondarily into the ministry of the earthly Jesus. A process such as this would be possible in principle, since for the community the earthly one and the exalted one are identical. This issue ought to be examined seriously in the case of the tradition of the walking on the water, which also contains other motifs occurring in the narratives of the Easter appearances.[122] The issue is less relevant in the case of the calming of the storm and of the transfiguration. There is no doubt, however, that the glorified Christ is the perfected, enthroned one who is able to lead humans to his perfection.[123] In the calming of the storm (the exalted) Christ is to be seen as the conqueror of the powers of chaos. It is important to note in this connection that the command issued to the storm to be quiet (Mark 4:39) is patterned after the exorcism narratives and assumes demons to be at work in natural powers that cause damage. Hence the pericope can be understood as a summary, as it were, of the victorious battle against the demonic powers that Jesus fought in his exorcisms.

The tradition of the miraculous feeding of the multitude with a few loaves and fish (Mark 6:32–44 par.; 8:1–10 par.) has to be seen in the context of the meals Jesus had in which he honored people with his table fellowship. The feeding of one hundred by the prophet Elisha (2 Kgs 4:42–44) served the narrator as a model. Rationalistic explanations of one's willingness to share with others on account of being impressed with Jesus' goodness might indeed be relevant in terms of the intention of his ethics,[124] but hardly of that of the narrative. Could the backdrop be a meal held in joyous anticipation

---

[122] The following are comparable sayings: the disciples think they see a ghost (Mark 6:49; cf. Luke 24:37); Jesus stands at the lake shore (Mark 6:47; cf. John 21:4). The Petrine scenes are comparable as well (Matt 14:28–30; John 21:7).

[123] Cf. Gnilka, *Markus,* 2.21–29; idem, *Matthäusevangelium,* 2.98.

[124] Cf. A. de Tocqueville, *Die Demokratie in Amerika,* reprint 1956, p. 206.

of the reign of God?[125] For the community the association with the eucharistic Lord's Supper would have come to mind as well.[126]

The narratives of raisings from the dead, of which there are three (Mark 5:21–43 par.: Jairus' daughter; Luke 7:11–17: the widow's son at Nain; John 11:17–44: Lazarus), can be proclaimed only in the context of Easter. The return of the deceased to earthly life, ending in death again, can be a portrait of redemption only in view of Christ, who has experienced the ultimate resurrection from the dead and who is the guarantor of eternal life. For this reason such assumptions as that the Jairus story originally told of the healing of the gravely ill daughter and subsequently was developed into a resurrection story[127] miss the point. Only from the perspective of Easter can the question of death and life be posed radically. Thus it is necessary to subject these narratives, and the development of the miracle stories sketched here in any case, to this radical background of inquiry, so as not to trivialize them.

Select bibliography: O. Betz and W. Grimm, *Wesen und Wirklichkeit der Wunder Jesu* (ANTJ 2; Frankfurt am Main/Bern/Las Vegas: Lang, 1977); O. Böcher, *Christus Exorcista* (BWANT 96; Stuttgart: Kohlhammer, 1972); U. Busse, *Die Wunder des Propheten Jesus* (2d ed.; FB 24; Stuttgart: Katholisches Bibelwerk, 1979); W. Ebstein, *Die Medizin im NT und im Talmud* (Stuttgart: F. Enke, 1903); F. Fenner, *Die Krankheit im NT* (UNT 18, Leipzig: J. C. Hinrichs, 1930); R. H. Fuller, *Interpreting the Miracles* (London: SCM, 1963); F. Hahn, "Jesu Wort vom bergeversetzenden Glauben," *ZNW* 76 (1985) 149–60; K. Kertelge, *Die Wunder Jesu im Markusevangelium* (SANT 23; Munich: Kösel, 1970); D.-A. Koch, *Die Bedeutung der Wundererzählungen für die Christologie des Markusevangeliums* (BZNW 42; Berlin: de Gruyter, 1975); H.-W. Kuhn, *Enderwartung und gegenwärtiges Heil* (SUNT 4; Göttingen: Vandenhoeck & Ruprecht, 1966); E. Lohse, "Glaube und Wunder," 335–50 in *Theologia Crucis—Signum Crucis* (FS E. Dinkler; Tübingen: Mohr, 1979); H. van der Loos, *The Miracles of Jesus* (NTS 8; Leiden: E. J. Brill, 1965); U. B. Müller, "Erwägungen zur prophetischen Struktur der Verkündigung Jesu," *ZTK* 74 (1974) 416–48; T. K. Oesterreich, *Possession and Exorcism: Among Primitive Races, in Antiquity, the Middle Ages, and Modern Times* (ET; New York: Causeway, 1974) R. Pesch, *Jesu ureigene Taten?* (QD 52; Freiburg: Herder, 1970); H. Seng, *Die Heilungen Jesu in medizinischer Sicht* (2d ed.; Arzt und Seelsorger 4; Königsfeld, 1926); U. Wegner, *Der Hauptmann von Kafarnaum* (WUNT II/14; Tübingen: Mohr, 1985); O. Weinreich, *Antike Heilungswunder* (RVV VIII/1; reprint, 1904; Giessen: Töpelmann, 1969).

4. Future, presence, and imminence of God's reign

The reign of God is the center and essence of Jesus' proclamation. But as we have seen already, his reference to the reign of God is

---

[125] This possibility was misconstrued by the interpretation of Jesus as Zealot. Cf., e.g., H. Montefiore, "Revolt in the Desert?" *NTS* 8 (1961/62) 135–41.

[126] Surprisingly, the eucharistic dimension is hardly given any attention in the text's history of interpretation.

[127] Pesch, *Markusevangelium*, 1.313.

so essential that it cannot be restricted to his proclamation but encompasses his ministry as a whole. Indeed it transcends his ministry; the reign of God yet to come is *the* issue. Only in its absence, its futurity, its coming, is it possible to appreciate and surmise what it is or will be. This brings the temporal dimension into view. The reign of God is associated with the future as well as with the present. There are sayings of Jesus that relate to its future and others to its presence. In order to understand what it actually is or will be, it is necessary to endeavor to determine and delineate how the future and the present relate to the reign of God, or how the reign of God relates to the future and the present.

In the attempt to answer this question, there is a major exegetical debate, in which "extreme" positions have been taken, allowing either for the future only or for the present only. In other words, they were able to conceive of the reign of God only as future or only as present. In the view of the former, Jesus, as forerunner, becomes the messenger of the future reign of God, announcing its coming. This coming is always construed as imminently impending, as very near. In the view of the latter, everything is fulfilled in him, the reign of God is with him and in him, visible and concrete. In this case, of course, the problem of its nearness and the resultant problem of its absence does not arise.

By describing both of these positions as "extreme" we are indicating that the solution is not halfway between the two, to be sure, but that it is to be sought by taking seriously both temporal relations, by highlighting both the future and the present. The problem is aggravated by the quality of the reign of God, which is such that it cannot be grasped adequately if it is merely set in relation to temporal phases, to the present and the future. In a certain sense it qualifies time and is not merely set in some relation to the future; rather, it is the future. This cannot but have ramifications for ascertaining the present.

There is no explanation anywhere in the gospel of what the reign of God is. Jesus refused to define it or to explicate it theoretically. It is arguable that he was able to assume that his hearers understood the meaning of "the reign of God." But this is only partly correct, for in a general conception of the reign of God it is important to learn how he construed it. Furthermore, a theoretical presentation would not have been appropriate to his language. To begin with, therefore, it has to suffice to start with the message. The message speaks about God's acts or it promises them. God acts regally, reigns as king, and manifests his royal power. When God is construed as king in the conception of the OT, one needs to remember that the redemptive action described as the reign of God is seen as something coming entirely and exclusively from God to us. It is important, therefore, to consider this redemptive action in the future and the present by means of sayings that can be traced back to Jesus. Future, present, and nearness are the aspects under consideration.

a) The futurity of God's reign is established in an easily remembered way in the Lord's Prayer. The disciple is to pray for its coming, ἐλθέτω ἡ βασιλεία σου (Matt 6:10; Luke 11:2), "may your royal reign come." The tense (aorist) indicates that the petition refers to a single future coming. Hence the tense is not to be misunderstood by construing this coming as a progressive, gradual one to which the person can contribute. God alone will act and then manifest his anticipated royal power. It is clear at this point, incidentally, that the translation of βασιλεία as "kingdom"—though well established—is rather unfortunate.[128] The kingly reign of God is to come and to manifest itself to humans.

Occasionally this petition, as well as the preceding one for the hallowing of his name, has been rejected as a word of Jesus, especially by pointing to its radical Jewishness.[129] The Jewish character of the Lord's Prayer is as contested as the observation that the advent of God's kingdom is a recurring feature in Jewish prayers. Yet it is precisely the comparison with materials that appear to be parallel that affords insight into the particular understanding of the reign of God in Jesus' prayer. Thus the eleventh and fourteenth prayers of the Eighteen Benedictions (Shemoneh Esreh), in the (older) Palestinian recension, say:

> Bring again our judges as of old and our governors as in the beginning and be king over us, you alone. . . . Have mercy, Yahweh, our God, on Jerusalem, your city, and on Zion, the dwelling place of your glory, and on the kingdom of the house of David, the anointed of your righteousness.[130]

---

[128] This translation may have come about for reasons of language-related aesthetics, because it allowed the text to be spoken in community with greater ease. The Vulgate translation, *Adveniat regnum tuum!* signals a change of meaning.

[129] So Harnack. In E. Lohmeyer, *Das Vater-Unser* (5th ed.; Göttingen: Vandenhoeck & Ruprecht, 1962) 207. S. v. Tilborg, "A Form-Criticism of the Lord's Prayer," *NovT* 14 (1972) 104f., considers the petition for the hallowing to be secondary. S. Schulz, *Q: Die Spruchquelle der Evangelien* (Zurich: Theologischer, 1972) 87, assigns the Lord's Prayer in its totality to the earliest community of Q in Palestine.

[130] On the translation, cf. Str-B, *Kommentar*, 4.212f.

Whereas the petition for the coming of God's kingdom here is only one petition among others, the Lord's Prayer as a whole is shaped eschatologically. The kingdom petition is central to it. The restoration of conditions of the past, however brilliant its form of expectation might be, is lacking in Jesus. What is conspicuously absent is the national political focus. A reestablished royal throne of David is not in view. This negative finding is characteristic and thus to be taken as support for authenticity. Certainly the kingdom that Jesus expects is primarily focused on Israel, yet ultimately it concerns the earth, humanity.[131]

In the Lord's Prayer the kingdom petition is most directly linked with the petition ἁγιασθήτω τὸ ὄνομά σου (Matt 6:9; Luke 11:2), "hallowed be thy name." Thus the two "you-petitions" can be understood in terms of synthetic parallelism, each explaining the other.[132] In this instance the term "name" is virtually synonymous with "kingdom." The name does not refer back to the name Father in the address of the prayer. In biblical understanding, "name" is synonymous with being. God's name, God's being, is holy, in contrast with what is worldly, creaturely; he is holy in his uncreatedness and in his freedom from sin and darkness, yet veiled and unapproachable in the present. The petition for the hallowing aims at unveiling and revelation. Once again, as in the case of the petition for the coming of the kingdom, the focus is upon an event that is to be expected from God alone, without any human contribution. Linked with the coming of the reign of God, the hallowing of the name sets the theological quality of the former in even bolder relief and perceives it as the great gift to humans. It is indeed important to note that this utterance is part of a prayer. Thus the total focus upon God is particularly clear. The petition for God to hallow his name corresponds not only with the experience of God's hiddenness but also with that of his being reviled and despised.[133] The one who prays feels this painfully and petitions for the coming of the reign of God in salvation and judgment.

---

[131] Authenticity is further supported by the observation that the Easter perspective is not inserted into the Lord's Prayer. This would be expected if it were shaped by the community.

[132] H. Schürmann, *Das Gebet des Herrn* (4th ed.; Freiburg: Herder, 1981) 53, and R. H. Gundry, *Matthew* (Grand Rapids: Eerdmans, 1982) ad loc., want to link the first petition with the address of the prayer. The parallelism militates against this.

[133] This association also applies to the prophet Ezekiel: "I will vindicate the holiness of my great name, which has been profaned among the nations, and which you have profaned among them; and the nations will know that I am the LORD . . . " (36:23; cf. 39:7; 43:7f.).

In conjunction with the so-called entrance sayings, the futurity of God's reign is seen from a different vantage point, as it were. These words enunciate conditions whose fulfillment facilitates entering the kingdom. Transformed by the eschatological Parousia of God, the earth becomes the full realm of salvation, the kingdom of God, into which Jesus promises entrance to those who take heed of his word. The kingdom of God, as the world that is filled with the royal reign of God, is the longed-for goal for which the human being is destined. Entrance sayings that originated with Jesus—subsequently (e.g., Mark 10:15; Matt 5:20) growing in number—are found in Mark 10:25, "It is easier for a camel to go through the eye of a needle than for a rich man to enter the kingdom of God," and in Matt 18:8f., where the summons is to a decisive struggle against offenses.[134] In both instances the vivid and shocking manner of speaking may be used in support of authenticity. The danger of riches and the occasionally curt decisiveness of his directive are likewise characteristic of Jesus' preaching. It warrants attention even when Matt 18:8f. uses "to enter life," rather than "to enter the kingdom." The kingdom of God to be gained by the person grants enduring, ultimate life. The resurrection of the dead is at the threshold of God's kingdom (cf. Luke 11:31f. par.).

Among the candidates whose destiny for the kingdom of God is given preference, there are the poor. This promise is found in the Beatitudes that usher in the extensive instruction (Sermon in the Plain). At this point we are not yet interested in the question of who precisely is meant by the poor, those that hunger, and those that weep, and how precisely these are capable of meeting the conditions for entry. We only highlight the future perspective, which comes to light with particular clarity here as far as the kingdom is concerned. For them, the kingdom of God to be given to them also means that they will be satisfied there and will be able to laugh again (Luke 6:20f.). This concrete description of salvation warrants attention, because it shows consideration for the real misery existing in the world and keenly recognized by Jesus; for him its final abolition is an essential part of the kingdom.

A problematic saying is the prophecy of death that Jesus made at the Last Supper. While the reconstruction might be difficult, he does announce, in any case, that he will no longer be drinking wine, the "fruit of the vine," until that day (so Mark 14:25), until the

---

[134] Matt 18:8f. (cf. Mark 9:43, 45, 47) has a doublet in Matt 5:29f. On the status of the history of the tradition, cf. Gnilka, *Matthäusevangelium,* 1.160 and n. 4. The wording in 18:8f. is more original. Jeremias, *Theology,* 32f., points out that the formulation of "entering the kingdom of God" has no parallels outside the NT.

kingdom of God comes (so Luke 22:18). Even if the direct mention of the kingdom is secondary and the prophecy of death is central, the reflection transcends the dark interval of death and provides insight, as if through a crack, into the future kingdom of God.[135] As in the case of Jewish literature, it is presented as a banquet (cf. Matt 8:11 par.). At the meal Jesus sits at table. By means of this insight, "that day," otherwise the day of judgment (Matt 7:22; Luke 10:12; 17:31; 22:34), takes on clarity, thus fostering confidence.

b) It is necessary to draw attention to some of the parables that traditionally are set in a particular, direct relation to the reign of God and that, as far as their pictorial material is concerned, are drawn largely from the life and work of the Galilean peasant. If we begin by addressing the perhaps too familar parable of the sower (Mark 4:3–8 par.), we do so because of the many questions that burst upon us here, not least precipitated by an intensive discussion in the scholarly re-search, questions that can sharpen our appreciation of the problem. Jesus is hardly ever denied this parable. In terms of its meaning, however, there is absolute confusion. Concerning this narrative Bult-mann said in a resigned way, "Is it a consolation for every man when his labour does not all bear fruit? Is it in this sense a monologue by Jesus, half of resignation, half of thankfulness? Is it an exhortation to the hearers of the divine Word? Of Jesus' preaching? or of the message of the Church? or was there originally no meditation at all on the Word . . . ?"[136] There are authors who think that finding the original meaning of the parable is impossible.[137] The interpretation added to it (Mark 4:13–20 par.) is correctly taken to be secondary.[138] Nevertheless, the parable offers ample indicators.

The story tells of a sower. As far as his part is concerned, the story is content with reporting the sowing of the seed: "A sower went out to sow" (Mark 4:3). He seems to leave the seed to itself. No mention is made of plowing and cultivating. Hence the way he sows

---

[135] In Mark 14:25 the ὅταν clause should be seen as an embellishment. Cf. Gnilka, *Markus*, 2.243; K. Berger, *Die Amen-Worte Jesu* (BZNW 39; Berlin: de Gruyter, 1970) 54f.

[136] Bultmann, *History*, 200.

[137] H.-W. Kuhn, *Ältere Sammlungen im Markusevangelium* (SUNT 8; Göttingen: Vandenhoeck & Ruprecht, 1971) 114 and n. 77; cf. Linnemann, *Parables*, 117.

[138] So Jeremias, *Parables*, 75–77; J. Wellhausen, *Das Evangelium Marci* (2d ed.; Berlin: Georg Reimer, 1909) ad loc. The arguments have been repeated frequently. It is particularly important to point out that, in the interpretation, by means of allegoriz-ing language the parable is raised to a new level of understanding and that the terminology corresponds to the early Christian language of missions.

seems all the stranger, at least to us, the way he apparently carelessly casts the seed on the hard-trodden path, on rocky ground, among the thorns, and finally also on good soil.

The debate is endless about whether this was the way sowing was done then or whether we are here presented with a sower who had two kinds of seed, one that perishes and the other fruit-bearing.[139] Today one opts largely for the former view and rejects almost unanimously—and correctly so—a judgment of obduracy as inherent in the parable. The conclusive answer is that in Israel at that time sowing preceded plowing, and so such loss somehow came about as a matter of course.[140] Nevertheless, we need to realize that the parable is not intended to be understood as instructions for Palestinian agricultural technology.[141] Thus, if the sower's action was comprehensible to the contemporary hearer, two things warrant attention: the emphasis on the loss of seed in the description, and the narrative's movement to the time of the harvest.

In the depiction of the loss of seed we encounter detailed painting with small brush strokes, with possible secondary intensification.[142] The opposing forces are shown vividly: the birds picking up the seed, the sun causing it to be scorched, the thorns choking it. These opposing forces require no allegorizing interpretation. They reflect the experience of being unsuccessful. The train of thought does not stop here, however; rather it continues on to the plentiful harvest with its threefold structure, analogous to the threefold loss: thirtyfold, sixtyfold, and a hundredfold.[143] This optimistic perspec-

---

[139] This view also arose especially on account of the Markan context concerned with the judgment of obduracy (Mark 4:10–12). Cf. H. Windisch, "Die Verstockungsidee in Mc. 4:12 und das kausale ἵνα der späten Koine," *ZNW* 26 (1927) 203–9.

[140] The chief witness for this view is G. Dalman, "Viererlei Acker," *PJ* 22 (1926) 120–32. Yet cf. Dalman, *Arbeit und Sitte*, 2.195: "The fact that careful plowing precedes sowing in the biblical era is established by Isa 28:24f. and is further alluded to in Hos 10:11f., where sowing is mentioned after both methods of plowing." Clearly both types of cultivation were in use, sowing before plowing and plowing before sowing. There also was the method of plowing before and after sowing. Cf. Klauck, *Allegorie,* 189f. G. Lohfink, "Das Gleichnis vom Sämann," *BZ* 30 (1986) 51f., argues for the sower's behavior in the parable as the agricultural norm in the mountainous region of Palestine.

[141] Cf. Klauck, *Allegorie*, 190.

[142] Lohfink, "Gleichnis," 39, considers as secondary the following part of Mark 4:5f.: "where it had not much soil, and immediately it sprang up, since it had no depth of soil . . . it was scorched."

[143] Here, too, there are unending debates about whether the numbers refer to the individual seed or to the overall harvest of the field in which seed has been sown. Regarding the so-called new shoots, Lohfink, "Gleichnis," 52–57, has furnished considerable support again in favor of the former.

tive of the harvest refers to the reign of God. Yet the message of Jesus' parable cannot be reduced to the assurance that the reign of God is coming—who would have doubted it?—rather it links its coming with what is happening now. What is taking place now may not be limited to Jesus' preaching but may nevertheless be seen as summarized in his word.[144] His word will prove fruitful when the reign of God emerges unveiled. The loss of seed stands out against the expected harvest. The apparent insignificance of what transpires in the present is not linked with the harvest, as in other seed parables. This lends the loss its unique significance. Yet this is not to hide the fact that the future has already begun.[145]

In other parables, juxtaposing beginning and end of the reign of God may be done by means of other pictures. Among them are the parables of the mustard seed and the leaven, both of which were linked in a double parable already in the sayings source (Luke 13:18–21; Matt 13:31–33; Mark 4:30–32). They were well suited for a link like this, since the one addresses the experiential domain of the man who works the field, while the other addresses the experiential domain of the woman who prepares bread.[146] Determined by the issue and appearing almost grotesque, the narrative speaks of *one* mustard seed which is sown in the field, on the ground (Matt/Mark), in the garden (Luke). The differentiations, which may well have occurred already in the oral transmission, have to do with the fact that the mustard—presumably the black mustard used as a kitchen herb—was considered partly a field plant and partly a garden plant. Its growth, given its minuteness, is proverbial; it grows into a tree (Matt/Luke), "the greatest of all shrubs" (Mark). The birds of the air that can now make nests in its branches (allusion to Ezek 17:23; 31:6; Dan 4:9, 18) may be considered part of the early content of the parable, since there is no evidence of a

---

[144] Thus the secondary interpretation could make the word its point of departure. As far as the characteristics of the picture are concerned, there are diverse possibilities of application for sowing and reaping. Cf. Klauck, *Allegorie,* 192–96.
[145] Somewhat different emphases are provided by H. Frankemölle, "Hat Jesus sich selbst verkündet?" *BibLeb* 13 (1972) 184–207, who stressed the personal plight of the sower; C. Dietzfelbinger, "Das Gleichnis vom ausgestreuten Samen," 80–93 in *Der Ruf Jesu und die Antwort der Gemeinde* (FS J. Jeremias; Göttingen, 1970), who emphasized the threat to Jesus' mission; and B. Gerhardsson, "The Parable of the Sower and Its Interpretation," *NTS* 14 (1967–68) 165–93, and Lohfink, "Gleichnis," 63–66, both of whom establish the link with the people of God, albeit in quite different ways.
[146] The association has led to parallelizing. The impersonal introduction in Mark 4:31, "a grain of mustard seed, which, when sown upon the ground," may be construed as the older version. On the reconstruction, cf. Gnilka, *Matthäusevangelium,* 1.494f.

direct citation, and applying excisions to the parable too boldly may reduce its vitality to a skeleton.[147]

Once more the aim of the story is the complete reign of God—the tree with its large branches. It is to be observed, however, that its inception is already given now, in the ministry of Jesus. The beginning is established, regardless of how insignificant, indeed how minute, it might appear. It guarantees the end, just as a plant grows organically. Inherent in it is an unstoppable dynamic. The growth and the mature tree do not have the church in view, or indeed its continued expansion. The relationship between the people of God and the reign of God is yet to be discussed. It is to be noted, however, that the two entities are not synonymous. The birds' making nests in the top of the tree may point to the eschatological coming of the nations and their incorporation in the ultimate reign of God.

Something quite analogous is communicated by the parable of the leaven. A pinch of leaven is sufficient to permeate a large measure of flour, namely, three seahs (about 40 liters). Jesus may have used the image of the leaven, otherwise almost exclusively used negatively as a metaphor of corrosive power (cf. 1 Cor 5:6ff.; Gal 5:9), in the positive sense in order to shock or to rouse.

The same theme of beginning and end that characterizes and links these parables, and confirms their authenticity, appears again under yet another aspect in a further group of parables. In terms of content and structure the parables of the fishing net and the weeds among the wheat (Matt 13:47–50, 24–30) are closely related and have frequently been treated as a double parable. Both have to do with success and failure, fruit and fruitlessness being in close proximity and mingled. In the case of the one, the extensive net draws all kinds of fish to the shore, a process that could be seen regularly at Lake Gennesaret. In the case of the other, the mixture is more dramatic, more cunning. At night an enemy sows weeds upon a field in which good wheat had been sown. The weed is exactly identified, and it is precisely this that denotes the narrative's cunning. The enemy sowed ζιζάνια, darnel, resembling wheat so closely that even the eye of the expert is hardly able to distinguish it from the wheat until the ear develops. The original purpose of these parables was not to describe the judgment; that came about on a secondary level.[148] These stories

---

[147] Otherwise, e.g., Klauck, *Allegorie,* 212f.

[148] In the parable of the weeds this shift was due to the secondary interpretation (Matt 13:36–43). This is also true of the parable of the net (13:49f.). Matthew emphasizes the idea of judgment time and again; in this instance he may have

do not focus on the judgment, nor on the separation of the good fish from the bad, nor on the harvest, but rather on the preceding period, the present. The present is the time of gathering, of sowing and allowing growth. A premature intervention in this process is rejected: "Let both grow together until the harvest" (13:30). Now is the time of decision. The present is under the influence of the future, a distressing future. Yet the emphasis is not upon the latter but upon the present made possible by the future. To comprehend the future, to make the right decision in view of the future, means to gain time, to gain the future. In terms of the meaning of the reign of God, this means that it is already here and eschatologically imminent. In the future it will be revealed eschatologically and ultimately, yet in the ministry of Jesus it already qualifies the present and in the present is attacked, fought against, rejected, and calls upon the individual to take a position. In terms of the theme of the delay, the problem of time plays no significant part in the parables. Hence this is no reason not to attribute them to Jesus.[149]

There is a short parable expressing confidence, almost provocatively so, that still needs to be recalled, a parable that has been given many names: the parable of the seed growing of itself, of the patient farmer, of the seed corn (Mark 4:26–29). Only Mark contains it, while Luke did not incorporate it and Matthew replaced it with the parable of the weeds, presumably because they considered it to be too shallow. For a Galilean peasant it narrates the most obvious thing in the world, the process of the ripening of the seed.

"The kingdom of God is as if a man should scatter seed upon the ground, and should sleep and rise night and day, and the seed should sprout and grow, he knows not how. The earth produces of itself, first the blade, then the ear, then the full grain in the ear. But when the grain is ripe, at once he puts in the sickle, because the harvest has come."

Despite the fact that the event is natural and common, for the person of the Bible it conceals something unpenetrable, something bordering on a mystery. The process of ripening takes place of itself.

---

depended on an apocalyptic tradition with the following features: mission of the angels of judgment at the end of time, separation of the wicked from the righteous and their punishment/reward. Cf. Theison, *Richter;* see bib. p. 141, 191.

[149] Cf. E. Grässer, *Das Problem der Parousieverzögerung in den synoptischen Evangelien und in der Apostelgeschichte* (2d ed.; BZNW 22; Berlin: Töpelmann, 1960) 147. The parable of the weed originally ended with v. 30a: "Let both grow together until the harvest." On this issue, cf. Gnilka, *Matthäusevangelium,* 1.489f., 492f. In this parable only the surprise effect associated with the discovery of the weeds, i.e., of evil, could point to the later situation of the community.

In contrast, the farmer is presented in exaggerated sharpness; with the sowing completed he seems to be released from all duties. He sleeps, awakens, and expectantly awaits the grain. Once again the element of time afforded by the coming *basileia* is featured here, not elastic time but time given as a gift. This time is filled with the assurance that God's reign is present and will soon unfold in a harvest.[150] Precisely the dominant feature of freedom from care is a further argument that we are here confronted with a word that originated with Jesus.[151]

c) There is a logion, characterized entirely by the reign of God, in which Jesus sketches his relationship with John the Baptist and especially the time since then, the time in which he is working, describing it as a time pervaded by the *basileia*. In its reconstruction, the double and differing tradition in Matt 11:12f. and Luke 16:16 is disputed. Its succinctness and terseness contribute to the fact that it has almost become a riddle for interpreters. What is undisputed, however, is that it deals with the reign of God that is already becoming effective. The underlying reconstruction essentially allows for two translations for the second part:

1. "The law and the prophets were until John. From then until now the reign of God suffers violence, and men of violence oppress it."

2. "Since then the reign of God approaches violently, and the resolute seize it."[152]

The ambivalence in the translation has to do with the double meaning of the Greek terms βιάζεται (exercise force, enter by force) and βιασταί (violent, resolute persons). If the interpretation reflects the first meaning, the present reign of God appears to be threatened and combated by its adversaries. If one opts for the second meaning, it succeeds victoriously, longing to be recognized and confirmed by resolute humans. For Jesus the second perspective is more to the

---

[150] The question whether v. 29 was part of the parable from the start is disputed. Joel 3:13 has the following saying: "Put in the sickle, for the harvest is ripe." This citation follows the Masoretic Text but has taken on a new meaning. Joel announced the judgment of wrath, while in the parable the saying is a shout of joy.

[151] J. Wellhausen's interpretation is erroneous; cf. *Evangelium Marci,* ad loc. He appeals to a saying from J. W. von Goethe for support, "Time is my field." Here the eschatological dimension is played down completely, and the parable dissolved in an ethical maxim.

[152] In the second part Matt 11:12 has preserved the wording better. Luke 16:16 brings to bear his favorite term, εὐαγγελίζεται. On the complex analysis, cf. Gnilka, *Matthäusevangelium,* 1.412f.; Merklein, *Gottesherrschaft,* 88; Hoffmann, *Studien,* 53ff., who arrives at a different conclusion.

point. He is confident. He sees the ultimate, victorious success of the *basileia;* yet he also expects his hearers to orient their lives without compromise in the new situation.[153] Noteworthy in this logion is the relation of John the Baptist to Jesus, which is expressed in such a way that it does not precisely define his role as a forerunner. Had this saying been formulated later, that association might have been expected.

One makarism related to the presence of the time of Jesus is addressed to the disciples in both Matt 13:16f. and Luke 10:23f., although originally it may well have addressed a broader audience. We assume that its earliest wording was as follows: "Blessed are the eyes that see what you see and the ears that hear what you hear, for I say to you, many prophets and kings longed to see what you see, and did not see it, and to hear what you hear, and did not hear it."[154]

The significance of the present is to be gauged by its fulfillment of past longings. Prophets and kings are representatives of Israel's longing for salvation, of the prospect of messianic salvation; foremost among the kings was David, who was deemed the author of the book of Psalms. The seeing and hearing that are now possible refer to Jesus' deeds and words, which have to be recognized in terms of their eschatological quality, of course. When the eyewitnesses and earwitnesses of his deeds and words are declared blessed, the reference is to those who have truly come to see and hear. In the final analysis the reference is once again to the reign of God that is already present in Jesus, though it is not mentioned explicitly. This indicates the close relationship between the present *basileia* and Jesus' deed and word; hence the christological implication in a saying such as this. Already it can be seen, in regard to the christological question yet to be posed, that the *basileia* and Jesus' relationship to it represent an important link. Ultimately the makarism is meaningful and reasonable only as a saying spoken during the time of his ministry.

Finally, the future kingdom and its impact upon the present is also addressed in two parables closely related in content, the parable of the treasure in the field and that of the pearl merchant, which

---

[153] Matthew, on the other hand, may have understood the saying in the negative sense mentioned first. This is indicated by the context into which he places it: The Baptist has been imprisoned (11:2), and the parable of the quarrelling children reflects the stubbornness and disobedience of this generation.

[154] Matthew refers to many prophets and righteous ones and, by means of δίκαιοι, takes up one of the important terms for his theology. The causal addition, "because seeing . . . hear," is likewise adapted to the context. Cf. Matt 13:13; Gnilka, *Matthäusevangelium,* 1.480.

Matthew presents as a double parable. While plowing a field he does not own, a certain man, a day laborer, unexpectedly uncovers a treasure. A merchant of pearls, preoccupied with his collector's passion, discovers a particularly lovely pearl (Matt 13:44–46). Both are ready to act decisively. Both risk everything to gain what they discovered. They are not filled with a sacrificial spirit but with joy. It is easy to observe that both of these compelling stories depict the kingdom as God's great gift, now offered and affirmed to humans and to be seized as that which surpasses everything else in terms of value.[155] In the parable of the treasure the kingdom virtually becomes the decisive vehicle of action, triggering by itself, as it were, the day laborer's reaction. God's action, to be experienced already, changes the people. In the story of the pearl merchant the kingdom is also present as agent, though the pondering merchant is somewhat more prominent here.

If we briefly survey the parabolic utterances, as well as those of the illustration and sayings type, concerning the reign of God, we notice their twofold temporal dimension. Both future and present are focused on it, or in other words, it is focused on the future and present. To be sure, the future and the present are not to be played off against one another, nor are they to be turned into the criterion of authenticity by arguing that only sayings about the future or only those about the present can lay claim to authenticity. One of the characteristics of Jesus' kingdom preaching may be recognized in precisely this combination. There are sayings of Jesus that focus more directly on the future or on the present. There are also those, however, that address future and present equally; the number of the latter predominates. On account of the *basileia* the present becomes future-oriented and the future takes on meaning for the present, so that within this framework it is less significant whether there is more emphasis on the future at one point and on the present at another. The only important matter is to recognize the trajectory ranging from the present to the future. It is indeed appropriate to speak of a tension here since, in the view of many contemporaries, the depiction of the kingdom as present in Jesus' ministry did not measure up to what they expected it to be. In the context of its depiction Jesus likewise maintains the tension of the small, seemingly insignificant beginning and the great final fulfillment. Against this backdrop it is necessary now to raise the issue of the imminence of the kingdom.

---

[155] Cf. Jüngel, *Paulus und Jesus,* 143f.; Weder, *Gleichnisse,* 140.

How near is the *basileia*? Is it feasible to postulate announcements of a specific time as a response to a question such as this? Are they specific for Jesus at all, or are they part of another, changed perspective in the orientation?

d) Nearness and nearness with a specific date are not the same. For something to be near does not mean the same as something coming true at the agreed point in time. In the case of the former, nearness is open to time *and* space. In the case of the latter, it is strictly bound up with time, a specific time. What has been said thus far about time, about past and present in their relationship to the kingdom, has to be extended further to the idea of nearness.

Jesus spoke about the nearness of the *basileia*. What is urgent in this advancing situation he articulated in images, especially those describing the judgment, the test still to come; we will have to come back to these. The nearness is a factor of his kingdom proclamation that cannot be bracketed out. The summary of his proclamation in Mark 1:15 expresses this programmatically: "The time is fulfilled, and the kingdom of God is at hand; repent, and believe in the gospel." Though today we assume that this text, written in summary form, is the work of Mark the evangelist, who picked up elements of the later Palestinian and Hellenistic missionary proclamation,[156] he nevertheless pinpointed Jesus' salient concerns and continued especially the nearness of the reign of God.

In a few of the logia the nearness is observed not only as temporally very near but also as predictable. This is true of three logia that will be examined briefly at this point. Mark 13:30 says, "Truly, I say to you, this generation will not pass away before all these things take place."[157] This saying is part of the "synoptic apocalypse," providing instruction for the period of time leading to the end, which is presented as visible and structured. This apocalyptic text is

---

[156] The expression "to proclaim the Gospel of God" is in keeping with the Hellenistic missionary proclamation (cf. 1 Thess 2:9; Gal 2:2). The proclamation of the nearness of the reign of God has its origin in the Palestinian tradition (Matt 10:7; Luke 10:9). Jesus presupposes the nearness of God's intervention. Whether or not the expression "the kingdom of God is at hand" can be traced back to him is a matter of dispute. It is given a favorable assessment in Merklein, *Gottesherrschaft*, 35. It should be noted that Luke 10:9 (ἤγγικεν ἐφ' ὑμᾶς) and Mark 1:15 presuppose that the kingdom begins to be realized from this point on, that is, beginning with Jesus' ministry. In Mark this is conveyed by means of "The time is fulfilled."

[157] Essentially the parallels, Matt 24:34 and Luke 21:32, have not changed the saying. Luke has "till all has taken place." Of course the logion takes on other nuances in different contexts.

based on a little apocalypse that had its origin in Jewish Christian circles and was particularly relevant against the historical background of the Jewish War and the destruction of Jerusalem and the temple.[158] This logion cannot be attributed to Jesus.

The second logion says, "When they persecute you in one town, flee to the next; for truly, I say to you, you will not have gone through all the towns of Israel, before the Son of man comes" (Matt 10:23). Today this logion, too, is almost unanimously attributed to the post-Easter context.[159] It presupposes the post-Easter mission to Israel, as well as the rigorous persecution of the missionaries who are to be comforted with the promise of the expected Son of man; in other words, despite all opposition, they are to be encouraged not to flag in their missionary task to Israel.

The assessment of the third saying is more difficult: "Truly, I say to you, there are some standing here who will not taste death before they see the kingdom of God come with power" (Mark 9:1). The color of the language of this saying is Jewish as well. The fixed-time announcement foretells its advent for this generation, and to that extent its content agrees with Mark 13:30. Since those addressed are not particular persons, for instance specific disciples, but more generally simply some who happened to be "standing here," the focus is on the setting of the date. The intention is not to provide someone with a personal promise (cf. John 21:22f.). This saying, too, can hardly be traced back to Jesus. It could be argued that precisely its strong temporal structure, which quickly evoked attempts at toning it down, suggests authenticity.[160] Ultimately, however, it is the reference to the predictability of the nearness, entirely in keeping with apocalyptic thought but hardly conforming to Jesus' kingdom proclamation, that hardly leaves us with any alternative to locating

---

[158] Cf. E. Brandenburger, *Markus 13 und die Apokalyptik* (FRLANT 134; Göttingen: Vandenhoeck & Ruprecht, 1984) 21–42; R. Pesch, *Naherwartungen* (KBANT; Düsseldorf: Patmos Verlag 1968) 207–33. The precise reconstruction of the exemplar is controversial.

[159] Perhaps it even belongs to the Matthean redaction. Cf. Gnilka, *Matthäusevangelium,* 1.374f. H. Schürmann, "Zur Traditions und Redaktionsgeschichte von Mt. 10:23," *BZ* 3 (1959) 82–88, wants to attribute it to the sayings source. A. Schweitzer, *Quest,* 357–60, used this logion as a central point in his eschatological interpretation of the life of Jesus. This is completely outdated, however.

[160] The parallels, Matt 16:28 and Luke 9:27, reinterpret the saying. Mark's interpretation is contextual. Presumably he considered it fulfilled in Jesus' transfiguration on the mountain, before the three chosen disciples. On the arduous history of interpretation of this logion, cf. M. Künzi, *Das Naherwartungslogion Markus 9:1 par.: Geschichte seiner Auslegung* (BGBE 21; Tübingen: J. C. B. Mohr, 1977).

the origin of this disputed saying in the post-Easter Jewish Christian community in Palestine.[161]

As a countermove and counterargument against these predictive references, Luke 17:20f. contains an observation that rejects the predictability of the *basileia*'s advent. The reign of God does not come μετὰ παρατηρήσεως, Jesus says in response to some Pharisees' request for a date. In secular Greek the term παρατήρησις, occurring only there in the NT, can refer to observing stars, symptoms, and signs signaling the future.[162] As a saying of Jesus it is directed against the notion, capable of escalating even to naïveté, that the advent of the future reign of God is plainly visible and can be calculated reliably in advance.[163]

If we assume that Jesus refused to pinpoint the time of the coming of his kingdom,[164] what did he understand by nearness? Two aspects need to be considered in response. For one, we have already seen that the concept of the "reign of God" conceals God's action. For another, the announcement of its nearness, which was given in numerous figures, implies an inward certainty. The result of combining both aspects is that the focus of the inward certainty is upon God's (prior) action. H. Merklein described this very appropriately as God's resolve in salvation.[165] Jesus was convinced of God's resolve in salvation. Hence Jesus himself becomes the guarantor of God's resolve in the eschatological salvation. Thus we begin to grasp that he announced not merely the eschatological reign of God to come but that this future reign of God could already be experienced and was present in his ministry and in his message.

This is also the premise for its nearness. The certainty of the nearness of God's reign is based on the fact that what is essentially future, the future itself, has already become present. The tension

---

[161] For Grässer, *Parousieverzögerung*, 133, this is a post-Easter logion because it reflects the problem of the delay of the Parousia. The experience of the revelation of God's reign is afforded to only a few, no longer to everyone. The influence of the eschatologists can hardly be missed in this interpretation.

[162] On the documentation, see BAGD (2d rev. ed., Chicago: University of Chicago, 1979) s.v.

[163] Luke 17:20b is surely part of the early rendition of the logion. Verse 21b ("the kingdom of God is in the midst of you"), which has triggered considerable discussion, is Lukan redaction. Luke moves away from the expectation of the future *basileia* to an active personal engagement. Cf. G. Schneider, *Das Evangelium nach Lukas* (2 vols.; 2d ed.; Gütersloh: Mohn, 1984) 2.305.

[164] This is stated explicitly in Mark 13:32 as well. Yet this expression is possibly part of the Markan redaction. Cf. Gnilka, *Markus*, 2.204f.

[165] Merklein, *Gottesherrschaft*, 157.

between the present and the future is not yet resolved. Nevertheless, the presence of the future in the present anticipates the nearness of the future.

Overview

Here we can only touch upon the beginnings of developments in the proclamation of the kingdom. We limit our attempt to the Gospels. A line of development has already been indicated, namely, the attempt to pinpoint the time of the advent of the *basileia* more precisely. Linked with it is the attempt to provide an overview of the brief time still to come and to come to grips with it, as it were. In this process the apocalyptic element penetrates the Jesus tradition more strongly. The synoptic apocalypse (Mark 13 par.) provides a vivid example of this. The experience of Easter is linked with another shift, which emerges more clearly in the Epistles. There the issue is not only the reign of God but also the reign of Christ, which he gained through the cross, the resurrection, and the exaltation. The presentation of the concept is diverse and leads to new eschatological conceptions. Among the Synoptics only Matthew offers an analogous idea, which he calls the reign of the Son of man (Matt 13:41; 16:28; 20:21) and which encompasses a universal reign. Conversely, in the Gospel of John, where the proclamation of the reign of God recedes significantly (only in 3:3, 5), Christ's *basileia* is not of this world (18:36). Embedded in Johannine dualism, his universal power appears in powerlessness.

Select bibliography: R. Bultmann, "Die Interpretation von Mk 4,3–9 seit Jülicher," 30–34 in *Jesus und Paulus* (FS W. G. Kümmel; Göttingen: Vandenhoeck & Ruprecht, 1975); G. Lohfink, "Das Gleichnis vom Sämann," *BZ* 30 (1986) 36–69; E. Lohmeyer, *Das Vater-Unser* (5th ed.; Göttingen: Vandenhoeck & Ruprecht, 1962); J. M. McDermott, "Mt 10,23 in Context," *BZ* 28 (1984), 230–40; H. Schürmann, *Das Gebet des Herrn* (4th ed.; Freiburg: Herder, 1981); J. Theison, *Der auserwählte Richter* (SUNT 12; Göttingen: Vandenhoeck & Ruprecht, 1975); S. v. Tilborg, "A Form-Criticism of the Lord's Prayer," *NovT* 14 (1972), 94–105; A. N. Wilder, "The Parable of the Sower: Naiveté and Method in Interpretation," *Semeia* 2 (1974) 134–51.

5. Reign of God and judgment

Only at this point are we able to speak about judgment. In no wise can the topic of judgment be excluded from Jesus' preaching. But it needs to be fitted in at the right place. The announcement of judgment, too, is oriented to the reign of God and cannot be divorced from it. The notion of judgment provides the reign of God with seriousness, ultimate obligation, urgency. Without the judgment it would remain hanging in the balance, not taken seriously.

For this reason, in a sense, the reign of God has two aspects, salvation and judgment. Nevertheless, in Jesus' proclamation the aspect of salvation is dominant. Salvation is the aspect of the *basileia* that faces people. Quantitative measuring or counting of expressions of salvation and judgment may not be appropriate. What matters is the weighting, for it determines the relationship of salvation and judgment. Salvation is the primary aspect; it is the offer that has been made and is being realized. The judgment is the loss of salvation as a result of not receiving salvation, of not accepting but rejecting the message. In the case of the individual's refusal, it is an unintended consequence of salvation, as it were. To the extent that the possibilities of salvation and judgment, acceptance and refusal, are postulated, this combination accords with common human experience. On the various levels of human existence both are generally experienced: fulfillment and loss, meaning and futility, greatness and emptiness. Yet on the level of the *basileia* the alternative is given ultimate binding force. Human existence in its totality is challenged.

The term "judgment" has several nuances. This is even more the case with the corresponding Greek term κρίσις. Among the important nuanced meanings of interest to us are the following: decision, separation, trial, legal investigation, verdict, punishment.[166] By means of a few sample texts from Jesus' proclamation we shall describe his understanding of *krisis*.

The alternative of salvation or judgment emerges in the brief parable of the flood, which was attached to the conclusion of the didactic discourse to the disciples (already in the logia source; cf. Matt 7:24–27; Luke 6:47–49). The alternative is shown in the skill of a builder who does his work carefully or carelessly, and thus the individual's responsibility for judgment and salvation is stressed. Since the bad result concludes the story, judgment is the more important idea in this parable.

While Matthew and Luke agree in terms of an underlying structure that can easily be recognized, they disagree in the details. In Matthew the two builders build upon the rock or upon sand. According to Luke the one builds his house upon a foundation, while the other foregoes a foundation. Presumably Matthew comes closer to the situation in the Galilean hills and thus, presumably, to Jesus,

---

[166] Cf. Passow, *Handwörterbuch*, s.v.

whereas Luke more likely has an urban setting in mind.[167] Matthew describes the testing and the catastrophe more vividly: "and the rain fell, and the floods came, and the winds blew and beat against that house, and it fell; and great was the fall of it."[168]

In this picture the person hearing and doing Jesus' words and the person not doing, though hearing, them are set in contrast. The pressing thing in this contrast is that there is hardly any doubt that it depicts the imminent, eschatological judgment, which elsewhere is seen as analogous to the flood (Matt 24:38f. par.).[169] Hence judgment is the crucial deciding factor in response to Jesus' words. Failing at the judgment is the consequence of obedience spurned. The result is ruin, as reflected in a possible translation of the Greek term used for the fall of the house built upon sand (Matt 7:27—πτῶσις). The words of Jesus, the message of the *basileia*, establish the criterion for this *krisis*. They are decisive for the individual's salvation and ruin, albeit in such a way that the one rejecting salvation ruins himself, as it were. Jesus is speaking about his own words. Especially in its focus on the imminent judgment, this formulation insures authenticity.

Judgment, however, is also the separation of persons on account of the end breaking in suddenly and unexpectedly. In that night two will be in one bed; one will be taken and the other left (Luke 17:34f.). There will be no escape for the unsuspecting and unprepared. The idea of the coming of the end at night could show that it will be a surprise for many.[170]

The element of surprise and the nighttime are linked in the portrait of the nocturnal burglar, whose coming the householder should anticipate so that he does not let his house be broken into. The uncertainty of the night-watch, that is, of the hour in which the thief is coming, has nothing to do yet with the problem of the delay of the Parousia; rather it intends to arouse a public that is dulled and entangled in its earthly affairs (Matt 24:43 par.).[171]

Something similar occurs in the picture of going to court (Matt 5:25f.; Luke 12:58f.). In a sense the topic of judgment is being

---

[167] Cf. Schürmann, *Lukasevangelium*, 1.382f.

[168] According to Luke the threat was due to flood waters. Hence the house is in the vicinity of a river.

[169] Those who take the image to refer to any repetitive threat rob it of its decisive eschatological emphasis.

[170] The parallel, Matt 24:40, which is perhaps secondary, speaks of two men working in the field.

[171] In Israel the night was divided into three watches, while the Romans had four (cf. Mark 13:35b).

addressed on two levels here, a factor that has been aptly described as evidence for Jesus' way of speaking.[172] To begin with, we hear of two people quarrelling who are en route together to court, perhaps to Jerusalem. Yet one of them is hopelessly in a weaker position than the other because he owes him money and apparently has not yet repaid it. The initial counsel, given on this level of judgment, to get free from him, to attain an agreement with him while still on the way, comes against the gloomy backdrop of the debtor's prison. No one handed over to it had a chance to get out without first paying off the debt in full.[173] The saying touches the second level of judgment, namely, that of the—imminent—divine judgment, by means of the solemn formulation that breaks open human conditions: "truly, I say to you, you will never get out . . . " What follows from this for the understanding of judgment is the pressing nearness, the inexorable advance of the hour of judgment. As far as the issue of time is concerned, it is characteristic for Jesus' proclamation of the kingdom that the time factor of the intensive nearness is prominent in the judgment sayings. This is not due as much to the subject matter itself as to a pedagogical purpose appearing almost of itself. The nearness of the reign of God as the fullness of salvation was less motivating than the announcement of the imminent judgment. Yet the latter could not be concealed, because salvation was already present in Jesus. Therefore one could be and ought to be deeply stirred, in the brief period of time, while still on the way, for salvation would be withdrawn in the hour of judgment.[174] Hence the image of going to court does not represent instruction about the execution of judgment but an incisive call to repentance.

In the parables the master and householder or slave appear in juxtaposition quite frequently. This, too, is related to the notion of judgment. The situation of a householder who has been put in charge of something, such as an estate, a vineyard, or monetary wealth, fits excellently in describing the human situation before God. The householder

---

[172] U. Luz, *Das Evangelium nach Matthäus* (2d ed.; Zurich: Benziger, 1989) 1.252.

[173] Imprisonment for debt and debtor's prison are foreign to Jewish law but were firmly established in the Greco-Roman legal domain. Familiarity with it can be assumed for Jesus' audience. For details, cf. L. Mitteis and U. Wilcken, *Grundzüge und Chrestomathie* (2 vols.; 1912; reprint, Hildesheim: Olms, 1963) 1.44–46. On the reconstruction of the saying in Matt 5:25f. par., cf. Gnilka, *Matthäusevangelium,* 1.152.

[174] M. Reiser, *Die Gerichtspredigt Jesu* (NTA 23; Münster: Aschendorff, 1990) 277, wants to set the opponent in the saying in parallel with Jesus and argues for the old notion of God's lawsuit against his people being taken up here. This explanation goes too far. The association with Jesus' ministry is granted, however.

is accountable to his master, just as the human being is to God. In this respect this metaphorical element already clarifies with urgency the situation of the person in his earthly life. It clarifies for him that he is not the sole master of his life, but that life represents something entrusted to him. Even though this insight might be meaningful already, it is in the framework of Jesus' proclamation of the *basileia* that it gains its special profile. Further, the possession by foreign masters of large estates in Galilee, entrusted to administrators, belonged to the metaphors of a world familiar to the hearers. It goes without saying that the existence of masters and slaves was a matter of course for the society of antiquity. There is no doubt that Jesus used the metaphorical terminology of master, householder, and slave.

To be sure, there is no room for the misconception that, by speaking of masters and slaves with apparent ease, Jesus approved of this oppressive societal structure in antiquity. We shall be seeing shortly that apparently with equal ease he wove the fiscal behavior of knowledgeable banking experts into his parables. The synoptic parables certainly also contain what could be called "immorality"; one need only consider the parables of the unrighteous judge and of the dishonest steward (Luke 18:1–8; 16:1–8). This means that in the parables people were able to rediscover themselves, their conditions of life, their situation. Paradigmatically, however, the parables shed light on these conditions of life in view of the kingdom of God.

From among the parables of stewardship we select that of the talents (Matt 25:14–30; Luke 19:12–27), which in its history of transmission underwent further development in several respects until it received its fixed written form by the evangelists. Nevertheless, its basic original form can be reconstructed fairly well and can be traced back to Jesus, especially since we rediscover the already familiar element of time in it. To begin with, the individual's accountability in God's coming judgment may be seen as its message in general terms; it tells of a man who went on a journey and entrusted three of his slaves with differing sums of money with which they were to work. They are given minas—the mina is a monetary unit of one hundred denarii; under discussion probably were five, two, and one minas.[175] In Matthew the entrusted sum of

---

[175] According to Luke everyone receives a mina, i.e., the same amount. This may represent an alteration, for even in Luke the first of the slaves presents ten minas (ten talents in Matthew) at the end. The intensification of one to ten, however, is coarser than that of a doubling. What is coarser tends to be more recent. Cf. Jülicher, *Gleichnisreden,* 2.493f.

money is escalated to enormous proportions, namely, to five, two, and one talents (one talent = sixty minas),[176] which (secondarily) is an intended exaggeration of the scope of the responsibility taken on. The story by Jesus took place in humbler conditions. The successful trading of the first two slaves is contrasted with that of the third one, whose behavior focused on assumed security and who kept the mina in his napkin (Luke 19:20). When giving an account before the master who returned, the two who proved themselves are promoted, whereas the third, who merely kept the mina, has to hand it over to the first one.

The emphasis of Jesus' story is not on the execution of judgment. This shift does not begin until later.[177] The emphasis is on the time preceding the judgment. This time is easily comprehensible, even if it has been identified—perhaps already by Jesus—as a long time (Matt 25:19). More important, it is a qualified time, characterized by the powers of God's reign already at work within it, which occupies and obligates the people who hear and know about it. Living by consciously drawing upon the salvific powers of the reign of God means to make one's abilities available, to change one's life, to live purposefully. As demonstrated in the example of the third slave, emphatically placed at the end, it does not mean to let time pass by and to live as if time had not changed. Procuring false security, deduced from an erroneous assessment of time, is foolish and thoughtless, as is keeping a sum of money in a napkin.

"Turn in the account of your stewardship" is the master's demand in the parable of the dishonest steward, when the latter is found out to have been dishonest in dealing with the goods entrusted to him. The reaction of the accused, given very little time to secure his own future and forced to act swiftly, is astounding and appears offensive because he chooses deceptive wheeling and dealing (Luke 16:1–8). The steward commands two of his master's debtors to falsify their bills very much in their favor.[178] The purpose of taking this irregular step is to

---

[176] In this case we assume the smaller Attic talent.

[177] In Luke 19:12ff. this shift is achieved by inserting the story of the pretender to the throne, from which one is not to derive an independent parable fused with the parable of the entrusted moneys; rather it is possible to detect in it an allusion to Archelaus's journey to Rome in 4 BCE. M. Zerwick, "Die Parabel vom Thronan-wärter," *Bib* 40 (1959) 654–74, argues for an independent parable. On the analysis, cf. Gnilka, *Matthäusevangelium,* 2.356–58; H. Weder, *Die Gleichnisse Jesu als Metaphern* (FRLANT 120; Göttingen: Vandenhoeck & Ruprecht, 1978) 193–202.

[178] What is waived are fifty baths of oil and twenty cors of wheat. It is very plausible that this represents a gift of equal value to both, since wheat was more

obtain the willingness of those favored in this manner to provide assistance to the steward, who surmises he will be removed from his post and face an uncertain future. When the master lauds the steward for his shrewdness and cunning at the end, this conclusion remains by all means within the framework of the story. Cheated by the shrewd action of his subordinate, the master's praise certainly exceeds what is realistically conceivable and causes the story to become a humorous tale.[179] The scope of the story is missed and its humor removed if one tries to transform the steward's fraudulent behavior into lawful behavior, if one entertains the notion that the steward merely chose to forego part of his rightful share of the business.[180] Applied to the kingdom of God, the parable expresses the importance of doing everything quickly to gain the future determined by the *basileia*. What is paradigmatic here, of course, is not the craftiness but rather the decisiveness and determination of the steward's action. Once again it is the present shaped by the future, the time to be gained, the tense nearness of what is still to come, that support the idea that we are dealing with a parable of Jesus.

If we recall the parable of the unforgiving servant (Matt 18:23–35), which has already been addressed, there is agreement here with the story of the dishonest steward inasmuch as the former narrative—in our opinion—only approaches the execution of the judgment, focuses upon the time ahead, and wants to make clear what is necessary for this final, qualified time: "and should not you have had mercy on your fellow servant, as I had mercy on you?" (v. 33).

Hence what is characteristic for Jesus' proclamation of judgment in the instances cited is that he foregoes a description of the execution of judgment, although he reckons with it, that he is, rather, concerned with showing, by means of seriousness and humor, by making use of tangible experiences and pictures, the requirements of the time moving toward the judgment in order to motivate people to suitable behavior.

Did Jesus address the possibility of an individual's eternal punishment, of hell, which in biblical terminology was known as the

---

valuable than oil. In this case the steward would have acted cunningly as well, for he would have prevented the debtors from feeling they received unequal treatment.

[179] Heininger, *Metaphorik,* 167–77, has brought this out remarkably well. The parable concludes with v. 8a. Heininger does take vv. 3f., the steward's monologue, as Lukan redaction. If so, the question needs to be asked whether the story loses its comprehensibility.

[180] So, e.g., J. Fitzmyer, *The Gospel according to Luke* (2 vols.; AB; New York: Doubleday, 1981–85) 2.1098.

valley of the sons of Hinnom, where dreadful child sacrifices had been made to Molech (2 Kgs 23:10; 16:3; 21:6; Jer 7:32ff.; 19:6)? Authentic documentation is quite sparse. In this category belongs the following series of sayings concerning offense:

"And if your hand causes you to sin, cut it off; it is better for you to enter life maimed than with two hands to go to hell, to the unquenchable fire.

"And if your foot causes you to sin, cut it off; it is better for you to enter life lame than with two feet to be thrown into hell.

"And if your eye causes you to sin, pluck it out; it is better for you to enter the kingdom of God with one eye than with two eyes to be thrown into hell" (Mark 9:43, 45, 47).

Once again the radicalized imperative is characteristic. There is no didactic intent here concerning the hereafter. Nevertheless, the warning against the possibility of the loss of salvation is piercing. More elaborate descriptions of the final judgment in which the Son of man, Jesus, is described as judge have their origin in the post-Easter community. Twice this occurs in conjunction with allegorizing interpretations of parables of Jesus, such as the parables of the weeds among the wheat and of the net (Matt 13:41–43, 49f.). The Son of man will send his angels to gather from his kingdom all those who are lawless and to throw them into the furnace of fire, where they will weep and gnash their teeth. The righteous, on the other hand, will shine like the sun, says the text, adopting apocalyptic conceptual material. The impressive picture of the gathering of the nations before the throne of the Son of man / King (Matt 25:31–46) belongs to the post-Easter setting as well.[181] What is important, however, is that the standard used at the judgment is the mercy that has either been granted or refused relative to the least brothers, with whom the Son of man / judge identifies. This standard of judgment continues the ethos of Jesus' proclamation, just as the central concern of this challenging text has to be seen in the call to acts of compassion.

---

[181] In Matt 25:31ff. J. Friedrich, *Gott im Bruder* (CThM A/7; Stuttgart: Calwer Verlag, 1977), wants to begin with a text in which the judge was not the Son of man but God himself. He sees "God in the brother" as the apex of meaning in the picture of the judgment as presented by Jesus. Similarly U. Wilckens, "Gottes geringste Brüder," in *Jesus und Paulus* (FS W. G. Kümmel; Göttingen: Vandenhoeck & Ruprecht, 1975) 363–83. This explanation is not convincing exegetically, however. Jesus did not develop the concept of God as brother, nor did the Synoptics. On the discussion, cf. Gnilka, *Matthäusevangelium,* 2.366–79.

Whose is the anticipated eschatological judgment, according to Jesus' proclamation? The judgment is God's. Yet Jesus referred to the Son of man sharing in the divine judgment: "every one who acknowledges me before men, the Son of man also will acknowledge before the angels of God, but he who denies me before men will be denied before the angels of God" (Luke 12:8–9).[182] The participation of the Son of man in the judgment may have to be interpreted to mean that he appears as a qualified witness, upon whose confession or denial the divine verdict will depend.[183] The confession and denial occur on two levels. On the level of the divine judgment, confession and denial belong to the Son of man. But confessing Jesus in this life or denying him is at the individual's discretion, so that he himself decides about his future and about the result of the verdict to be passed on him, based on his disposition with regard to Jesus. Confessing Jesus before people cannot be restricted to a context of persecution but rather encompasses the varied possibilities in which a free, undiminished "yes" to belonging to Jesus is incumbent upon the disciple. In this case denying him means renouncing him.

It is once again particularly significant that the focal point is the present, shaped by the future, as the time of decision. This is the perspective that also characterized other sayings of Jesus. Here we also become acquainted with the apparently distanced Son of man language, characteristic of Jesus' way of speaking, which appears to separate him from the Son of man and leaves open the identity of this Son of man. But since everything, including the saying concerning the Son of man in the divine judgment, depends upon one's present attitude to Jesus, whether one confesses or denies him before people, the question of the identity of the Son of man becomes secondary and hence can be deferred.

We have discussed expressions of judgment whose reference point is the individual. Alongside these we encounter expressions of judgment that refer to Israel, this generation, the Galilean towns. These will be addressed in a different context.

---

[182] On the reconstruction of this logion, cf. Schulz, Q, 68f., who assumes that in the logia source the original reference to the Son of man ("him the Son of man will deny as well") in the second part was replaced with the passive formulation, "he will be denied before the angels of God." On the other hand, Perrin, Rediscovering, 189, and C. Colpe, "ὁ υἱὸς τοῦ ἀνθρώπου," TDNT 8.442, are of the opinion that the Son of man title did not occur at all in the logion. As attempts at alteration, both proposals are unconvincing.

[183] Cf. Acts 3:5b.

Overview

The post-Easter situation changes the expectation of the judgment primarily in the sense that the communities now expect Jesus as the Son of man in the Parousia and in the judgment. That which was still tentative in the proclamation by Jesus is transformed into certainty on the basis of the Easter experience: Jesus, who was raised from the dead, is the Son of man appearing as the qualified witness at the judgment; indeed he himself will conduct the judgment, with all nations appearing before his throne. There are pictures drawn about this judgment, as already indicated above, that also conceptualize the trial and the execution of judgment. They develop dialogues between judge and accused analogous to those in rabbinic Judaism (cf. Matt 7:22f.; 25:34ff.).[184] Jesus himself has not addressed his Parousia as yet. The link between his coming in the clouds of heaven (Mark 13:26 par.) and the appearance of the completed reign of God could be made only after Easter. In this connection it is worthwhile noting the emphasis in the Gospel of Matthew: the execution of judgment is shown in bold relief at various points in the First Gospel. Almost like a leitmotif, it pervades the entire work (Matt 5:22; 7:22f.; 13:41–43, 49f.; 18:34f.; 20:16; 22:11–13; 23:50f.; 25:10–12, 30, 31–46).

Select bibliography: M. Reiser, "Die Gerichtspredigt Jesu" (Habilitationsschrift; Tübingen, 1989); A. Weiser, *Die Knechtsgleichnisse der synoptischen Tradition* (SANT 29; Munich: Kösel, 1971); P. Wolf, "Gericht und Reich Gottes bei Johannes und Jesus," in *Gegenwart und Kommendes Reich* (FS A. Vögtle; SBB; Stuttgart: Katholisches Bibelwerk, 1975) 43–49.

---

[184] Cf. H. D. Betz, "Eine Episode im Jüngsten Gericht," *ZTK* 78 (1981) 1–30.

6

Disciples, Discipleship, Lifestyle

Jesus took his message to the population at large. He did not, however, consider this approach to be all that was needed. In the Gospels we observe a group of people who were closer to him. This observation is relevant in terms of evaluating his personality, for it indicates that he wanted people around him and that he did not want to make his journey alone as the great recluse. Within the context of our experience this suggests the category of friendship. The Jesus traditions, however, fail us especially if we inquire into psychological, emotional contexts of interest to us. More appropriate may be the question of how this closer circle came about, what significance or task he attributed to it, and what significance it had for these people. Is it possible to examine at least one or two of this circle more closely, even if only by means of an episode characterizing the person, via a peculiarity, an event that, like a flash, for one moment only, illumines the face remaining in the shadow of history?

As far as the association with companions is concerned, Jesus resembles other significant persons.[1] Buddha, Socrates, and Confucius gathered those of like mind around them as well. Philosophers founded schools. More relevant are John the Baptist or Jewish scribes of the time, such as Hillel and Shammai, who were also surrounded by adherents. This is not the place for a comparison such as this, however. Only the Jewish contemporaries mentioned last will be addressed briefly, for the important feature for us is what

---

[1] The expression is K. Jasper's.

is unique to Jesus. Comparisons could cause the latter to be blurred or lost in the current of the general portrait. But since Jesus lived with his companions, his followers, an attempt must be made to discover something about their lifestyle and the way they conducted their lives.

1. Discipleship and following

According to the presentation in the Gospels—Luke being somewhat of an exception—Jesus opens his ministry by gathering disciples around him (Mark 1:16–20; Matt 4:18–22; John 1:35–51).[2] Here the Christian narration has shaped a particular form of stories of the call to discipleship, which prove to be structurally dependent upon the story of Elisha's call by Elijah the prophet. This is all the more conspicuous since there is not a single other comparable story of a call in the OT. Placing the texts in parallel highlights the issue of dependence:

"And passing along by the Sea of Galilee, he saw Simon and Andrew the brother of Simon casting a net in the sea; for they were fishermen. And Jesus said to them, 'Follow me and I will make you become fishers of men.' And immediately they left their nets and followed him. And going on a little farther, he saw James the son of Zebedee and John his brother, who were in their boat mending the nets. And immediately he called them; and they left their father Zebedee in the boat with the hired servants, and followed him" (Mark 1:16–20).

"So he departed from there, and found Elisha the son of Shaphat, who was plowing, with twelve yoke of oxen before him, and he was with the twelfth. Elijah passed by him and cast his mantle upon him. And he left the oxen, and ran after Elijah, and said, 'Let me kiss my father and my mother, and then I will follow you.' And he said to him, 'Go back again; for what have I done to you?' [3] *. . . Then he arose and went after Elijah, and ministered to him"* (1 Kgs 19:19–21).

The formative structural elements respectively are (1) the deliberately evoked impression that this is the initial encounter between the one calling and the one called; (2) the everyday tasks in which they are called upon to follow and their immediate obedience;

---

[2] The corresponding account in Luke 5:1–11 is preceded by narratives concerning Jesus' teaching and ministry in Nazareth and Capernaum (4:14–44). Over against the Markan pattern, however, Luke does not offer anything new; he merely rearranges the respective pericopes (cf. Mark 6:1–6a; 1:23–28). Jesus' rejection at Nazareth is developed programatically and moved to the beginning.

[3] According to the original form of the story, Elijah does not permit the farewell. Cf. G. Fohrer, *Elia* (ATANT; Zurich: Zwingli, 1957) 21f.

(3) overcoming an obstacle, represented by the farewell from the father or from the parents respectively.[4]

Despite its deliberate shaping into an ideal scene,[5] the tradition provides several glimpses of the historical background, such as the names of those called and of their father, their occupation, and, most important, their call by Jesus. The decisive feature of embarking upon following him is not the disciples' decision but rather Jesus' electing will. The initiative is his. This is the point of difference between him and the rabbinic teacher-disciple relationship, in which the disciple selected his rabbi—generally the one from whom he hoped to learn the most—and was also able to transfer to another; but Jesus can be associated with the prophetic understanding of discipleship. Disciple-ship is not opened up and made possible on account of Jesus having been a well-known rabbi but rather because he called with charismatic authority. The unique charismatic character of this discipleship finds expression in Elijah's case in that it is not the prophet but God who calls, depicted in the symbolic act of casting the mantle. There is no such symbol in the case of Jesus. He calls by his word. Discipleship sayings that have been handed down confirm this authority.

In an attempt at reconstructing the beginnings of Jesus' ministry in conjunction with the gathering of a band of disciples, the question has been raised from time to time whether or not he ministered alone for a time, without any disciples around him.[6] This possibility cannot be dismissed categorically. A period such as this would have to have been very brief in view of the rather limited duration of his ministry as a whole. For the disciples, Jesus' call did not come from someone unknown to them.[7] We have to remember that Jesus is calling some men who previously were part of John the Baptist's circle of disciples (cf. John 1:35ff.). They presumably had come to know Jesus in the company of the Baptist. Jesus gathered his circle of disciples in Galilee, where he also established the center of his ministry.[8]

---

[4] The schematic arrangement is confirmed by the calling of the tax collector, Mark 2:14 par.

[5] The term is Bultmann's, *History*, 28.

[6] Hengel, *Charismatic Leader*, 72, remarks that in the earliest tradition Jesus often appears as one who works alone.

[7] When Luke arranges other pericopes so as to precede the calling, especially the reference to the previous opportunity of those being called to hear Jesus' preaching (5:1, 4), he too may have been aware of the difficulty arising from the fact that they would have responded to the calling from someone unknown. See note 2 above.

[8] There is no hint here of Jesus wooing away disciples of the Baptist. These men also had clearly returned to Galilee as well and resumed their occupation.

Jesus transcends the Elijah account of the calling by means of a commissioning declaration: "I will make you become fishers of men." He demonstrates his uniqueness by adapting to the current occupation of these men, whereby they were able to realize that they were to be "fishers" in a different realm from now on. Further, the image of the fisher of men or hunter of men has only negative parallels; hence if Jesus were making use of known imagery such as this, he would have introduced its positive application.[9] More likely is his spontaneous formation of the imagery in view of their occupation. Thus a fundamental purpose of following Jesus is opened up, again leading us to the center of his ministry, namely, the proclamation of the reign of God, for people are to be caught into God's reign, rescued into the salvation offered to them. Jesus gathered disciples around him in order for them to support him in his own ministry.[10] Discipleship of Jesus is directed outward, to the people.

Yet it also has its inward focus, namely, upon Jesus. This orientation is articulated in the term "following"; it may be assumed that he used it in the same way as the term "disciple." It is noteworthy that in the place where the Elijah account states that Elisha became his servant, the Gospel says that they followed him. This indicates an essentially new quality of discipleship in Jesus. It was commonplace in the rabbinic teacher-disciple relationship for the disciple to attend to his teacher, as illustrated in the proverb "Every task a slave carries out for his master, a disciple is to do for his teacher, except for untying the sandals" (*b. Ketub.* 96a).[11] But Jesus says, "For which is the greater, one who sits at table, or one who serves? Is it not the one who sits at table? But I am among you as one who serves" (Luke 22:27).[12]

It may be prudent in other areas likewise to distinguish carefully between the rabbinic disciple-teacher relationship and discipleship with Jesus. The contacts are superficial. Nevertheless many contemporaries even at that time may not have noticed the particulars. To the observer, Jesus and his discipleship may indeed have

[9] Jer 16:16; 1 QH 5:7f.; 3:26 (dragnet of the wicked). Luke 5:10 has the logion in adapted form: "henceforth you will be catching men." Hengel, *Charismatic Leader,* 76, traces this back to an Aramaic variant. The saying on catching men is not Hellenistic, as Haenchen, *Weg,* 81, assumes on the basis of a very dubious parallel in Aristippus.
[10] This view is emphasized correctly by Hengel, *Charismatic Leader,* passim.
[11] In Str-B, *Kommentar,* 1.121.
[12] Hengel, *Charismatic Leader,* 52f., has demonstrated that in rabbinic texts "to follow after" frequently has the concrete meaning of walking behind the teacher and consistently denotes the pupil's subordination to the teacher, without any more profound meaning.

looked the same outwardly as any scribe with his circle of students. The rabbi walked on ahead, and his disciples followed him. Riding, of course, was not a rarity for the Jewish teacher. For external observers the parallel is given in the address of "rabbi" (lit. "my great one," "my master"), which was used among the common people with reference to Jesus. In this connection the Gospels certainly have preserved an accurate reminiscence (Mark 10:51; John 3:2, 26).[13] The address "rabbi," however, was not yet used as a title with reference to the ordained rabbi at that time. The restrictive use of the term became dominant only toward the end of the first century CE; hence it is not appropriate to conclude from the use of "rabbi" as an address that Jesus had been taught by a rabbi at some time.[14] Likewise the designation of Jesus' closer companions as μαθηταί (pupils, learners, disciples) may have channeled the understanding in this direction. It corresponds to the term used for the student of a rabbi *(talmid)*. In the disciples' relationship with Jesus, however, we do not encounter a schoolhouse atmosphere or an academic enterprise.[15]

Some of the transmitted sayings of Jesus on discipleship demand radical decisiveness. We find them partly in scenes of anecdotal description which, in contrast to the call narratives, omit details about the people who encounter Jesus, such as their name or occupation, and in which everything hinges on Jesus' statement (Luke 5:57–62 par.). We hear of a particular man whom he calls to follow him but who objects that he first wanted to go and bury his father. There is a distant resemblance in this objection to the call of Elisha, though the issue in the latter was to say farewell to the living (1 Kgs 19:20). The response he receives from Jesus is such that it was argued to contravene, more than any other of his sayings, the law, piety, and customs all in one:[16] "Follow me, and leave the dead to bury their own dead" (Matt 8:22). In place of the (reiterated) call to follow, Luke 9:60 offers: "but as for you, go and proclaim the

[13] In Greek "Rabbi" as address is replaced by "Teacher" (e.g., Mark 9:17; 10:17, 20; 12:12, 19, 32).

[14] The rabbinic tradition alleging that Jesus had been a pupil of Jehoshua ben Perachiah is unfounded. Even for chronological reasons this is not tenable, because it moves Jesus into the era of King Jannai. A critical assessment of this tradition is provided by Klausner, *Jesus*, 25–29. According to John 7:15 the Jews accuse Jesus of not having studied.

[15] Mark's well-defined stretch of the disciples' instruction in the house is reminiscent of later community contexts, more specifically reflecting the catechesis of the church, perhaps already of the house church; cf. Mark 7:17; 9:28; 10:10.

[16] Hengel, *Charismatic Leader,* 14.

kingdom of God." This may be secondary, though the difference is not considerable, since the only thing the man following Jesus is to do is to spread the news of the kingdom.[17]

The point of this saying gains its full impact if one recognizes that the dead are here considered on two different levels of understanding. For one, there are those who are physically dead, like the father, whom the son is about to bury. For another, there are those who are spiritually dead, who died because they were not or are not prepared to accept Jesus' saving message. When both instances of being dead are evaluated, the latter is weightier for Jesus. Hence the young man is to undertake what is more essential, and that at once. It is not appropriate to conclude from this response that the issue for Jesus was to oppose commonsense piety or that he argued against an exaggerated cult of the dead like Cynic philosophers ("the smell will bury me").[18] Neither is the response to be weakened by observations such as that in the East a funeral took eight days.[19] Rather, as in numerous other instances, Jesus' position here is a concrete one, referring to the situation and to each of the respective individuals. It would be wrong to seek to develop a system from a directive such as this. The person addressed, however, unmistakably learns what is required of him.

Similarly concrete and aimed at a specific situation is the call to follow addressed to the rich man; he is called upon to sell all he possesses and to give it to the poor (Mark 10:21 par.). This, too, does not express a condition for discipleship which, on principle, has abiding validity, though Jesus was aware of the great dangers of wealth and expressed himself accordingly (Mark 10:25).

If one of the primary intents of Jesus' gathering of disciples was for them to support him in his ministry, it follows almost inevitably that they were sent out by him at some point. Questioning this mission, for instance, by arguing that the instructions for the mission were indebted to the later, post-Easter missionary activity means to disregard that, in its decisiveness and radicality, the core of these instructions has its origin in Jesus, though they were certainly interpreted and adapted later on. Since these instructions are especially concerned with lifestyle, it is necessary to pick up this point again. Obviously the center of the activity of those sent out

---

[17] Gnilka, *Matthäusevangelium*, 1.310.
[18] Lucian, *Demonax* 65.
[19] Schwarz, *"Und Jesus sprach,"* 96.

was the proclamation of the *basileia:* "The kingdom of God is near" (cf. Matt 10:7). This offer of salvation brooked neither delay nor rejection. The response to those refusing the offer was to be the gesture of shaking the dust from the feet, as a sign of the impending judgment (10:14). The language of this gesture was understood, for it customarily denoted the cessation of fellowship.

Discipleship in this sense brings dangers and incurs conflicts. It is noteworthy that such dangers and conflicts, the willingness to suffer and die, are discussed precisely in the context of discipleship. If his disciples are to support him in his ministry, discipleship means to go before the public, to talk to people, and to endeavor to win them personally for the kingdom. The conflict began in one's own family. Those who took Jesus' call to be for them and accepted it could not reckon with their family members responding in the same manner. This is the situation intended by the saying "If someone comes to me and does not hate his father and mother, he cannot be my disciple."

This is a reconstruction, in its presumed original form, of a saying handed down differently in Luke 14:26 and Matt 10:37. In Luke the sequence of those from whom one might have to be separated is clearly secondary, and various possibilities are enlarged with painstaking comment to include wife, children, brothers, sisters, and one's own life. Matthew reduces as follows: "He who loves father or mother more than me is not worthy of me," though he maintains the terse focus on the parents.[20] In order to understand the seemingly hard saying, it is important to remember that it assumes conflict. In this case, and only in this case, the one called is advised to prefer discipleship. It is more important and eminently more essential for life. The hard term "to hate" here does not denote an affectively charged separation from one's parents but rather a prioritizing. Jesus, too, experienced dispute with his relatives. This experience supports the authenticity of the saying, which, on account of its focus on the parents, provides the insight that the band of disciples was composed of young men, just as in his ministry Jesus himself was a man of about thirty years of age. Incidentally, rabbinic teachers likewise placed obedience to the Torah above obedience to the parents.[21]

The saying concerning discipleship of the cross leads on the way of discipleship: "and whoever does not take up the cross and follow is not worthy of me" (Matt 10:38 par. Luke 14:27 ["cannot be

---

[20] Cf. Gnilka, *Matthäusevangelium,* 1.393.
[21] Documentation in Str-B, *Kommentar,* 1.587.

my disciple"]).[22] This saying too has a claim to authenticity. It does not yet speak of the cross of Christ, although after Easter it could not have been construed in any other way than with reference to his cross. Rather, in a pre-Easter context it speaks metaphorically of every disciple's own cross: "He who does not take up *his* cross . . . "[23] The actual experience of those who were executed on the cross and had to carry their cross to the place of execution was one with which the Jews had been all too familiar since the time of the Maccabees and in particular during the time of the Roman governors. There was no problem with understanding the metaphor Jesus used.[24] While it includes the idea of readiness to martyrdom, it cannot be restricted to martyrdom. It also encompasses hostility, contempt, restriction, and harm that might befall a follower in discipleship. Although it was a predictive saying, it allows for the conclusion that already in Jesus' time—and especially then—discipleship did not place one on a path of triumph. In this sense the repeated portrait of the Gospels, especially in the early parts, according to which Jesus is surrounded by innumerable crowds of people calls for correction and cannot blind us to the fact that the lack of understanding outweighed the approval. Only gradually, to be sure, did the disciples probably grasp the full meaning of the admonition, which was to become the classical expression of the concept of discipleship.[25]

Jesus' parenesis of martyrdom is strengthened significantly by means of an antithetically structured logion dealing with gaining and losing life. In its several variants[26] it has retained its dialectical movement—whoever would save his life will lose it; whoever loses it will save it—though, while maintaining the idea of losing, the verbs could be exchanged: find, seek to gain, save. The qualification,

---

[22] "Take his cross" in Matthew is more original than "bear his own cross" in Luke. The Lukan formulation of "cannot be my disciple," however, is preferable to the Matthean "is not worthy of me." Matthew favors the term "worthy." On the reconstruction, see Gnilka, *Matthäusevangelium,* 1.393f.

[23] Cf. Bultmann, *History,* 160f.

[24] The interpretation offered in E. Dinkler, "Jesu Wort vom Kreuztragen," in *Neutestamentliche Studien für R. Bultmann* (2d ed.; BZNW 21; Berlin: Töpelmann, 1957), according to which the cross denotes a sign of sealing, as a kind of tattoo, is highly artificial.

[25] Plato's notion, *Resp.* 361d–362a, that the just might expect to be worse off in life than the unjust, is factually related but has a strictly ethical orientation. Referring to Socrates, Plato is indeed of the opinion that the just person must reckon with being hanged or crucified.

[26] Matt 10:39 par. Luke 17:33; Mark 8:35 par. Matt 16:25 par. Luke 9:24; cf. John 12:25.

"whoever loses for my sake . . . will save," is to be understood as an early component,[27] for it authenticates the logion as a saying of Jesus. The post-Easter supplement in Mark 8:35 was "and the gospel's [sake]." After Easter the gospel in a sense takes the place of Jesus, on account of whom the disciples' existence was in jeopardy before Easter. The ultimate goal of discipleship, of decisive commitment, of readiness for denial and martyrdom, is the gaining of life (ψυχή).[28] The focus of the dialectic of this saying turns out to be on the question of meaning. In other words, to attempt to fulfill one's life by means of false securities, wrong, selfish goals, effort, earthly possession, and the like means to miss the meaning. On the other hand, to order one's life in following Jesus and in keeping with his message means to be able to lend life its full meaning, even at the possible cost of offensive experiences, even to the point of losing one's life. Furthermore, this promised life to be gained here transcends the boundaries of death and, in a great wealth of meaning, encompasses human existence in its totality. If we take another look at the complex of discipleship and following Jesus, its primary characteristic is the disciples' inclusion in his ministry, their participation in the proclamation of the kingdom of God. It is important to note, of course, that the disciples here are fully dependent upon Jesus and are not to be working in their own name but in fellowship with him. Without him the proclamation of the basileia is powerless.[29] This "school" did not lead to systematic instruction, nor to a cultivated formation of tradition, but rather to an initial nonsystematic outline of the contents of proclamation. Yet neither is discipleship to be construed as hurrying through villages and towns, driven, as it were, by restless, hectic rush, in red-hot expectation of what is imminent. While time was indeed urgent, discipleship also afforded them time.

In addition, it is important not to ignore the personal aspects of discipleship. Its focus is on Jesus. Following renders one a disciple of Jesus. This element is already present in the aspect of the kingdom of God. It means that, as something future and present, the basileia is bound up with Jesus. It reminds us of the charismatic nature of the calling of the disciples. More than anything else, however, the disci-

---

[27] The omission of the qualification in Luke 17:33 is due to the Lukan context, which does not deal with following after but with eschatological fright.

[28] G. Dautzenberg, Sein Leben bewahren (SANT 14; Munich: Kösel, 1966) 51–82, has shed light on the meaning of psyche in the relevant logia of the synoptic tradition.

[29] The story of the strange exorcist in Mark 9:38–41 is informative. On this, see Gnilka, Markus, 2.58–62.

pling and martyrdom parenesis brings out the personal aspect of discipleship. This parenesis goes back to Jesus' dealings with his disciples. Here discipleship literally becomes a following-after. Equality between Jesus and the disciples is out of the question. In his person and in his path Jesus becomes the model to be remembered.

Overview

Following and discipleship remain essential elements of being a Christian. Yet the understanding of them had to change in the post-Easter situation, after Jesus' earthly life was concluded. The designation "disciples" for the followers of Jesus continues only in the Acts of the Apostles. Outside the Gospels, in the NT the term "to follow" occurs only in Acts 14:4 in its specific sense. Paul develops the conception of the imitation of Christ (cf. 1 Cor 11:1; 1 Thess 1:6). The early Christians experienced the charismatic power of their calling in that they understood themselves as called out and called together by the Holy Spirit. Yet the Gospels intentionally and conceptionally created the enduring invitation to get involved in Jesus' path leading to Jerusalem and to follow him.

Select bibliography: H. D. Betz, *Nachfolge und Nachahmung Jesus Christi im Neuen Testament* (BHT 37; Tübingen: J. C. B. Mohr, 1967); E. Dinkler, "Jesu Wort vom Kreuztragen," 110–29 in *Neutestamentliche Studien für R. Bultmann* (2d ed.; BZNW 21; Berlin: Töpelmann, 1957); J. Gnilka, "Martyriumsparänese und Sühnetod in synoptischen und jüdischen Traditionen," 223–46 in *Die Kirche des Anfangs* (FS H. Schürmann; Leipzig: St-Benno Verlag, 1978); M. Hengel, *The Charismatic Leader and His Followers* (ET; Edinburgh: T. & T. Clark, 1981); A. Oepke, "Nachfolge und Nachahmung Christi im Neuen Testament," *AELKZ* 71 (1938) 850–57, 866–72; A. Schulz, *Nachfolgen und Nachahmen* (SANT 6; Munich: Kösel, 1962); T. Süss, "Nachfolge Jesu," *TLZ* 78 (1953) 129–40.

2. The lifestyle of Jesus and his disciples

Jesus' focus in life was on people; during the time of his public ministry he lived in fellowship with people who had responded to his call. He lived in community with his disciples. But the mutuality of life did not lead to a contemplative lifestyle in seclusion. Instead we see the small band as itinerant, en route, without a home. They are en route in order to proclaim the kingdom of God to people and to bring it home to them. It can be said, of course, that the focal point of Jesus' ministry was in Galilee, in the vicinity of Lake Gennesaret and around Capernaum. Yet he and his disciples did without a real home, or they forsook it.

The instructions Jesus gave them on their way are of major interest as far as the disciples' lifestyle is concerned. Among the four variants of the missionary instructions (Mark 6:8–11; Matt 10:5–15; Luke 9:2–5; 10:2–12),[30] upon which the influence of later missionary practice is to be assumed, we are at this point interested only in the rules relative to the disciple's personal needs. In terms of their stringency and radicality, which in part underwent certain ameliorating corrections already within the synoptic tradition, they cannot have originated with anyone other than Jesus. What is remarkable here is that these rules do not describe what they are to take along on their journeys but precisely the opposite, what is not to be taken along: no staff, no bread, no bag, no copper coin in their belts, no sandals, no second tunic.[31] Mark 6:8f. secondarily concedes the staff and the sandals. And the formulation that the disciple who has been sent out is not to wear two tunics may well have been an easing of the directive that he was not to have two tunics (Matt 10:10; Luke 9:3).

Foregoing the food for the journey—"bread" is to be understood in this sense—and the money renders them completely impoverished. Even the reference to the copper coins, that is, the least valuable coins, is informative. If Matt 10:9 forbids obtaining gold, silver, or copper coins, it presumably deals with problems already occurring in the communities. To be without a bag meant to avoid begging for provisions. Foregoing the staff, sandals, and a second tunic causes them to appear poor. Being barefooted was an expression of great poverty. Perhaps foregoing the staff also had something to do with their message of peace, for this staff could also be used as a weapon.

The poverty prescribed for the disciples can be compared with the lifestyle of the itinerant preachers of moral philosophy. We are told that Antisthenes, a pupil of Socrates, was contented with a stave, satchel, and a single cloak, which identified him as a philosopher. Crates, Aristotle's pupil, is said to have publicly declared himself to be freed from his property by using the appropriate form for the emancipation of a slave and to have donated it to his fellow-citizens

---

[30] Luke records a mission of the twelve apostles and another of seventy-two disciples. Consensus has it that Matthew and Luke drew the instructions for the mission from Mark and Q. In this connection, Luke distributes the two sources regarding this matter between the two missions, whereas Matthew combines them. Ultimately, however, the instructions in Q and Mark must have had a common prior tradition. Cf. Gnilka, *Matthäusevangelium*, 1.359–62; F. Hahn, *Das Verständnis der Mission im Neuen Testament* (WMANT 13; Neukirchen: Neukirchener, 1963) 33–36.

[31] The Greek text refers to the χιτών, meaning the woolen or linen garment worn on the body directly.

or, following another tradition, thrown it into the sea.[32] On this point there are contacts with other religions as well. We know of Buddha that as the prince's son who went without any possessions, he made his daily rounds as a beggar, with a dish in his hand, without uttering a request, looking despondent, expecting someone to give him a morsel of food.[33] In the context of contemporary Judaism, the Essene monastics of Qumran were pledged to strict poverty and personal destitution.

If one probes the overall meaning of the poverty demanded of the disciples, it is clearly different from the parallels cited. The disciple is not to be driven by the inner tranquility of indifference characteristic of the philosopher's distance from the world and its goods, nor by overcoming the world, as Buddha demanded of his monks on the path of meditation and self-denial. Qumran cannot serve as a model either. There we indeed encounter an eschatological-apocalyptic expectation, but behind denial of possessions and community of property there are ritual, cultic conceptions as well as the resultant concern of being defiled by the world.[34] Jesus' circle of disciples is not a monastic group.

Living in poverty and dependent upon the help of others, the disciples are an explanation, so to speak, of the kingdom of God that Jesus and the disciples proclaim. The kingdom ushers in a new order, which is not to be the order of possessions, gain, wealth, and contempt for humankind any longer. Their lifestyle could be understood even better as a sign of the *basileia* if we assume that they, or at least some of them, had previously lived in ordered economic circumstances. Indigent, unarmed, unpretentious, they knew they were at the mercy of this God, or they were to deem themselves committed to the one who was in the process of establishing his reign. Likewise their conspicuous silence, namely, that they were not to greet anyone on the way (Luke 10:4b),[35] was to point to their message of the *basileia,* which they were to treat like a valuable gift and which they were not to pass on until they reached their journey's destination, where they were to proclaim the message.

---

[32] Documentation in Hengel, *Charismatic Leader,* 28f.

[33] Cf. K. Jaspers, *Die massgebenden Menschen* (10th ed.; Serie Piper 126; Munich: R. Piper, 1988) 109.

[34] Cf. H.-J. Klauck, "Gütergemeinschaft in der klassischen Antike, in Qumran und im Neuen Testament," in *Gemeinde—Amt—Sakrament* (Würzburg: Echter, 1989) 69–100.

[35] Only Luke has this logion, which may well have been in Q and originated with Jesus. Perhaps Matthew no longer understood it, or he deemed it inappropriate. The directive may include the notion that the disciples were not to be hindered by anything.

We may assume that the poverty Jesus demanded of his disciples also characterized his own lifestyle. He too wandered through the country as one who was homeless, without provisions, money, or satchel, barefoot and without staff. In this sense *he* above all else was the sign of the reign of God. The disciples merely followed him. His destitution and homelessness are indicated by a logion of the tradition of the sayings source, which might have assumed the Son of man title only secondarily:[36] "Foxes have holes, and birds of the air have nests; but the Son of man has nowhere to lay his head" (Matt 8:20; Luke 9:58). In its present form the logion is framed by the animals / Son of man contrast. In this theological nuance the reason for the homelessness of the Son of man lies with people's hostility and rejection. If the saying had indeed been expressed in the first person at one time, the contrast with the foxes and birds would become even more prominent, and being without a home, for him, would reflect extreme existential insecurity. Whatever might be the case as far as the derivation of the saying is concerned in the history of tradition,[37] it has in any case preserved the historically accurate remembrance of Jesus' homelessness as his lifestyle.

The unusual way of life could easily trigger disputes with members of the family, of course. Jesus himself experienced it, as various strands of the tradition demonstrate. One scene, which is difficult to interpret because of its brevity, depicts his family as going out to seize and bring him home, with the remark, "He is beside himself" (Mark 3:21). While it may reflect a strong redactional bias,[38] the lack of understanding, the distance of his brothers represent a solid part of the tradition (Mark 3:31–35 par.; John 7:3–9). After Easter there was a partial change; now we see James, the Lord's brother, as the leader of the Jerusalem church, who according to 1 Cor 15:7 was granted a personal appearance of the risen Jesus (Acts 12:17; 15:13; 21:18; Gal 1:19; 2:9, 12).

Jesus lived a celibate life; he renounced establishing his own family, wife, and children. In the context of contemporary Judaism this behavior must have seemed offensive, shocking. Establishing a family and having children were almost considered compulsory, based on Gen 1:28, "Be fruitful and multiply." To be single, in

---

[36] Thus Hoffmann, *Studien*, 182.
[37] On this see Gnilka, *Matthäusevangelium*, 1.309f.
[38] Cf. Gnilka, *Markus*, 1.144f. Socrates was accused of making his pupils obey him more than their fathers. Musonius points to the same conflict. Cf. Hengel, *Charismatic Leader*, 29.

rabbinic Judaism, was tantamount to bloodshed and meant to be refused ordination as a rabbi. Only Qumran had monks living a celibate lifestyle.[39] There is a logion in Matt 19:12 that in all probability refers to Jesus' celibacy. Following the teaching on marriage, directed to the people, Jesus instructs the disciples concerning the possibility of celibacy: "For there are eunuchs who have been so from birth, and there are eunuchs who have been made eunuchs by men, and there are eunuchs who have made themselves eunuchs for the sake of the kingdom of heaven. He who is able to receive this, let him receive it."[40] This saying, constructed in keeping with the "rule of three"—three cases for being a eunuch are cited—makes its point in two ways. First, there is the use of the disparaging term "eunuch," designating one who is castrated, hence unfit for marriage. According to Deut 23:2ff. and Lev 22:24 castration was an abomination to Israel. Second, the saying contains a shift in value. If the first two instances refer to those who through external mishaps were plunged into the lamentable condition of physical infertility, the third type of "eunuch" becomes a metaphor for the celibate life that has been chosen voluntarily. But since the term "eunuch" with its connotations of an insult is retained, it has been assumed appropriately that we are here dealing with an attack against Jesus.[41] Because of his celibate life his opponents slandered him with the term "eunuch," just as he was chided as "a glutton and a drunkard" (Matt 11:19 par.) because of his table fellowship with tax collectors, prostitutes, and sinners.

This lifestyle, departing from the norm, once again is focused on the kingdom of God. Marriage and family are not renounced for the sake of some ascetic ideal, nor to attain the kingdom of God, but rather in order to work singlemindedly and with every ounce of strength for the *basileia*. This happens for people's sake. Jesus granted his love precisely to those who were deemed unlovable by others.

We have no information concerning the details of the disciples' family circumstances. Only of Simon Peter do we know that he was married and lived in Capernaum, presumably in the house of his

---

[39] On this issue, see H. Hübner, "Zöllibat in Qumran?" *NTS* 17 (1970/71) 153–67. In the OT Jeremiah remains single for the sake of his prophetic office (Jer 16:2).

[40] In a slightly altered form and clearly dependent upon Matthew, this logion occurs in Justin, *First Apology* 15.4.

[41] So also Blinzler, "εὐνοῦχοι," *ZNW* 48 (1957) 269. Braun, *Radikalismus*, 2.112, n. 3, likewise observes that the logion does not fit a Jewish matrix and proves to be an authentic saying of Jesus. Cf. J. Gnilka, "Mann und Frau nach dem Neuen Testament," 185–205 in *Gott schuf den Menschen als Mann und Frau* (ed. P. Gordan; Graz: Styria, 1989) esp. 191–93.

parents-in-law. Mark 1:29–31 par. recounts the healing of Simon's mother-in-law in the house where he and his brother Andrew lived. Simon's wife is not mentioned as such.

Here too the Gospels demonstrate how little they are interested in biographical matters.[42] Since a house in Capernaum is mentioned elsewhere (Mark 2:1), the reference could very plausibly be to Simon's house. In this case Jesus may occasionally—or frequently?—have been a guest there. The house may well have remained in the family's possession.[43]

The introduction to the so-called catechesis of the disciples helps in determining the milieu, in obtaining a more detailed characterization of Jesus' audience or of those who were willing to hear him out. To be sure, already in the logia source this sermon is shaped redactionally. At this point we refer only to the three introductory Beatitudes in Luke 6:20f.:

> *"Blessed are you poor, for yours is the kingdom of God.*
>
> *"Blessed are you that hunger now, for you shall be satisfied.*
>
> *"Blessed are you that weep now, for you shall laugh."*

In comparison with the parallel in Matt 5:3–10, this form of the Beatitudes may be considered the older one. For Jesus' situation the fourth Beatitude, concerning those who are persecuted on account of the Son of man, is not to be considered. In it the praises are transferred to the disciples.[44]

Jesus addressed the poor. Who specifically is meant by the poor?[45] From a purely linguistic perspective the Greek term πτωχός denotes the one who has to stoop and cower (from πτώσσειν), and the Hebrew (ʿānî, from ʿānāh) refers to one who is answerable to another, i.e., one who is dependent. Yet the concept has a prehistory without which Jesus' Beatitude cannot be understood.

---

[42] If, after the apostles, Acts 1:14 refers to the women who gather for prayer in the upper room in Jerusalem, those intended are not the wives of the apostles but the circle of the female disciples of Jesus, as shown in J. Roloff, *Die Apostelgeschichte* (NTD 5; Göttingen: Vandenhoeck & Ruprecht, 1981) 28. Codex D, however, reads "with wives and children."

[43] John 21:1ff. assumes that, after Good Friday and prior to the new gathering of the disciples in the Easter event, Simon and the others once again pursued their trade as fishermen.

[44] Cf. Schürmann, *Lukasevangelium*, 1.326–32.

[45] Cf. Hauck and Bammel, "πτωχός, κτλ," *TDNT* 6.885ff.; J. Dupont, *Les Beatitudes I* (2d ed.; Bruges: Abbaye de Saint André, 1958–73); J. Maier, *Die Texte vom Toten Meer* II (Munich: E. Reinhardt, 1960) 83–87.

Deplorable social conditions and poverty occurred in greater intensity during the period of the monarchy, when the social stratification between the poor and the rich, between the oppressed and the rulers, widened. The prophetic critique was directed against this development and declared God to be the protector of the poor. It spoke up for justice for the poor that had been trampled underfoot, justice that was equated with the justice of God. God will take up their cause and restore justice to them. Hence the poor person who knows about this leaves the matter of his justice to God. He submits to God's will, in contrast to the profiteers and the rich who dismiss God's justice high-handedly. Thus being poor also designates a disposition relative to God; indeed at a time of imminent expectation of God's intervention it is the only disposition in which God can be encountered. The spirituality of the poor appears in some particularly significant statements in Deutero- and Trito-Isaiah:

> *The LORD has anointed me to bring good tidings to the afflicted; he has sent me to bind up the brokenhearted, to proclaim liberty to the captives, and the opening of the prison to those who are bound; to proclaim the year of the LORD's favor, and the day of vengeance of our God; to comfort all who mourn; to grant to those who mourn in Zion* (Isa 61:1–3; cf. 58:7; 66:2).

Many psalms likewise reflect the piety of the poor: "This poor man cried, and the LORD heard him, and saved him out of all his troubles. The angel of the LORD encamps around those who fear him . . . " (Ps 34:6–7; cf. 9:11ff.; 14:6; 22:25ff.; 37:21ff.; etc.). There is no doubt that Jesus' promise of salvation to the poor is to be understood in the tradition of this theology. If he calls blessed those who hunger and weep as well, and thereby addresses the same group of the poor, the concern for the concrete need comes to the fore again. Nevertheless, it is clear that the poor who are blessed have maintained a disposition of an open heart toward his message. Surely it goes without saying that the blessedness is not intended because of poverty and misery per se. It is meant for the poor because God pledges them his salvation, his *basileia*. At this point we find ourselves not only in the milieu of those in Jesus' audience who are disposed toward God but also at the heart of his proclamation of the kingdom.[46]

Who receives preferential attention in Jesus' company? Whom do we meet? The Gospels preserved the relevant reminiscences.

---

[46] Schürmann, *Lukasevangelium*, 1.332, refers to the original form of Jesus' proclamation of the *basileia* and believes that the threefold Beatitude was his inaugural public message.

It is the sick, demoniacs, epileptics, blind, as well as people who are unable to realize their life to the full and hence need assistance. It is those who have become debtors, tax gatherers, suspicious, despised, marginalized, who foundered in life, who do not see a way out, who are despairing. This is not to say that his message was palatable only for these types of people, but their plight caused them to be more open for the message. Nevertheless, they were not without selfishness and smug scheming either. But for their part these people became an expression of the salvation that was becoming available and challenged others to look after them and so to follow him. Jesus' commission to the disciples to heal the sick and to cast out demons is to be seen against this backdrop (Luke 10:9; Mark 6:7). For Jesus, associating with people who were exploited, suspect, and doubting does not arise from a preference for the demimonde, or a pathos that no longer has any regard for the boundaries between good and evil. Guilt is not excused. Yet the naturalness with which Jesus accepts these people who need him and that thus transcends normative boundaries is capable of restoring lost self-confidence and helps prepare for an inward transformation.[47]

> A primarily sociological evaluation of Jesus' association with sinners fails to get to the heart of the matter and threatens to distort the situation grossly. Thus for K. Kautsky, Jesus' disciples are a bunch of dispossessed cadgers, without family or home, wandering ceaselessly from place to place and themselves capable of violence (with reference to Luke 9:51–56).[48] Here the notion of voluntary poverty—whatever the case of the disciples' individual possessions may have been—has faded away completely, and the purpose of following Jesus, as well as of the expectation of the kingdom of God, which shaped discipleship considerably, has been lost altogether.

There is a profound theological reason for Jesus' lack of possessions. We are referring to a text that may be construed as an original

---

[47] Cf. Bornkamm, *Jesus*, 76f. Those marginalized may not be identified as the Am-ha-Aretz in an absolute manner. This term, meaning as much as "common people," designates those who had little regard, if any, for the law, especially the regulations on tithing and purity. The term does not occur in the Gospels; John 7:49 has an affinity to it. A. Oppenheimer, *The "Am-Ha-Aretz"* (ALGHJ 8; Leiden: Brill, 1977) seeks to demonstrate that there were also adherents of the higher social classes among the Am-ha-Aretz and, conversely, there were also those of low social stratum who sought to order their lives in keeping with the law. The problem becomes noteworthy, however, when the poor person is no longer able to adhere to the religious regulations because of poverty.

[48] K. Kautsky, *Der Ursprung des Christentums* (11th ed.; 1921) 404f. (ET *The Foundations of Christianity*, New York: S. A. Russell, 1953). Theissen, *Studien*, 96f. argues that Kautzky's assessment also favors the widespread rejection of outsiders.

instruction to the disciples and the reconstructed form of which probably was something like the following:

"Do not be anxious about your life, what you shall eat, nor about your body, what you shall put on. Is not life more than food, and the body more than clothing? Look at the birds; they neither sow nor reap nor gather into barns [have no barns?]. And God feeds them. Are you not of more value than they? And why are you anxious about clothing? Consider the lilies, how they grow. They neither toil nor spin. Yet I tell you, even Solomon in all his glory was not arrayed like one of these. If God so clothes the grass of the field, which today is alive and tomorrow is thrown into the oven, will he not much more clothe you, O men of little faith?" (Matt 6:25f., 28–30; Luke 12:23f., 27f.).[49]

This well-formed rhetorical text, with stimulating questions and the popular conclusion of an argument from the lesser to the greater (from the birds and lillies to the disciples), as well as its parallelisms (food and clothing; sowing and reaping, toiling and spinning; man's work and woman's work), fits readily into Jesus' preaching, in the sense that it continues the topic of poverty, and its content presupposes absolute trust in God's care. The text has a wisdom orientation and thus has its parallels in wisdom literature and in the Psalms (Job 38:41; Ps 104:10ff.; 147:9; *Pss. Sol.* 5.10). Jesus emerges as a teacher of wisdom. Nevertheless, the overall setting of his proclamation of the kingdom needs to be observed.

If the calmness and freedom from care (which is not to be toned down) were likened to a disposition of indifference, they would be misunderstood. Jesus does not oppose working in this life but presupposes nature as yet pristine. The high regard for life has a liberating effect. Life (ψυχή) is more than food and clothing. By worrying about these, the person can easily squander his life and lose the meaning of life in what is secondary. The words reflecting freedom from self-tormenting worry are those of a free and happy person. Another reason for the value of these words is that they preserve for us an often forgotten portrait of Jesus. It depicts a serene person who feels safe in God's security. We refer once again to Wisdom as saying: "for sorrow has destroyed many, and there is no profit in it. Jealousy and anger shorten life, and anxiety brings on old

---

[49] Concerning the reconstruction, Matt 6:27 par. is a secondary insertion. The ravens in Luke 12:24 are secondary to the birds in Matt 6:26 (cf. the end of Luke 12:24). The reference to "your heavenly Father" in Matt 6:26b accords with the style of language; the use of "God" in Luke 12:24 preserves the more original form. For further details, cf. Gnilka, *Matthäusevangelium*, 1.246; Merklein, *Gottesherrschaft*, 178f.

age too soon. A man of cheerful and good heart will give heed to the food he eats. . . . Wakeful anxiety prevents slumber, and a severe illness carries off sleep" (Sir 30:23b; 31:2). Yet Jesus goes beyond the teaching of wisdom, for trust in the God who cares, for him and the disciples, is coupled with action on behalf of the kingdom of God. Those who commit themselves fully to the kingdom may also count on God's help.

What can be ascertained about the lifestyle of Jesus and his disciples in turn is centered in the *basileia*. As they move through Galilee, undemanding and unpretentious, they witness to the kingdom of God, in word as well as in life, and reflect in their being the inauguration of a new order. They have separated from their families in order to be free for the work of God. Those lending them their ears are primarily the country's poor; the exploited and harrassed gather around them. By trusting in the God who cares for them, they are to be free from worry and devote themselves fully to their task.

Overview

In the post-Easter context the radical itinerant life continued for a while among early Christian missionaries.[50] This was liable to be abused as well. The *Didache* warns of false prophets who demand money from the congregations (11.6). Luke 22:35 represents a break: "'When I sent you out with no purse or bag or sandals, did you lack anything?' They said, 'Nothing.' He said to them, 'But now, let him who has a purse take it, and likewise a bag. And let him who has no sword sell his mantle and buy one.' " The time of Jesus has become the past, which is remembered as an ideal, exemplary time. The realities have overtaken its extraordinary possibilities; only isolated Christians displayed its strength in later times. The problem of the delay of the Parousia does not explain everything by any means. Saint Francis is the unequaled great example.

Select bibliography: J. Blinzler, "Εἰσὶν εὐνοῦχοι," *ZNW* 48 (1957) 254–70; B. Buby, "A Christology of Relationship in Mark," *BTB* 10 (1980) 149–54; F. Hahn, *Das Verständnis der Mission im Neuen Testament* (WUANT 13; Neukirchen-Vluyn: Neukirchener, 1963); H. Kasting, *Die Anfänge der christlichen Mission* (Munich: Kaiser, 1969); L. E. Keck, "The Poor among the Saints in Jewish Christianity and Qumran," *ZNW* 57 (1966) 54–78; J. Lambrecht, "The Relatives of Jesus in Mark," *NovT* 16 (1974) 241–58; C. M. Tuckett, "The Beatitudes," *NovT* 25 (1983) 117–25.

---

[50] Cf. Theissen, *Studien,* 79–105.

3. Male/female disciples; the Twelve

As a group the disciples surround the ministry of Jesus and share in it. They accompany their master, are sent out by him, at times show they are perplexed, are rebuked or encouraged by him. This is the portrait we gain of them in the Gospels. The commonality, indeed the stylizing, of their portrait is surely associated with the circumstance that the believers of the post-Easter communities are to recognize themselves in the disciples. It is difficult to determine anything about individual disciples and their relationship to Jesus. There are many names but no faces.

Among those who followed Jesus there also were women. Though Mark 15:40f. does not designate them as disciples,[51] he clearly characterizes them as such: "when he was in Galilee, [they] followed him, and ministered to him; and . . . came up with him to Jerusalem." Luke 8:2f. provides us with a list of the names of female disciples. What is noteworthy is that the women are named after the Twelve: "Mary, called Magdalene, from whom seven demons had gone out, and Joanna, the wife of Chuza, Herod's steward, and Susanna." Along with Mary there were other women who had been healed by him. Both Mark 15:41 and Luke 8:3 speak of many others. Both references assume that the women accompanied Jesus.

Luke elucidates their ministry: They "provided for him out of their means." Is this a projection onto the time of Jesus of later missionary contexts, in which affluent women assisted missionaries economically? Or did the radical directives of the discourse on missions take a different form for the female disciples? Much remains obscure on this. At any rate, by accepting women among his followers Jesus did something very provocative for his contemporaries. Women disciples among the Jewish rabbis were inconceivable. Even in the ministry of the synagogue only men were eligible. A woman did not read from the Torah. She did partake of the Passover meal. She was barred from the prayer of the Shema. The Sabbath commandment did not apply unconditionally to women. Religious instruction was not a matter of course for women. When Jesus admits women as disciples, he seeks to alleviate the position of

---

[51] In the NT the feminine form of the term "disciple" is found only in Acts 9:36, where it refers to Tabitha of Joppa, who is thus described as a Christian. Acts uses the term "disciple" for the members of the Christian community.

women suppressed by society and to promote the restoration of their human dignity.

In the Gospels' lists of women Mary of Magdala is generally mentioned first (Mark 15:40 par.; 15:47 par.; 16:1 par.; Luke 8:2; 24:10).[52] Her person has been burdened by supposition in the history of interpretation. Ever since Gregory the Great she has been identified as the sinful woman of Luke 7:36–50.[53] Hence she found her way into the liturgy as the penitent one. This view has been recognized as erroneous. Mary was set free of seven demons, which means that she was healed of a serious sickness. This has nothing in common with the life of a sinful woman. Her epithet, Magdalene, derives from the town of Magdala, where she came from, on the Lake of Gennesaret, situated half an hour by road north of Tiberias, at the mouth of the Valley of Doves.[54] That she is mentioned first in the list of women points to her preeminence.[55] In the community she was held in high regard because, together with other women, she stood at the cross and in all probability experienced the initial appearance of the resurrected Lord.[56] Thus she was an extremely important witness of the life, passion, death, and resurrection of Jesus.

We know nothing about the other two women, Joanna and Susanna, in the list of Luke 8:2f. Since the former is introduced as the wife of a high-ranking official (ἐπίτροπος) of the tetrarch Herod Antipas, both women are associated with Galilee. This likewise applies to the women at the cross.[57]

A unique call narrative is dedicated to Levi, the son of Alphaeus (Mark 2:14). Immediately following his calling there is the story of

---

[52] In John 19:25 Mary Magdalene is mentioned last in a listing of four women. Here John adheres to the principle of the degree of relationship. Cf. M. Hengel, "Maria Magdalena und die Frauen als Zeugen," in *Abraham unser Vater* (FS O. Michel; AGSU 5; Leiden: Brill, 1963) 250.

[53] Cf. J. Schmid, *Das Evangelium nach Markus* (4th ed.; RNT 2; Regensburg: Pustet, 1958) 254f. (Excursus: "Die Magdalenen-Frage").

[54] On his way from Nazareth to Capernaum Jesus must have passed through Magdala; so also on his trips from Galilee to Jerusalem. Curiously Magdala is not mentioned in the context of Jesus' ministry. According to Schürmann, *Lukasevangelium*, 1.446, n. 13, as a town Magdala was notorious for its illicit sexual behavior. But this is to mistake this town with Magdala Sabbaᵃyya; cf. Str-B, *Kommentar*, 1.1047.

[55] The listings of women repeatedly contain three names, presumably in keeping with the regulation concerning witnesses, Deut 19:15.

[56] Cf. John 20:11–18; Luke 24:22f.; Matt 28:9f. The reason for her name not being included in the list of witnesses in 1 Cor 15:5 is that according to Jewish law women were not qualified to be witnesses.

[57] Cf. Gnilka, *Markus*, 2.326.

Jesus at table with tax collectors and sinners. Although we have no other information about him, the important thing is that he is a tax collector. Tax collecting was considered a despised profession. The Pharisees did not accept tax collectors among their ranks. For this reason the calling of a tax collector must be seen as an expression of the forgiveness of sins. There is no clear answer to the question of why in Matt 9:9 the name Levi was replaced by that of Matthew. It may be assumed that Levi and Matthew were two distinct persons and that the first evangelist had particular reasons for this substitution.[58] The locus of this calling too is at the Lake of Gennesaret, in the vicinity of Capernaum. The tax office is appropriate for the vicinity of this border town.

In John 1:45–50 we are told how Nathanael became Jesus' disciple. He is a Galilean as well, a native of Cana (John 21:2). It is noteworthy that his name is not found in the list of the Twelve either. It is wise to desist from the constantly recurring attempts at identifying him with one of the Twelve, via another name, even if these were included in the Greek liturgy.[59]

Only in John's Gospel do we encounter the disciple who is remembered by the particularly distinguishing designation "whom Jesus loved" (13:23–29; 19:26f.; 20:2–10; 21:7, 20–23) and hence is called the beloved disciple for short. Comparable symbolic names are known from the Qumran writings (Teacher of Righteousness, wicked priest). Here the problems intensify to the point of the insoluble. In current scholarship two exclusive views are being asserted: He cannot be identified with John; yet he is not a symbolic figure either. Who is he? Determining his name should be avoided. He was a disciple of Jesus, and after Easter he became the decisive authority for the "Johannine community." R. Schnackenburg assumes that he came from Jerusalem.[60] But he could also have been a Galilean, especially if one is prepared to see the beloved disciple in the "other disciple" who with Andrew belongs to those who were called first according to the Fourth Gospel[61] and if one takes 21:7

---

[58] On this issue, cf. Gnilka, *Matthäusevangelium,* 1.330f.; R. Pesch, "Levi-Matthäus," *ZNW* 59 (1968) 40–56.

[59] In the Greek liturgy Nathanael is identified with Simon the Zealot. Schnackenburg, *John,* 1.314, leaves the possibility of an identification open. At various times Bartholomew has been suggested; these are constructions, however.

[60] R. Schnackenburg, "Der Jünger, den Jesus liebte," *EKK* (Einsiedeln, 1970) 2.97–117, esp. 113: "There is no ultimate certainty." Cf. idem, *John,* 3.375–88.

[61] Narratively it would be very plausible if this disciple had not yet been known as the beloved disciple in the story of the call.

(the fishing scene) seriously. If he was from Jerusalem, he was an exception to the circle of Galileans.[62]

The Twelve are the best-known group of Jesus' disciples. In Mark, the earliest Gospel, they are simply called the Twelve (3:14; 6:7; 9:35; 10:32; 11:11; 14:17). In Matthew they may be called the twelve disciples (10:1) or at one point even the twelve apostles (10:2). In the Lukan writings the term "twelve apostles" becomes dominant (Luke 6:13; 9:10; 17:5; 22:14; 24:10). These become a sacrosanct institution, as indicated particularly in the subsequent election of Matthias (Acts 1:12–26; cf. Rev 21:14).[63] The evidence shows that a distinction needs to be made between the Twelve and the apostles; post-Easter the latter have to be seen as a larger group, as confirmed by the differentiation between the Twelve and "all the apostles" (1 Cor 15:7), based on the early credal statement in 1 Cor 15:5.

The question of how and when the circle of the Twelve was established is hotly debated. For many scholars the circle of the Twelve originated only in the post-Easter situation, as the body of the community's leadership, in conditions of intense expectation of the imminent coming of the end.[64] Here one appeals especially to the absence of the Twelve in the logia source, to their early disappearance from the horizon of the community's awareness, and to 1 Cor 15:5 cited above. This view, however, only increases the difficulties. How is it to be explained that a body created after Easter was projected back into Jesus' life and that Judas, who handed Jesus over, is consistently called "one of the twelve" (Mark 14:10, 20, 43; Matt 26:14; et al.)?[65] Indeed, as one of the Twelve, it is precisely Judas who represents an important argument for Jesus himself having established the circle of the Twelve. This is further supported by the sketch of the development from the Twelve to the twelve apostles, as well as by the observation that as a prophetic

---

[62] Occasionally appeal is made to John 7:3 for disciples of Jesus from Judea. But this verse is hardly suitable for a reconstruction of this kind. Cf. Bultmann, *John*, 289 n. 9.

[63] In this case Luke has difficulties with the apostleship of Paul. On the Lukan portrait of Paul, cf. K. Löning, *Die Saulustradition in der Apostelgeschichte* (NTA 9; Münster: Aschendorff, 1973); C. Burchard, *Der dreizehnte Zeuge* (FRLANT 103; Göttingen: Vandenhoeck & Ruprecht, 1970).

[64] Cf., e.g., P. Vielhauer, "Gottesreich und Menschensohn in der Verkündigung Jesu," *Aufsätze zum Neuen Testament* (TB 31; Munich: Kaiser, 1965), 68–71.

[65] This calls for the construction of daring postulates, such as that Judas's fall represents the spectacular apostasy of a member of the early community, which was then projected back into the life of Jesus as a lasting memory.

sign, the constitution of such a group certainly fits the manner of Jesus' ministry. If the Twelve are not mentioned in Q, as far as we are able to reconstruct its content, the reason may lie in the character of this source as sayings.[66]

Therefore if we assume that Jesus himself established the group of the Twelve, he intended to communicate something symbolic thereby. The numeral twelve has to do with Israel, the people of God. The nation is composed of twelve tribes. In any case, Israel's existence as a nation of twelve tribes was perceived as the ideal state of affairs. This was true even of the time of Jesus, though most of these tribes no longer were in existence, having disappeared in warlike events, in deportations. There are numerous attestations of this awareness.

> Flavius Josephus, *Ant.* 11.107, narrates in an idealized way that, after their return from the Babylonian exile and after erecting a new temple, the Israelites, among other things, sacrificed twelve goat kids, in accordance with the number of tribes. The *Epistle of Aristeas* (47–50) reports that in conjunction with the Greek translation of the Bible the Jews sent a delegation from each of the twelve tribes, with the task of confirming the reliability of the translation. The *Testaments of the Twelve Patriarchs,* a writing whose original existence may date back to the second century BCE, confirms the interest in the number twelve. In the Qumran community there was a body of twelve men, charged with particular tasks, which also had affinities with the commemoration of the nation of twelve tribes (1QS 8:1; cf. 1QM 2:2). Finally, in Rev 7:4–8 the seer of Patmos notices the host of the 144,000 who are saved, twelve thousand from each tribe.

The passages mentioned also express the hope that, in the messianic time of the end, the people as a whole will be restored. The ministry of Jesus is likely to be categorized as belonging to this context of expectation. Jesus' circle of the Twelve symbolizes the turning to the nation of Israel as a whole, the promise of its reconstruction, its destiny for the salvation of the coming reign of God. Within this perspective we observe that, while the individual is challenged to make a decision, ultimately it is the people of God who are in the purview of his work. The symbolic nature of the circle of the Twelve may be alluded to in the (pre-Markan)[67] comment in Mark 3:14 that they are to be with him. Yet we remember that, as far as the objective of following Jesus is concerned, we saw that its primary intent was their

---

[66] With regard to its reconstruction, the logion of Matt 19:28 par., which could be construed as an allusion to the Twelve, is too problematic and hence has to be left out of consideration.

[67] Cf. Gnilka, *Markus,* 1.136–38.

involvement in the proclamation of the kingdom of God. To be sure, as the nucleus of discipleship, the Twelve are not to be excluded from this task. In conjunction with the proclamation of the *basileia* the Twelve were able to present the offer of salvation made to Israel even more effectively. It remains to be noted that at this earliest stage the Twelve did not yet perceive any additional, specific function, such as participating in the eschatological reign and rule of the Son of man, as expressed later in Matt 19:28 par.; nor is their existence to be restricted to depicting a prophetic sign.

Within the NT we are given three lists of the names of the Twelve, three in the Synoptics (Mark 3:16–19; Matt 10:2–4; Luke 6:14–16) and one in Acts 1:13, while the Gospel of John significantly has none.[68] In the following we present the sequence of the twelve names with their epithets as given in Matt 10:2–4:

> Simon, who is called Peter
> Andrew his brother
> James the son of Zebedee
> John his brother
> Philip
> Bartholomew
> Thomas
> Matthew the tax collector
> James the son of Alphaeus
> Thaddaeus
> Simon the Cananaean
> Judas Iscariot, who betrayed him

Apart from the different sequence in listing Andrew and Thomas, the names found in the four lists agree, with one exception: both Lukan lists omit Thaddaeus. He is replaced by Judas (the brother?) of James, which may be secondary.[69] All of the lists begin with Simon Peter and end with Judas Iscariot. The positioning of both is intended as a value judgment.

The following observations are worth mentioning. The first four are the two pairs of brothers who were called first, according to

---

[68] John's Gospel has only four inferential references to the Twelve, twice in the phrase "one of the Twelve," relative to Judas Iscariot and Thomas (6:67, 70, 71; 20:24). It is unlikely that Q contained a list of the Twelve, as M. Trautmann, *Zeichenhafte Handlungen Jesu* (FB 37; Würzburg: Echter, 1980) 216f., assumes.

[69] Was the reference here to Judas the Lord's brother (cf. Mark 6:3)? Was it a case of securing the apostolic authority of the letter of Jude (cf. Jude 1)? This is the assumption of Pesch, *Markusevangelium,* 1.208. John 14:22 also mentions a second Judas.

Mark 1:16–20 and Matt 4:17–22. Could it be that Jesus had only these four disciples initially?[70] Simon Peter and Andrew, as well as Philip (cf. John 1:44; 12:21), were from Bethsaida, located east of the Jordan and hence no longer part of Galilee but rather of Gaulanitis.[71] Peter and Andrew had moved to Capernaum. It may not be coincidental that Andrew and Philip were the members of the circle of the Twelve who had Greek names, the latter even the name of a tetrarch.[72] It is not inconceivable that especially the disciples from Bethsaida had a good command of the Greek language. According to Mark 3:17 Jesus conferred on the two brothers James and John the additional name of Boanerges, which Mark understands to mean "sons of thunder." Its meaning is not clear (temperament, Zealot mindset, authority?). It is of interest that the double vowel in "Boan" contains an echo of the Galilean dialect of Aramaic, characterized by the obscuring of the *a*.[73]

In Matt 16:17 Simon Peter receives the further name Bar-Jona. Following John 1:42; 21:15, his name is Simon the son of John. For this reason Bar-Jona is also construed in the sense of this patronym. It is unlikely that the name Bar-Jona proves that Simon Peter was a Zealot because the Zealots were designated by the plural form of Bar-Jona.[74] This designation for the Zealots does not emerge until later. Simon's milieu does not support this either.[75] By contrast, the other Simon in the circle of the Twelve is clearly a Zealot, as his epithet "the Cananaean" indicates, aptly translated as "Zealot" in Luke 6:15.[76]

Judas, concluding the sequence of the Twelve, bears the rather mysterious name Iscariot. There are three possibilities of derivation:

Judas, concluding the sequence of the Twelve, bears the rather mysterious name Iscariot. There are three possibilities of derivation:

---

[70] This is J. D. Kingsbury's assumption, "The Figure of Peter in Matthew's Gospel as a Theological Problem," *JBL* 98 (1979) 67ff.

[71] John 12:21 refers to Bethsaida in Galilee. This is incorrect. If one reckons that the riverbed of the Jordan moved and the river flowed into the lake east of Bethsaida, a shift of this kind would have to have occurred in the pre-Christian era. At the time of Jesus Bethsaida was the residence of Philip the Tetrarch.

[72] Thaddaeus could be a Greek name, if it is derived from Theudas.

[73] Cf. G. Dalman, *The Words of Jesus* (ET; 2d ed.; Edinburgh: T. & T. Clark, 1902) 39 n. 4.

[74] Contra Cullmann, *Der Staat im Neuen Testament* (2d ed.; Tübingen: Mohr, 1961) 11, who borrowed this notion from R. Eisler.

[75] On the discussion of this, cf. M. Hengel, *The Zealots* (ET; Edinburgh: T. & T. Clark, 1989) 53–56, esp. 55f., n. 251.

[76] On designating the Zealots as zealous ones, cf. ibid., 59–75.

1. He is so called on account of his place of origin, "the one of Kerioth,"[77] in southern Judea—a place also mentioned in Josh 15:25—the precise location of which is hard to determine. In this case Judas would also be an outsider in terms of his origin.

2. Iscariot is associated with *sicarius*.[78] This would associate Judas with the Zealot movement as well, more specifically with a presumably particularly rigorous group that obtained its name from the way its members fought (from *sica*, "dagger").[79]

3. Iscariot is construed as a name depicting a motive (man of falsehood).[80] In this case the Christian community would have given him this name later. The first or third derivation could be correct.

Of particular interest for us is the name Peter that was given to Simon, the disciple mentioned first. To begin with, it is helpful to recall that there is no evidence for the occurrence of Peter as a first name in the pre-Christian era (though similar names do occur, e.g., Petrios, Petraios, Petron[81]). This means that Simon was given this name for the purpose of expressing something. In Matt 16:18 the bestowal of the name Peter is linked with the intention of building the church. This, however, is a secondary interpretation of the name Peter, which can be recognized from the fact that "Petros" becomes the πέτρα, the rock (change of gender and meaning), whereas "Petros" signifies "stone" (more frequently "slingstone"). In his *Handwörterbuch der griechischen Sprache,* F. Passow makes the following firm observation on the term πέτρος: "always denotes *stone* and hence clearly distinct from πέτρα, *rock.*" Hence Matt 16:18 assumes that this disciple already had this name, which is merely given a new interpretation here.

How did Simon obtain this name? What did it mean at the outset? If a reinterpretation could follow this name and Simon thus

---

[77] This is Dalman's suggestion, *Words of Jesus,* 51f. According to M. Noth, *Das Buch Josua* (HAT I/7; Tübingen: Mohr, 1953) 93f., Kerioth was situated in the region of Horma, i.e., south of Hebron, east-northeast of Beersheba. Cf. the map on p. 91. According to Abel, *Géographie* 2.417, it was seven kilometers (4.3 miles) south of Tel Ma'in.

[78] O. Cullmann, "Der zwölfte Apostel," in *Vorträge und Aufsätze,* 214–22, esp. 218f. Before him, F. Schulthess, "Zur Sprache der Evangelien," *ZNW* 21 (1922) 241–58, esp. 250ff.

[79] On the *sicarii,* cf. Hengel, *Zealots,* 46–53.

[80] B. Gärtner, *Die rätselhaften Termini Nazoräer und Iskariot* (HSoed 4; Stockholm, 1957). From John 6:71; 13:2, 26 ("son of Simon Iscariot") we gather what the name of Judas's father was. The association of Iscariot with the name of the father could favor the derivation from Kerioth as a place-name.

[81] In P. Lampe, "Das Spiel mit dem Petrusnamen—Mt. 16:18," *NTS* 25 (1979) 228.

already had the name Peter, the notion suggests itself that its origin goes back to Jesus. Jesus called Simon "Kepha." This is the original Aramaic form. Ten times we encounter it in the NT, in the slightly hellenized form "Kephas."[82] The predominant meaning of the Aramaic *kepha* is "stone," as well as "precious stone"[83] and "rock."

Simon's role as spokesman for the disciples is still intimated in Gospels. The most obvious explanation for this is that, together with his brother Andrew, he was the first to be called by Jesus. Andrew may well have been the younger of the two. It may be assumed that conferral of the name Kepha is associated with Simon as the earliest follower of Jesus. Perhaps this took place at his calling. Or did it happen when the circle of the Twelve was constituted?[84]

It may be said in summary that Jesus' disciples, men and women, were primarily Galileans. Especially from the perspective of his followers, the movement he produced appears to be a Galilean one. Of many of the female and male disciples we have no information other than their names. Neither is it possible to say how many disciples he had, other than that apart from the Twelve there also were other disciples. By means of the Twelve, Jesus presented the people of Israel with a prophetic sign indicating that they were to be gathered for the imminent kingdom of God. Within the Twelve, Simon is in first place. The conferral of the name Kepha distinguishes him as the first of Jesus' disciples.

Overview

In terms of its symbolic significance for Israel, the group of the Twelve diminishes after Easter. The functions of leadership in the community of Jerusalem hardly take note of it. Acts 6:2 offers too fragile a premise for a position such as this. Its significance is now

---

[82] Besides John 1:42, consistently in the proto-Pauline letters. Whether "Kepha" was a term already used as a forename is questionable. The evidence in the Elephantine papyri is uncertain. Cf. the controversy between J. A. Fitzmyer, "Aramaic 'Kepha' and Peter's Name in the New Testament," 121–32, in *Text and Interpretation* (FS M. Black; Cambridge: Cambridge University Press, 1979) esp. 127ff., and P. Grelot, *Documents araméens d'Egypte* (Paris: Editions du Cerf, 1972) 476.

[83] G. Dalman, *Aramäisch-neuhebräisches Handwörterbuch* (3d ed.; Göttingen: Vandenhoeck & Ruprecht, 1938) 197, left column.

[84] This is the assumption of R. Pesch, "Πέτρος," *EDNT* 3.84f. In the Gospels Jesus consistently addresses this disciple as "Simon" (Mark 14:37; Matt 16:17; 17:25; Luke 22:61; John 21:15–17). The one exception is Luke 22:34, on which cf. par. Mark 14:30. From this it may be concluded that the name Kepha-Peter had not yet displaced the name Simon.

seen in a new light. Although they are still mentioned next to all the apostles in 1 Cor 15:5, 7—it may be assumed that the Twelve here are part of all the apostles—Luke especially promotes a development whereby the name "apostle" becomes restricted to the Twelve. As the twelve apostles, they are the leading and authoritative witnesses of the life, death, and resurrection of Jesus. Within the group of the apostles Simon Peter becomes a special "qualified witness" in the sense described and thus the rock upon whom the church of the Messiah is to be built. This extraordinary task of Simon Peter, with its link in the pre-Easter context, has its basis in the post-Easter situation through the appearance of the resurrected one first to him, which also distinguishes him in a personal way from the Twelve (1 Cor 15:5; Luke 24:34). Having been the first twice, at the beginning of Jesus' ministry and at the new beginning after the cross and Easter, he became the Kepha of the church.

Select bibliography: J. Gnilka, "Tu es Petrus," *MTZ* 38 (1987) 3–17; F. Hahn, "Die Petrusverheissung Mt 16,18f.," 185–200, in *Exegetische Beiträge zum ökumenischen Gespräch* (Göttingen: Vandenhoeck & Ruprecht, 1986); M. Hengel, "Maria Magdalena und die Frauen als Zeugen," 243–56, in *Abraham unser Vater* (FS O. Michel; AGSU 5; Leiden: Brill, 1963); J. D. Kingsbury, "The Figure of Peter in Matthew's Gospel as a Theological Problem," *JBL* 98 (1979) 67–83; J. Lambrecht, " 'Du bist Petrus'—Mt 16,16–19 und das Papsttum," *SNTU* 11 (1986) 5–32; P. Lampe, "Das Spiel mit dem Petrusnamen—Mt. 16:18," *NTS* 25 (1979) 227–45; H. Merklein, "Der Jüngerkreis Jesu," 65–100 in *Die Aktion Jesu und die Re-aktion der Kirche* (K. Müller, ed.; Würzburg: Echter, 1972); R. Pesch, "Levi-Mattäus," *ZNW* 59 (1968) 40–56; B. Rigaux, "Die 'Zwölf' in Geschichte und Kerygma," 468–86 in *Der historische Jesus und der kerygmatische Christus* (H. Ristow and K. Matthiae, eds.; 2d ed.; Berlin: Evangelische Verlagsanstalt, 1964); G. Schmahl, *Die Zwölf im Markusevangelium* (TThSt 30; Trier: Paulinus Verlag, 1974); P. Vielhauer, "Gottesreich und Menschensohn in der Verkündigung Jesu," 55–91, in *Aufsätze zum NT* (TB 31; Munich: Kaiser, 1965); A. Vögtle, "Das Problem der Herkunft von Mt 16,17–19," 109–40, in *Offenbarungsgeschehen und Wirkungsgeschichte* (Freiburg im Breisgau: Herder, 1985).

Israel, People, and Church of God

The constituting of the circle of the Twelve as a prophetic sign has directed our attention more intently to the notion of the people of God. We now need to consider Jesus' ministry in terms of its place in the history of salvation. In theological language the term *Heilsgeschichte* ("salvation history") did not emerge until the nineteenth century. It is an important term and as such is relevant to biblical findings, to the extent that, from the biblical perspective, God's salvation reveals itself in history. With regard to Jesus it denotes particularly the fact that his ministry was anticipated and that he is part of a broader history. The realization of this expectation, of course, stands in contrast to this broader history. Expressed in the premonitions of the prophets, this expectation could be obscured and made to suit human—far too human—desires. When God acts, he always does so in a new and surprising way, even for pious expectation. In Jesus, however, that which is ultimate has appeared, the kingdom of God can be experienced, something radically new has dawned. The dawning of the new that concludes history's past, fulfills and leads it toward its zenith, is in mind in the saying "From the days of John the Baptist until now the kingdom of heaven has been coming violently. For all the prophets and the law prophesied until John" (Matt 11:12–13; cf. also Mark 1:15).

Jesus' link is particularly with the people of Israel. He encounters this people with its history. In his ministry his focus is on this people. These correlations are expressed in numerous ways in his work. He himself is part of this people, an Israelite; he speaks its language and in his proclamation uses familiar images and motifs, drawn from the Bible's metaphorical language, with which his hearers were well acquainted. Even if he addresses the individual and calls him or her to decide, he sees that person as an integral part of this people. If his offer of salvation were understood in terms of individualized salvation, it would be grossly misconstrued. Since this is the people on whom he focused, to whom he knew he was sent, and whom, with his disciples' assistance, he sought to prepare for the approaching kingdom of God, there was no reason to establish first a collective entity such as this. In salvation-history terms, it was indeed necessary for him to fulfill his task in Israel. Jesus' ministry is understood only when this orientation of his ministry is given undiminished acknowledgement. The frequent comment that Jesus' audience among Galilee's mixed population also contained Gentiles does not essentially affect this orientation at all. We have to reckon with such Gentiles in his audience, to be sure, but his salvific will is nevertheless focused on Israel. To formulate it pointedly, Israel was his "church," the people who were to be called out anew and ultimately into God's kingdom. By church (ekklesia) one first and foremost has nothing else in mind than the called-out people of God.[1]

In the Gospels the orientation of Jesus' ministry to Israel is further indicated in that it remains spatially confined to the land of Israel. While the Decapolis, the region of the ten hellenized towns east of the Jordan, is mentioned (Mark 5:20; 7:31; Matt 4:25)[2] and according to Mark 7:24ff. par. Matt 15:21ff. Jesus travels to the region of Tyre and Sidon (which Luke omits) and according to Mark 8:27 par. Matt 16:13 undertakes a trip to the region of Caesarea Philippi (Luke 9:18 speaks vaguely of Jesus being alone), there is no reference at all to missionary activity among the Gentiles. Whatever may have been the case regarding the trip to the region of Tyre and Sidon, the geographical reference is quite vague, and the trip is possibly inferred from the healing granted to a Syrophoenician woman (Mark 7:26 par.), which furthermore is characterized as an exception (Mark 7:27–30 par.) If there is no missionary work that can be determined as a historical reminiscence of a trip to the north, what

---

[1] It is important to remember that in the Greek translation (LXX) Israel is frequently termed *ekklesia, ekklesia of the Lord,* or something similar: Deut 23:1, 2; Judg 20:2; 1 Kgs 8:14, 22, 55; 1 Chron 13:2, etc. The Hebrew equivalent in most instances is *qāhāl.*

[2] Only Scythopolis was situated to the west of the Jordan and was also part of the Decapolis.

might be in mind here is the intention to escape the temporary harassment by the tetrarch, Herod Antipas (cf. Luke 13:31f.).

Inconspicuous details shedding light on this orientation, like a momentary flash, are something to be reckoned with. We are choosing the healing narrative of Matt 8:5ff., which is characterized by a seemingly precise reference to person and place. In Capernaum a centurion living there entreats him to heal his seriously ill servant. The centurion is identified as a Gentile. Beyond the indicators cited, the narrative gains historical concreteness through Jesus' reaction, which can indeed be understood fully only if it is construed as a question, "Should I come and heal him?" (v. 7).[3] There is a slight sound of indignation to be detected in this question. It is the indignation of the Jewish Jesus, who is asked to enter the house of a Gentile. The famous answer of the centurion fits this interpretation.

The focus of Jesus' ministry on Israel becomes even more vivid for us if we recall that, in terms of their spiritual and religious perspective, the people were not unified but divided into various factions and parties. Jesus does not join any of these groupings, favoring none. He did experience tension with one group or another, of course, but this does not remove the focus of his intention for Israel as a whole. This intention was underscored by constituting the circle of twelve men and by their mission.

Jesus established the center of his ministry in Galilee; perhaps it can even be pinpointed as the northeastern region adjacent to the lake. Why is it that the Gospels do not mention towns such as Sepphoris, Magdala, Gabara in conjunction with his activities?[4] Could it be that he was received badly there? Could he have left the ministry there to his disciples? We can only pose these questions, not answer them. He avoided Samaria.[5] How often was he in Jerusalem? We know that according to the account in the Synoptic Gospels Jesus enters the capital only once during his public ministry, namely, for the Passover of his passion. Yet this account is based on literary intention. His movement to Jerusalem is dramatized. The Gospel of John assumes more than one visit to Jerusalem, though there are redactional transpositions, such as placing the pericope of the temple cleansing at the beginning (2:13–17), and interpolations (6:1 continues 4:54) that need to be reckoned with. If Jesus was concerned with Israel as a whole, it was indispensable for

---

[3] Cf. Gnilka, *Matthäusevangelium*, 1.301.

[4] This question was posed already by W. Bauer, *Jesus der Galiläer* (FS A. Jülicher; Tübingen: Mohr, 1927) 31.

[5] Luke 9:51–55 has preserved this reminiscence.

him to minister in the southern region as well. For W. Bauer, it was his lack of popularity closer to home that drove him to Jerusalem.[6]

It may be disconcerting that the explicit statements focusing on Israel as a totality are utterances of judgment. Yet this happens almost automatically if it is assumed that Jesus' positive focus on Israel as a whole is a given. For this reason, bringing these judgment sayings into the discussion may distort the picture. It is important from the start to keep in mind the priority of the offer of salvation, inclusive of all Israelites and presented with intensity, and that it is not canceled as long as he is at work. The tone of the judgment sayings is one of warning and thus not to be ignored. It is not necessary to think that he used many of these sayings repeatedly.[7]

Let us turn our attention to the object of his judgment sayings. In Matthew 12:41f. par. it is "this generation":

> *"The men of Nineveh will arise at the judgment with this generation and condemn it; for they repented at the preaching of Jonah, and behold, something greater than Jonah is here. The queen of the South will arise at the judgment with this generation and condemn it; for she came from the ends of the earth to hear the wisdom of Solomon, and behold, something greater than Solomon is here."[8]*

As a designation, the phrase "this generation" threatens and accuses and is integrated into a pronouncement of judgment. It receives its form from the OT, where it is used in the same sense and can be embellished with appropriate adjectives: "For forty years I loathed that generation and said, 'They are a people who err in heart, and they do not regard my ways' " (Ps 95:10); "Not one of these men of this evil generation shall see the good land . . . " (Deut 1:35). In Deut 32:5 they are called "a perverse and crooked generation."[9] In the saying of Jesus the reason for the rebuke is the rejection of the offer of salvation. Since the offer pertains to the kingdom, "this generation" is the final one. Contemporary Israel as a totality, the final generation, this generation, approaches the ominous judgment in which Gentiles—the men of Nineveh and the mysterious queen of the South (cf. 1 Kgs 10:1–13; 2 Chron 9:1–12)—will rise up as

---

[6] Bauer, *Galiläer,* 32.

[7] This is Reiser's view on Matt 12:41f. par., *Gerichtspredigt,* 205.

[8] Matt 12:41f. par. Luke 11:31f. agree in the transmission of the saying, except that Luke 11:31 adds, "with the men of this generation" and for contextual reasons Matthew prefaces it with the reference to the "men of Nineveh."

[9] Cf. M. Meinertz, " 'Dieses Geschlecht' im Neuen Testament," *BZ* 1 (1957) 283–89.

witnesses for the prosecution. In their era, albeit at the very last moment, they repented, as did the Ninevites, and escaped the judgment, or they endured considerable hardship, as did the queen of the South, to take in the spiritual nourishment of wisdom from the mouth of Solomon, the wisest of the wise. Israel's guilt and accountability are more serious because it resisted a greater offer of salvation. Precisely this formulation, pointing to the message of Jesus rather than to his person, serves as an indication of his language.[10]

In Matthew 23:37 par. Luke 13:34 the addressee is Jerusalem:

> *"O Jerusalem, Jerusalem, killing the prophets and stoning those who are sent to you! How often would I have gathered your children together as a hen gathers her brood under her wings, and you would not!"*[11]

First of all, the transition is noteworthy, from the description of Jerusalem's disastrous past to the speaker's present experience: "How often would I have gathered . . . " The rendering of a personal experience may be a plausible indication that we are dealing with an authentic saying of Jesus. In this manner the speaker, Jesus, joins ranks with the long list of prophets and those whom God sent prior to him and for whom Jerusalem had prepared an awful fate—murder and stoning. He concludes this list, the last of those who have to reckon with the possibility of the prophets' violent fate.[12] The avoidance of a christological title warrants our attention. The saying is wisdom-oriented and participates in the fate of wisdom, representing God, and its messengers, who are rejected (cf. Prov 1:20ff.; *1 Enoch* 42.1f.; et al.).

The image of the hen is taken from the OT: "The children of men take refuge in the shadow of thy wings" (Ps 36:7; cf. Isa 31:5). The image describes the intensive effort to provide salvation and protection. In this instance it is not appropriate to limit Jerusalem to the city itself; as frequently in the Bible, it represents all of Israel. Consequently the phrase "How often would I have" denotes nothing other than the continued, diligently pursued endeavor to save Israel— an endeavor that appears all the more incriminating in view of the past

---

[10] For "greater" in Matt 12:41f. the Greek text has the neuter πλεῖον. Cf. U. B. Müller, "Vision und Botschaft," *ZTK* 74 (1977) 416–48, esp. 434 n. 49. It is also possible to argue for the Semitic phraseology: twice "and behold" is followed by a nominal sentence, and the definite article is omitted before "queen" and "men of Nineveh."

[11] The texts of Matt 23:37 and Luke 11:49 are largely in agreement. The shift from the second aorist to the first aorist is not very significant.

[12] Cf. O. H. Steck, *Israel und das gewaltsame Geschick der Propheten* (WMANT 23; Neukirchen: Neukirchener Verlag, 1967).

history of stubbornness and disobedience. The result of this loving effort is depressing: "you would not." The judgment is the natural result of spurning the offer of salvation. The notion of judgment is present even if v. 38 as an explicit announcement of judgment is no longer considered part of the ancient logion of Jesus.

In Matt 11:21–24 par. Luke 10:13–15 the addressees are Chorazin, Bethsaida, and Capernaum:

"Woe to you, Chorazin! woe to you, Bethsaida! for if the mighty works done in you had been done in Tyre and Sidon, they would have repented long ago in sackcloth and ashes. But I tell you, it shall be more tolerable on the day of judgment for Tyre and Sidon than for you. And you, Capernaum, will you be exalted to heaven? You shall be brought down to Hades."[13]

Structurally this saying agrees with the pronouncement of judgment upon this generation to the extent that the unrepentant Jewish public is contrasted with the willingness of the Gentiles. The contrast seems even sharper here because the willingness of Tyre and Sidon, the Syrian cities, is only assumed, while the Ninevites and the queen of the South represent concrete examples of the biblical tradition. Worse still, Tyre and Sidon are considered proud and godless in the biblical tradition: "Wail, O ships of Tarshish . . . Be ashamed, O Sidon . . . they will be in anguish over the report about Tyre" (Isa 23:1–5; cf. 23:6–18; Ezek 26–28). In Jesus' pronouncement of judgment the prophetic oracles concerning the nations are reversed. Yet it is not solely this antithesis that demonstrates that this is a saying of Jesus. These towns are reprimanded because they were places of his ministry, rather than of Christian missionaries after him. They witnessed his miracles (δυνάμεις) whereby the kingdom of God to be experienced was proclaimed to them. Chorazin, Bethsaida, and Capernaum form a triangle of towns that could be covered on foot in four or five hours and that may be considered the hub of his ministry. This is all the more noteworthy considering that Chorazin, situated three kilometers (1.9 miles) to the north of and above Capernaum, is mentioned in the Gospels only in this woe. His town, Capernaum, is given its own woe. Precisely because a declaration about Capernaum is expected in a context such as this, it may be appropriate to attribute this woe to Jesus.[14]

---

[13] Matt 11:23b, 24 is reproduced from 10:15, while Luke has no such equivalent. The introductory "But I tell you" in Matt 11:22 is Matthean redaction (cf. v. 24). Luke 10:13 has "sitting in sackcloth and ashes."

[14] F. Hahn, *Die Mission im Neuen Testament* (WMANT 13; Neukirchen: Neukirchener Verlag, 1963) 27 and n. 1, takes it to be secondary.

The pronouncement of judgment upon the three towns sounds like the outcome of an activity that is about to end or has ended. Was Jesus' action perhaps analogous to his commissioning of the disciples, according to which they were to shake the dust from their feet after an unsuccessful mission (cf. Matt 10:14)? If so, the pronouncement could have been made at the farewell from Galilee and the departure on the last journey to Jerusalem. Especially in the declaration about Capernaum, however, the feature of the woe is more prominent.[15]

In our last example of a judgment pronouncement, it is no longer possible to ascertain precisely who the addressees were.

"Many will come from east and west and sit at table with Abraham, Isaac, and Jacob in the kingdom of God and you yourselves [Matt: the sons of the kingdom] thrust out. There men will weep and gnash their teeth" (Matt 8:11f.; Luke 13:28f.).[16]

Given its Semitic form, the designation "sons of the kingdom" does indeed seem to refer to the erstwhile addressees; it could have secondary character, however, since the concept recurs in Matt 13:38 (presumably as Matthean redaction). If the original reading, as in Luke, simply said "you," to whom was it directed? Was it perhaps merely the Jewish hierarchy? This saying likewise confronts the Jews with the Gentiles. The many who are to come from the east and the west are Gentiles. (Luke 13:29 expands the scope further to include the north and the south.) The Gentiles will come and put the Jews to shame. At the eschatological banquet in the kingdom of God they will take the place of the Jews. However extensive this role reversal might be, this logion was particularly provocative on account of its implicit, sharp criticism against a false confidence in being a descendent of Abraham and of the patriarchs. This critique can be observed already in John the Baptist: "and do not presume to say to yourselves, 'We have Abraham as our father'; for I tell you, God is able from these stones to raise up children to Abraham" (Matt 3:9 par.).

This saying of Jesus picks up the ancient prophetic idea of the nations' pilgrimage to Mount Zion. The logion poses a predicament for its interpreters, which can be described as follows: Either, on account of the radical nature of the logion's content, namely, that

---

[15] With Wellhausen and Klostermann we take this sentence to be a semiticizing negative parataxis (cf. the translation).

[16] Luke reversed the two parts of the saying in order to set it in his own context. The Matthean redaction includes "the outer darkness" and "the kingdom of heaven" in place of "the kingdom of God." Cf. Gnilka, *Matthäusevangelium*, 1.300.

Gentiles will take the place of the Jews, one argues that it cannot have come from Jesus,[17] or one says that Jesus is not serious about allowing Gentiles to take the place of the Jews and merely uses this possibility as a threat.[18] Is there no compromise?

It is necessary for us to examine the prophetic announcement of the nations' pilgrimage more carefully. The texts that are of interest here are not those dealing with the nations coming to Zion in order to serve Israel and to pay tribute but rather those dealing with the Gentiles' inclusion in Israel's salvation, such as the following: "And many nations shall join themselves to the LORD in that day, and shall be my people; and I will dwell in the midst of you" (Zech 2:11), or "It shall come to pass in the latter days that the mountain of the house of the LORD shall be established as the highest of the mountains, and shall be raised above the hills; and all the nations shall flow to it, and many peoples shall come, and say: 'Come, let us go up to the mountain of the LORD, to the house of the God of Jacob; that he may teach us his ways and that we may walk in his paths'" (Isa. 2:2f.).[19]

These announcements of a gathering of the nations into Israel's salvation or law are inconceivable without the qualification that Israel herself is fully God's and serves him or, should this not be the case, is restored to such a situation. The saying of Jesus has a different point of departure, tantamount to a reinterpretation of the nations' pilgrimage. And precisely in this provocative new interpretation, similarly to the pronouncement over Tyre and Sidon, we may well recognize a piece of evidence of his language.

---

[17] E.g., D. Zeller, "Das Logion Mt. 8:11f./Luke 13:28f. und das Motiv der 'Völkerwallfahrt,'" *BZ* 15 (1971) 91.

[18] E.g., Reiser, *Gerichtspredigt,* 280f.

[19] The interpretation of the logion, which also occurs in Mic 4:1f., is controversial. Presumably the nations are coming merely to settle actual conflicts, to subject themselves, as it were, to international conventions of war, in order that there might be peace (cf. Isa 2:4; Mic 4:3; and H. Wildberger, *Jesaja I* [BKAT; Neukirchen-Vluyn: Neukirchener, 1972] 84f. O. Kaiser, *Der Prophet Jesaja Kap. 1–12* (ATD 17; Göttingen: Vandenhoeck & Ruprecht, 1960) 20, goes beyond this by suggesting that the reference is to the conversion of the nations to Yahweh. This is certainly taken even further in the Targum of Isaiah 2:2b: "And all the kingdoms will turn to him to worship there (on Zion)" (ed. J. F. Stenning). A different framework applies to Isa 66:18–24, where two differing ideas are placed side by side. First there is the active mission: "from them I will send survivors to the nations . . . and they shall declare my glory among the nations" (v. 19), followed by the pilgrimage of the nations, though only linked with the expectation that the nations will bring home to Zion the Israelites scattered among them. Cf. C. Westermann, *Das Buch Jesaja Kap. 40–66* (ATD 19; Göttingen: Vandenhoeck & Ruprecht, 1966) ad loc.

There are a number of different associations that arise. In any case, nations will be coming, called by God in the final hour to share in the kingdom of God. Jesus takes up again the ancient prophetic idea in a positive form, which in the meantime, especially via apocalypticism, had degenerated into the expectation that in the end, when the kingdom of God appears, "the multitude of the nations" (2 Esdras 13:49) will be annihilated, at least in part, depending on the respective nations' relationship to the people of Israel in history (2 Bar. 72.3–6).[20] Nations will come, even if Israel, or the majority of its people, refuses the message of Jesus. Hence the reinterpretation of the notion of the nations' pilgrimage is to be found in the idea that the nations are expected to come, even in the face of the status of Israel, which was not showing itself ready at that time to receive Jesus' declaration.

The judgment sayings allow for the view that Jesus' ministry, focused exclusively on Israel, was not successful. The majority of the people rejected him and did not understand him. Had they accepted Jesus' message, the saying concerning the nations' pilgrimage (Matt 8:11f.) raises the question of what Israel's task should have been, given that nations were to attend the eschatological arrival of the kingdom of God.[21] In any case, posing this question means to acknowledge Israel's centrality for Jesus. The question itself cannot be answered. Nevertheless, there are indications that a universalization of his proclamation of the kingdom is possible. Indeed, as we have seen in the discussion of the petitions of the Lord's Prayer (Luke 11:2), for instance, his concept of the *basileia* has a universal orientation. National political colorations, as seen in the contemporary *Psalm of Solomon* 17, for instance (establishing the throne of David in its former splendor, evicting the Gentiles from the land, etc.), are absent altogether.

Did Jesus abandon his people? This question is to be answered in the negative. If this were the case, he would have abandoned his own mission. With reference to the logion of the nations' pilgrimage, this means that one part is not to be played off against another, that is, the warning of Israel's exclusion from salvation is not to be played against the coming of the nations in order to render the warning ineffective. The question shifts to the death of Jesus. The crisis at the

---

[20] *Sib. Or.* 3:716–740 remain open-minded about the Gentiles.
[21] This issue concerned R. Guardini, *Der Herr* (5th ed.; Aschaffenburg, 1948) 46f., 113f., 259ff., 691.

conclusion of Jesus' ministry, perhaps expressed most incisively in this logion, calls for a response in view of his death. This question will have to be addressed again in the discussion of his death.

Overview

The universal church, the church of the nations, has a post-Easter beginning. To construe the church in this way is not feasible until after Easter, in any case. Jesus' relationship to Israel, the erstwhile people of God, which its rejection of him brings to an end but which is open to new beginnings, is preparatory for what is to unfold. The salvation Jesus proclaimed is focused on a people and can be realized only in a people. A people is to be gathered into the coming kingdom of God that is at hand. "People of God" / "church" and "kingdom of God" are corresponding concepts, not incompatible entities. A. Loisy's often cited assertion, that Jesus proclaimed the kingdom of God and its result was the church, is theologically incorrect. Israel's rejection of the Gospel is an experience that the apostles and early Christian missionaries had as well. Their turning to the nations, principally made possible in the message of Jesus, was the necessary theological consequence. We do know that historically the way to the Gentiles was fraught with difficulties. The church originated from the death and resurrection of Jesus, through the work of the Holy Spirit. It remains a provisional entity. What is ultimate is the kingdom of God. The better the church understands its interim status and is determined by the ultimate, the more it will be able to correspond with Jesus' ministry.

Select bibliography: W. Bauer, *Jesus der Galiläer* (FS A. Jülicher; Tübingen: Mohr, 1927) 16–34; H. van der Kwaak, "Die Klage über Jerusalem," *NovT* 8 (1966) 165–70; F. Mussner, "Gab es eine 'galiläische Krise'?" 238–52, in *Orientierung an Jesus* (FS J. Schmid; Freiburg: Herder, 1973); R. Schnackenburg, *Die Kirche im Neuen Testament* (QD 14; Freiburg: Herder, 1961); R. C. Tannehill, *The Sword of His Mouth* (Philadelphia: Fortress, 1975) 122–28; A. Vögtle, "Der Spruch vom Jonaszeichen," 103–36, in *Das Evangelium und die Evangelien* (KBANT; Düsseldorf: Patmos, 1971); D. Zeller, "Das Logion Mt 8,11f/Lk 13,28f und das Motiv der 'Völkerwallfahrt'," *BZ* 15 (1971) 222–37; 16 (1972) 84–91.

8

The Instruction

From the offer of salvation arises the instruction, the new orientation of life to be gained. Something new entered the world with Jesus. The *basileia* he proclaimed and ushered in denotes something essentially new, that which is ultimate. By means of the offer of salvation the person is confronted with what is ultimate and thus faces a decision. Newness does not necessarily mean that what is new in essence has to be demonstrated in content, with materially new directives or by stating or claiming something unprecedented. A biased, apologetically oriented perspective on Jesus' ministry and instruction—and arising from it, Christian ethics as a subsequent development—has expended too much effort in attempting to prove it. Quite apart from the fact that it would be extremely difficult to furnish such proof and would have to assume a subtle familiarity with the other world religions, and that it could easily lead to assessing other religions unfairly, it is unnecessary and brings little gain. What matters is that we examine the details. It may be worth noting, incidentally, that in observing religions comparatively in this manner, faith that is experienced and realized is far more persuasive than a theoretical comparison. Basic here is what is new objectively and conclusively, which has come into the world with Jesus but which can be received and affirmed only in the readiness of faith.

We find Jesus' instruction especially in the texts that Luke shaped into his Sermon on the Plain and Matthew, composing and editing even more, into his Sermon on the Mount. Yet before we can unearth and present Jesus' original material found there, it is necessary to mark out the theological limits within which the ethical instruction is to be viewed and assessed.

1. A person's relationship to God in light of the announced reign of God

The God whose reign and kingdom Jesus brings and proclaims is the God of the Bible, the God of Israel, the God of Abraham, Isaac, and Jacob, but also the universal God beside whom there are no other gods and who is favorably disposed to all persons. God's universality and all-encompassing power will be revealed in the eschaton. History moves inexorably toward God's final revelation. Jesus' perspective is focused on this God who is to come and who is in the process of coming, but also on the God who has been at work and continues to work in history. Jesus' announcement is of God's works, less of God's attributes, even less of God's work of creation and the work of maintaining that creation. This may be the reason why the question of the origin of evil and of suffering is not posed and the problem of a theodicy is not addressed. At his ultimate coming God will bring everything to light and clarity.

Jesus was not afraid to pronounce the name God explicitly. He declined to circumscribe this name—as was done customarily among his Jewish contemporaries—with the term "heaven," for instance. Yet he also referred to God as Father, his Father, our Father. This was not new. We are also able to observe that the divine name Father enters increasingly into the transmission of his sayings, especially in the references to the heavenly Father and, in Matthew, the Father in heaven. Nevertheless, the conception of God the Father takes on a new quality that can be seen especially in Jesus' prayers, in which he evidently addressed God consistently as his Father.

If for the moment we disregard "Father" as an appellation in prayer, which Jesus also passed on to his disciples (Luke 11:2), Father as the name for God also occurs in the tradition of the sayings source, the earliest tradition of Jesus' words accessible to us. This is seen especially in the context of God's mercy and care: "Be merciful, even as your Father is merciful" (Luke 6:36);[1] "If you then, who are evil, know how to give good gifts to your children, how much more

---

[1] By comparison the parallel saying of Matt 5:48, "You, therefore, must be perfect, as your heavenly Father is perfect," is secondary.

will your heavenly Father[2] give good things to those who ask him!" (Matt 7:11; cf. Luke 11:13); "your Father knows that you need them all [food and clothing]" (Matt 6:32; Luke 12:30).[3]

The confident dependence on God the Father is taught in the petition for bread in the Lord's Prayer: "Give us this day our daily bread" (Matt 6:11).[4] This is the only petition regarding material concerns that Jesus allows, but it is not to be diluted. Thus the Vulgate, for instance, one of the important Latin translations of the Bible, translates, "Give us this day our supernatural bread,"[5] reminiscent of the Eucharist. The reason why the petition for food that Jesus allows is so provocative is that the disciple is to pray only for the necessities, namely, for what is needed today (the Lord's Prayer is primarily a morning prayer). He is to view himself before God like a day laborer who lives and labors by trusting in him. Since it is a prayer for disciples, the disciple is to consider himself free of worry and be fully given to the task of proclamation. To be sure, the petition for bread also has an ethical implication. It is expressed in the "we" form (hence not "give me the bread I need today"). The one who possesses the world's goods is able to bring this petition honestly before God the Father only if he or she is prepared to share with the starving.

The Father-concept would become particularly apparent if we translated Matthew 23:9—a verse whose meaning is disputed—as follows: "And call no man your father on earth, for you have one Father, who is in heaven." Presumably this verse originally was handed down as an independent saying of Jesus. By placing it in the context of analogous sayings, Matthew did not understand it as radically as this but wanted to render it in the sense of "And do not

---

[2] Matt 7:11 alters it to say, "your Father who is in heaven." Otherwise he preserves the original in comparison with Luke 11:13, which refers to the gift of the Holy Spirit.

[3] Once again Matt 6:32 refers to "your heavenly Father." Other sayings linked with the designation of "Father" in Matthew are associated with the name of God in Luke: Luke 12:6 par. Matt 10:29; Luke 6:35 ("sons of the Most High"); cf. Matt 5:45 ("sons of your Father who is in heaven").

[4] The parallel in Luke 11:3, "Give us each day our daily bread," broadens "today" to a number of days. This is secondary and is associated with the waning of the eschatological expectation. The form of the bread petition used in today's liturgy, "Give us today our daily bread," is not tautological (daily-today) only if we construe "daily" in the sense of "necessary," "which we need." The underlying term ἐπιούσιος is best translated in this sense. On this issue, cf. Gnilka, *Matthäusevangelium,* 1.222f.; W. Foerster, "ἐπιούσιος," *TDNT* 2.598f.

[5] *Panem nostrum supersubstantialem da nobis hodie.*

call yourselves father on earth . . . "[6] In its presumably original meaning, which reinforces its authenticity, the logion calls for the disciple's separation from the family and for his complete dependence upon God. We do not know the specific circumstances in which the saying might have been spoken. Could it be that there is a family dispute behind it? Who does not recall the case of Francis Bernardone, who, according to tradition, renounced his father on the basis of this saying in order to obey his calling?

Through Jesus the person has entered into a new relationship with this God. Through him the God of Israel, the God of Abraham, to whom Jesus refers as Father, wants to bring home to people his gracious reign. This reign is the ultimate, the absolute upon which the person is focused, from which the people of Israel are to attain a deepened orientation to God, and upon which the history of the nations of the world is ultimately focused, for in him that history reaches its goal. We have considered both aspects of the kingdom, which appear like the two sides of one coin, namely, salvation and judgment, eschatological salvation and eschatological judgment. It is to be stressed again that the offer of salvation and the reality of salvation are meant to be what is decisive for the person or what sets him or her in motion, the initiating factor. The judgment is added secondarily as a necessity, to be sure, as of its own accord. It results from the rejection of salvation. In the pericope dealing with Jesus' instruction, hence also with his ethics, this cannot be stressed enough. Moral behavior does not correspond with fear of the judgment. In this manner the person would never be able to come to her or his senses and could never develop in her or his being. People begin to act morally because they have been gifted and recognize in the *basileia* the fulfillment of their being. It is not very appropriate to differentiate in this matter between the acting God and God's actions or, expressed theologically, to distinguish between theology and eschatology as a unifying factor in the instruction.[7] This does not work because here, as in the topics of Jesus' message considered thus far, the reign of God constitutes the center of the discussion. The reign of God implies both God's person and God's decisively liberating, saving, redeeming action, which has been brought near through Jesus.

---

[6] The Greek text allows for either translation. On this matter, cf. Gnilka, *Matthäusevangelium*, 2.276f.

[7] On this controversy, cf. W. Schrage, *The Ethics of the New Testament* (ET; Philadelphia: Fortress, 1988) 24–30; R. Schnackenburg, *The Moral Teaching of the New Testament* (ET; London: Burns & Oates, 1975) 23ff.

The stress on theology in contrast to eschatology may arise from the concern that instruction that seems to derive one-sidedly from eschatology takes on the character of an interim ethic. This would mean that the instruction, the radicality of which we will be addressing, would demand attention only for the period between Jesus' appearance and the end, a period he is alleged to have viewed as very brief. In the final analysis such interim ethics, a concept formed by A. Schweitzer, would concretely no longer apply for a protracted period of time, for the centuries following Jesus, for us. Thus it is dismissed as illusory, utopian, as intended for a catastrophic situation, or is otherwise diluted in the seriousness of the directives. Time does not do away with the ultimate, however. It may be dulled by time, and there is ample indication that this is what has happened. Hence the remembrance of Jesus' instruction is continually important.

This instruction has its premise in the God who through Jesus has become immanent and acted decisively to bring about eschatological salvation for the human being. God's will remains upheld. God wants to motivate human action and to achieve the adoption of the divine will by the human will, including its translation into practice. Here God obliges the individual and thereby enables his or her action but then also demands the action. These correlations are demonstrated in exemplary fashion in the parable of the unforgiving servant, which has already been discussed (Matt 18:23–33). By forgiving him a large debt, the master's beneficence toward the servant enabled and demanded a merciful disposition on the part of the servant toward his fellow servants. Here enablement is to be understood as spiritual, moral restoration, delight, from which enduring changes are meant to arise. These transformations create a new order or intend to overcome the old order of hatred, cheating, and egotism, exposed so glaringly by the unforgiving servant. They caused God's reign to become effective and to be made apparent in the new relationships among people.

That Jesus' instruction is linked with the shape of God's reign has been fostered by the interpretative orientation that argued that the teaching described behavior in the endtime, eschatological kingdom of God, in the hereafter. Thereby it dismissed the seriousness of Jesus' claims, of course. Instead its fulfillment is meant to present what God intends for the person in his reign. Consequently the *basileia* gives rise to Jesus' ethics as its "implication and consequence,"[8] though it could also be its anticipatory, provisional focal point.

---

[8] Schrage, *Ethics,* 28.

Before God all persons are sinners. According to the scant occurrence of the term in the synoptic tradition, of course, Jesus did not refer to sin as much as to the sinner. This too indicates that he is favorably disposed to the person and his or her need. Nevertheless, all have to be deemed sinners because all are in need of repentance.

Since all are under the verdict of sin, it has to be permissible to ask the question what precisely is to be understood by sin or how it is seen. The answer is to be sought in the context of repentance. To begin with, it may be possible to formulate it as follows: Sin appears where repentance is spurned. In the discussion of the woes against the towns of Chorazin, Bethsaida, and Capernaum (Matt 11:20–24 par.), it became apparent that Jesus' ministry there caused guilt to come to light. Since they did not repent and did not receive his salvific offer though great miracles were wrought among them, their sin was revealed and they became culpable. Sin is an event. It is the transgression of a commandment, to be sure, yet it is now primarily one's evasion of God's personal claim. Sin comes about by refusing to accept the message, just as salvation occurs in its acceptance. The person's refusal or acceptance indicates what his or her actual situation is.

How is it possible to get to the heart of the matter of sin in such rigorous fashion? Because for Jesus sin is not administered by keeping an account of it but has to do with the relationship to the loving Father God. We argued that all are sinners before God and are in need of repentance. The message of the kingdom offers salvation and forgiveness to all. Just as God accepts the whole person in this forgiveness and does not merely close a debit account that might be regarded in isolation from the person, so the person should turn to God and make a new beginning. To refuse means to decide on sin.

In the summary of Jesus' proclamation in Mark 1:15 the call to repentance is virtually linked categorically with the reign of God. Even if this summary is shaped by the evangelist, it intimates that this call to repentance is addressed to all.

The universality of the call to repentance is the topic of a vivid scene in the material unique to the Gospel of Luke (13:1–5). Two events that occurred in the history of the city of Jerusalem and in which persons perished gave rise to a statement made by Jesus. Pilate, the Roman procurator, had some Galileans murdered as they prepared to offer a sacrifice in the temple: "whose blood Pilate had mingled with their sacrifices." At the pool of Siloam a tower collapsed—apparently one of the fortified towers of the city wall—and buried eighteen people. Following a stringently applied doctrine of

retribution, according to which earthly events reveal whether someone is a sinner—good people fare well, bad people do not—the
Galilean victims and those of Jerusalem obviously must have been
sinners who received their just deserts. This viewpoint is rejected:
Those who think that these victims were worse sinners than the rest
of the inhabitants of Galilee and Jerusalem are in error. "I tell you,
No; but unless you repent you will all likewise perish."

The universality of the call to repentance, embedded in the
rhythm of the text, is skillfully developed in a composition that
intentionally refers to contemporary events in both Galilee and
Jerusalem, hence including all of Israel.[9] But this cannot be used to
argue against deriving this tradition directly from Jesus. We also
encountered the parallel mention of two historical occurrences in
the twofold pronouncement concerning the queen of the South and
the Ninevites (Matt 12:41f. par.). Weightier is the argument that
Josephus, the Jewish historian, does not mention Pilate's rather
remarkable intervention against Galileans bringing offerings in the
temple. This argument is irrelevant to the second incident, the
collapse of the tower at the pool of Siloam.[10] Could it be that the
reference to the desecration of the temple is mistaken for an incident that occurred in CE 35, in which Pilate moved with brute force
against the Samaritans on Gerizim, their holy mountain?[11] Could
Luke have linked this event redactionally with the tower of Siloam?
As a concrete contemporary point of reference, the Siloam disaster
suggests its authenticity, however. This is even more the case in
terms of the shift in the theological argument in Jesus' statement.
For him the brutal death of unfortunate people is by no means
God's seal upon the failure of people's lives, but it is rather a
warning sign that calls for repentance that is long overdue. The
warning signal is addressed to all, at least to all of Jerusalem's

---

[9] The parallelism in the description of the two incidents is slightly disturbed in
that the first incident is reported to Jesus, while he himself brings up the second.
Reiser, *Gerichtspredigt,* 294–96, considers the report as Lukan redaction and recon-
structs the following introduction to the saying: "Those Galileans whose blood Pilate
had mingled with their sacrifices, do you think . . . "

[10] The collapse of the tower might be linked with the construction of an aqueduct
that Pilate ordered to be built. Cf. Josephus, *Ant.* 18.60; *War* 2.175.

[11] On this see Josephus, *Ant.* 18.85–87. Merklein, *Gottesherrschaft,* 127 n. 223,
rejects a confusion here. J. Blinzler, "Die Niedermetzelung von Galiläern durch
Pilatus," *NovT* 2 (1958) 24–49, even seeks a dating of the incident by attempting to
find a Passover during which Jesus had not been in Jerusalem. A temporal reconstruction such as this is fraught with problems.

inhabitants. Nevertheless, the ominous possibility, "you will all likewise perish," may not refer to the destruction of the city but rather to the judgment associated with the eschatological coming of the kingdom of God. Hence the logion fits Jesus' proclamation of the *basileia* entirely. Jesus describes the relationship of the person to God ever so memorably in the parable of the Pharisee and the tax collector (Luke 18:10–14a):

> *"Two men went up into the temple to pray, one a Pharisee and the other a tax collector. The Pharisee stood and prayed thus with himself, 'God, I thank thee that I am not like other men, extortioners, unjust, adulterers, or even like this tax collector. I fast twice a week, I give tithes of all that I get.' But the tax collector, standing far off, would not even lift up his eyes to heaven, but beat his breast, saying, 'God, be merciful to me a sinner!' I tell you, this man went down to his house justified rather than the other."*

A correct understanding of the parable, which more than any other relates to its time, hinges completely on the contrast between the two individuals, their actions and their prayers. The extensive description of the content of the Pharisee's prayer in contrast with the deep sigh of the tax collector corresponds with the outline, in a few brief strokes, of the outward disposition of the former (he stood there) in contrast with the lingering description of the disposition of the latter (he stood far off; did not even lift his eyes to heaven; beat his breast). This description is not a caricature and hence is to be taken seriously. One distorts it if what is seen here is a denunciation of alleged Pharisaic pride confronted by the mature humility found in the tax collector.[12] Jesus does not teach virtue here.[13] The assertions made in the Pharisee's prayer are in keeping with the general sentiments. Tax collectors were deemed to be swindlers and robbers, while Pharisees were highly respected religious people. Who would dare to call into question the conscientious striving of the Pharisee who does more than what he is commanded to do?[14] The contrast receives its edge from its being made deliberately by the Pharisee ("like this tax collector"), not vice versa. One might think that he is the main character; yet the tax collector provides the positive example. The parable is to be read as an exemplary story. Pharisees and tax collectors represent the false and the authentic protagonist. It is disturbing that while both address "God" in identical fashion, the

---

[12] In this sense Jülicher has misunderstood the parable, *Gleichnisreden,* 2.607f.

[13] In agreement with Linnemann, *Parables,* 145.

[14] Fasting was required only on the day of Atonement, and only the proceeds of field and pasture were to be tithed.

Pharisee's prayer is introduced as a monologue (he prayed with himself, or even he prayed to himself).[15]

The verdict of the parable teller, hence of Jesus, given in v. 14a, does not agree with the common evaluation of Pharisees and tax collectors. In fact it is in sharp contradiction, turning it on its head. Since God is addressed in their prayers, it represents a kind of divine verdict. It is God's answer to both prayers. This is instructive both for Jesus' authority in his mission and for his argument with the Pharisees. The premise for this argument is theological; its roots are ultimately in a different understanding of God. He who knows he is a sinner before God and is willing to repent goes to his house justified. This is denied to the one who thinks he does not need to repent. This explanation is eminently theological, for in Jesus' view God is the one who cannot be manipulated by humans, who gives his love freely.

Thus in the exemplary story of the Pharisee and the tax collector the universality of the call to repentance is presented in a very subtle way. In his familiar relationship with God, the *homo religiosus* succumbs to the danger of surrendering the unavailability of the God he intends to serve. He too is in need of repentance. In the subtlety of the critique, which is clearly different from the later clashes with Pharisaism, this parable leads us to a central concern in Jesus' proclamation. In addition, it converges with his association with tax collectors and sinners, whom he called to his table fellowship. The "divine verdict" given at the conclusion of the narrative even confirms this fellowship with sinners as something God intended.[16]

It could be argued that, despite its forceful formulation, the call to repentance remains strangely abstract. But this impression enters only in the case of a quantitative evaluation. From a purely numerical perspective the imperative "repent!" does not occur frequently. Yet that which Jesus sought to effect by means of repentance is made concrete in the instructions that we encounter in the Sermon on the Mount.

---

[15] In agreement with W. Grundmann, *Das Evangelium nach Lukas* (THKNT 3; Berlin: Evangelische Verlagsanstalt, 1988) 350. This is translated differently by Jeremias, *Parables,* 140: "he took up a prominent position." Since monologues are characteristic of Lukan parables, as Heininger, *Metaphorik,* has demonstrated, this exemplary story fits in. The monologue necessarily sheds light on an inward situation. As a prayer, of course, the monologue obtains a particular emphasis.

[16] The passive in v. 14 is to be understood as a divine passive, circumscribing an act of God. On the semiticizing form of the parable, cf. Jeremias, *Parables,* 140.

Through Jesus the person's relationship to God has been redefined. God the Father alone offers salvation to all by means of the kingdom of God. But it is precisely the radicality of his love, as seen in Jesus' ministry, that exposes people as sinners, as well as their need of a new beginning, namely, repentance. Precisely those cannot escape this call who, as *homines religiosi,* think they own God.

Overview

The directness of the claim, couched in love, as rendered in a unique and unrepeatable form in the person of Jesus, could merely be replaced, not obtained, in the post-Easter context. The replacement came about through his word, through the Gospel and the sacraments. Perhaps the new interpretation of the parable of the Pharisee and the tax collector in Luke 18:14b is instructive: "for every one who exalts himself will be humbled, but he who humbles himself will be exalted." This saying turns the parable into an ethical maxim. Nevertheless, the issue may always be to attempt to underscore the directness of the claim. There are but few charismatic Christians, of course, who have the gift of arranging or at least expressing what S. Kierkegaard called the "contemporaneousness" with the life of Jesus.[17]

Select bibliography: H. Bald, "Eschatologische oder theozentrische Ethik?" *VF* (1979) 35–52; J. Blinzler, "Die Niedermetzelung von Galiläern durch Pilatus," *NovT* 2 (1958) 24–49; P. Hoffmann and V. Eid, *Jesus von Nazareth und eine christliche Moral* (QD 66; Freiburg: Herder, 1975); W. Marchel, *Abba, Père!* (2d ed.; AnBib 19; Rome: Pontifical Biblical Institute, 1971); J. Schlosser, *Le Dieu de Jésus* (LD, Paris: Cerf, 1987); F. Schnider, "Ausschliessen und ausgeschlossen werden," *BZ* 24 (1980) 42–56; H. Schürmann, "Das hermeneutische Hauptproblem der Verkündigung Jesu," 13–35 in *Traditionsgeschichtliche Untersuchungen zu den synoptischen Evangelien* (Düsseldorf: Patmos, 1968); D. Zeller, "Gott als Vater in der Verkündigung Jesu," 117–30 in *Standing before God* (FS M. Oesterreicher; New York: Ktav, 1981).

2. The position on the Torah

The literal meaning of "Torah" is "instruction." From the Torah— the law of Moses—the Israelite, the people of Israel obtained the definitive instruction. The instruction in the law and the prophets constituted the center of the synagogue service. At an elevated point in the synagogue was the Torah shrine, in which the scroll of the law was kept. Jesus may have preferred the open air as the place of his

---

[17] S. Kierkegaard, *Training in Christianity* (London: Oxford, 1941), invocation.

proclamation, but he also used the synagogue service as a connecting point for his preaching. On this the Gospels preserve an accurate historical reminiscence, not just regarding Nazareth (cf., e.g., Matt 4:23; 9:25; 12:9; 13:54).

Nevertheless, it is to be expected from the start that he takes a position on the Torah, expressing his view on its instruction either directly or indirectly. Since he was raised and educated as a Jew in a Jewish family, it may be assumed that he was familiar with the instructions of the Torah, including their ceremonial and Levitical purity regulations. Since he understood himself firmly as sent to the people of Israel, he could not help but voice his view. We do not have a basic statement on the Torah by Jesus. This makes the discussion of the question more difficult, of course, and explains the disparate scholarly views. In addition, even very early in the Christian communities—the earliest were Jewish Christian or a mixture of Jewish and Gentile Christian—there was a dispute over the correct understanding of the Torah, a dispute reflected in the Gospels. There are two fundamental positions on the Torah: "Think not that I have come to abolish the law and the prophets; I have come not to abolish them but to fulfil them" (Matt 5:17); and "But it is easier for heaven and earth to pass away, than for one dot of the law to become void" (Luke 16:17 par.). Although they are based on quite different premises, both are usually attributed to the early church and to the dispute indicated above.[18]

Here too it is the reign of God that makes possible an initial demarkation. In the text on entering the kingdom violently it is contrasted with the law and the prophets: "The law and the prophets were until John; since then . . . the kingdom of God . . . " (Luke 16:16 par.).[19] As far as the understanding of this saying is concerned, at this point we are merely interested in this contrast showing that, by means of the break announced by John the Baptist and established by Jesus, the law and the prophets came to a certain termination or at least were given a different perspective, in which they have to be seen from the vantage point of the *basileia*. In our discussion of the proclamation of the kingdom we have indeed been able to determine

---

[18] By placing the two sentences in parallel in 5:17f., Matthew attempts to regard this dispute as settled. Thus he develops his own interpretation of the law. Cf. Gnilka, *Matthäusevangelium*, 1.140–49; H. Hübner, *Das Gesetz in der synoptischen Tradition* (Witten: Luther-Verlag, 1973) 196–207; Barth, "Matthew's Understanding of the Law." Luke 16:17 has been termed the most Jewish sentence of the Gospel.

[19] Cf. 144f. above.

that it is henceforth the latter—and not (any longer) the law—that decides the individual's openness or rejection and that it is Jesus himself who is to be confessed but who can also be denied. This reign of God accords a different place to the Torah. In any case, it is no longer central. Salvation is connected with the reign of God, not with the law.

What should one do, however? Are the moral demands to be derived from the Torah? We choose the Decalogue as the point of entry to the problem. We encounter positions on the Decalogue in the antithetical statements of the Sermon on the Mount and in Jesus' dialogue with the rich man (Mark 10:17–27 par.). The characteristic feature is that the idea transcends the individual commandment of the Decalogue. We cannot unconditionally say that the Torah is being interpreted, but it is taken further and seen in a new light. The rich man who can say about himself that he has observed the commandments of the Decalogue, even from his youth, is summoned to sell his possessions and to follow Jesus. Whatever may have been the historical details of this call narrative, in any case the commandments of the Decalogue are acknowledged; indeed the call to discipleship can be based upon them, that is, the individual, concrete call that we have addressed already.

How is one to view the antithetical statements? This calls for some exegetical elaboration. The six antithetical statements usually contrast Jesus' instruction with an OT commandment. The first two clearly refer to a commandment of the Decalogue: Do not kill. Do not commit adultery (Matt 5:21, 27; cf. Exod 20:13; Deut 5:17f.). The fourth one is closely associated with the eighth commandment—Do not bear false witness—though the commandment is not cited; instead the instruction says, "You shall not swear falsely, but shall perform to the Lord what you have sworn" (Matt 5:33).[20]

Some scholars are not ready to trace the antitheses, or, more precisely, Jesus' instruction in antithetical form, back to Jesus; rather they take their origin to be anchored in Jewish Christianity and in its debate with Judaism.[21] This is why they are said to be found in the

---

[20] There is no literal equivalent in the OT; cf. Luke 19:12, however. The notion of the oath (ἐπιορκία) is found in the LXX: Wis 14:26–28; Zech 5:3; 1 Esd 1:46.

[21] E.g., M. H. Suggs, "The Antitheses as Redactional Products," *Jesus Christus in Historie und Theologie* (FS H. Conzelmann; Tübingen: Mohr, 1975) 433–44; I. Broer, *Freiheit vom Gesetz und Radikalisierung des Gesetzes* (SBS 98; Stuttgart: Katholisches Bibelwerk, 1980) 110. A staunch defender of tracing the antithetical statements back to Jesus is E. Käsemann, "The Problem of the Historical Jesus," *Essays on New Testament Themes* (ET; SBT 41; London: SCM, 1964) 15–47, esp. 37–38.

Gospel of Matthew. It is further argued that, while Jesus' instruction is found in Luke, it is not antithetical in form, hence the antitheses must be secondary. This, however, does not apply to the three antithetical statements mentioned above. In Luke there is nothing corresponding at all to these, even with regard to Jesus' instruction. For this reason, as well as for internal reasons, it is justified to attribute at least the first two antithetical statements to Jesus:

> "*You have heard that it was said to the men of old, 'You shall not kill; and whoever kills shall be liable to judgment.' But I say to you that every one who is angry with his brother shall be liable to judgment.*"

> "*You have heard that it was said, 'You shall not commit adultery.' But I say to you that every one who looks at a woman lustfully has already committed adultery with her in his heart*" (Matt 5:21f., 27f.).

Based on the fact that their propositions are part of the Decalogue, the sequence of which (fifth and sixth commandments) they indeed observe, the two antithetical statements are closely related to one another. Their formal structure confirms this.[22] It is to be noted that both offer a position on the Torah that agrees in principle. The introductory formula "You have heard, etc." refers to the commandment of the Decalogue as a declaration made to those of old, which is a reference to none other than the generation of Moses that received the Torah at Mount Sinai. The process of transmission is reflected here, of course. Those who have heard are Jesus' audience. They know about the promulgation of the law at Sinai. They have heard about it in the Torah readings in the synagogue service. "It was said" identifies the commandment of the Decalogue as a declaration from God (divine passive). Jesus juxtaposes this with his "But I say to you," which expresses authority. In a detailed exegetical discussion of these formulations it is important to remember that the phrases "It was said" and "But I say" were also used in rabbinic education, though one rabbi would contrast his view only with that of another and appeal to a scriptural text in support of his view. Never would he confront his view directly with God's word.[23]

The first proposition involves not only the fifth commandment of the Decalogue but also the directive on what is to be done with the murderer: He is liable to judgment. That the one who commits

---

[22] They are generally introduced by πᾶς followed by a present-tense participle.
[23] Cf. E. Lohse, "'Ich aber sage euch,'" 189–203, in J. Jeremias, *Der Ruf Jesu;* Gnilka, *Matthäusevangelium,* 1.151f.

premeditated murder should be killed could also be read in the Torah (Exod 21:12; Lev 24:17; Num 35:16ff.).[24] The judicial character of the statement is evident. The issue here is secular judgment. Jesus' position sounds judicial as well. If he renders even anger as liable to judgment, he can now have intended only divine judgment. But since anger does not represent something against which a lawsuit can be brought in a secular court, it is not necessary to suggest that a more severe punishment was to be announced. It is not the two judgments that are weighed against one another; rather the instruction of the law is being exceeded. This astounding argumentation intends for legalistic thinking and acting to be overcome. The instruction of the law remains untouched, yet the individual is to become good in his whole being. Legalistic behavior would be inadequate. Jesus' instruction gains its particular nuancing only as an antithesis to this proposition. Apart from this thesis it would almost be trite and would have many parallels in Judaism and Hellenism. In this manner, however, it becomes a sharpened sword. The term "brother" receives its full meaning as well, for brotherliness does not come about merely by abstaining from killing one another.

Perhaps the second antithetical statement highlights the essential concern even more pointedly. For one thing, unlike the first antithesis, there is no mention of punishment here but an apparent judicial fact. It is to be remembered that according to Lev 20:10 adultery was to be punished by death. Jewish law described with exactitude what constituted adultery, namely, that a man was sexually intimate with the wife or betrothed of another, that this woman was a Jewess, and that both partners were of a certain age, etc. Again Jesus is not interested in the punishment part at all but instead in the person's goodness in his existence as a whole. It is possible to commit adultery "in the heart" by looking at the wife of another in order to covet her. The formulation echoes the ninth commandment, "you shall not covet your neighbor's wife" (Exod 20:17). This too is a process that cannot be checked on by others. This instruction is not to be discredited as "Jewish supermorality."[25] Jesus also defended women, especially if they were poor, who were exposed to the advances of the gentry.

---

[24] The sentence concerning the punishment refers to a targumic tradition of interpretation, according to M. McNamara, *The New Testament and the Palestinian Targum to the Pentateuch* (AnBib 27; Rome: Biblical Institute, 1966) 126–31.

[25] Thus E. Stauffer, *Die Botschaft Jesu damals und heute* (DTb 333; Munich: Francke Verlag, 1959) 83.

The first observation we want to affirm is the following: In his position on the Torah Jesus combats legalistic behavior patterns. In their antithetical function anger and the adulterous look point to a meaning beyond themselves. The focus is on the comprehensive affirmation of the divine imperative, which also encompasses the human will. We begin to see what Jesus recognized behind or by means of the Torah—the will of God.

The instruction of the fourth antithetical statement points in a similar direction. Even if the antithetical form is secondary, the instruction retains its urgency and likewise addresses singleminded moral behavor. The issue is the problem of truth and falsehood. Jesus forbids swearing. Nevertheless, it has to be made clear in what radical ways the demand for truthfulness is made.

In this instance we also encounter Jesus' instruction in the letter of James, possibly in an earlier form than that of Matt 5:33–37:

> But above all, my brethren, do not swear, either by heaven or by earth or with any other oath, but let your yes be yes and your no be no, that you may not fall under condemnation (Jas 5:12).

Apart from its antithetical form Matt 5:33–37 offers some specific reasons for the prohibition of swearing by heaven or by the earth and presents other oath formulations (by Jerusalem, by one's own head). More particularly Matthew formulates the prohibition somewhat differently: "Let what you say be simply 'Yes' or 'No'; anything more than this comes from evil." This formulation too may be secondary.[26] In its basic structure, however, Matthew agrees with Jas 5:12.

Apart from the holiness of the divine name, from the notion of the misuse of the divine name, the prohibition of swearing has its presupposition in the perspective that the person is always before God, who always sees through him, not only when he specifically calls upon God. Swearing is to call on God as a witness. Since the person is to live in this dynamic presence of God, swearing is superfluous, unnecessary, indeed an offense against the awareness of the presence of God.

---

[26] The twofold "yes" or "no" did not have the force of an oath in contemporary Judaism, as has been argued occasionally. Yet the formulation "let your yes be yes," etc., is clearer. On the twofold yes-no, cf. E. Kutsch, "Eure Rede aber sei ja, ja, nein, nein" (*EvT* 20; 1960) 206–18, and 1 Cor 1:17f. The reference to judgment in Jas 5:12 agrees with the first antithetical statement (Matt 5:21). Matthew prefers speaking of evil speech, including in the personal sense.

Juridical thought has devised excuses. In Jewish law a distinction was made between binding and less binding oath formulations.
By means of the formulations "by heaven," "by the earth," Jesus
presumably takes up two examples that were considered to be less
binding. Jesus' theological reasoning is different from the philosophers' critical assertions on swearing. Plutarch argues that, as spiritual coercion, swearing ill befits a free man.[27] The church has always
had difficulties with the prohibition of swearing. Jesus' directive was
softened by arguing that he merely wanted to warn against abuse.
More incisive is the viewpoint that the reinstatement of oaths and
swearing takes into consideration humankind's guilt and insincerity,
and in fact exposes them.[28] Demands so radical that they pose problems are unmistakably traced back to Jesus.

In the Torah provision is made for swearing and oaths. Deuteronomy 6:13 commands that swearing be done only by the name of
God. Leviticus 19:12 warns against swearing falsely. The prophets
reprimand the thoughtless use of the oath (Jer 5:2; Zech 5:3f.; Mal
3:5). Numbers 5:11–31 describes the oath required of the wife
suspected of adultery, the law of jealousy which in fact was linked to
a sacrifice. By means of his prohibition of swearing, of course, Jesus
transcended all of these possibilities. Still, from this point his position on the Torah cannot be attributed to a systematizing formula. In
a sense he continues the critical line of the prophets, though he
intensifies it. It would be absurd to argue that by means of the
prohibition of swearing he intended to rescind the prohibition of
swearing falsely, found in the Torah. Yet he transcends it by regarding
the person as directly confronted by God. He is confronting his
listeners with the will of God. Yet it cannot be denied that his
instructions, in a provocative way, were able to bring about consequences that had to affect the Torah itself.

There is a particularly crucial logion about the stipulations of the
law relative to cultic or Levitical purity. Luke no longer includes it
because it was especially relevant in a Jewish context. It is offered in

---

[27] Plutarch, *Quaestiones Romanae* 44. Cf. Epictetus, *Enchiridion* 33.5. The picture
we have of the Essenes is conflicting. According to Josephus, *War* 2.135 (cf. *Ant.*
15.371), they rejected oaths and vows; according to *War* 2.139, however, they swore
"tremendous oaths" when they were admitted into the community. Philo, *Prob.* 84,
rates their rejection of the oath as evidence of their love of God. CD 9:8ff.; 15:1ff.;
16:7ff. assumes swearing while safeguarding certain provisos.
[28] Cf. B. Häring, *The Law of Christ,* 3 vols. (ET; Cork: The Mercier Press,
1963) 2.274ff.; D. Bonhoeffer, *The Cost of Discipleship* (ET; London, SCM Press,
1959) 122ff.

Mark 7:15 and Matt 15:11, though the latter does so in a weakened, secondary form. The following is the older Markan version: "there is nothing outside a man which by going into him can defile him; but the things which come out of a man are what defile him." In the Markan context the logion, which originally may have been handed down independently, pertains to food laws. Matthew's wording reinforced this point of reference: "not *what goes into the mouth* defiles a man, but *what comes out of the mouth* defiles a man." We may assume that this principle originally was attributed major significance.[29]

The structure of the saying is that of an antithetical parallelism and indicates that the emphasis was on its second part, hence that it was important to note the nature of the actual impurity. What constitutes the actual impurity is the evil that comes out of the person and takes shape in evil words and evil deeds. By contrast cultic impurity is irrelevant.

The idea that the person who approaches God in worship must purify himself plays an important part in the OT, as well as in other religions. In this context pollution that the person can contract comes about not only through sin but also via contact with persons, animals, utensils, and things that were deemed impure. Ritual ablutions, which were practiced customarily in the temple, had an atoning effect that removed these impurities. Since the priestly lifestyle among the Pharisees and the Essenes was considered to be exemplary, we may assume that striving for cultic purity had intensified at the time of Jesus. Since the later Mishnah devotes twelve tractates to purity questions, certain conclusions may be appropriate regarding the time before 70 CE. Although the center of the purity laws in Leviticus is in the statement "Consecrate yourselves therefore, and be holy; for I am the LORD, your God" (20:7), it is reasonable to suggest that these practices could have resulted in a trivialized piety that paid more attention to the external practice of religion than to the internal essence. Here too it was the prophets who had already intervened by means of their critique: "Wash yourselves; make yourselves clean; remove the evil of your doings from before my eyes" (Isa 1:16).[30] Without turning away from evil, washings are meaningless.

---

[29] Jeremias's view (*Theology,* 210) that the sentence is to be taken as a warning is unfounded.

[30] An example of this material piety is a prayer addressed to Marduk, found in a Sumerian text: "May the tamarisk tree purify me, the foliage release me, the sap of the palm tree blot out my sin," etc., in H. Wildberger, *Jesaja,* 46.

In terms of its authenticity and meaning, this logion of Jesus is disputed. There is the attempt to remove it from Jesus by arguing that, had they had this instruction from him, later Christian communities could not have relapsed into a more strict practice of the Torah.[31] It is frequently to be observed, however, that radical directives by Jesus were not maintained consistently in their radicality. We also know too little about the Palestinian Jewish Christianity of the early period. Furthermore, there arises the question of how critically the logion is to be taken.

According to D. Flusser[32] Jesus was critical of the Pharisees in a manner congruent with intra-Jewish practice. He cites *As. Mos.* 7:3–10, where the Pharisees are accused of immoral practices: "Their hearts, their hands practice impurity, their mouth speaks great things. In addition they say: Touch me not, so that you do not render me unclean." For Klostermann Jesus did not draw the ultimate conclusion of his message.[33] Conversely C. G. Montefiore argues that the message did away with ritual purity and represents one of the most significant assertions in the history of religion.[34] Haenchen takes this even further by asserting that Jesus is in irreconcilable contrast to part of the legacy of the Torah.[35] His God is said to be different and new.

The truth may be in the middle. We no longer know the event from which the critical statement arose. It does indeed place in question the meaningfulness of cultic purity. Yet the emphasis is on the realization of the true impurity, namely, the moral one. By directing it to the centrality of moral action, the instruction agrees with what has been established thus far. Jesus was able to develop this polemic in his critique of formalized, legalistic morality and piety. He probably did not have in mind a fundamental abolition of cultic purity. He intervenes where, in his view, the essence of faith in God is distorted. His position statements emerge ad hoc. As a Jew, he was reticent at first toward the invitation of the Gentile centurion. In his table fellowship with sinners and tax collectors he was prepared to disregard the purity laws. By associating with these people, it was no doubt true that he became cultically impure, something that he accepted.

---

[31] E.g., S. Schulz, "Die neue Frage nach dem historischen Jesus," 33–42, in *Neues Testament und Geschichte* (FS O. Cullmann; Zurich: Zwingli, 1972) esp. 39–41.

[32] Flusser, *Jesus,* 45.

[33] Klostermann, *Markusevangelium,* 70.

[34] Montefiore, *The Synoptic Gospels* (2d ed.; London: Macmillan, 1927) 1.152f.

[35] Haenchen, *Weg,* 266.

Jesus' relationship to the Sabbath can confirm this view. The Sabbath commandment, a commandment of the Decalogue, inculcates the Sabbath rest (Exod 20:8–11; Deut 5:12–15). The reasons given differ. According to Exod 20:11 the reason is God's rest on the seventh day of creation, while according to Deut 5:15 it is the liberation from slavery in Egypt. The OT does not refer to any cultic acts whatsoever on the Sabbath. At the time of Jesus one gathered in the synagogue to worship God on the Sabbath. It was held to be the day belonging to Yahweh.[36] Above all, the Sabbath rest was prescribed in a petty, casuistic manner. We do not have detailed information about the specifics of Pharisaic interpretation of the Sabbath of that time. The Essene interpretation we now know from the Damascus Document, which does not merely stipulate the types of forbidden labor but also prescribes the number of steps permitted to be taken, the preparation of meals, and many other aspects (CD 10:14–18).[37] The Pharisaic Sabbath law may have to be construed as narrow also, though perhaps somewhat more generous compared with Qumran. According to Acts 1:12 the way from Jerusalem to the Mount of Olives corresponded with a journey permitted on a Sabbath day. The sick were not allowed to be attended to on the Sabbath. This is where Jesus' critique of the Sabbath begins. The Gospels provide several Sabbath healings or violations on the part of Jesus (Mark 2:23–28 par.; 3:1–6 par.; Luke 13:10–17; 14:1–6; John 5:9ff.; 9:14ff.). Even though the reconstruction of the respective instances may be difficult, an important feature of his ministry has been preserved reliably in this broad tradition. In particular we have a very instructive saying of Jesus that justifies his critique of the Sabbath: "The sabbath was made for man, not man for the sabbath" (Mark 2:27). It may have been the didactic emphasis in this reasoning that prompted Matthew and Luke not to include this logion, since later Jewish Christian communities had difficulties with Jesus' critical position on the Sabbath.[38] Both features verify that we are onto something completely genuine.

Jesus does not at all intend to abolish the Sabbath. What he does intend is to restore its appropriate intent, which he sees established

---

[36] G. von Rad, *Deuteronomy* (OTL; ET; Philadelphia: Westminster, 1966) 58, reaches this conclusion from the meaning of the year of the sabbath. The actual meaning of the Sabbath celebration is not expressed in the OT at all.

[37] CD 11:13f. prohibits assisting cattle at birth and retrieving the calf if the cow had its young in a ditch or cistern. Luke 14:5 contradicts this, presumably in keeping with a Pharisaic opinion.

[38] Cf. W. Rordorf, *Der Sonntag* (ATANT 43; Zurich: Zwingli, 1962) 80–87.

already in the creation order. That the Sabbath was made for the human being once again depicts God's action, his creative action in this case, that Jesus is restoring in the eschatological era. "For man" denotes that, as the day of Yahweh, the Sabbath is likewise focused on the salvation of the person. Refusing healing on the Sabbath meant to oppose the salvation of the person and hence the will of God. An intensified form of this position can be seen in a Sabbath dispute in a synagogue in which Jesus confronts his critics with the question of whether or not it is permissible on a Sabbath to do good or evil, to save a life or to kill (Mark 3:4). In its sharpness this saying, too, suits him well. Refusing to do good by appealing to the Sabbath commandment means to do evil. Likewise the episode in which the disciples who walk through the grain fields on the Sabbath, plucking heads of grain—presumably because they are hungry—and whom Jesus defends against reproachful critics, may have preserved a significant reminiscence in its originality (Mark 2:23ff.).[39] The reproach is not directed against the theft for personal consumption of which the disciples might be alleged to have been guilty—according to Deut 23:26 this was permitted—but against the plucking of heads of grain, which was classified as harvest-related labor, on account of which the Sabbath rest was broken, according to the critics' conceptions of the Sabbath.[40]

It is the perverse handling of the Torah that Jesus castigates. In the final analysis it is the legalistic mindset that is in danger of valuing the outward appearance more highly than the essence. In this sense he is able to emphasize the Torah over against its interpreters. This is what he does regarding the commandment in the Decalogue of honoring one's father and mother. Following good Jewish opinion, the honor to be accorded to the parents also included the duty to take care of their welfare. Contemporary interpretative regulations had provided the possibility of withdrawing from this duty by declaring the share designated for the parents as an offering to the temple and then reinforcing it by means of the oath of the Corban (i.e., an offering devoted to God). Jesus rejects this practice decisively (cf. Mark 7:9–13 par.). The practice of the Corban, to be sure, may not have been undisputed in contemporary Judaism.[41]

---

[39] Cf. Roloff, Kerygma, 58.

[40] Did this reproach come from peasants with a Pharisaic orientation? So Haenchen, Weg, 122.

[41] The Mishnah allows for the dissolution of the oath of the Corban (Ned. 9.1). Was this already in use before 70 CE?

In the second antithetical statement Jesus expressed himself in an nonlegalistic manner. There he showed that in marriage the relationship between husband and wife is to be undivided, established on their love. The formulation, of course, was focused negatively, on the more specific designation of adultery. It argues that adultery, that is, marital infidelity, has its roots in the realm of thought, in the lustful glance. Remarkably, the party addressed here was the husband.

We have another saying of Jesus on the issue of marriage. It speaks of its indissolubility and is quickly captured by juridical thinking, from which the saying first has to be extricated. Its reconstruction is not a simple matter either. Two versions present themselves and are discussed.

> *"But I say to you that every one who divorces his wife, except on the ground of unchastity, makes her an adulteress; and whoever marries a divorced woman commits adultery"* (Matt 5:32).

> *"Every one who divorces his wife and marries another commits adultery, and he who marries a woman divorced from her husband commits adultery"* (Luke 16:18).

The Matthean exception clause may be set aside as a secondary addition. It signals the rise of juridical thought.[42] Otherwise one might gain the impression that Matthew is more Jewish and hence more original, for his text still gives greater consideration to the option accorded in Judaism to the husband to dissolve the marriage, that is, to dismiss his wife by handing her a letter of divorce.[43] The husband's privileged position becomes particularly clear in that he could never commit adultery against his own marriage, only against that of another. Sexual relations with unmarried persons was considered adultery only in the case of the wife, never of the husband. This legal mindset was predicated upon the notion that the wife was regarded as the husband's property and that the man forcing his way into another marriage hence violated the property of the husband. To begin with, Jesus' prohibition

---

[42] Cf. Gnilka, *Matthäusevangelium,* 1.165f. The logion in Mark 10:11f., where the prohibition to dismiss is also applied to the wife, seems to be juridically influenced as well. The influence here is from non-Jewish, perhaps Roman, legalities.

[43] Matthew is favored by Merklein, *Gottesherrschaft,* 257f.; Berger, *Gesetzesauslegung,* 596f., who includes the exception clause as well; Hübner, *Gesetz,* 46f. (only v. 32a); Schulz, Q, 116f. In favor of Luke are H. Baltensweiler, *Die Ehe im Neuen Testament* (Zurich: Zwingli, 1967) 68; Bultmann, *History,* 135; J. A. Fitzmyer, "The Matthean Divorce Texts and Some New Palestinian Evidence," *TS* 37 (1976) 200–202; Schnackenburg, "Ehe," 415f. The Lukan version is to be preferred on philological grounds. Cf. Gnilka, *Matthäusevangelium,* 1.165f.

of dismissing one's wife denotes a significant reduction in the husband's legal privileges and comparable preventive measures for the wife, especially considering that some silly reasons were sufficient for handing a letter of divorce to the wife. It is said of Rabbi Aqiba that he could dismiss his wife if he found one that was prettier than she. The husband, of course, was obligated to render financial compensation. Nevertheless, Jesus clearly establishes the responsibility and guilt of the husband in the first half of the saying.

If the first half is shaped by the protection for the wife, who easily falls into social need as someone who has been dismissed, cast away, the prohibition against marrying a divorced woman is cut from a different piece of cloth. A divorced woman would indeed be helped by a remarriage. Somehow the prohibition presupposes a marriage order. The fact that it is no longer possible to determine how Jesus construed the order has to be attributed to the aphoristic nature of his sayings, which is particularly painful in this instance. As in the case of the Sabbath, he probably had the creation order in mind, so that the argumentation in Mark 10:6–9 par. may have preserved an accurate reminiscence.[44] The further consideration has to be included as well, however, that the goal is the restoration of the wife.[45]

Even if it is not feasible to bring Jesus' position on the Torah to a general formula, the observation remains nevertheless helpful that now that the reign of God is being proclaimed, the declaration of the law is no longer the final and salvifically relevant one; instead it is the declaration of the reign of God that he proclaims. In their details his utterances on the Torah are multifaceted. Against a distorted interpretation he can affirm the directive of the Torah, as in the case of the fourth commandment. Yet he is also able to critique incisively parts of the Torah, including those associated with the practice of the Torah, as in the case of the Levitical purity laws. Since he always assesses ad hoc, it is not possible to say categorically that he intended to nullify the Torah or parts of it. Yet his insight into the will of God leads beyond the instruction of the Torah. In this connection two observations are particularly important. For one, his concern is that the person becomes good in his totality. A legalistic attitude, which is to be overcome, truncates the will of God. It can even lead away from God, as the parable of the Pharisee and the tax collector

---

[44] In the Qumran texts, too, monogamy is supported by appealing to Gen 1:27 (CD 4:21). Here the synoptic tradition may well show the same dependence.

[45] In Jewish law the reinstatement of a wife who had committed adultery was problematic. The Matthean exception clause may have arisen from this problem.

illustrates. In this context Jesus is confident that the person does what is good in open agreement with the will of God and not because he is under the compulsion of a law that demands sanctions. This also applies to the instruction on marriage. In this sense the admonition against its indissolubility likewise is not to be understood legalistically. Nor does it mean, of course, that it is not to be taken seriously; on the contrary, it offers vital affirmation.

Further, Jesus' position on the Torah is focused on the salvation of the person. He rejects as inhuman those views of the law that contradict that salvation. The person must not become a slave to the Sabbath; the wife is to be set free from the enslaving dominion of the husband. These examples are surely applicable to other instances. To be sure, the person is not rendered autarchical; he remains bound to positive instruction. Later on, however, we shall have to probe a summation of Jesus' ethics that opens up freedom in moral behavior.

The ambivalence in Jesus' attitude to the law can also be seen in the fact that his disciples are not urged to study the Torah.[46] He accepts the law on leprosy granting authority to the priest (Mark 1:44) and registers protest most incisively against trading in the temple. He also provides instruction without appealing to the law and is unconcerned about whether it offends the law. This is to be addressed in the following section.

Overview

It is understandable that the question of the law was more volatile in Jewish Christian than in Gentile Christian communities. There has been much strife in Christianity on the question of the law. In the final analysis the apostolic council was called because of this problem (Acts 15; Gal 2:1–10). In this regard, of course, much remains shrouded in the darkness of history for us. How long might the Jewish Christian community have practiced circumcision? Sabbath observance likewise only yielded gradually to the celebration of the Lord's Day. An early reference to the Lord's Day is found in Rev 1:10. The scene changed with the Jewish War of 66–70 CE and its consequences. It meant the demise not only of the Jewish state but also of Jewish Christianity. We hear of the exodus of the Jerusalem

---

[46] This peculiarity becomes prominent if one recognizes the seriousness with which the Qumran community undertook the study of the Torah. Cf. 1QS 6:6–8: "From the place where there are ten, there shall never be absent a man who searches the Law day and night, by turns, one after another . . . "

community to Pella, in Transjordan, which took place shortly before the Roman siege isolated the city completely. We also know that these residual Jewish Christians disappeared into Ebionite sects, but then their trace is lost. For Christianity and the church the disappearance of Jewish Christianity signifies the loss of a substantial component. This loss does not release us from the question concerning the Jewish soil of Christianity, which is again pressing upon the consciousness of today.

Another problem is equally relevant. If Jesus was concerned with overcoming law-related thinking and with mobilizing the person for the moral good, in his total being, with all of his outward and spiritual powers, what emerged were legalistic structures in new forms. We have seen that juridical categories even penetrated the Jesus tradition. In the church it was the ecclesiastical law that developed. One of the eminent tasks would be to clarify and explain the theological assumptions of this ecclesiastical law. Likewise, with reference to that law, one of the eminent pastoral tasks would be to prevent legalistic thinking and behavior from dominating the church, which would be against the spirit of Jesus. Ultimately the existence of the ecclesiastical law is the seal on the fact that in terms of its head and members, the church is a community of sinners. It is by the mercy of God alone that sinners are saved.

Select bibliography: H. Baltensweiler, *Die Ehe im Neuen Testament* (Zurich: Zwingli, 1967); G. Barth, "Matthew's Understanding of the Law," 58–164 in *Tradition and Interpretation in Matthew* (G. Bornkamm et al.; NTL; Philadelphia: Westminster, 1963); I. Broer, *Freiheit vom Gesetz und Radikalisierung des Gesetzes* (SBS 98; Stuttgart: Katholisches Bibelwerk, 1980); J. A. Fitzmyer, "The Matthean Divorce Texts and Some New Palestinian Evidence," *TS* 37 (1976) 197–226; H. Greeven, "Ehe nach dem Neuen Testament," *NTS* 15 (1968/69) 365–88; H. Hübner, *Das Gesetz in der synoptischen Tradition* (Witten: Luther-Verlag, 1973); E. Lohse, "Jesu Worte über den Sabbat," 79–89 in *Judentum-Urchristentum-Kirche* (FS J. Jeremias; BZNW 26; 2d ed.; Berlin: Töpelmann, 1964); U. Luz, "Die Erfüllung des Gesetzes bei Matthäus," *ZTK* 75 (1978) 398–435; J. P. Meier, *Law and History in Matthew's Gospel* (AnBib 71; Rome: Biblical Institute, 1976); W. Paschen, *Rein und Unrein* (SANT 24; Munich: Kösel, 1970) 414–34; W. Rordorf, *Der Sonntag* (ATANT 43; Zurich: Zwingli, 1962); G. Strecker, "Die Antithesen der Bergpredigt," *ZNW* 69 (1978) 36–72; H. Venetz, "Theologische Grundstrukturen in der Verkündigung Jesu?" 613–50, in D. Barthélemy, *Mélanges* (OBO 38; Göttingen: Vandenhoeck & Ruprecht, 1981).

3. Concrete instruction

Jesus also offers concrete instruction apart from the Torah, indeed apparently unconcerned with what the Torah says. This has to do with his authority. Even if what he says is not to be construed as a new law, it represents instruction that is to be taken seriously and holds the individual who hears accountable. The seriousness of the declaration is expressed because it is spoken authoritatively. Yet it is also expressed in that the message—especially his moral instruction—is set in the context of his proclamation of the kingdom. The *basileia* is what is ultimate. It represents a new and salvific order of liberating salvation. Yet it does not intend to become visible and effective proleptically in healings of the sick only, but more particularly in that people accept his message, are changed, and through their life and deeds cause the new order to become effective already. In this connection it is clear from the start that realizing the "reasonableness" of his instruction is not sufficient for accepting it. Those who quietly reflect on his instruction may be in a position to agree that, if accepted by many, it could change the world. If it is gauged by the standards of the old order, it may seem unreasonable and foolish in several ways. Ultimately it can be accepted only in the affirmation of his *basileia* proclamation, in the yes to God's new order. What appears foolish, in terms of the old order, in the ethical instruction of the *basileia* proclamation, denotes what is offensive in his message. The new order is gauged by the standard of absoluteness. The absolute, however, that is to say, everything applying the standard of absoluteness, *eo ipso* is a sacrifice (S. Kierkegaard).[47] Especially the one who demonstrates and lives the instruction becomes an offense himself—and possibly even a sacrifice.

The instruction of Jesus, which has to be extracted from the speech compositions of the evangelists (Sermon on the Mount, Sermon on the Plain), is presented to us in its already sufficiently familiar form. We may regret that, just as Kierkegaard's philosopher did.[48] He, however, ignored the fact that these unique instructions represent aphoristic summaries or accumulations of Jesus' teaching, which, in terms of their literal meaning, call for interpretation or elaboration. How these aphoristic accumulations came about remains an open question. Surely Jesus did not speak only in aphorisms. He must have addressed the issues in detail. Presumably he himself summarized his detailed explanations in aphorisms such as these. This provides the hearer with a certain freedom. The logia of Jesus that have been preserved for us take on an all the more fundamental character. What is important is the interpretation that Jesus himself gave to his moral

---

[47] Kierkegaard, *Training in Christianity.*
[48] Ibid.

instruction by means of his life. In the sphere of methodology, the convergence of Jesus' message and life is regarded as a strong indication of the authenticity of a logion that has been handed down. In the sphere of theology this concord becomes a significant factor in the credibility of Jesus' moral teaching. It is in his life that the new order of the kingdom became visible. The way the disciples who are called to follow him translate the call into action will always be fragmentary; the task of repentance they are to undertake will be imperfect. Yet theirs remains the task of proclaiming the kingdom, inextricably linked with the endeavor to bring about the new order.

The moral teaching of Jesus is characterized by a further feature that might appear to be regrettable. By no means does it cover all of the realms and issues pertaining to a theory of moral theology. In connection with his position on the law, Jesus did indeed make some statements about his people's religion, about marriage, about the woman in society. We are now indeed hearing something on possessions and riches, the use of force and the relationship to one's enemy, the authority of the state, as well as on prayer; nevertheless, other realms remain untouched. Yet these omissions, like the aphorisms, bring about freedom. The disciple is personally called upon to act responsibly. This too may be understood in terms of attempting to overcome legalistic thinking. It is important, of course, for us to be directed by the characteristic flow of this radical teaching. These considerations will become clearer still in the discussion of the summary of Jesus' ethics in the following section.

The commandment to love one's enemy is incisive. As far as the structure is concerned, it resembles the OT commandment of loving one's neighbor (Lev 19:18), except that now not the neighbor but the enemy is the object of love. It has been handed down in two versions, in Matthew and Luke. Both evangelists stress the major significance of this commandment. Matthew does so by using it to conclude the antitheses of the Sermon on the Mount, whereas Luke uses it to introduce the teaching of the Sermon on the Plain. The two renditions follow:

"Love your enemies and pray for those who persecute you, so that you may be sons of your Father who is in heaven; for he makes his sun rise on the evil and on the good, and sends rain on the just and on the unjust" (Matt 5:44f.).

"Love your enemies, do good to those who hate you, bless those who curse you, pray for those who abuse you. . . . and you will be sons of the Most High; for he is kind to the ungrateful and the selfish" (Luke 6:27f., 35b).

Comparitively speaking, the core of both versions is identical: The directive to love one's enemies and to pray for them is followed by an indication of the goal (to become a child of God) and of a reason (God's indiscriminate goodness to all).[49] It is this core that concerns us here.

As a topic, goodwill toward an enemy, the loving care of him, can be found in almost all major religions, a chord echoed by almost all founders of religions,[50] including the voice of many philosophers independent of Christianity. A comparison of the causality and finality is particularly instructive and helps in grasping the particular form of Jesus' instruction.

Although there are links in the OT, these do not yet amount to loving one's enemy: "Remember the end of your life, and cease from enmity, . . . remember the covenant of the Most High, and overlook ignorance" (Sir 28:6f.); "If your enemy is hungry, give him bread to eat; and if he is thirsty, give him water to drink; for you will heap coals of fire on his head . . ." (Prov 25:21f.). On the one hand, one is to be prepared for reconciliation in the face of death; on the other, feeding the opponent serves to shame him. Heaping coals of fire on someone's head describes this shame and humiliation figuratively.

Hellenistic Judaism goes beyond this. In *Joseph and Asenath* we find the repeated warning against compensating evil with evil. God would avenge such pride (28.14; cf. 23.9). "And if anyone wishes to do you harm, you should pray for him, along with doing good, and you will be rescued by the Lord from every evil" (*T. Jos.* 18.2). The goal of loving the enemy is to be freed from the enemy's power with the Lord's help.

Stoic philosophers have frequently spoken about loving one's enemy. The relevant arguments are neatly collected in Marcus Aurelius, *Meditations* 7.21–22: "Soon you will have forgotten everything

---

[49] There are numerous attempts at a reconstruction, e.g., Schürmann, *Lukasevangelium,* 1.342ff.; Gnilka, *Matthäusevangelium,* 1.188f.; P. Hoffmann, "Tradition und Redaktion: Zur Verbindlichkeit des Gebots der Feindesliebe in der synoptischen Überlieferung und in der gegenwärtigen Friedensdiskussion," in *Ethik im Neuen Testament* (QD 102; Freiburg: Herder, 1984) 51ff.; D. Lührmann, "Liebet eure Feinde," *ZTK* 69 (1972) 416ff.; Merklein, *Gottesherrschaft,* 222ff. Luke repeats the commandment to love one's enemy (6:35a), though in the prayer for those who revile he probably preserves what is more original. Matthew is more elaborate in describing what God does, whereas Luke is in describing the attitude toward the enemies. To speak of God as the Most High or of his being merciful (χρηστός) is in keeping with Hellenistic sentiments.

[50] From this standpoint a prayer of peace organized by the different religions, as practiced since the Assisi meeting, is meaningful.

and soon you will be forgotten by everyone. Loving even those who have violated us is the special task given to us as humans. This you will achieve if you realize that they are related to you and ignorantly make mistakes against their will and that both of you, you and they, will soon be dead and especially that the sinner did not inflict any damage upon you at all. He did not render the reason in your soul less valuable than it was before."[51]

Arguments about the brevity of life, the relatedness of character in all humans surface here as well, as does the virginity of the soul that is to be cultivated and the possibility that the enemy who acted against us did not fully appraise his action.

The love of one's enemy comes to prominence particularly in the Asian religions. Buddha admonishes his followers:

> Even if robbers and murderers were to use a saw with double serration to dismember someone a limb at the time, if this one's spirit would be filled up with anger, he would for precisely that reason not be a follower of my doctrine of salvation. In this case you must be on your guard as well and speak thus: Let not our spirit be agitated, no evil word be spoken, but we will remain kind and compassionate, benevolent, with no hatred within. We will permeate this one with a spirit of goodwill and, from this starting point, permeate the whole world with a spirit of goodwill.[52]

This incredible text, demanding that even the most painful torments are to be endured without anger and wrath, pinpoints as both its finality and its foundation the benevolent spirit that Buddha's disciple is accumulating in his being and with which he is to permeate the enemy and ultimately the entire world. The person does not obtain this benevolent spirit from God but gains it by means of the lifelong, tenacious labor of meditation. It points the way to the knowledge of suffering, including suffering inflicted by an enemy, as well as the path to overcoming suffering. The path of overcoming suffering is a path of self-deliverance. Overcoming self and working on oneself is the enduring task imposed.[53]

Taoism too is familiar with the love of one's enemy. Lao-tzu calls for it in these words: "Hostility is to be answered with goodwill." The ability for this is not attained by activism but by inactivity,

---

[51] Cf. Seneca, *De otio* 1.4.
[52] *Majjhimanikaya* 21, translated from the German quotation in Heiler, *Religionen,* 273, which has further examples.
[53] Buddha's last words were: "Subject to decay are compound things: strive with earnestness," in E. J. Thomas, *The Life of Buddha as Legend and History* (3d rev. ed.; London: Routledge, 1949) 153.

through the power of an inward and outward distance: "The attitude of the perfected sage is the same toward the one as toward the other, as if it were a scarecrow." F. Heiler speaks of a "mystical quietism."[54]

As far as Islam is concerned, it is hardly possible to speak of loving one's enemy. The Qur'an refers too often to holy war, as well as to the eternal blessedness assured to those who are killed in such war. Retaliation is also taught: "O ye who have believed, retaliation in the matter of the slain is prescribed for you, the free for the free, the slave for the slave and the female for the female" (2:173).[55] The OT refers to this *ius talionis* as well (cf. Exod 21:24; Lev 24:20; Deut 19:21).

Let us now return to Jesus! What characterizes his teaching on loving one's enemies is not the notion of the brevity of life, nor the appraisal of the plans of the enemy, nor the commonality of human descent. It is precisely in the comparison with other authorities that the eminently theological content of his teaching appears. The goal of his teaching is for the person to become God's child. In this context being a child of God is construed as a process. There is a relatedness of character between parents and children. The children receive the imprint of their father's bearing and manner; they are, as it were, the image of their parents.

In terms of the relationship with God, this denotes the imitation of God, the fashioning of oneself after his character. To a large extent the Christian would indeed also be able to affirm the arguments postulated by the other religions. Yet the Christian instruction is bound up with the God of Jesus, that is, more specifically, with the way in which God's reign is made apparent in Jesus' ministry. Once again we arrive at the reign of God as the basis of Jesus' proclamation.

While the reason for Jesus' teaching is not acceptable to the atheist in the final analysis, it is binding for the disciple. To begin with, the atheist could not adopt it because the practice of loving one's enemy is bound up with prayer. Just as becoming a child of God is a process, so the ability to love one's enemy is a process that needs to be practiced in prayer first of all. The disciple who is called upon to pray for those who scorn him is to learn in the spirit, before

---

[54] Heiler, *Religionen,* 122. The texts cited are found in this source.

[55] R. Bell, *The Qur'an* (Edinburgh, 1937), Surah 2:173. On killing in the holy war cf., e.g., Surah 2:191; 4:74, 89, 91, 191; 8:15–17; 9:41. According to Jaspers, *Die massgebenden Menschen,* 198, Muhammad is not to be compared with Socrates, Buddha, Confucius, and Jesus, as far as depth of being is concerned. Despite historically comparable scope, his impact does not come close to theirs.

God, to strip down every prejudice against his enemy, to desist from hatred, and to overcome anger. Christians need to consider this aspect in discussions of peace. In the age of the H-bomb, all reason speaks against war. Yet, although much is to be gained from it, the prevention of war is not yet tantamount to the fulfillment of Jesus' instruction to love one's enemy. Jesus' approach reaches further. The enemy Jesus addresses is any kind of enemy, such as a personal enemy, the opponent in a court case, a group enemy, the adversary of the clan, opponents of a war. By demanding prayer for those who "persecute you," Matthew presumably arranged secondarily a certain concentration on the religious enemy and adversary (5:44). Enmity between religions can be particularly hostile, as history has taught us. For the milieu of Jesus' contemporary hearers, of course, the most obvious examples were the stabbing at the village tavern or the hostilities between clans and villages. The sociopolitical dimension cannot be excluded, however. Conversely, neither is personal hostility to be ignored by shifting everything onto the societal structures of hostility; it is a common tendency today to call the anonymous society to account, rather than the individual. Precisely the theological finalization and foundation point to the individual and underscore the authenticity of Jesus' instruction.

The most radical demands are summarized in Matt 5:39–42:

> *"But I say to you, Do not resist one who is evil. But if any one strikes you on the right cheek, turn to him the other also; and if any one would sue you and take your coat, let him have your cloak as well; and if any one forces you to go one mile, go with him two miles. Give to him who begs from you, and do not refuse him who would borrow from you."*

Despite the tightly structured summary, we are dealing with four individual sayings which, in turn, may again be résumés of more elaborate presentations of Jesus. In Luke 6:29f. the sayings appear in truncated form, with the saying about accompanying someone on the way omitted altogether and moved to a different context. It is interesting to note this, since Matthew contains the more original milieu here, that is, the milieu of Jesus' hearers.[56]

Striking the right cheek—Luke refers only to striking the cheek—was the infamous blow with the back of the hand, which

---

[56] On the individual reconstruction, cf. Gnilka, *Matthäusevangelium,* 1.180; Hoffmann, "Tradition," 61–63; Merklein, *Gottesherrschaft,* 269f.; Schürmann, *Lukasevangelium,* 1.347f.

one could accompany with an object and which was perceived as particularly abusive.

The lawsuit over the shirt (RSV "coat"), the long garment with sleeves that was worn on the body directly, takes us into the context of the poor (Luke 6:29b speaks of robbery).[57] One is not to quarrel; not only the shirt is to be relinquished but the cloak as well. The poor person foregoes his rights, for according to Exod 22:25f. the cloak of the poor person was not allowed to be taken in pledge. It was the only thing he had to cover himself for the night.

At the time of Jesus, accompanying someone on the way was enforced upon the Jews by the soldiers of the Roman occupying power; frequently it was associated with carrying burdens and may have affected the poor in particular. A notable example of such enforced accompaniment is provided by Simon of Cyrene, who is forced by the soldiers to take the way of the cross along with Jesus, bearing his cross (Matt 27:32 par.).

The final saying deals with begging and borrowing. In place of the latter, Luke (6:30) again refers to the thief: "and of him who takes away your goods do not ask them again."

These rigorous demands are grouped around the theme of nonviolence. Violence is not to be countered with violence but with giving in. This type of giving in is not weakness but an attempt to overcome evil with good. The examples offered are those of surrender. The one who has been struck surrenders to the opponent for a further blow. The demonstrative helplessness is meant to conquer his hatred. The escalation of violence is to be broken. Yet these rules of behavior cannot be dissolved into psychological programs. The demonstration of nonviolence is the demonstration of a God-given new order, which the "world" must perceive as crazy and mad, all the more so as it is bent on itself and its old order.

The second example has to appear as even more insane; here the one who has been robbed of his clothes is left naked and at the mercy of his adversary. Once again, this is not weakness or indifference gained from inward distance with regard to outward events and the currents of the times.[58] It is love's desperate attempt to change the "normal" relationship between humans, governed by egotism and thoughtlessness.

---

[57] Because Luke speaks of something robbed, he is forced to reverse the pieces of clothing: "and from him who takes away your coat do not withhold your shirt as well."

[58] This inward distance prompted Epictetus to instruct the Cynic as follows: "He must be willing to be beaten like a donkey and at the same time love those who beat him—as a father of all or as a brother" (*Discourses* 3.22.53–54).

Much has been written and said about these radicalisms. Their radicality has frequently been copied painstakingly. Hence, with reference to the saying about being struck on the cheek, H. Braun, for instance, argued that it does not indicate the point "after whose fulfillment agreeability then ceases and self-defense may begin."[59] The interpreters are right, of course. The following needs to be taken into consideration, however: It has to be admitted that 99.99% of all Christians do not observe this radical directive of Jesus literally in their lives. But there is a relationship of credibility between these instructions and the practice in life of those who perpetuate and proclaim it. In fact, G. Theissen argues that these radicalisms could be handed down only because of those in early Christianity who lived by them. He describes this group with the term "wandering radicalism." Preventive censorship in those communities where these demands were deemed as too hard, and thus were rejected, saw to it that they were removed from the tradition.[60] This may apply to the history of early Christianity. If we have not yet been separated from these traditions, though their demands are not being realized, this is partly the case because of the Gospels and their canonization.

The credibility of these radical demands is to be found in Jesus alone. He himself fully lived in accordance with these instructions. He practiced this nonviolence, surrendered himself to the people in this manner, and shared what was his without limits. He indeed formulated these directives because they conformed to his way of life. The convergence of message and deed not only produces credibility; it also vouches for the authenticity of the instruction as Jesus' message in the fullest sense of the term. These words are conceivable only as his own.

For the disciples, that is, for us, these words continue to be a thorn in the flesh. We are no longer able to remove them, nor are we able to play them down by associating them, in good Catholic fashion, with a certain class of people, namely, with those who strive for perfection, those in religious orders, or by distinguishing, in good Lutheran fashion, between the private person and the official person, in keeping with the doctrine of the two realms, and then excusing the official person from the teaching. By means of this teaching the disciple is placed on a path to which he is to become accustomed and on which he keeps the goal set before him. Even if

---

[59] Braun, *Jesus*, 97.
[60] Theissen, *Studien*, 87–92.

he does not reach the set goal, there is no reason to despair or to relinquish discipleship. Discipleship would be jeopardized, however, if one lost sight of the set goal.

What is not commensurable relative to this path is explained clearly in the logion of the *imitatio Dei*: "Be merciful, even as your Father is merciful" (Luke 6:36). The person can never exhaust or arrive at the mercy of God. Rather, he has been taken into it, and therefore he has been charged with it. It is also important to remember here that God's mercy has become mediated through Jesus and has been made effective and visible in his ministry. The Matthean version of the logion, "You, therefore, must be perfect, as your heavenly Father is perfect" (5:48), takes hold of the ideal of the Jewish, Torah-oriented person. This ideal is shown with particular clarity in the Qumran writings, in which striving for perfection plays a major part.[61] The Matthean formulation is secondary, referring to the interpretation of the law found in the antithetical statements of the Sermon on the Mount, and therefore is altogether focused on the instruction of Jesus as well.

In several respects a word picture calling for reconciliation fits the framework which we have gained from Jesus' concrete instruction:

"So if you are offering your gift at the altar, and there remember that your brother has something against you, leave your gift there before the altar and go; first be reconciled to your brother, and then come and offer your gift" (Matt 5:23f.).

The reference to Jesus cannot be separated from the reference to the person. We have already come to realize this relationship in the discussion of the Sabbath commandment. The connection is intensified when we now hear that the worship of God is worthless if the unreconciled brother is excluded. Since God offers the reconciliation of a person, he cannot come before God as one who lives in conflict and hostility with his neighbor. The encounter with God is to be the reason for actively bringing about reconciliation.

A second feature needs to be observed. The conflict which the offerer remembers proves to be one that smolders in the personal, intimate realm. In any case the conflict is not the reason for bringing this offering. This is why Jesus does not establish a cultic rule,[62] unlike the rabbinic context, in which the discussion frequently revolved around the issue of when the act of offering was allowed to

---

[61] Cf. 1QS 1:8: "They are to walk before him in perfection, in accordance with all that is revealed" (as well as, e.g., 1:13; 2:2; 3:3, 9; 4:22; 5:24).

[62] Thus Braun, *Radikalismus,* 2.43 n. 2, paragraph 4.

be interrupted. Such provision was made, for instance, in the case of someone who had not yet returned stolen property to its owner. Only then was the atoning sin offering allowed to be offered. The case Jesus describes is more sweeping. Only the offerer knows about the brother who is not reconciled. The offering would become a farce if there were no reconciliation beforehand. His awareness of being in God's presence challenges the disciple to action that cannot remain an endeavor whose hypocrisy is apparent to God, but that, rather, engages his moral personality in its totality.[63]

Besides love of one's enemy, nonviolence, and reconciliation, Jesus demands an incisive correction in the relationship to possession and wealth. Yet how far did he take this? In view of the coming reign of God, does he consider every form of wealth as reprehensible, a nuisance, evil, or is he more concerned with making the owners aware of their social obligations? We have already seen that after separating from his family, he himself lived without means in his ministry, and when he sent his disciples on mission, he urged them to maintain a thoroughly simple lifestyle. But there were also those in his surroundings who had possessions. The family of Simon Peter did not relinquish its house in Capernaum. Women, female disciples, supported him with their financial means.

In reviewing the relevant synoptic texts, one makes a somewhat irritating observation. On the one hand, the tradition contains a strand in which instructions of this kind are neutralized to some extent, while on the other hand, one encounters an intensification in another strand. The fact that Luke undertook the latter will be shown with a few select examples.

In the call narratives of Mark 1:16–20 par. Matt 4:17–22 Simon and the others leave their nets and Zebedee their father, and thus their professional occupation up to then; according to Luke 5:11 they leave *everything*. Only Luke 14:33 has this logion, attributed to his redaction: "So therefore, whoever of you does not renounce all that he has cannot be my disciple."

The words addressed to the rich man are also intensified: "Sell *all* that you have and distribute to the poor"(Luke 18:22; Mark 10:21: "sell what you have"; Matt 19:21: "sell what you possess"). After the excuses by those initially invited in the parable of the great banquet, those called to the table are the poor, maimed, blind, and lame (according to Matt 22:10 both bad and good were called).

---

[63] This is reminiscent of the old prophetic message. Cf., e.g., Amos 4:4; Jer 6:20; 7:3.

The other strand we encounter in Matthew. According to Matt 19:21, giving up one's possessions is the condition for perfection: *"If you would be perfect, go, sell what you possess."* The words addressed to the rich man do indeed place him under obligation, though not of a fundamental kind. The differing expressions of the tradition confirm the assumption that Jesus did not fundamentally demand the renunciation of possessions, nor did he regard possessions and wealth as something inherently reprehensible.[64]

Yet he did warn urgently against the hazards of wealth, which can entangle a person so much that he misses the truly fulfilling meaning of life. In this context belongs the saying of the camel and the eye of the needle (Mark 10:25 par.) as well as the following:

"No one can serve two masters; for either he will hate the one and love the other, or he will be devoted to the one and despise the other. You cannot serve God and mammon" (Matt 6:24 par. Luke 16:13).[65]

The radical alternative sketched here, the pictorial part of which is drawn from the fate of a particularly unfortunate slave, does indeed raise the question whether money and wealth do not disqualify altogether and are being branded as evil. The term "mammon," which has been retained as a borrowing, is not yet vested with a negative bias, though it has the definite meaning of possession, belongings.[66] In contrast to God, mammon appears as an idol. Serving mammon is serving idols. The fascination emanating from mammon is capable of occupying a person altogether and especially of causing him to forget God, and even of opposing God.

We may assume, of course, that Jesus, here as elsewhere, is thinking and assessing with the person in mind. Possessions, money, and wealth are not evil in themselves, but using them entices him to evil, to unscrupulous egotism, and furthermore to forget the poor, in whose favor Jesus opts.

For this reason the Stoic-Cynic ideal is distant from Jesus, though there are comparable expressions to be found there: "You cannot play Thersites and Agamemnon at the same time," said Epictetus.[67] Thersites was a hunchback and bald-headed, while Agamemnon was tall and handsome. Epictetus expresses the same about

---

[64] Cf. Braun, *Radikalismus,* 2.76 n. 1.

[65] The Matthean version is: "No one can serve two masters . . ."

[66] The etymological derivation was most likely drawn from *ma^{e}mon*—that which has been deposited. Luke, in 16:9, 11, speaks of the "unrighteous mammon."

[67] Epictetus, *Discourses* 4.2.10.

the relationship of tension between rich and poor. Yet for the philosophers the primary goal was gaining spiritual distance from the outward situations of life and hence inner peace. Also the awareness of transitoriness was significant for them. When he observed a mouse, Diogenes decided in favor of abject poverty. Similar sentiments, derived from philosophy, later entered the Christian tradition, of course.

In the case of Jesus, the social responsibility of the one who has possessions is made clear in the encounter with the rich man. The decisive feature is not that he lets go of his possessions, nor is he to undertake some ascetic effort. What is decisive is that he loves and in love shares his wealth with the poor. Hence the important thing is not only what he distributes but also what he retains.[68]

The parable of the rich man and poor Lazarus takes the same line (Luke 16:19–31), although it is highly disputed in terms of its derivation from Jesus' message, as well as its interpretation. It consists of two parts. The first one depicts the compensation for wealth and poverty in the hereafter. The reversal of values is carried out with exactitude. In this life Lazarus, wretched, licked by dogs in his weakness and illness, lies at the door of the rich man who lives sumptuously. In the hereafter the rich man is tormented and sees Lazarus in Abraham's bosom (vv. 19–26). The second part calls for repentance because the rich man considers hearing Moses and the prophets to be far more important than a warning voice from the hereafter (vv. 27–31). We are interested only in the first part.[69] Compensation for material wealth and material poverty is uncommon in early Judaism, except at Qumran,[70] and hence can quite plausibly be attributed to Jesus. This impression is heightened if one observes that in the final analysis the story makes us aware again of Jesus' option in favor of the poor.[71] Thus there is a material correlation with the Beatitude concerning the poor. God's defense of the poor is given in the meaningful name of the protagonist: Lazarus means "God helps." In this parable alone is a person given a name.

---

[68] Cf. Schrage, *Ethics,* 106f.

[69] Heininger, *Metaphorik,* 183f., has shown plausibly that the second part is Luke's redaction. This is supported by the unexpected appearance of the five brothers, the suspicion that vv. 30, 31 are already pointing to Jesus' resurrection, and the competition of the main point of the second part with that of the first part, as well as by further Lukan stylistic peculiarities.

[70] Cf. Braun, *Radikalismus,* 2.74, n. 4.

[71] Cf. Schnackenburg, *Moral Teaching,* 146f.

If one wants to learn something about Jesus' relationship to the state and its authority, it is good to remember that he himself ultimately became a victim of this power. This does not mean that he was opposed to the governmental authority of his time. Yet from the little that has been handed down to us and that may be considered as authentically from Jesus, we may hear without difficulty a certain reticence and skepticism, in keeping with an inward sovereignty: "You know that those who are supposed to rule over the Gentiles lord it over them, and their great men exercise authority over them" (Mark 10:42).[72] This is followed by a statement that it is not to be like this among the disciples. The community of disciples—the foundation of the post-Easter church—is to be understood as a contrasting community. The evaluation of those ruling this world is realistic and at the same time critical. Nevertheless, it does not lack a theological background. The anticipated reign of God—which brings to an end every human reign and hence also every oppression and abuse of power and which is now to be reflected proleptically in the community of disciples, which is to be governed by a law different from that of oppression—shows that short-term political powers are mere appearance.[73] Earthly potentates are not the ultimate rulers of the world.

In the famous pericope on giving taxes to Caesar, which fits in with this perspective yet goes beyond it, Jesus states: "Render to Caesar the things that are Caesar's, and to God the things that are God's" (Mark 12:17 par.). This saying is embedded in the pugnacious encounter with opponents who present Jesus with the question of whether Caesar's taxes are permissible. The extraordinary stringency and unity of this tradition, as well as its incredible force, favor a concrete historical reminiscence.[74] For most Jews the imperial tax meant the ongoing confirmation of their political and national dependence and bondage. The Zealots refused to pay these taxes.[75] If

---

[72] The Lukan parallel departs more incisively from Mark than, and differently from, the Matthean parallel in 20:25. Luke 22:25 says: "The kings of the Gentiles exercise lordship over them; and those in authority over them are called benefactors." Luke has adapted the saying in line with Hellenistic sentiments.

[73] The ironic δοκοῦντες is lacking in Matthew and Luke, yet it is surely an ancient tradition.

[74] According to Bultmann, *History*, 26, there is no reason for supposing that this is a product of the community. Schrage, *Ethics*, 112ff., speaks of historicization and thinks that v. 17 was originally addressed to the disciples; this renders the statement colorless, however.

[75] Josephus, *War* 2.118.

Jesus answered positively, he could be charged with disregarding the theological problem; if he answered negatively, he would have been deemed a zealotic rabble-rouser. His position, which has been interpreted both to the left and to the right of the spectrum, sets clear boundaries between Caesar and God. He neither calls for a revolutionary departure nor proclaims a doctrine of divine right.[76] His response transcends the issue of taxes and again represents an answer in principle. He affirms the authority of the state but points up its limitations. Governmental, imperial power is subject to the reign of God and accountable to it. In case of conflict the disciple owes God greater obedience than Caesar.

The instructions on prayer relate entirely to the prayer of petition. The conspicuous feature here is the assurance of the prayer being answered. Here too the milieu of the poor is apparent: "Ask, and it will be given you" (Matt 7:7); apart from the fact that it is a prayer, this is beggar's wisdom. Such misconstrual is avoided if the affirmation is linked with faith: "And whatever you ask in prayer, you will receive, if you have faith" (Matt 21:22). Prayer rendered jointly is accorded particular power: "if two of you agree on earth about anything they ask, it will be done for them by my Father in heaven" (Matt 18:19), just as the Lord's Prayer gives the disciples a prayer that is designed to be prayed jointly. The assurance of answered prayer can be translated into a parable. The parable of the entreating friend (Luke 11:5–8), for instance, depicting the intensity, indeed the persistence, of a request certainly fits this frame, which can be seen as characteristic of Jesus' teaching (cf. Luke 18:1–8). If one is to ask about the source of this assurance of being answered, which may seem naive and unrealistic, the answer may have to be sought in his own prayers. After all, in this most personal aspect as well, he was able to speak only of what was his own experience. Furthermore, in this prayer the will of the person does not intend to overcome the will of God; rather, the opposite is the case, that the disciple ought to learn to submit prayerfully to the will of God and to acknowledge it gladly.

This instruction, sustained by this kind of spirit, does not expect any reward because it is aware that with God's reign it will receive everything. Calculated thinking about pay is chided in the parable of the laborers in the vineyard (Matt 20:1ff.). If Jesus spoke of treasures in heaven, in line with Jewish thought, he did so to

---

[76] The former viewpoint is found in E. Stauffer, *Die Botschaft Jesu*, 110, while the latter is commonly represented in Reformation theology. Cf. Gnilka, *Markus*, 1.154f.

juxtapose them to earthly treasures, which are caricatured, and ultimately called on those who have earthly possessions to share them
with others (Matt 6:19f.).[77]

If we gather together some essential perspectives of Jesus'
concrete instruction once again—the topics of love of the enemy,
nonviolence, reconciliation, possessions and wealth, as well as the
relationship to the power of the state—what should be given renewed consideration is especially their formative point of view, the
anticipated and approaching reign of God. The instruction not only
describes the disposition with which the ultimate, the absolute, is to
be anticipated; it also intends to make effective the reign of God and
its new order already in the present. Thus the instruction is essentially bound up with Jesus. The convergence of his life and message
is the reason for the radicality of his demand and alone allows for its
expression. Even if the instruction might be quite fragmentary in
terms of content, it allows for the recognition of a characteristic
style, a tendency, an essential current whereby it can be transmitted.
The disciple is not absolved of his imagination and autonomy.

Overview

The concrete instructions of Jesus bring to the open what is
genuinely "Christian"; they demonstrate that the historical Jesus
certainly had something to do with Christianity, and they even cause
Christianity to be examined. Rigorous as they are, these instructions
are a thorn in the flesh of the one who takes his or her Christianity
seriously, as well as of the church. Since these instructions are
addressed primarily to the disciples, hence to the subsequent church,
taking them seriously is linked with their credibility. In the course of
the history of Christianity these teachings have time and again been
allowed to be forgotten, or they were flagrantly opposed; otherwise
many wars, even wars among Christians, confessional wars, would
not have been possible. There was also a point in time when in
Christian ethics the Decalogue (which retains its validity, of course)
was made prominent and the specific instruction of Jesus was made
to recede into the background. The remembrance of Jesus' concrete
instruction is inconvenient. Nevertheless, for the sake of the identity
of what is Christian, it remains a given. The instruction also concerns the relationship to the state. In modern times it degenerated

[77] Cf. Gnilka, *Matthäusevangelium*, 1.238f.

into the doctrine of divine right. In contemporary terms, it applies to the responsible citizen.

Select bibliography: J. Becker, "Feindesliebe-Nächstenliebe-Bruderliebe," *ZEE* 25 (1981) 5–18; J. Eckert, "Wesen und Funktion der Radikalismen in der Botschaft Jesu," *MTZ* 24 (1973) 301–25; C. H. Giblin, " 'The Things of God' in the Question Concerning Tribute to Caesar," *CBQ* 33 (1971) 510–27; L. Goppelt, "Die Freiheit zur Kaisersteuer," 208–19, in *Christologie und Ethik* (Munich, 1968); M. Hengel, *Eigentum und Reichtum in der frühen Kirche* (Stuttgart: Calwer Verlag, 1973); P. Hoffmann, "Tradition und Redaktion. Zur Verbindlichkeit des Gebots der Feindesliebe in der synoptischen Überlieferung und in der gegenwärtigen Friedensdiskussion," 50–118, in *Ethik im Neuen Testament* (QD 102; Freiburg: Herder, 1984); W. G. Kümmel, "Der Begriff des Eigentums im Neuen Testament," 271–77, in *Heilsgeschehen und Geschichte* (Marburg: N. G. Elwert, 1965); G. Lohfink, "Der ekklesiale Sitz im Leben der Aufforderung Jesu zum Gewaltverzicht," *TQ* 162 (1982) 236–53; D. Lührmann, "Liebet eure Feinde," *ZTK* 69 (1972) 412–38; J. Piper, *"Love your Enemies,"* (Cambridge/New York: Cambridge University Press, 1979); L. Schottroff, "Gewaltverzicht und Feindesliebe in der urchristlichen Jesustradition," 197–221, in *Jesus Christus in Historie und Theologie* (FS H. Conzelmann; Tübingen: Mohr, 1975); W. Schrage, *Die Christen und der Staat nach dem Neuen Testament* (Gütersloh: Gütersloher, 1971); A. Vögtle, *Was ist Frieden?* (Freiburg: Herder, 1983); W. Zimmerli, "Die Frage des Reichen nach dem ewigen Leben," *EvT* 19 (1959) 90–97.

4. The summation of ethics

Love is the summation of Jesus' ethics. Hardly anyone will contradict this statement. It needs to be put in concrete form and substantiated, of course. Although much of what we have already addressed in the preceding sections points to this insight, putting it in concrete form and substantiating it are no easy task in the light of the exegetical situation.

To begin with, in the synoptic tradition the term "love" (ἀγάπη) occurs only twice (Matt 24:12; Luke 11:42; presumably both refer to the love of God). Possible equivalents, which have different emphases, ἔρως and φιλία, are missing altogether. The verb forms occur more frequently, especially ἀγαπᾶν, while φιλεῖν occurs less often.[78] Ἀγαπᾶν is used particularly frequently in connection with loving one's enemy (Matt 5:43–46 par. Luke 6:27, 32–35), including the saying "For if you [only] love those who love you, what reward [Luke: credit] have you?" and the citation of the commandment to love one's neighbor (Matt 5:46; 19:19), as well as the double commandment to love God and neighbor (Matt 22:37–39

---

[78] Matthew has eight, Mark six, and Luke thirteen occurrences of ἀγαπᾶν; the occurrences of φιλεῖν are five in Matthew, one in Mark, and two in Luke. The latter term is conspicuous because it designates misdirected love (Matt 6:5; 23:6). In Mark 14:44 par. it designates Judas's kiss.

par.). It will become apparent, however, that there is a particular reason for the last.

We have examined various statements Jesus made relative to the Torah, and we have seen that precisely in this context he issued a rigorous teaching. We have observed that occasionally he renders his teaching on the written law in a seemingly carefree manner. If we inquire after the principle whereby this instruction becomes comprehensible, the answer is love. We recall the use of the Corban, which he removes from the world by appealing to the love for parents; the Sabbath commandment, the distortions of which he combats out of consideration for the person; and the purity laws, which are made subservient to this higher principle. When he also extends the prohibition against killing to that of being angry, he points in the direction of the principle of love. The commandment of love for one's enemy explicitly addresses the love that sweeps aside the commandment of retaliation formulated in the OT: "life for life, eye for eye, tooth for tooth, hand for hand, foot for foot, burn for burn, wound for wound, stripe for stripe" (Exod 21:23f.; cf. Lev 24:20; Deut 19:21), which is in keeping with an exaggerated view of justice.

The argument that love was the driving force behind all of the directives cannot be refuted by appealing to the discipleship sayings, which call for the separation, if necessary, from family and other loved ones.[79] Following after in discipleship is meant to set one free to minister to the person, who is not to be lorded over but is to be shown love. Jesus speaks of a new family being constituted (Mark 3:35 par.).

Love as a principle, as the highest criterion in acting even with regard to the Torah, renders comprehensible the teaching of Jesus, which is difficult at times; but it does not necessarily always make it seem reasonable. Absolute veracity, nonviolence, and love for the enemy may very well be deemed unreasonable in different situations. There is another factor entering the equation here, namely, God's love, which is again linked with the reign of God, which in turn is correlated with this given, new order. In the context of these rigorous demands, the person is not left alone. He or she is the one who has responded to the message of the kingdom of God, has become a follower of Jesus and entered into a relationship of discipleship, and through Jesus has experienced God's love. The *imitatio Dei,* the summons to be merciful, just as God is, contains not only

---

[79] Contra Braun, *Radikalismus,* 2.10 n. 2, paragraph 2.

the imperative but also the empowerment.[80] The empowerment came through the message and ministry of Jesus. Some parables, especially that of the unforgiving servant (Matt 18:23ff.), have clarified these correlations.

Thus we are able to approach more calmly the tradition that explicitly highlights love of God and love of neighbor as the first commandment (Mark 12:28–34 par.).[81] To a scribe's question concerning the first commandment Jesus cites first the Shema, which every male Israelite at the time had to recite in the morning and in the evening, "Hear, O Israel: The LORD our God is one LORD" (Deut 6:4), followed immediately by the text in Deuteronomy that contains the commandment to love God, "and you shall love the LORD your God with all your heart, and with all your soul, and with all your might"[82] (Deut 6:5). But then, as the second commandment, he further cites the commandment to love one's neighbor, "you shall love your neighbor as yourself" (Lev 19:18), and apparently merges both commandments, to love God and neighbor, with the remark "There is no other commandment greater than these." The distinctive feature lies in combining the two commandments to become the commandment transcending all others. The centrality of the Shema, together with the commandment to love God, is clear enough in Israel. In times past this might have been the summons with which the cultic assembly was opened.[83] The commandment to love one's neighbor, however, is one among many others in Lev 19:18. Jesus' merging of two commandments found in entirely different contexts also represents a kind of Torah interpretation.

This merger is also found in T. Iss. 5.2: "Love the Lord and your neighbor, and show compassion for the poor and the weak," though the commandment here is not particularly prominent.[84] This is not the case with Philo of Alexandria. For him, revering God and benevolence

---

[80] It may be pointed out that καθώς has both a comparative and a substantiating function, as, e.g., in the clause "as your father is merciful." Cf. BAGD, s.v.

[81] The parallels, Matt 22:34–40 and Luke 10:25–27, are dependent on Mark. It is not necessary to assume a separate source. In support of this, cf. Gnilka, Matthäusevangelium, 2.257f. When Luke inserts the pericope elsewhere, he is pursuing particular intentions that are indicated by corresponding alterations.

[82] Over against the OT text of Deut 6:5, there is the addition of the mind as a fourth human capacity. Compared with the LXX text, δύναμις is replaced with ψυχή and διάνοια. Cf. Dautzenberg, Sein Leben bewahren, 120–22.

[83] Cf. G. von Rad, Deuteronomy, 63f.

[84] Cf. A. Nissen, Gott und der Nächste im antiken Judentum (WUNT 15; Tübingen: Mohr, 1974) 236.

are the leading virtues, with the one being the sister and twin of the other (*Virt.* 51.95): "And there are two basic doctrines, so to speak, to which are subordinated countless details and specific sayings: with reference to God it is the commandment to revere God and piety, with reference to humans it is benevolence and justice" (cf. *Spec.* 2.63). Following the criterion of dissimilarity, therefore, it is argued that the double commandment to love God and neighbor did not come from Jesus and that the respective synoptic tradition had been borrowed from Hellenistic Judaism, represented by Philo.[85]

There are certain distinctions that need to be observed, of course. Revering God / piety and benevolence/righteousness are not absolutely the same as loving God and neighbor. Philo draws these concepts from Greek philosophy. Yet his Jewish thinking comes through when he calls εὐσέβεια (revering God) the queen of virtues (*Spec.* 4.135). For him εὐσέβεια and φιλανθρωπία are virtues, natural tendencies.[86] The decisive thing is an ideal concept of the person. The modern dispute of whether benevolence is sufficient and hence one can forego revering God is already breaking out here.[87]

There is yet another track, one that points to Palestine. At Qumran phylacteries, condensed versions of the law, have been found containing the Decalogue and the "Hear, O Israel," among other things, and these may represent a common form of phylactery.[88] In Jesus' response we have the "Hear, O Israel" and the double commandment to love God and neighbor alongside one another. Could this be in reaction to the condensed Jewish version? In any case, the love of God and love of neighbor are quite plausible as condensations of the two tables of the law.[89] The first three

---

[85] Cf. Merklein, *Gottesherrschaft*, 104.

[86] See Philo, *Abr.* 208: "For the nature which is pious is also kindly, and the same person will exhibit both qualities."

[87] Philo, *Decal.* 108–110: To have this orientation means to possess only half of the virtue, as does the one for whom εὐσέβεια is sufficient. An impressive development of benevolence is found in *Virt.* 51–174 and deals with the ally, the proselyte, the enemy (moderately so), and even animals and plants. Repeatedly one also encounters the two antonyms for revering God and benevolence: μισανθρωπία and ἀσέβεια (*Virt.* 94; *Prob.* 90; cf. *Mos.*, 1.95).

[88] Cf. H. Schneider, "Der Dekalog in den Phylakterien von Qumran," *BZ* 3 (1959) 18–31. Schneider considers the removal of the Decalogue from later phylacteries to have been a measure directed against Christians. The intention was to counter the high regard for the Decalogue on the part of the Christians. There are corresponding rabbinic statements on this matter (p. 27).

[89] Cf. Deut 27:15–26; Lev 19:1–18; Ezek 18:5–9, which clearly take their orientation from the two tablets. Cf. G. von Rad, *Old Testament Theology* (ET; New York: Harper, 1962) 1.194.

commandments proclaim what is due to God, the remaining ones deal with the social obligations.

Whatever the case may be, the linking of Deut 6:5 and Lev 19:18 as the summation of ethics reflects something original, which very plausibly came from Jesus, especially since it agrees entirely with his perspective. In contrasting it with Philo, this unique feature becomes even more prominent. In Philo, revering God and benevolence are bequeathed to human nature. Jesus does not begin with an ideal view of humanity, which the person might be able to develop from within himself. What he commands is loving God and neighbor. This has serious implications for the love of one's neighbor. Turning to the neighbor is not the result of a natural inclination but considers the situation of the other and makes that its starting point. Love of neighbor does not necessarily arise from sympathy but turns to the one who is distant and alien and who might, in his plight, even appear repulsive. Since it is commanded, it does not come easily; rather it is necessary to practice it. This is a laborious, perhaps lifelong process.

But loving God, how does one do that? Experiences with God allow for a variety of feelings.[90] In this case loving him surely also means willingly trusting to devote oneself to his ways. As discussed earlier, the fact that the love of God can be experienced in Jesus means empowerment. For this reason love of God and love of neighbor belong together. The modern dispute about the reducibility of love of God to love of neighbor misses Jesus altogether.[91] Clearly if the love of God excludes love of neighbor, the former becomes an untruth. Conversely, however, love of neighbor that disregards the love of God is inconceivable in following Jesus. It is obvious that outside the circle of Jesus there is benevolence and love of neighbor. That is not the issue here. There could be nothing worse for discipleship than to be shamed by others in loving action. Nevertheless, for the disciple, loving action arises primarily from the relationship to Jesus. If love of God and love of neighbor are the greatest commandment, the implication is that all action has to be gauged by it. That which is contrary to love is against God.

In this connection, we have to observe once again that the instruction seems to be general and hardly concrete. In the concrete

---

[90] Cf. von Rad, *Deuteronomy*, 63.
[91] Cf. H. Symanowski, ed., *Post Bultmann locutum: Eine Diskussion zwischen H. Gollwitzer und H. Braun* (TF 37; Hamburg: Evangelischer, 1965).

instructions we summarized examples of concretions that are also concretions of the practice of love. The commonality of the instructions, however, focuses on human responsibility and imagination. If one of Jesus' fundamental goals was to overcome legalistic thinking, he liberates for the freedom of love.

The following formulation offers a guiding principle, namely, to love one's neighbor as oneself; in other words, self-love is the standard measure of love for neighbor. This is not to be construed in the sense of eliminating the self, however. Taking ὡς ἑαυτόν in the sense of "instead of yourself" is ultimately the direction of Kierkegaard's interpretation. Yet the neighbor does not replace the self—this would also be disastrous according to the insights of modern psychology—rather it is the required comparison that must be taken seriously. Everyone knows what is good for himself. The ability to place oneself in the situation of the other should result in providing the neighbor with the same good. The ability to place oneself in the other's situation arises from the imagination. If the imagination is nurtured by love, it produces actions in keeping with love of neighbor. The love of God safeguards that which is objectively good.[92]

In the Greek realm it is common to distinguish between *agape* and *eros,* between self-giving love and desiring love. It has already been noted that the eros-concept does not occur in the synoptic tradition, nor in the NT as a whole. Certainly the focus is on self-giving love. Yet desiring love is not completely excluded. God, too, is a jealous God: "Thus says the LORD of hosts: I am jealous for Zion with great jealousy . . . " (Zech 8:2; cf. Joel 2:18). Israel is Yahweh's wife, over whose love he watches jealously (Hos 2:4–7, 18–21).[93] The lack of precision in the NT use of the Greek concept of agape has to do with the fact there is no distinction in Hebrew and Aramaic; the term ʾahₐbāh encompasses the entire semantic field.

The parable of the good Samaritan also offers a concrete example (Luke 10:30–35):

"A man was going down from Jerusalem to Jericho, and he fell among robbers, who stripped him and beat him, and departed, leaving him half dead. Now by chance a priest was going down that road; and when he saw him he passed by on the other side. So likewise a Levite, when he came to the place and saw him, passed by on the other

---

[92] There is also self-hatred, a negative kind of self-love, which should not be projected on the neighbor, of course.

[93] Cf. Bornkamm, *Jesus,* 116.

side. But a Samaritan, as he journeyed, came to where he was; and when he saw him, he had compassion, and went to him and bound up his wounds, pouring on oil and wine; then he set him on his own beast and brought him to an inn, and took care of him. And the next day he took out two denarii and gave them to the innkeeper, saying, 'Take care of him; and whatever more you spend, I will repay you when I come back.' "

This story speaks for itself. We may disregard the context provided by Luke, which is itself disputed to a considerable extent but presumably is a Lukan product. This applies to v. 29 at least. In this context a lawyer asks who his neighbor is, and Jesus concludes the parabolic story with the counterquestion "Which of these three, do you think, proved neighbor to the man who fell among the robbers?"[94] The arguments adduced are not adequate to reject the parable as having come from Jesus.[95] On the contrary, its rigorous style certainly fits in with his preaching.

Its vivid local coloring provides the parable with clarity and originality, even though the story of two pitiless people and one merciful one may be in keeping with a more general motif.[96] Occasionally it was even suggested that Jesus picked up on something that had occurred very recently, but this is neither necessary nor convincing. The very relevant and credible background includes the dangerous road through desolate areas from Jerusalem to Jericho, the town of the priests, and the eight days of temple service that had to be carried out regularly by members of the priestly clan, from which the

---

[94] Noteworthy here is the exchange of object and subject: Who is my neighbor? Who was neighbor to him? For Jülicher, *Gleichnisreden,* 2.596, this shift from the *diligendus* to the *diligens* points to the secondary character of the context. For Bultmann, *History,* 178, however, it indicates that at least the beginning of the question in v. 36 was available to Luke. Jeremias, *Parables,* 205, speaks of a formal inconsistency and warns against eisegesis. According to Linnemann, *Parables,* 55, vv. 29 and 36 are part of the story, with the latter functioning like a signpost at a crossroads.

[95] G. Sellin, "Lukas als Gleichniserzähler: Die Erzählung vom barmherzigen Samariter," *ZNW* 66 (1975) 29–60, argues against its authenticity by asserting that the story is unsatisfactory without a context. This is a highly elaborate opinion. The statistical accounting of words used is too narrow a base. The (not very frequent) Lukanisms can also be explained as an oral tradition in literary form. At the turn of the second century the Samaritans are said to have been viewed more leniently by the Jews, and the priests had become representatives of the cultic epoch of Israel. The perspective found in the parable agreed with that of R. Simeon ben Azzai (ca. 110 CE). The dating of rabbinic sayings, however, is problematic. The more lenient assessment of the Samaritans robs the parable of its sharpness. Thus, apart from the bold premise that it originated at the time of ben Azzai, the opinion that the parable actually goes back to Jesus is certainly arguable.

[96] The argument that this is borrowed from 2 Chron 28:5–15, is far-fetched. Only v. 15 is comparable here. Bultmann, *History,* 204, sees this as the assimilation of a popular fairy tale.

two cultic servants are hurrying to get home. The question of why Jesus has a priest and a Levite pass by, rather than a Pharisee and a scribe, has been significantly overplayed. Thus the most fitting context is the road cultic servants used all the time. Hence it is not appropriate to speak of anticultic needling here. The important thing is the appearance of a Samaritan. He belongs to a people whom the Jews had been regarding as their arch enemies for centuries. Mutual, spiteful provocations are well known. The most outrageous incident was when some Samaritans entered the Jerusalem temple around midnight during a Passover festival in order to desecrate the temple court by scattering human remains in it.[97]

The story lingers on the Samaritan, the protagonist, and on his merciful actions. Both priest and Levite are devoid of this compassion.[98] The story needs to be read as an example narrative and depicts love of one's enemy. One could also say that it depicts love of neighbor—and the secondary frame certainly allows for this—though it must be pointed out that it interprets love of neighbor, which includes the enemy, from the perspective that is characteristic for Jesus. The contemporary discussion on the meaning of the term "neighbor," whether it still included the alien in the land and under what conditions, a discussion yielding both petty and generous answers, has lost its punch. The enemy, too, is deserving of love. Nobody else could be used to communicate this more memorably than a Samaritan who is presented as the loving one. Perhaps precisely this was intended to introduce a change of mind.

This story, of course, likewise is part of the overall framework of Jesus' proclamation of the kingdom of God. If this were disregarded, it would run the risk of a biased moralistic understanding. Within this framework it is exemplary of the new order that God intends among people and that Jesus has brought. He brought it by living this love himself and giving it to others, and empowering them for it. For Jesus "it is precisely the neighbor who is God's book to read" (E. Fuchs). It was to be the same for the disciple.

---

[97] Cf. Josephus, *Ant.* 18.30. According to Jeremias, *Parables,* 204, this event took place between 6 and 9 CE.

[98] This contrast is the decisive point. It is distracting to look for some excuses that the cultic servants might have adduced, such as that contact with a corpse, or with someone assumed to be dead, would have rendered them cultically unclean. Likewise, the notion that a Jew was actually not allowed to be helped by a non-Jew is rather academic. Cf. W. Grundmann, *Die Geschichte Jesu Christi* (2d ed.; Berlin: Evangelische Verlagsanstalt, 1959) 90.

Let us summarize: For Jesus the summation of ethics is the bringing together of the love of God and the love of neighbor. Both are derived from the law, as can be read in Deut 6:5 and Lev 19:18. Hence the combination of the two passages causes the law to be seen in an entirely new light. When Matthew interprets it as the fulfillment of the law in 5:17 and 22:40, he is definitely on the right track. In the final analysis this combination also establishes a new relationship to the world. The interpretation of the world furnished by the law is broadened and transcended. By means of the law the world is fundamentally overcome[99]—apparently. By means of the law one becomes aware of the world in oneself only. Love in its summation as the love of God and love of neighbor places the person into the movement of historical life. What is truly called for cannot be read in the law. Love opens up new insights, new horizons; it causes needs ignored by the law to be perceived and sees the downtrodden on the road with heart-felt compassion, overlooking the fact that he is the enemy.

Overview

Love as the summation of ethics is a fundamental chord of the NT. Paul describes loving one's neighbor as the summation of all the commandments (Rom 13:9). In this perspective he is likely dependent on the Jesus tradition, rather than on the Hellenistic synagogue. James 2:8 speaks of love of neighbor as the royal law which does not permit regarding a person by outward criteria. The new commandment of which the Johannine Christ speaks is mutual love (John 13:34). While this is restricted to brotherly love (cf. 1 John 4:20f.), its premise is essential: because/as I have loved you (cf. John 13:14f.). It would be worthwhile to trace the aftereffect of the double commandment in the course of the history of the church and of Christendom. One thing is certain from the start: Wherever Christians have practiced the double commandment, there has been a convincing witness for Christ. Where it has been disregarded and betrayed, however, even power and outward splendor are not able to improve the shabbiness of the witness.

Select bibliography: G. Bornkamm, "Das Doppelgebot der Liebe," 85–93 in *Neutestamentliche Studien für R. Bultmann* (2d ed.; BZNW 21; Berlin: Töpelmann, 1957); C. Burchard, "Das doppelte Liebesgebot in der frühen christlichen Überlieferung," 39–62 in *Der Ruf Jesu und die Antwort der Gemeinde* (FS J. Jeremias; Göttingen: Vandenhoeck & Ruprecht, 1970); J. Ernst, "Die Einheit von Gottes und Nächsten-

---

[99] Cf. Linnemann, *Parables,* 55, following A. Schlatter.

liebe in der Verkündigung Jesu," *TGl* 60 (1970) 3–14; R. H. Fuller, "Das Doppelge-
bot der Liebe," 317–29 in *Jesus Christus in Historie und Theologie* (FS H. Conzelmann;
Tübingen: Mohr, 1974); V. P. Furnish, *The Love Command in the New Testament*
(Nashville: Abingdon, 1972); D. Gewalt, "Der barmherzige Samariter," *EvT* 38
(1978) 403–17; W. Grundmann, "Das Doppelgebot der Liebe," *ZZ* 11 (1957) 449–55;
K. Hruby, "L'amour du prochain dans la pensée juive," *NRT* 91 (1969) 493–516;
R. Kieffer, "Analyse sémiotique et commentaire. Quelques réflexions à propos
d'études de Lc 10,25–37," *NTS* 25 (1979) 454–68; H.-W. Kuhn, "Das Liebesgebot
Jesu als Tora und als Evangelium," 194–230 in *Vom Urchristentum zu Jesus* (FS
J. Gnilka; Freiburg: Herder, 1989); A. Nissen, *Gott und der Nächste im antiken Juden-
tum* (WUNT 15; Tübingen: Mohr, 1974); R. Pesch, "Jesus und das Hauptgebot,"
99–109 in *NT und Ethik* (FS R. Schnackenburg; Freiburg: Herder, 1989);
G. Schneider, "Die Neuheit der christlichen Nächstenliebe," *TTZ* 82 (1973) 257–75;
G. Sellin, "Lukas als Gleichniserzähler: Die Erzählung vom barmherzigen
Samariter," *ZNW* 65 (1974) 166–89; 66 (1975) 19–60; H. Zimmermann, "Das
Gleichnis vom barmherzigen Samariter," 58–69 in *Die Zeit Jesu* (ed. G. Bornkamm et
al.; FS H. Schlier; Freiburg: Herder, 1970).

9

Jesus' Authority in Mission

The formulation of the issue is fraught with particular exegetical difficulties, which already begin with the attempt to find a title for the issue to be discussed here. Traditionally the issue has been addressed under the topic of "the self-consciousness of Jesus" or "the messianic self-awareness." Yet the Gospels do not contain any psychological texts. Their interest is in being, not in consciousness, in other words, if occasion arises, in Jesus' messiahship, rather than in his messianic self-consciousness. For this reason we prefer to use the term "authority in mission" *(Sendungsautorität)* here.[1]

Considering the problem, which is reflected in an intricate exegetical situation, it is advisable to begin with the following consideration: In the *post-Easter context* faith in Jesus is deepened in confessions and confession-like statements. After Easter the disciples gather afresh in their confession of faith in Jesus; that is to say, the church is constituted. The church is the community of those who are united in the confession of Jesus. This confession is projected back into the Gospels. In the confession of Jesus found in the Gospels, these writings prove to be particularly that kind in which history and kerygma, reporting and expression of faith, have become mingled. If we limit this to the Synoptic Gospels, the number of such confessions is not great, but they are placed strategically. These include Peter's messianic confession (Mark 8:29; Luke 9:20), which

---

[1] Cf. F. Hahn, who suggests the concept of "a claim to missions," "Methodologische Überlegungen zur Rückfrage nach Jesus," 11–77, in K. Kertelge, ed., *Rückfrage nach Jesus* (QD 63; Freiburg/Basel/Vienna: Herder, 1974) esp. 49.

in Matt 16:16 is expanded into the confession of Jesus as the Messiah and Son of God; the confession of Jesus as the Son of God by the Roman centurion at the cross (Mark 15:39; Matt 27:54);[2] and the disciples' confession of the Son of God, handed down only in Matt 14:33, associated with the epiphany narrative of Jesus' walking on the water.[3] In addition we encounter the Son of man terminology, which, however, nowhere occurs in confessional formulation (e.g., "You are the Son of man").

The christological titles, Messiah, Son of God, and Son of man, the first two formulated as confessions, prove to be the most significant for our concerns. There are additional christological titles in the confessional material of the NT, especially the confession of Jesus as Lord *(kyrios),* which becomes particularly important for the Gentile-Christian, Pauline communities but need not concern us here.

Hence if we begin with these post-Easter confessions, we notice that their content is clearly shaped by the reminiscence of the earthly Jesus. This is true of the titles Messiah and Son of God, as well as Son of man, which did not attain the level of confession. This peculiar shaping is perceived by drawing a comparison with the prehistory of these honorific titles Messiah, Son of God, and Son of man. This prehistory has its locus in Jewish theology, in the OT, and in intertestamental writings. Let us begin with Son of man.

The Son of man is the anticipated eschatological salvific figure in apocalypticism. He is a heavenly being whose home was with God, who already exists with God before creation; he is not a human being. For this reason the oldest Son of man expression available to us, in the night vision of Dan 7:13, says that he looked *"like* a son of man" (italic added). He comes suddenly, on the clouds of heaven.[4]

---

[2] According to Luke 23:47 the centurion says: "this man was innocent!"
[3] Another strand is represented by the pericopes of Jesus' baptism and transfiguration, in which the heavenly Father attests to Jesus as his son (Mark 1:10f. par.; 9:2–8 par.). The high priest's question in the trial before the Sanhedrin is also shaped by the Christian confession (Mark 14:61f. par.). On the synoptic confessions as post-Easter faith statements, see R. Schnackenburg, "Christologie des Neuen Testaments," Mysterium Salutis 3/1, 227–388, esp. 234.
[4] Daniel 7:13 does not yet contain a titular use of Son of man, despite the fact that all Son of man speculations link up with this reference. In the Son of man of Daniel 7 U. B. Müller (*Messias und Menschensohn in jüdischen Apokalypsen und in der Offenbarung des Johannes* [SNT 6; Gütersloh: Gütersloher, 1972] 60) sees the notion of the ruler of the nations, according to which the nations have their representative in heaven. In this case the one like a son of man represents Israel. The derivation of the Son of man concept in the history of religions is controversial. Cf. the bibliographic account in W. Bracht, "Der Menschensohn" (diss.; Munich, 1972) 206–66.

This terminology is picked up in 2 Esd 13:3: "I looked, and behold, this wind made something like the figure of a man come up out of the heart of the sea. I looked, and behold, that man flew with the clouds of heaven; and wherever he turned his face to look, everything under his gaze trembled." In *1 Enoch* the anticipation solidifies into the titular Son of man of whom it is said that in the hour of the eschatological judgment his name was named in the presence of the Lord of Spirits; yet this name had, after all, been named already before the creation of the sun and the constellations and before the stars of heaven had been made (*1 Enoch* 48.2f.). His supreme task is the judgment of the nations, which he will render sitting on the throne of his glory (69.27f.). He guards the lot of the righteous, who will be saved by his name, for he is the avenger of their life (48.7).

The synoptic Son of man terminology is linked with Dan 7:13. This can be seen most clearly in the synoptic apocalypse, in Mark 13:26, into which—following a widely held opinion[5]—has been incorporated a minor Jewish writing or, more plausibly, a Jewish Christian apocalyptic one. The subject here is the coming of the Son of man (Jesus) in clouds with great power and glory. While the description of the apocalyptic-eschatological appearing of the Son of man in judgment is largely in keeping with Jewish apocalyptic—according to Matt 25:31; 19:28, the Son of man who judges the nations is seated on the throne of his glory, as in *1 Enoch* 69.27f.—in the logia referring to the Son of man we notice the radical change. The Son of man is the friend of tax collectors and sinners (Matt 11:19 par.), one who is homeless in this world (Matt 8:20 par.), who forgives sins (Mark 2:10 par.), who is Lord of the Sabbath (Mark 2:27 par.), and who above all else is rejected and killed (e.g., Mark 8:31 par.; Matt 17:22 par.; 20:18 par.; 26:24 par.). There is no longer any doubt at all that this Son of man, whose original conception has him remain in his heavenly mode of being, is a real human among humans.

Nevertheless, even in Judaism the Son of man did not remain a heavenly manifestation. The expectation of the Son of man merged with that of the Messiah.[6] The Messiah is an earthly figure coming from the house of David. The Son of man is attributed corresponding names, such as "anointed one" (*1 Enoch* 48.10) and "son of a

---

[5] Cf. Gnilka, *Markus,* 2.211f.
[6] This has been demonstrated convincingly by K. Müller, "Menschensohn," *BZ* 16 (1972) 161–87; 17 (1973) 52–66, and by Müller, *Messias,* 52ff., 90ff., 117ff., 144ff. On 2 Esd 13, Müller, 119–22, thinks rather that the features of the expectation of the Son of man were transferred to the Messiah.

man" (62.5; 69.29); he is even identified with Enoch, who was
carried away to heaven (71). In particular the Son of man is given the
task belonging to the Messiah, to destroy Israel's enemies (2 Esd
13:8–13) and to reestablish the kingdom for Israel (Dan 7:14).[7]
   This brings us to the Messiah. Excellent insights into the general, Pharisaically oriented, messianic expectation are found in *Psalms
of Solomon* 17 and 18.[8] He is called king and the Lord's anointed,[9] "a
just king taught of God" (17.32), Son of David (17.21). His coming
is linked with the "kingdom of our God" (17.3f.). His outstanding
task is to gather Israel again as a holy people, to lead them in
righteousness and to instruct everyone in works of righteousness
(17.26–28.41; 18.8). God equips him with the Holy Spirit; he puts
his hope entirely on God, and he himself is free of sin (17.37, 34,
36). Yet the intensity of the anticipation of the one praying in *Psalms
of Solomon* 17 is focused on the fact that the Messiah chases away the
people's enemies, whom he denounces as sinners:

> . . . *and purify Jerusalem of the nations which trample her down in destruction,*
> *In wisdom, in righteousness, may he expel sinners from the inheritance:*
> *May he smash the sinner's arrogance like a potter's vessel.*
> *With a rod of iron may he break in pieces all their substance:*
> *May he destroy the lawless nations by the word of his mouth,*
> *So that, at his rebuke, nations flee before him;*
> *And may he reprove sinners by the word of their own hearts* (17.22–25).[10]

In this way the Messiah becomes not only the undisputed
leader of Israel but also the ruler of the world, who "will smite the

---

[7] Thus the Jewish and the synoptic traditions represent two developments in
parallel. The development leads from the heavenly to the earthly Son of man. This is
seen differently by K. Müller, "Menschensohn," *BZ* 17 (1973) 66, for whom the
synoptic development begins where the Jewish one ends, with the earthly Son of man.
It may be possible to look for reasons the Son of man conception was not sustained
in Judaism. Müller, *Messias,* 146f., cites two of them, that the God of Jewish orthodoxy
did not brook a partner alongside and that the national hope was dominant. The
circumstance that *Enoch* and 2 Esdras have come down to us only in translations had
to do with Pharisaic opposition. Could it be that the expectation of the Son of man
was at one time more widespread in Judaism than can be assumed from the paucity
of documents? This question cannot be answered.

[8] According to J. Schüpphaus, *Die Psalmen Salomos* (ALGHJ 7; Leiden: Brill, 1977)
137, this pseudepigraphic collection of psalms attests to Pharisaic theology and piety
from the mid-first century CE.

[9] The supplement τοῦ κυρίου in 17.32 is textually suspect but nevertheless
feasible. This is the position taken by S. Holm-Nielsen, *Die Psalmen Salomos* (JSHRZ
4/2; Gütersloh: G. Mohn, 1977) 1–4, note d on v. 32. The concept occurs in 18.7.

[10] The translation is taken from H. F. D. Sparks, *The Apocryphal Old Testament*
(Oxford: Clarendon, 1984).

earth with the sword of his mouth for ever" (17.35). It is precisely in conjunction with the victory over the enemies that the Messiah takes on a form that bursts human possibilities and becomes a suprahistorical eschatological figure. Even if the Son of man and the Messiah are essentially different in origin, in contexts such as these "there certainly is no difference between the national and the transcendent savior."[11] The Gentile nations will indeed come, in order to behold the glory of the Messiah; yet they will not participate in the salvation but only bring home to Zion the exiled Israelites, "his sons who had fainted" (17.31).[12]

It may not be disputed that there is a broad affinity between the portrait of the Messiah in the part of the *Psalms of Solomon* that focuses on the gathering of the people of Israel, despite a conception that remains very general, and the ministry of Jesus as sketched by the synoptic writers. Yet the unmistakable shaping that the portrait of Jesus gains from the reminiscence of his historical life is expressed in his passion and rejection. Thus according to Mark 8:29–31, Peter's confession of Christ is followed by the first explicit prediction of the passion, announcing suffering, rejection, and death: "the Son of man must suffer many things . . . " The change in titles from Christ to Son of man corrects both the popular messianic expectation and the common Son of man expectation. In the passion narrative "Christ" is the dominant title, as well as the title derived from it, "king."

Caiaphas and Pilate, Jesus' earthly judges, ask him whether he is the Christ, the king of the Jews (Mark 14:61; 15:2). When the high priests and scribes mock him as "Christ, the king of Israel," at the cross (15:32), erroneous Jewish messianic expectations are colliding sharply with Christian realization. This, at any rate, is the perspective of faith.

The OT also refers to sons of God, though neither in the OT nor in Judaism is the Messiah or the anticipated bringer of salvation explicitly designated "Son of God." Only in the promise uttered by Nathan does God say the following concerning him: "I will be his father, and he shall be my son. When he commits iniquity, I will chasten him with the rod of men, with the stripes of the sons of men" (2 Sam 7:14). The figurative nature of the language is evident. It may

---

[11] Volz, *Eschatologie,* 221.

[12] The messianology of the Qumran writings, characterized by the expectation of two messiahs, remains bland and colorless. Nevertheless, it also knows the feature of liberation from the enemies. It is expressed in the notion of the eschatological war (1QM).

also be appropriate to consider that the promise of establishing David's house, kingdom, and throne forever is all-encompassing (7:16).[13] In the OT, being a son of God means as much as being in a special relationship to God, being chosen by God. Thus the nation of Israel is God's son, indeed God's firstborn (cf. Exod 4:22; Jer 31:9; 3:19), the righteous one who is persecuted by sinners and whose relationship to God is tested in persecution (cf. Wis 2:13; 16:18). Particularly interesting is the observation that the king of Israel is a "son of God," who as the leader of the people of God and as their representative personally represents their relationship to God yet again. The interpretation of the declaration of God regarding the king in Ps 2:7 is disputed: "You are my son, today I have begotten you." One of the disputed issues may be the temporal reference to "today" as pointing to the day of the king's enthronement, when the king became the son of God. In any case, this saying does not exceed the metaphorical. It is understood either in terms of adoption—possibly spoken by a prophet in the context of the ritual of the investiture[14]—or, more plausibly, in terms of legitimation, which is itself part of the royal ritual.[15]

In Jesus the experience of God goes beyond being chosen. This is why the OT models were insufficient when he was confessed as the Son of God in the Christian community. In Jesus, God himself was experienced. For this reason it is noteworthy that the Synoptic Gospels included not only texts that confess Jesus as the Son of God but also those that present him as the Son in an absolute sense. For both types of texts it is characteristic that the Son is juxtaposed with the Father. Their mutual devotion is central, whether in terms of the Son's obedience to the Father (Mark 13:32 par.)[16] or of the Son's legitimation by the Father (Matt 11:27 par.). The absolute reference to the Son in relation to the Father may be regarded as a Christian characteristic.[17] The authority that the Father has vested in the Son is

---

[13] 4QFlor 10f. links 2 Sam 7:11–14 with the shoot of David, the Messiah. "Filius meus" as a messianic designation in the Latin text of 2 Esd 7:28; 13:32, 37, 52; 14:9, is not significant since it represents a translation of the Greek παῖς and of the Hebrew ʿabdî. Cf. E. Lohse, "υἱός κτλ," *TDNT* 8.361.

[14] H.-J. Kraus, *Psalms 1–59* (ET; Minneapolis: Augsburg, 1988) 45f., 130f.

[15] G. Fohrer, "υἱός κτλ," *TDNT* 8.349–51, adduces the comparison of the father's legitimation of an extramarital child. The messianic 4QFlor 18f. also cites Ps 2:1f., rather than v. 7.

[16] Not knowing the day or the hour implies the Son's recognition of the Father's eschatological prerogative.

[17] Cf. Hahn, *Titles,* 307–17. The absolute reference to the Son is also encountered in (Sethian) gnosticism. Cf. " 'Die dreigestaltige Protennoia' 21–24," *TLZ* 99 (1974) 737. In the Mandaean literature references to the Son are always given with

that of divine revelation, the premise of which is their mutual, continuing knowledge: "no one knows who the Son is except the Father, or who the Father is except the Son and any one to whom the Son chooses to reveal him" (Luke 10:22). Their reciprocal knowledge is the mutuality in being known. What is captured here is the movement of loving knowledge that seeks to be continued from the Father, through the Son, to people.[18]

Having taken the first step in the inquiry into Jesus' authority in mission, we may note the result that the central extant christological titles—Son of man, Messiah, and Son of God—were reshaped by what was experienced with Jesus. While they form a connection for the Christian confession, they do not prove to be adequate in the manner in which they have been adopted. This leads to two further considerations. First, their lack of adequacy renders it even more comprehensible that in articulating its faith the early Christian community was not content with *one* christological title but picked up a relatively large number of them. The inadequacy of one was to be balanced by the fulness of the others. There is the further observation that the given titles are not distinctly separate from one another. The conceptions and expectations associated with them are overlapping. This became particularly apparent in our comparison of the Son of man title with that of the Messiah.[19]

Second, both the plethora of extant messianic titles and the lack of clarity of given messianic conceptions serve as a warning against fixing Jesus to one concept.[20] Before raising the question of the possible use of titles in Jesus' proclamation, it is necessary to follow the path of implicit Christology. This means first of all that we need to attempt once more to recall and construct, especially from Jesus' message and deeds, that which describes his authority in mission. Within this aspect his portrait may become clearer than through the

descriptors, such as first-born Son, Son of God, Son of life. Cf. M. Lidzbarski, *Ginza* (Göttingen: Vandenhoeck & Ruprecht, 1925) 613 (index). Quite apart from the fact that these writings are later than the NT, they are based on a radically different theological conception. The *protennoia* is father, mother, and son at the same time.

[18] On the interpretation, cf. Gnilka, *Matthäusevangelium*, 1.436–39.

[19] Thus H. Gunkel called the book of 2 Esdras "a compendium of the eschatological world of ideas," in E. Kautzsch, ed., *Die Apokryphen und Pseudepigraphen des Alten Testaments* (1900; reprint Hildesheim: Georg Olms, 1962) 2.348.

[20] This may also apply to the attempt to understand Jesus as the messenger of joy announced in Isa 11. On this cf. in particular H. Frankemölle, "Jesus als deuterojesajanischer Freudenbote?" 34–67, in *Vom Urchristentum zu Jesus* (FS J. Gnilka; Freiburg: Herder, 1989).

mediation of given titles. Implicit Christology directs our attention to the specifics concerning Jesus. Only when this has taken place will we be able to inquire into possible titles.

From the beginning, the central point of all our considerations was the βασιλεία τοῦ θεοῦ, the reign of God. It is undisputably the center of Jesus' preaching, the crux of his ministry. Hence the access to his authority in mission is to be approached first of all from this central point. The reign of God is that which is ultimate, which remains, the definitive salvation which God will bring about and is already beginning to be effective, the new and valid order to be established, which is being obstructed by the legal conformity of the world.

Jesus' proclamation of the reign of God was inimitable. The reign of God is to be proclaimed alongside him and after him as well—and those taking on the task are to do it the way he did it. But they are able to do it only by his orders and in his name, participating in what he has done and yet never again fully attaining it. Jesus did not merely proclaim the coming reign of God; it also became an event in him, linking his message, his work, and his person. In numerous parables he demonstrated the dynamic relationship between the future and the present of the reign of God and clarified the new order of boundless love, blazing its trail into the hardened structures of the legal conformities of the world. In these parables we observed the correlation between the message and his ministry among the people. We observed that, for instance, the message of the parable of the prodigal son and of the laborers in the vineyard has its anchoring and credibility in his ministry, without thereby allowing the parables to be turned into allegories. Since the kingdom of God denotes God establishing God's gracious reign, the presence of the future reign of God in Jesus' ministry ultimately means that God is actually at work in him and that God's love itself was experienced by him.

His eschatological salvation is portrayed in his acceptance of sinners, represented by the table fellowship with tax collectors, prostitutes, and outcasts, in attending to the sick, the poor, the demonized, and lunactics, all of whom he helps powerfully. He is criticized because of these scandalous actions, as perceived by the world's legal conformities, and justifies himself by pointing to his authority: "But if it is by the finger of God that I cast out demons, then the kingdom of God has come upon you" (Luke 11:20); "and behold, something greater than Jonah is here. . . . something greater than Solomon is here" (Matt 12:41f.). Salvation that is bound up inseparably with his person is the distinguishing feature of his eschatological ministry, in contrast to Qumran, for instance, where the notion of the presence of salvation is known also, but without this personal core: "Blessed are the eyes which see what you see! For I tell you that many prophets and kings desired to see what you see, and did not see it, and to hear what you hear, and did not hear it" (Luke 10:23f.). People, presumably the disciples, are made aware of the salvific relevance of the hour of his ministry by means of these words; they indicate that the ancient, deep-rooted longing of the people for the definitive salvation that the prophets announced is being fulfilled in him. Faith, to which the miracle stories refer time and again in a more general sense and which suffering people offered to him, is to be construed as faith that transcends the concrete situation of need— faith in Jesus, the bringer of salvation.

In his proclamation of the reign of God, Jesus knows he is sent to the people of Israel as a whole. In contrast to the many splinter groups, he rejects separatistic ambitions. In this openness and in view of the completed reign of God, he is even able to take up the ancient prophetic notion of the nations' pilgrimage. He presents the ultimately binding will of God to the people of Israel, announces what is to be undertaken, and proclaims the new order of salvation that leaves behind and transcends everything up to now. In doing so, he can confront his teaching directly with the ancient word of God in the Torah. It is no longer the message of the Torah but the message of the reign of God, his message, that is needed for salvation and determines people's destiny. Accepting or rejecting his proclamation of the *basileia* governs the person's future and eternal destiny.

As God formerly used the prophets to call disciples after them, so Jesus calls people to be his disciples in a special way. In this manner, too, he shows his authority. Nothing is to be given priority over discipleship, not even the ties to one's own family (Matt 10:37). "Whoever loses his life for my sake . . . will save it" (Mark 8:35).

One of the results of what can be said about Jesus' authority in mission will be the particular emphasis that he ushered in the ultimate and that God himself effected God's ultimate salvation in him. The totality of his authority in mission balks at categorization by means of titles. He was more than a prophet. The law and the prophets were until John (cf. Luke 16:16).[21] There were features in

---

[21] Also inadequate is the category of the end-time prophet, which has been described, including its distinction from the category of the Messiah, by Hahn, *Titles,* 352–96. According to Hahn, Jesus' ministry is best compared with the end-time prophet like Moses (372–88).

his ministry, of course, that were essentially messianic, compared with the messianic expectation of the *Psalms of Solomon,* for instance. What is lacking, however, is the national political feature that was so decisive, particularly for his contemporaries. This is the difference that helps in understanding Jesus' authority in mission as not derivative.

Before we proceed with the inquiry, however, there are other observations to be adduced. Authority denotes a particular manner of speaking that can be traced back to Jesus. Accordingly he used the term "Amen" to introduce certain declarations, especially those with an eschatological content, hence sayings that provide a particular insight about the last days and that, in turn, are also linked with the proclamation of the kingdom. It is to be expected, of course, that many sayings were not fitted with this amen until later (in John's Gospel they become double amens), though this form of speech as such may be considered unique to him.[22] Thus he assures the unknown woman who anoints his head with oil in the house of Simon the leper, in Bethany, with the solemn introduction of "[truly] amen, I say to you," that her deed will be remembered, that is, in the judgment (cf. Mark 14:9).[23]

An early christological determination identified Jesus with divine wisdom,[24] though the latter cannot be traced back to him directly. It is correct, however, that in many respects Jesus resembles a teacher of wisdom. He is skilled in poetic, impressive language, composes *meshalim,* and in his story telling proves to be an undisputed master. When he claims to be more than Solomon (Matt 12:42 par.), he transcends the greatest, universal sage of Israel, indeed of the entire world, for the queen of a distant country of the South was once attracted to the wisdom of Solomon.[25] Jesus' lament over unrepentant Jerusalem, the second part of which includes his intensive care for his people, sounds wisdom-like (Matt 23:37 par.). Here

---

[22] Berger, *Die Amen-Worte Jesu,* has argued against the authenticity of this form of speech by pointing out that it is also found in two instances in the *Testament of Abraham* and is to be traced back to Hellenistic Jewish Christianity. Apart from the fact that the criterion of dissimilarity has been overworked, both passages are too recent. According to J. Jeremias, "Zum nicht-responsorischen Amen," *ZNW* 64 (1973) 122f., recension A of the *Testament of Abraham,* to which Berger appeals, originates from the medieval period. Cf. also E. Janssen, "Testament Abrahams" (JSHRZ 3/2; Gütersloh: Mohn, 1975) 222, n. 140.

[23] On the analysis and interpretation, cf. Gnilka, *Markus,* 2.221f., 225f.

[24] On this issue, cf. F. Christ, *Jesus Sophia* (ATANT 57; Zurich: Zwingli, 1970).

[25] Cf. Hengel, "Jesus als messianischer Lehrer der Weisheit und die Anfänge der Christologie," *Sagesse et Religion. Colloque de Strasbourg 1976* (Paris: Presses universitaires de France, 1979) 151f.

he appears like a messenger of wisdom, of divine wisdom representing God. Jesus is identified with wisdom no later than in Matthew.[26] For the rest, in comparison with the language of wisdom, it is
precisely the parables that clarify that such language is not to be
separated from his message of the kingdom. In his wisdom teaching
Jesus proves to be the one who bears the divine Spirit.[27]

This brings us to the Son of man. Did Jesus refer to the Son of
man? Did he perceive himself as the Son of man? Does "Son of
man" perhaps offer the ultimate information, the formula to be used
in our inquiry into Jesus' authority in mission?

The discussion on this is endless.[28] In order to understand it, it
is important to know that the Son of man sayings are traditionally
divided into three groups: eschatological (key statement: The Son of
man will come to judge in the clouds); passion-related (key statement: The Son of man must suffer much and be rejected); and a
third group that cannot be subsumed under a particular heading. In
any case, these sayings deal with the earthly Son of man, with his
authority to forgive sins, his homelessness, etc. We have already
alluded to this above in our discussion of the unique shaping of the
Christian Son of man Christology, which is predicated upon an
alleged Jewish Son of man conception and occurred in reminiscing
about the historical Jesus.

Two things are very conspicuous regarding the synoptic Son of
man tradition. For one, it is only Jesus who speaks of the Son of
man; in other words, nowhere does anyone else refer to the Son of
man. The expression "Son of man" is encountered only in the logia
of Jesus. For another, Jesus always refers to it in the third person;
nowhere does he say, "I, the Son of man." The embedding of the Son
of man sayings in the written Gospel, of course, assumed early on
that the community knows by faith that Jesus is the coming Son of
man and judge. The same can be observed in the parallelism between
the eschatological sayings and those dealing with the suffering and
earthly Son of man. But what about Jesus' proclamation? Luke 12:8
evoked particular attention: "every one who acknowledges me before

---

[26] Compare Luke 11:49, "Therefore also the Wisdom of God said, 'I will send
them . . . ' " with Matt 23:34, "Therefore I send you . . . "
[27] Both the Messiah and the Son of man are presented as gifted by the Spirit. Cf.
Isa 11:1–4; *Pss. Sol.* 17.37; 18.7f.; *1 Enoch* 49.1–4; 51.3; 62.2.
[28] On this issue, cf. the still foundational work of H. E. Tödt, *The Son of Man in
the Synoptic Tradition* (ET; London: SCM, 1965). On the more recent discussion, cf.
A. Vögtle, "Bezeugt die Logienquelle die authentische Rede Jesu vom 'Menschensohn'?" *Offenbarungsgeschehen und Wirkungsgeschichte* (Freiburg: Herder, 1985) 50–69.

men, the Son of man also will acknowledge before the angels of God." Here Jesus' references to himself and to the Son of man diverge, as if they refer to two different persons.

Scholarship has frequently made Luke 12:8 the starting point of the appraisal. While R. Bultmann[29] was indeed of the opinion that Jesus referred to the Son of man as someone else, H. Conzelmann[30] argues that Luke 12:8 presupposes the identification of the Son of man with Jesus and therefore must be attributed to the church. The same applies to the Son of man tradition as a whole. More recently E. Lohse[31] and A. Vögtle,[32] too, have wanted to view all of the Son of man sayings in a post-Easter context, for in Jesus' proclamation it will not do either to differentiate between him and an announced Son of man or to expect him to have spoken of his appearance in judgment in terms of a Son of man. The latter is held to be comprehensible and expressed only from the perspective of Easter. Furthermore, Jesus proclaimed the kingdom of God, alongside which there is no room for an expectation of a Son of man. This is demonstrated by the fact that there are no sayings of Jesus in which the kingdom of God and the Son of man are linked.[33]

> Conversely L. Goppelt wants to trace Luke 12:8, as well as other sayings relative to the earthly Son of man, back to Jesus.[34] Jesus chose the mysterious third-person form in order to announce himself as the Son of man in a veiled manner. This approach was chosen not for the people at large but for the disciples, who were able to understand him. Finally, in yet another scholarly perspective, the logia of the earthly Son of man are the starting point. Here the point of departure frequently is the equivalent Aramaic concept of *bar nasha*, which simply means "human" in Jesus' language and which could be used in such a way that the speaker was able to include himself in a general statement about a person, such as: With reference to me, Jesus, a person is allowed to forgive sins (Mark 2:10); A person like me, Jesus, has nowhere to lay his head (Matt 8:20). A general statement about a person has developed into a christological title or can be placed in parallel with it.[35]

The following remains to be said about this confusing array of suggested interpretations: A general statement about a person, postulated for some

---

[29] Bultmann, *Theology,* 29–33.
[30] Conzelmann, *Outline,* 135f.
[31] Lohse, *Grundriss der neutestamentlichen Theologie* (Stuttgart: W. Kohlhammer, 1974) 48f.
[32] Vögtle, "Logienquelle," 67.
[33] Cf. P. Vielhauer, "Gottesreich und Menschensohn in der Verkündigung Jesu," *Aufsätze zum Neuen Testament* (TB 31; Munich: C. Kaiser, 1965) 55–91.
[34] Goppelt, *Theology* 1.180–86. This applies to Mark 2:28; 2:10; Matt 8:20 and to a basic form of Mark 9:31.
[35] Cf. C. Colpe, "ὁ υἱὸς τοῦ ἀνθρώπου," *TDNT* 8.401–5, 430–61.

sayings about the earthly Son of man, is not convincing. Apart from the disputed philological problem, the question needs to be asked, who of Jesus' hearers would have understood and concluded that he actually referred to himself in this curious manner of speech. The resultant meaning is reduced to platitudes, as in the case of Matt 8:20. It is better to assume that all of the Son of man sayings, regardless of whether they originated with Jesus or later, are using "Son of man" as a title. The question of clarity also needs to be addressed concerning the view of Goppelt, namely, that Jesus' manner of communication with his disciples was veiled. The Gospels do not indicate that the Son of man sayings were addressed exclusively to the disciples.

The concepts of the Son of man and the reign of God are compatible. H. E. Tödt has already shown the parallelism in content and structure of the two lines of expression of Son of man and *basileia*. Such central features of proclamation as judgment and repentance are found in both lines.[36] The very conspicuous fact that Jesus alone speaks of the Son of man and that there is no confessional statement about Jesus, the Son of man, to be found in the Synoptics anywhere can ultimately be explained satisfactorily only by the observation that the Son of man expression existed in some way in Jesus' proclamation. There is the further differentiation between the speaking "I" and the Son of man that is characteristic of Luke 12:8. Those interpreters who are intent on denying Jesus any and all Son of man sayings continue to owe a convincing explanation of why this disconcerting differentiation between Jesus and the Son of man arose in the community and why the Son of man logia were then put into Jesus' mouth exclusively.

Luke 12:8 has to be taken as an authentic statement of Jesus and as the starting point of the Son of man Christology; in other words, the development within the groupings of statements about the es-chatological, earthly, and suffering Son of man begins with the first of these. We have delineated a similar development in the Jewish Son of man messianism, proceeding from the heavenly Son of man to an earthly Son of man / messiah figure. The synoptic development is to be seen as parallel to this. The fact that the Son of man title in the synoptic tradition underwent further expansion—whether new Son of man sayings were formed or the Son of man title intruded into sayings of Jesus—can be observed nicely in the Gospel of Matthew, where it found its broadest expansion.[37] The differentiation between self and the Son of man, as is the case in Luke 12:8, may be seen as Jesus' particular language of the Son of man.

---

[36] Tödt, *Son of Man*, 319–39.

[37] Cf. Matt 10:23; 13:37, 41; 16:13 (with Mark 8:27); 24:27, 30, 37, 39, 44; 25:31; 26:2; and H. Geist, *Menschensohn und Gemeinde* (FB 57; Würzburg: Echter, 1986).

For this reason one more thing needs to be said concerning this logion. In this connection, it is inappropriate to get too quickly involved with the alternative that has frequently been conjured up, namely, whether Jesus referred to the Son of man as someone else or identified himself as the one who was anticipated. In any case, the focus is on the coming eschatological judgment and hence the most important statement accorded to the Son of man. It is less significant whether he himself carries out the judgment or whether he appears as the judicial witness before the judge and makes his position known in a decisive manner regarding every individual. His acknowledgment and denial are definitive. Yet the inserted judgment scene contains a shocking prelude. Because of what happens before the event, the scene of the judgment, despite its seriousness, becomes a secondary and second-rank event. That which precedes the judgment also takes place in the encounter with the human Jesus, in response to his message, to his person. Acknowledging or denying Jesus determines the result of the eschatological judgment, anticipating it, as it were.

As far as the relationship of Jesus to the Son of man is concerned, this reveals the identity of the redemptive community.[38] What can be recognized, in any case, is that in the proclamation of Jesus the question of the identity of the Son of man is secondary in comparison with the resultant necessity for the hearer to make a decision. Those who are in community with him now will belong to the community of the saved at the judgment. If we want to examine the relationship of Jesus to the Son of man more closely, this proclamation, its structure and intention, actually obstructs the access to it. Did Jesus speak—occasionally at best—of the Son of man only so as to accommodate the conception of a certain group of hearers? Did he want to communicate that the expectation of the Son of man is couched in his preaching? In any case, the function of the anticipated Son of man becomes secondary compared with what Jesus is doing presently by means of his preaching and ministry. Or does he see himself in a particular relationship to this Son of man? If so, is it the relationship of identity? In any case, it is in harmony with his proclamation that he does not provide any detailed information about the "how" of the final, eschatological concern. This removes him from apocalyptic, from whose repertoire the expectation of the Son of man is derived and which dared to provide more detailed

---

[38] Cf. Tödt, *Son of Man*, 59–60.

descriptions of the conditions of heaven and hell and the intervening time. Jesus does not lift the curtain separating us from the final, eschatological realm, nor does he do so regarding his person. Although "mystery" is not a historical category, it is certainly appropriate here. Purely historical inquiry reaches its limits in a purely historical attempt at establishing and determining Jesus' authority in mission. This boundary ought to be observed.

Nevertheless there is a further nuance of Jesus' authority in mission that needs to be considered. We have already been able to observe above[39] that his way of addressing God is characterized by the name Father. This is continued in his prayers that have been handed down to us. At this point it is not the content of these prayers that is of interest to us but the fact that "Father" as appellation in prayer is used in the sense of "my Father" (Matt 11:25, 26 par.; 26:39, 42; Luke 23:46). The appellation "my Father" also occurs in other logia that are not prayers (Matt 7:21; 8:32f.; 16:17; 18:19, 35; et al.) and seems removed from statements in which Jesus calls God "your Father" in relation to the disciples (Matt 5:16, 45, 48; 6:1, 8, 14; et al.).

Whatever may be the case concerning the authenticity of the various logia, Jesus' manner of referring to God as his Father, especially in the address of prayers, must be taken as authentic. In the OT and in Judaism the reference to God as Father is very rare. In the collective sense it occurs in the Greek text of Sirach 23:1, 4 and Tobit 13:4.[40] "My Father" as a way of addressing God in prayer by an individual represents something new.[41]

Mark 14:36 contains the appellation "Abba" in Jesus' prayer in Gethsemane. This Aramaic term—grammatically best understood as a vocative—can be used as a son's way of addressing his natural father in Aramaic and in spite of its form is not restricted to an infant's babbling.[42] This may be construed as ipsissima vox on the part of Jesus and attests to his special, personal relationship with God.[43]

To be sure, we become aware of this special relationship with God, illumined for us as if by a flash, in the little word "Abba" only if

---

[39] See above, 200f.

[40] Cf. J. A. Fitzmyer, "Abba and Jesus' Relation to God," A cause de l'évangile (FS J. Dupont; Paris: Publications de Saint-André, 1985) 25f. Sirach 51:10 represents a recognition and possibly an echo of Ps 89:27.

[41] Fitzmyer, "Abba," 28.

[42] For the targumic documents, see ibid., 24. A parallel can be seen in ʾimmāʾ, which addresses the mother, comparable to our Mom, Dad.

[43] In two instances in the Talmud, in b. Taʿan. 23ab, the reference is indirectly to God as Abba. Apart from this, these texts are late and hence yield little.

we add and bring to bear the entire context of his mission. Let us attempt to formulate it from God's perspective: God gave him the task of arranging and bringing to bear in word and deed the eschatological salvation through the reign of God. He was entrusted with portraying God's love among people. He represents God uniquely in this world; he is with the people on behalf of God. The revelation of God the Father as bound up exclusively with Jesus is addressed in the logion that speaks of the Son in an absolute sense and that, not without reason, is cryptically labelled "Johannine" because it prepares for the depth of Johannine Christology (Matt 11:27 par.). It is closely linked with the "Abba" appellation, which it develops by means of a Hellenistic understanding.[44] By pointing to the comprehensive authority that the Father vested in the Son—"All things have been delivered to me by my Father"—it likely points to the position of lordship that has been accorded to Jesus the resurrected one (cf. Matt 28:18). Hence, in its uniqueness Jesus' authority in mission is not derived historically. The available messianic titles capture it only in part and in fragmentary fashion. The title of Messiah probably comes closest to his missionary claim if two essential changes are included: (1) Jesus is going to the cross. He saves his people not by conquering his foes but by presenting himself paradoxically as the one who has been put to death. (2) What links him with God, whom he calls his Father, is the bond of a unique sonship.

Overview

In the light of Easter, through the events of Easter and Pentecost, the perspective of the disciples' faith is deepened. If, as suggested, we pursue the insights of faith that experienced a post-Easter deepening through the highlighted christological titles and in retrospect were sharpened by the experience with the earthly Jesus, we notice that the Son of man who will be coming to judge is largely seen as the returning earthly Jesus. This return of Jesus, the Son of man, moves center stage even alongside the anticipated reign of God and temporarily may have fostered a forced imminent expectation.

---

[44] Cf. Gnilka, *Matthäusevangelium,* 1.431–42. Both Hengel, "Lehrer der Weisheit," 161, and Jeremias, *Theology,* 63–68, want to construe this sentence metaphorically: As the father does not keep anything from the son, especially regarding the trade skill that the son is to assume, so God communicated the totality of knowledge of his own self to Jesus. Nevertheless, this verse does not make clear structurally whether a comparison is intended or not.

Although the expectation of the Parousia is not important in the Gospel of John and the reign of God also mostly recedes into the background (cf. John 3:3, 5), the notion of the Son of man continues and gains its own shape. In the context of a certain parallelism with the apocalyptic concept of the preexistent Son of man, the Son of man is seen as the one whose home is with God, has come from God, and returns to God (so 3:13). Jesus, the Messiah, or, more appropriately, Jesus, the Christ, is probably the original confession of the Christian faith, which above all else is bound up with Christ's death and resurrection (e.g., 1 Cor 15:3–5). In precisely this manner it is possible to express peculiarities and specifics of the messianic Christian faith. As Messiah, Jesus is the one who was proclaimed in advance by the prophets in holy writings, as the son of David (Rom 1:2f.), whose fate of death and resurrection proved to be "in accordance with the scriptures" (1 Cor 15:3f.) and who maintains the continuity of salvation between the old and the new people of God. It goes without saying that the confession of Jesus, the Christ, which originated in Jewish-Christian circles, remained particularly relevant for them and also retained its significance in the community's endeavor to win Jews or in the dispute with the synagogue. In Gentile-Christian communities it may fade, the original dynamic may wane, and the expression "Jesus Christ" may be perceived almost as a proper name.

It is interesting to observe that large sections of the early church gave a central position to the concept of Jesus the Son of God (or the Son). The reason for this may be that this title was extant in the biblical as well as in the Greco-Roman worlds. It is more important, however, that probably early on they gained the insight that the title was especially suited to express what Jesus really was. In the earliest Gospel the christological train of thought culminates, as it were, in the concluding and summarizing confession by the Gentile centurion at the foot of the cross of Jesus, the Son of God (Mark 15:39; cf. Matt 27:54). The priority of the title Son in the Gospel of John and in the Johannine letters is without question. Yet such important theological documents of early Christianity as Romans and Hebrews likewise introduce their presentations with confessions of the Son of God (Rom 1:4; Heb 1:2). The Son of God concept made it possible to discuss the mystery of the person of Jesus—to the extent that this can be done at all—that he is the incarnate Word and the image of the invisible God (John 1:14; Col 1:15). Further titles are added to this. On the human side, the mystery made manifest has its counterpart in faith—not a faith, however, that is stuck in knowledge alone but one that shapes and transforms life in its concreteness through the message of this Messiah and Son.

Select bibliography: W. Bracht, "Der Menschensohn" (diss.; Munich, 1972); R. Bultmann, "Die Frage nach dem messianischen Bewusstsein Jesu und das Petrus-Bekenntnis," *ZNW* 19 (1919/20) 165–74; P. M. Casey, *Son of Man* (London: SPCK, 1979); F. Christ, *Jesus Sophia* (ATANT 57; Zurich: Zwingli, 1970); J. A. Fitzmyer, "Abba and Jesus' Relation to God," 15–38 in *A cause de l'évangile* (FS J. Dupont; Paris: Publications de Saint-André, 1985); M. Hengel, *Der Sohn Gottes* (Tübingen: Mohr, 1975); idem, "Jesus als messianischer Lehrer der Weisheit und die Anfänge der Christologie," *Sagesse et Religion. Colloque de Strasbourg 1976* (Paris: Presses universitaires de France, 1979) 147–88; A. J. B. Higgins, *The Son of Man in the Teaching of Jesus* (SNTSMS 39; Cambridge/New York: Cambridge University Press, 1980); H. Hübner, "Der 'Messias Israels' und der Christus des NT," *KD* 27 (1981) 217–40; K. Müller, "Menschensohn und Messias," *BZ* 16 (1972) 161–87; U. B. Müller, *Messias und Menschensohn in jüdischen Apokalypsen und in der Offenbarung des Johannes* (SNT 6; Gütersloh: Mohn, 1972); 17 (1973) 52–66; H. Riesenfeld, "Bemerkungen zur Frage des Selbstbewusstseins Jesu," 331–41 in *Der historische Jesus und der kerygmatische Christus* (H. Ristow and K. Matthiae; 2d ed.; Berlin: Evangelische Verlagsanstalt, 1964); G. Schelbert, "Sprachgeschichtliches zu 'Abba,'" 395–447 in *Mélanges D. Barthélemy* (OBO 38; Göttingen: Vandenhoeck & Ruprecht, 1981); H. Schlier, "Wer ist Jesus?" *Der Geist und die Kirche* (Freiburg: Herder, 1980) 20–32; H. E. Tödt, *The Son of Man in the Synoptic Tradition* (ET; London: SCM, 1965); K. W. Tröger, "Jesus als Prophet," *Kairos* 24 (1982) 100–109; A. Vögtle, "Bezeugt die Logienquelle die authentische Redeweise Jesu vom Menschensohn?" 50–69, in *Offenbarungsgeschehen und Wirkungsgeschichte* (Freiburg: Herder, 1985).

10

Conflict and the Final Days

As the Gospels present it, the ministry of Jesus is characterized by conflict almost from the start. The conflict intensifies and ends with Jesus' execution on the cross. The conflict has various scenes, namely, Galilee and Jerusalem. Jesus gets caught in conflict with various groups, ultimately with the Roman powers, thereby leading to his death. Jesus' trial will be a topic of its own. In this chapter the conflict is to be brought, as it were, to the threshold of the trial. It is in keeping with the interest of the Gospels, and of the traditions they contain, that they devote considerable space, relatively speaking, to Jesus' final days in Jerusalem. Hence we can focus on particular incidents that took place at that time: the entry into the city, the temple protest, the Last Supper with the disciples. This also means that everything we will be saying here is not merely linked with the conflict.

1. The conflict emerging in Jesus' ministry

The main opponents of the conflict emerging in Jesus' public ministry appear to be the Pharisees. They are frequently mentioned in conjunction with other groups: Pharisees and scribes / experts of the law (Matt 5:20; 12:38; 15:1; Mark 2:16; 7:1, 5; Luke 5:17, 21, 30; 6:7; 7:30; 11:53; 14:3; 15:2), Pharisees and Herodians (Mark 3:6; 12:13), Pharisees and Sadducees (Matt 3:7; 16:1, 6, 11, 12). These associations appear to be sweeping. The most inclusive is Matthew, who even has the Pharisees appear together with the Sadducees in Galilee, historically a rather unlikely scenario. Mark's differentiation is somewhat better, as he distances the Pharisees slightly from the scribes, probably because he knows that not all Pharisees were scribes and not all scribes were Pharisees.[1] Matthew may well have been aware of this as well. When he wrote his Gospel, however, there was no longer a party of the Sadducees. His concern was to show Jesus' Jewish opponents as a unified whole.

The amalgamation of the Pharisees into a bloc also seems to be sweeping. Among themselves they certainly were not unified at all. At the time of Jesus there were the feuding leaders of Pharisaic schools, Hillel and Shammai. Only occasionally does an individual scribe (Mark 12:28) or a Pharisee (Luke 7:36; 11:37; 14:1; cf. 18:10) appear on his own, and even then he is usually shown in an unfavorable light. Finally, when the resolutions of the Pharisees, scribes, and Herodians to destroy Jesus are moved forward into the ministry of Jesus, this too appears sweeping (Mark 3:6 par.; 11:18 par.; 14:2 par.). The presentation follows a literary plot. Just as the resolutions to kill him, together with Jesus' repeated announcements of the passion, are meant to provide the Gospel's structure with a passion orientation, so the prominence of the Pharisees has to do with the situation after CE 70, when the Gospels were compiled. Only the party of the Pharisees survived the catastrophe, was consolidated, and gained formative influence upon Judaism. A lively dispute ensued between the synagogue and the church and influenced the shaping of the Gospels and of their tradition.

It is also due to this shaping of the Gospels that there is no mention of two Jewish groups of that time, the Essenes and the Zealots.[2] This factor alone, however, does not explain this peculiar situation. As a party, the Sadducees did not survive beyond 70 CE either. Little more than assumptions can be made in this regard, of course. As far as the Zealots are concerned, it may be conjectured that a certain anti-Pharisaic polemic on the part of Jesus at least in part was also directed against them as the most radical representatives of left-wing Pharisaism.[3] Concerning the Essenes, it may be assumed that there was no direct contact with them, which is related to the fact that they lived in isolation.

---

[1] Both groups are given their own definite article in Mark 2:16; 7:1, 5, whereas the Pharisees and Sadducees are combined under one article in Matt 3:7; 16:1, 6, 11, 12, likewise the scribes and Pharisees in Matt 5:20; 12:38, as well as in Luke 14:3.

[2] The term "Zealot" occurs only as a nickname of Simon in Luke 6:15 and Acts 1:13.

[3] Hengel, *Zealots,* 378.

We must not be tempted to assume that the insertion of a later conflict between the church and the Pharisaically shaped synagogue means that there were no conflicts at all between Jesus and the Pharisees, or that it even favors the notion that Jesus himself has to be considered part of the Pharisaic orientation. Jewish exegetes in particular are fond of arguing the position that Jesus could be considered as belonging to a branch of the—mostly Hillelite—Pharisaic movement and that his dispute with the Pharisees remains within these boundaries.[4] It is one of the unique features of Jesus' ministry that he cannot be aligned with any of the Jewish sects but, going beyond their boundaries, addresses all and offers salvation to the nation as a whole. If there is a preference, it is the poor and disenfranchised to whom he is drawn. Yet he does not have in mind establishing a sect of the *anawim* (the pious poor) either. It is evident that the fabric of conflict accumulated in his proclamation was well suited to snub the Pharisees and the Sadducees, the latter even more intensively in several respects.

In an attempt to learn something about the nature of Jesus' conflict, we must not begin with the text that presumably comes to mind first, the woes directed against the scribes and Pharisees (Matt 23:13–31 par.). This composition, intensifying in bitter accusations, even to accusations of lawlessness and of condoning murder, is largely dictated by the subsequent distancing of the Christian community from the synagogue.[5] This is not to say that it contains no trace of elements of Jesus. Among these may be the charge that the scribes had taken away the key of knowledge and become an obstacle for those entering the kingdom of God (cf. Luke 11:52; Matt 23:13). The plea for the weak and those led astray is entirely congruent with Jesus' intentions.

As far as the nature of Jesus' conflict is concerned, it is necessary to begin with the basic chord of his proclamation, that of the kingdom of God. The new order that is being signaled with the *basileia* surpasses the old order of the law. The Sadducees rejected every eschatological option for the future. Jesus is distinct from the

---

[4] According to P. Winter, "The Enemies of Jesus," *On the Trial of Jesus* (SJ 1; Berlin: de Gruyter, 1961) 133, Jesus represents a pre-rabbinic form of Pharisaism; for A. Finkel, *The Pharisees and the Teacher of Nazareth* (ASGU 4; Leiden: Brill, 1964) 134–43, Jesus is close to the Hillelites, while for Klausner, *Jesus*, 381 n. 122, he actually was a Pharisee. In order to show the range of opinions, we cite E. Haenchen, "Matthäus 23," *Gott und Mensch* (Tübingen: Mohr, 1965) 52, who speaks of Jesus and the Pharisees as mortal enemies.

[5] For an analysis, cf. Gnilka, *Matthäusevangelium*, 2.280–85, 293f.

Pharisees and Sadducees in his conception of the sanctity of the person. By vouching for a radical realization of the love commandment and hence for the person, he may repeatedly have appeared to them as one who did not care about the law, much less about the "tradition of the elders" (cf. Mark 7:5). He sees the sanctity of the person as established not in the meticulous observance of Levitical purity regulations but in the innermost part of the person, out of which the person's nature unfolds (cf. Mark 7:15). The critique of tradition had to affect the Pharisees, and that of the institution of the Corban, associated with the temple, had to affect the Sadducees in particular. In his critique of the Sabbath, as we have shown earlier,[6] he stood for the dignity and salvation of the person but in doing so was bound to collide with the Pharisaic (as well as the Essene) understanding of the law. In his prohibition against the husband divorcing his wife under pain of becoming an adulterer, he supports God's creation order and the disadvantaged wife but at the same time clearly speaks out against a regulation of the law, against the Mosaic directive regarding the letter of divorce.

Given the considerable historical distance, the critique of the practice of Torah piety may appear less sharp to us today; yet in its subtlety and urgency it had to hit hard those who were rebuked by it. Jesus did not merely use words in his critique; in a provocative way he also held the new order up to them as an example. When he sat at table with lawless tax collectors and sinners, he overturned the rules by which the company had come together and he violated the "law of holiness," according to which contact with the lawless rendered a person unclean and left him open to the danger of being considered lawless himself. The subtlety of the conflict became particularly tangible in the parabolic narrative of the Pharisee and the tax collector (Luke 18:9–14), for it disclosed its theological backdrop. Here Jesus' plea for the sinner became recognized as the plea of God himself and thus the crushing critique of this legal piety.

The fact that the authorities took action against Jesus, however, cannot yet be made altogether plausible merely from the conflict described above. Neither does it suffice to point out that Moses' Torah represented both the religious and the juridical law code of the Jewish state, thereby making it impossible to distinguish between religious and juridical violations. We concur with P. Winter[7] in saying

---

[6] See above, 217f.
[7] Winter, "Enemies," 135.

that the effect of Jesus' ministry upon the masses has to be taken into consideration as well in order to grasp that on a certain day the authorities took action against Jesus. And this effect may have been quite considerable, though it is no longer possible to pinpoint its development.[8] On the whole, the picture of Jesus being surrounded by throngs of people, as the Gospels present it, is accurate. Even if they understood him only in part and largely did not carry out his demand of repentance, he could reckon with a sizable audience.

Perhaps it is helpful to refer to John the Baptist in an attempt to understand what is being delineated here. Josephus argues that the reason for Herod Antipas having the Baptist arrested and executed was the mass movement that John triggered. Herod feared that "the great influence John had over the people might put it into his power and inclination to raise a rebellion" and so "thought it best, by putting him to death, to prevent any mischief he might cause" (*Ant.* 18.116–119).

Josephus may have been correct in his observation.[9] Someone who rallies masses must appear suspicious to a despot. This is true both of John and of Jesus. In addition Jesus had been seen in the Baptist's company. In this context Herod's warning leveled against Jesus is revealing and certainly historically plausible (Luke 13:31). If those who voiced the warning were Pharisees, it becomes clear that the relationship of the Pharisees to Jesus has to be seen as differentiated and does not denote that the Pharisees en bloc were hostile to him.

In the evaluation of the conflict it is important to see that the Sadducees were not involved with him in Galilee. Only in Jerusalem did they enter the action (Mark 12:18 par.).[10] In the passion narrative and particularly in the account of the trial, prominence is given to the high priests, elders, and scribes (Mark 14:1, 43, 53; 15:1). The same can be said of Jesus' passion announcements (Mark 8:31; 10:33; cf. 11:18, 27). It is common knowledge that the high priests and elders belonged to the Sadducean party or were allied with them.

---

[8] In the Synoptic Gospels Peter's messianic confession contains a certain caesura. According to Mark 8:27ff. Jesus devotes himself more to teaching the disciples. No historical conclusions can be drawn from this depiction.

[9] On the interpretation of the text in Josephus, see R. Schütz, *Johannes der Täufer,* 20–27. Josephus (*Ant.* 18.109–115) also links the Baptist's fate with the adulterous conduct of Herod Antipas, though not as its cause, as in the case of Mark 6:17–29 par. On this issue, cf. Gnilka, "Das Martyrium Johannes," 78–92.

[10] The exception of Matt 16:1–12 is historically inapplicable and can be explained by the first evangelist's thinking in terms of blocs, to which we have already referred above.

Conversely, the Pharisees do not appear in the passion of Jesus, except in Matt 27:62 and John 18:3, where the reference to Pharisees is a secondary insertion. Although it has to be assumed that there were Pharisees among the scribes of the Sanhedrin, presumably even the majority, the findings described allow for the conclusion that the mortal conflict was kindled by the high priests and elders, or, to put it differently, by the Sadducees.

These findings would be assessed incorrectly if they led to the conclusion that there was no connection at all between Jesus' conflict in Galilee and the intensifying conflict in Jerusalem. To be sure, his relationship to the Pharisees needs to be evaluated differently; nevertheless, it is hardly possible to assert that he had no hardline opponents among them. Add to this the political stir that Jesus was able to evoke with the ruler of Galilee. When Jesus decides to travel to Jerusalem, he does not come as a stranger as far as the influential circles are concerned. He does not come as "an unknown quantity"; rather, in their view, he may have been considered suspiciously because of conflicts and crowds associated with him in Galilee.

2. The journey to Jerusalem

The old quest of the historical Jesus was eagerly concerned with the question of why Jesus went to Jerusalem. A. Schweitzer[11] reduced their efforts to the formula that some had Jesus go there because he wanted to minister there and challenge the people to the ultimate decision, while others opined that he wanted to die in the city. It is highly unlikely that he was completely surprised by the enormous danger he encountered in Jerusalem. It certainly was his intent to deliver his message in the metropolis. Our texts do not allow for detailed information on this matter. Looking at it from the outside, he went to Jerusalem with his disciples, men and women alike, as a simple pilgrim for the Passover festival.

It is difficult to say which way he took from Galilee to Jerusalem. What is certain is that he traveled via Jericho (cf. Mark 10:46) and consequently on the final leg of the journey used the well-known road past the Wadi el-kelt. According to Mark 9:33 he started from Capernaum. This redactional comment has little meaning, however. Of the three major routes from Galilee to Jerusalem, the eastern one followed along the Jordan River and was used to bypass

[11] Schweitzer, *Quest,* 389–95, esp. 389 n. 1.

Samaria. This route took three or four days.[12] In the spring the climate was pleasant and not yet as oppressively hot as in summer. Spending the night in the open was perfectly possible.

It is necessary at this point to ask how often Jesus might have been in Jerusalem during his public ministry, or, to word it differently, whether he had already visited the city prior to the Passover of his passion. According to the account in the Synoptics the latter option would have to be negated. Yet the panorama of his ministry, presented here in terms of a single journey from Galilee to Jerusalem, denotes a literary intention of focusing his ministry upon the passion. The Fourth Gospel speaks of several festivals during which Jesus would have been in the city. Besides the Passover of his passion, reference is made to a feast of Tabernacles (7:2), a certain unidentified festival of the Jews (5:1), and a further Passover (2:13). The last-mentioned deals, however, with Jesus' temple protest, that is, with the event that the Synoptics appropriately link with his final visit to Jerusalem but the fourth evangelist moved to the beginning of his ministry for theological reasons. Since the remaining references to festivals also are placed for theological reasons, the Fourth Gospel does not help us much. Jesus does not seem to have been known in person among the population of Jerusalem. This is, anyhow, presupposed in the scene of his arrest, in which Judas Iscariot is needed to identify him (cf. Mark 14:43–53). Although it cannot be proved, it cannot be ruled out that he came to Jerusalem only this one time. If this is accurate, it is at least viable to suggest that he wanted to call the people of the city to repentance. Nevertheless, this issue has to remain open.

The number of pilgrims traveling to Jerusalem for the Passover was large. They did not come merely from Judea and Galilee, but also from the Diaspora. J. Jeremias[13] estimates their number to have been around 125,000. If the 55,000 inhabitants of the city are added, there were around 180,000 people in the city during festivals. Many pilgrims may have arrived several days before the festival, as Jesus also probably did. An early arrival was called for by the Passover customs but was also advisable for practical reasons.[14]

---

[12] Cf. G. Dalman, *Orte und Wege* (3d ed.; Gütersloh: Bertelsmann, 1924) 222–62. The Madaba map indicates ferries across the Jordan near Salem and Jericho, that is, a rope stretched across the river and in the middle of the river a small boat, the mast of which is tied to the rope. The geographical reference in Mark 10:1 is probably redactional and contains several textual variants. Cf. Gnilka, *Markus*, 2.69–71.

[13] Jeremias, *Jerusalem*, 77–84.

[14] Since the men entered the priests' court of the temple in order to sacrifice the Passover lambs there, they needed to maintain rigorous purity. Cf. Num 9:6–13;

What happened when Jesus, coming from the Mount of Olives, approached the city? The account of his entry into Jerusalem in Mark 11:1–11 par. is heavily interspersed with theological motifs. In addition, the account is burdened with the zealotic interpretation of Jesus.

R. Eisler, considered the founder of the zealotic interpretative orientation this century, even made this pericope one of the central points of his view. It argues that the people literally proclaimed Jesus king of Israel at that time, comparable to the Roman troops who proclaimed victorious generals as emperors in the period of the Republic. In this connection Eisler refers to Luke 19:38, where the people acclaimed Jesus: "Blessed is the King who comes in the name of the Lord! Peace in heaven and glory in the highest!" He finds further evidence in the analogous appointment of King Agrippa II by the crowds—in keeping with the Hebrew Josippon [a medieval edition of Flavius Josephus, in Hebrew, ed. note]—who at his entry in Jerusalem responded: "Save us, O king! We do not want to be subject to Rome any longer." This is not all, however. In his construction Eisler also assumes that Jesus came to the city with a large crowd of guerillas and, after the acclamation by the people of Jerusalem, occupied the temple area.[15]

To begin with, the relevant texts further indicate that the people who acclaimed Jesus were pilgrims to the festival who came up from Jericho with him, hence not citizens of Jerusalem. In Mark 11:9 we read, "And those who went before and those who followed cried out, 'Hosanna!' " Only from John 12:12f. can the impression be gained that the people from the city went to him in order to meet him (εἰς ὑπάντησιν αὐτῷ). In any case, these too may have been pilgrims who had already arrived in the city.

It is beyond dispute that the narrative was stylized into a faith account in terms of the royal messianology. This was assisted substantially by the legend of the miraculous find of the foal of a donkey,

---

2 Chron 30:15–19; Josephus, *War* 1.229. According to John 11:55 many Jews came to Jerusalem before the Passover to purify themselves; according to 12:1 Jesus came to Bethany six days before the festival. The number may well have symbolic significance. The seventh day is the day of completion (cf. Mark 9:2).

[15] R. Eisler, *Iesous basileus ou basileusas* (Heidelberg: C. Winter, 1930) 2.469–75. Of course Jesus would have been overpowered by the Romans. His military rebellion is alleged to have been the reason for his execution. Thus Eisler categorizes Jesus precisely with the anonymous Egyptian who intended to conquer Jerusalem from the Mount of Olives with a group of people. Cf. Josephus, *Ant.* 20.169; *War* 2.262. This incident took place a few years after Jesus' death. The details of the two accounts by Josephus differ, especially with regard to the march to the Mount of Olives.

which is inspired by Zech 9:9 ("Lo, your king comes to you . . . riding on an ass, on a colt")[16] but also by Gen 49:11 ("Binding his foal to the vine"). The messianic acclamation by the crowds is stylized as well. Psalm 118:26 ("Blessed be he who enters in the name of the Lord!") was originally a call from the temple doors whereby the entering pilgrims to the festival were saluted. The acclamation "Hosanna," which is first of all a cry for help addressed to God, is also found in Ps 118:26a. The unambiguously messianic addition in Mark 11:10, "Blessed is the kingdom of our father David that is coming!" is secondary.[17] This is then clarified by the indirect referents.

If we look through the faith narrative to the enduring historical basis, we see Jesus, the wanderer and pilgrim, acclaimed outside the city gates by his disciples and other pilgrims en route to the festival. Their cry might have been, "Hosanna! Blessed is he who comes in the name of the Lord." The proximity of Jerusalem is the starting point for a possible interpretation of the historical situation. This is more than the elation over having reached the city after a long journey. The acclamation is meant for Jesus. Most likely this joy could be linked with the expectation that the reign of God which he has been proclaiming will soon be coming. But in this case the acclamation also gains a latent messianic ring. Against a possibility such as this it cannot be objected that the Romans would then have had to intervene at once. The demonstration was a peaceful one. Eisler's interpretation founders on the exegetical evidence, quite apart from the fact that a warlike intention would have been diametrically opposed to Jesus' message of nonaggression and loving one's enemy. We do not know whether and how the ovation given to Jesus continued to have an effect and became part of the complaints of his subsequent accusers. Neither do we know details of how Jesus reacted to the homage. In any case, he did not himself inaugurate a messianic scene.

3. The temple protest

During his stay in Jerusalem Jesus lived at Bethany, a small place on the other side of the Mount of Olives from Jerusalem, fifteen stadia (2.77 km, 1.72 miles) east of the city and away from the route of the pilgrims. Linked with Bethany are the names of Simon

---

[16] Matthew 21:4f. cites Zech 9:9 explicitly to show fulfillment, though the prophetic text is already implied by Mark 11:2-7.

[17] The reference to David as father is not Jewish at all. For an analysis of this, cf. Gnilka, *Markus*, 2.113-15; Trautmann, *Handlungen*, 347-78.

the leper (Mark 14:3), as well as of Mary, Martha, and Lazarus (only according to John 11:1; cf. Luke 10:38–42). The information about the accommodation at Bethany, which we owe to Mark 11:11 (cf. 11:19), deserves to be trusted. This opportunity for lodging may have come about conveniently, though it could also be the case that he wished not to spend the nights in Jerusalem.

The conspicuous incident prior to the Passover was the temple protest. Before dealing with it in detail, it is necessary to establish its historical credibility. Two arguments against this have been adduced, closely associated with one another: one individual on his own was not capable of a major action such as this; and this kind of action would have led to the direct intervention by the temple police, that is, the Roman troops stationed in the temple fortress. In this case the pericope Mark 11:15–18 par. is taken as an expression of the early church's critique of the temple cult.[18]

With regard to the transmission of the pericope, it is evident that Jesus' temple protest is interpreted in different ways. In John 2:13–22 the temple is made to refer to Jesus' body, which will be put to death and resurrected; in other words, by means of his protest Jesus provokes his own death. In addition to the pericope in the Gospel, Luke has a temple protest of the strongest verbal kind in the account of Stephen (Acts 6:13f.; cf. 7:47–51). Stephen and his circle adopt Jesus' temple protest in a radicalized form.

This means that the development runs from Jesus to the Hellenistic Jewish-Christian community, represented by Stephen, not vice versa. After all, Jesus' seemingly incomprehensible act cannot have been spun from the prophetic words adduced for its interpretation in Mark 11:1 par. Matt 21:13—Isa 56:7 (a house of prayer for all peoples)[19] and Jer 7:11 ("But you have made it a den of robbers")— for neither of them matches the situation precisely and hence both prove to be secondary.[20]

All of this speaks in favor of taking the spectacular temple protest as an act of Jesus but also of not yet having an interpretative

---

[18] On this issue, cf. Roloff, *Kerygma*, 89f.; Trautmann, *Handlungen*, 114–19.

[19] The addition of "for all the nations" occurs only in Mark 11:17.

[20] Cf. V. Eppstein, "The Historicity of the Gospel Account of the Cleansing of the Temple," *ZNW* 65 (1964) 44. The pericope was not influenced by Zech 14:21, "And there shall no longer be a $k^e na^{ca}n\hat{i}$ in the house of the LORD of hosts on that day" (so, e.g., Roloff, *Kerygma*, 96). The Hebrew term is ambiguous in meaning, denoting both a Canaanite and a trader. The prophet more likely had the former meaning in mind. This is also the view represented in the commentaries of F. Horst (HAT) and K. Elliger (ATD). The term Χαναναῖος used in the LXX supports this view.

statement of this event that goes back to him. As the deed of an individual, this action becomes comprehensible if we leave it in its context. The description obviously underwent an intensification because the Christian tradition increasingly saw in Jesus' action the abolition of the temple cult. Mark 11:15 speaks of driving out buyers and sellers and of overturning the tables of the money changers and the seats of those who sold pigeons.[21] John 2:14f. dramatizes the scene in an extraordinary way: "And making a whip of cords, he drove them *all*, with the sheep and oxen, out of the temple." The reaction of the authorities, which did not fail to materialize, is yet to be addressed.

A detailed understanding of how the temple market was handled at the time of Jesus is no longer possible. The only thing that can be said with some certainty is that, at least in part, it was held in the court of the Gentiles, that is, in the large temple court that encompassed the actual inner temple precinct to the north, east, and south and was accessible to Gentiles as well. In part, the temple market was held outside of the temple, on the terrain toward the Mount of Olives. The hypothesis that parts of the market were brought into the court of the Gentiles only by Caiaphas, the high priest, is interesting indeed but one that lacks convincing support. The concrete link with Jesus' action indicated thereby has to remain doubtful.[22] It is not conceivable, however, for the market to have been held in the temple without the toleration of the temple authorities. Presumably they even managed it themselves.[23] The Markan references may lead us to conclude that only the money changers and sellers of pigeons were situated in the court of the Gentiles, for these details seem to be precise. It is easy to imagine that at times of major pilgrim festivals, especially during the Passover, the temple market was booming.

---

[21] Add to this the mysterious verse of Mark 11:16. The prohibition of carrying anything through the temple refers either to the cultic utensils or to using the temple area as a shortcut. The reference to the cultic utensils would be tantamount to an abolition of the temple cult; hence this too would be a secondary theological interpretation.

[22] Eppstein, "Historicity," 42–58, argues this hypothesis; in fact he suggests 30 CE as the point in time when Caiaphas made the decision. This hypothesis is burdened with further aspects of a dubious nature, e.g., Caiaphas had been severely disturbed by the relationship between the Sadducees and the Pharisees, which had been good up to then; Jesus and the disciples stayed on the Mount of Olives for seven days and underwent purification before entering the temple.

[23] According to Str-B, *Kommentar,* 1.852 this applied to wine for drink offerings and to poultry offerings.

In order to gain a fair grasp of Jesus' action, we have to depend upon the Markan account, the terseness of which can hardly be outdone. Jesus did not wield a whip, neither did he grab oxen and sheep by the horns—this Johannine depiction is to be construed metaphorically for the abolition of the temple cult; rather he turned indignantly against some money changers and sellers of pigeons, whose tables and seats he overturned. To be sure, his action is not primarily directed against these people but against the temple hierarchy that set up this market. It is comprehensible why the Roman troops do not intervene; Jesus does not use military force. They may not have understood the action, or perhaps did not even notice it. But the high priests rise up to speak, though Mark, in keeping with his terse account, only alludes to it as a concluding remark (11:18).[24] Here the earlier reference perhaps deserves to be given historical attention, that it was the consideration of the people, of those sympathizing with Jesus, that prevented an immediate arrest. It is very relevant, however, that within the narrative segments of Mark's Gospel this is the first time that the high priests are mentioned. This confirms their initiative in acting against Jesus. The temple protest of Jesus prompted them to act, even if that action was delayed for another few hours or days. In a sense this is also the missing link between the Galilean conflict, which had not yet been driven to its climax, and the end. As the guardians of the system of government based upon the law and the temple, the Sadducees now had to regard them as challenged by Jesus. In the discussion of Jesus' trial this aspect will need to be examined further.

To find out how Jesus intended this course of events to be understood, it is necessary to begin with the action itself. While the action takes place in the court of the Gentiles, the precinct separate from the sanctuary, what the priests of the temple practiced here was related to the worship of God and to the temple in which such worship took place. G. Theissen used the designations of aggression and identification to identify Jesus' disposition regarding the temple, reflected in his action.[25] Both acceptance and rejection may in fact be recognized at the same time. It is not the temple per se that is unworthy; rather it is the manner in which people deal with God in the temple. Thus Jesus' action becomes a passionate call for a change

---

[24] If its particular history of tradition is considered, the issue of authority in Mark 11:27–33 is out of the question as a link with the temple protest. This history goes back to a dispute concerning the baptism of John. Cf. Gnilka, *Markus,* 2.136–38.

[25] G. Theissen, "Die Tempelweissagung Jesu," in *Studien,* 144.

of heart, a call to repentance. In this sense it fits with his critique of other institutions, the critique of the practice of the law, of the Sabbath, which he did not abolish but intended to be restored to the will of the Creator.[26] In the context of his proclamation of the kingdom of God, in view of the impending end, the call to repentance, turned into action, takes on its own profile.

Perhaps it is possible to advance the argument another step. Perhaps Jesus' words spoken during the temple protest may yet be determined. According to Mark 14:58 there are witnesses—identified as false witnesses by the text—who introduce the following saying of Jesus in the trial before the Sanhedrin: "I will destroy this temple that is made with hands, and in three days I will build another, not made with hands." It is noteworthy that we encounter this logion not only in quite different forms in other places (John 2:16; Acts 6:14; Matt 26:61; cf. Gos. Pet. 7.26) but, apart from John 2:16, also always as an accusation by the opponents. In this case the fourth evangelist would have retained this saying in, or even restored it to, its original context, even if the reformulation in view of the person of Christ was not its original form. Most probably the latter can no longer be reconstructed, for, as a statement that has been put in the mouth of the opponents, it may have been altered accordingly. The only corresponding basic structure of a temple saying may be one that announced its destruction and reconstruction. In Acts 6:14 the latter is reshaped into a change in the system. Was the saying originally impersonal, thus announcing God as the one acting in the future? Or was it in the first-person form?[27] If we intend to take up this saying as an interpretation of Jesus' temple protest, it becomes lucid in view of the expected destruction of the sanctuary of Jerusalem but also in view of its reestablishment in the eschatological advent of the reign of God, in keeping with Jewish eschatology (cf. Tob 13:17; Bar 5:1–9; 1 Enoch 90.28f.; 91.13).[28]

---

[26] Cf. Roloff, Kerygma, 96: "Thus Jesus' attitude to the temple matches the one regarding the Sabbath commandment."

[27] According to Theissen, "Tempelweissagung," 143 n. 3, the first-person singular form could be a misrepresentation by the opponents. In this case the intention to destroy the temple would have been purported to be his. For Theissen, the authenticity of the logion is supported by the fact that it cannot be derived either from Judaism or from early Christianity. Jewish prophecies against the temple never promise a new temple. A Christian vaticinium ex eventu is ruled out because the announced rebuilding of the temple remained unfulfilled.

[28] Interpreters attribute differing intentions to Jesus. For Hahn, Titles, 156–60; 206–7, Jesus' action is an eschatological promise given to the Gentiles. The court of

4. The Last Supper

Jesus spent the final evening of his life in the circle of his disciples in Jerusalem. In this connection it is not at all out of the question that among those present there were also women disciples who had traveled to Jerusalem with him (cf. Mark 15:40f.).[29]

Was the final night the night of the Passover? The answer to this question determines not only the type of supper that he ate with the disciples but also the pinpointing of the day he died. Interpreting his death theologically in light of the Passover could also be suggested by the proximity of the festival. Between the Synoptics and the Fourth Gospel there is the seemingly peculiar difference that the Passover meal is presupposed in one instance (Mark 14:12–16 par.; Luke 22:15f.), while in the other this is not the case; instead it is said equally explicitly that the context is the day before the Passover, the day of preparation, and that the Passover can be eaten only in the night after Jesus' death (John 13:1; 18:28; 19:14).

Attempts have been made at harmonizing these differing time references by appealing to Qumran. We know that that community observed the solar calendar (as did the Qumran-related book of *Jubilees*), whereas the Jerusalem temple adhered to the lunar calendar. For this reason the Passover was presumably celebrated on two different dates in Israel at the time of Jesus. While the Passover was always observed on the 15th of Nisan, the month of spring, in both calendars, according to the solar calendar this day always fell on a Tuesday, whereas the day varied in the lunar calendar. The solution is said to be that Jesus adhered to the solar calendar of the Essenes and thus celebrated the Passover meal on Tuesday. Conversely, of course, the high priests adhered to the lunar calendar in effect in the temple and hence were able to speak in line with what we understand from John 18:28.[30]

---

the Gentiles as the locus of the action hardly permits as sweeping an interpretation as this. E. Trocmé, "L'expulsion des marchands du temple," *NTS* 15 (1968/69) 1–22, speaks of a zealotic action. In this case the concept "zealotic" is unclear. C. Roth, "The Cleansing of the Temple and Zechariah 14:21," *NT* 4 (1960) 164–81, conversely, sees Jesus acting in an antizealotic manner. Trautmann, *Handlungen,* 121, suggests that the cleansing of the temple was symbolic of a relativizing of the temple cult, if not its abolition.

[29] The mention of the Twelve in Mark 14:7 does not necessarily rule this out. It should be seen as redactional and is intended to insure that the Twelve were present as witnesses (cf. Gnilka, *Markus,* 2.235).

[30] The solar-calendar hypothesis has been argued by A. Jaubert, *La date de la cène* (Paris: J. Gabalda, 1957), and by E. Ruckstuhl, *Die Chronologie des Letzten Mahles und des Leidens* (Jesu BiBe NF 4; Einsiedeln: Benziger, 1963).

As striking as this hypothesis appears to be, it fails to convince and can be dismissed. The Fourth Gospel does not intend to give the impression at all that the meal Jesus had with his disciples was the Passover meal.[31] And if one attempted to assume that Jesus wanted to celebrate the Passover on Tuesday, it would not have been possible for him to secure a lamb that had been slaughtered in the temple in keeping with the regulations. Yet this must be absolutely presupposed for this festival. The assertion that the Essenes had permission to slaughter lambs in the temple on their date is pure invention.[32]

Apart from Mark 14:12ff. par. and Luke 22:15f., of course, the Synoptics have left few traces of a Passover meal. Nevertheless, their chronology is to be preferred. The following factors can be used in support of this: Jesus and his disciples celebrate this meal in the city of Jerusalem, and they celebrate it at night. Both can be taken as confirmed. The time of night is also attested in the ancient Lord's Supper tradition in 1 Cor 11:23. Neither is to be taken for granted. The main meal was customarily eaten before sundown. The Passover meal was eaten next. It was also advisable to eat it inside the walls of Jerusalem. Even if Jesus and the disciples went to the Mount of Olives at night, they did not violate this Passover stipulation, since we may assume that, on account of the crowds of pilgrims, the territory of the Mount of Olives was incorporated into the Passover area.[33]

The reason why the synoptic Lord's Supper texts did not leave any trace of the Passover has to be sought in its liturgical use. This means that it was seen as instruction for making comprehensible in the community's celebration what Jesus practiced, according to the tradition, and not merely once a year, as in the Passover. In John's Gospel the chronology was adapted on theological grounds. Jesus dies in the hour when the Passover lambs are slaughtered and thus proves to be the true lamb (cf. John 1:29; 19:33–36). Incidentally, John 19:31 may contain a further indication of a major change.[34]

---

[31] Cf. Schnackenburg, *John*, 3.36.

[32] In this connection appeal is made to Josephus, *Ant.* 18.18, 19, who says that the Essenes who were barred from access to the common court offer their sacrifices themselves. But it is not appropriate to deduce from this reference the existence of a temple court that was accorded exclusively to the Essenes. By reckoning on lambs slaughtered at home or even on a Passover meal without a Passover lamb, the authors recognize the weakness of their argument. Cf. Ruckstuhl, *Chronologie*, 106f. It is also important to remember that calendar-related questions were always taken seriously.

[33] On this, cf. Str-B, *Kommentar*, 2.833f.

[34] Here one wonders why the Passover is not mentioned as in 18:28 and 19:14. Presumably the text originated from a tradition according to which Jesus died on the

Hence, if we may reckon that Jesus and the disciples came together for the Passover meal, it may be appropriate briefly to recall the order of the Passover celebration. Numbers 9:13 called to mind the seriousness of the Passover and signaled that those who failed to observe the festival would be cut off from the people. According to Exod 12:3 it was to be a festival for the family. The killing and offering of the lamb, carried out representatively for the meal community by one of its members, took place in the court of the priests "between the two evenings," that is, at the time immediately before sundown (cf. Exod 12:6). The large number of pilgrims present in Jerusalem surely posed difficulties in locating a room for the meal. Roofs and courtyards may have been places of celebration as well. The focal point of the order of the celebration in the family was the Passover haggadah—according to which the most distinguished participant at the table presided over the meal and was to recall for them the nation's deliverance from Egyptian bondage (Exod 12:26f.)—and the eating of the Passover lamb. In this context wine was consumed. Prior to that the one presiding at table distributed the unleavened bread, reminiscent of the misery in Egypt, and the bitter herbs were eaten (Exod 12:8). The prayer of thanksgiving after the eating of the lamb was linked with drinking a cup of wine, followed by the recitation of some psalms, namely, the small Hallel.[35]

The Passover meal was genuinely meant to be festive. Outwardly this was signaled by reclining at table, on mats, the head propped on one hand, and by taking time to eat, in contrast to the first Passover in Egypt, which was eaten in haste, loins girded and wearing shoes (Exod 12:11). Above all, the Passover celebration was characterized by joyous and confident remembrance, and in times of oppression surely also by hope for liberation.

15th of Nisan, as in the Synoptics, and not on the day of preparation of the Passover. Cf. Bultmann, *John,* 414 n. 5. The tradition of the Talmud (*b. Sanh.* 43a) that Jeshu was hanged on the eve of the Passover is of no historical value. Cf. J. Maier, *Jesus von Nazareth in der talmudischen Überlieferung* (ErFor 82; Darmstadt: Wissenschaftliche Buchgesellschaft, 1978) 219–37. Among the representatives of the view that the Johannine date is preferable, we mention H. Schürmann, *Der Paschamahlbericht* (NTA 19/5; Münster: Aschendorff, 1952) who reckons on a new Christian Passover festival in conjunction with a complex reworking of the Passover theology of the relevant synoptic tradition. Certain difficulties that one encounters in opting for the synoptic dating are easily removed, namely, that Simon of Cyrene comes from the country (Mark 15:21) and bears a sword (14:47), which could be considered part of the apparel; Simon does not come from work in the country at this time of day. Yet the Synoptics also force the conclusion that Jesus was executed on the feast of the Passover. More will need to be said on this below.
[35] Mark 14:26,"And when they had sung a hymn," could be reminiscent of this.

The argument that Jesus was completely surprised by his violent fate was occasionally found in the old liberal exegesis, though its assessment of the given situation was altogether unrealistic. To suggest that even a few hours before his death he was not aware of, and did not anticipate, anything disastrous means to deny him a sense of reality. Not only did conflict accompany his public ministry most of the time; surely Jesus himself, as we have already seen, and given the context of conflict, also made his disciples aware of the fact that remaining with him, following him, was dangerous. He did speak of taking up the cross after him and of the possibility of losing one's life (cf. Matt 10:37f. par.). Now it would be impossible to say that the danger that he saw threatening his disciples did not apply to him personally.

Hence it is entirely congruent with the situation for him to have spoken unambiguously of his death at this final meal. He did so by means of a very personalized logion containing a renunciation. The two renditions to be considered in reconstructing it are as follows:

"Truly, I say to you, I shall not drink again of the fruit of the vine until that day when I drink it new in the kingdom of God" (Mark 14:25).

"for I tell you that from now on I shall not drink of the fruit of the vine until the kingdom of God comes" (Luke 22:18).

In factual material the first part of the saying contains a prophecy concerning death, and the second one has a temporal orientation in divergent formulations: "until that day," "until the kingdom of God comes." It penetrates the somber night of death and sees the completion. In this context Mark's statement concerning a new drinking may be a secondary addition.[36] It is significant that in view of his death Jesus maintains his confidence, even if he articulates it only in these personal terms here. In its eschatological perspective this saying also means a final reinforcement of his message of the kingdom.

Whether or not the logion used to contain more remains questionable. In conjunction with Luke 22:15, J. Jeremias[37] wanted to detect in it the announcement of a celebratory fast, which in the final hour Jesus took upon himself for the conversion of Israel. We are aware that early Christians did observe a Passover fast for the purpose indicated. This is hardly applicable to Jesus himself, however.

---

[36] In Mark 14:25 the double time reference is conspicuous: "until that day" and "in the kingdom of God." Cf. Gnilka, *Markus,* 2.243; Berger, *Die Amen-Worte Jesu,* 54–58.

[37] Jeremias, *Eucharistic Words,* 207–18.

As far as the general understanding is concerned, the confidence-laden eschatological saying, with its focus on the kingdom of God, confirms that at this point Jesus surely reckoned with his violent death. It further confirms that he confidently maintained the expectation of the *basileia*, representing the central content of his proclamation, even though he initially may have applied it to his own person and referred to it in a manner relating to his own expectation. Thus this logion, whose authenticity has never been seriously contested, becomes an important starting point for the reconstruction of other matters of significance that transpired in the context of this meal.

In view of both his assurance of death and his confidence, it is to be expected that he also spoke of the kingdom as salvation that he offered to people on behalf of God. Indeed it was important in this situation to provide information about the further development of the kingdom of God, and it is highly likely that he associated his death with what was still to come and with what was expected. Furthermore, it is fairly obvious that he invested his death not just with a merely moral interpretation but also with one that linked him with the expected kingdom of God in a more or less direct or salvific relationship. After all, we have seen that in fulfilling his task as the bringer of the kingdom, he was also more than merely its messenger.

It shows a restricted perspective if one argues for a discrepancy and contradiction between the *basileia* that Jesus offered the people as the eschatological salvation and the possibility of him understanding his death salvifically and one then postulates that the two are mutually exclusive.[38] It is true to say that hitherto Jesus had not referred to his death as salvific. But this does not at all mean that he could not now—only now—speak about it. The uniqueness of this saying on the grounds of statistics and terminology should not be used to refute it. Rather what is to be considered is that, with the assurance of death in

---

[38] The objection raised by A. Vögtle, *Ökumenische Kirchengeschichte* (ed. E. Kottje and B. Möller; Mainz, 1970) 21, is also addressed by H. Schürmann, *Jesu ureigner Tod* (Freiburg: Herder, 1975) 43–46, and needs to be taken seriously. A different viewpoint, according to which it is impossible to document Jesus' interpretation of his death, is based on the argument that Luke 22:14–18 is older than the Lord's Supper tradition. This is the view, e.g., of Bultmann, *History,* 279f. Luke 22:14–18, however, is likely dependent upon Mark 14:25 as well. Cf. Schneider, *Lukas,* 444. Further arguments against this position are found in Schürmann, *Tod,* 59f.; H. Merklein, "Erwägungen zur Überlieferungsgeschichte der neutestamentlichen Abendmahlstraditionen," *BZ* 21 (1977) 235f. The view that Bultmann, *History,* 280f., seems to presuppose, that Jesus had been surprised by his violent fate and hence was not able to interpret his death either, can be considered outdated.

this hour, Jesus was made to realize that his ministry in Israel had failed. This realization did not lead him to resignation or despair. His confidence includes his willingness to accept death from the hand of God. If he accepts the fate of death in agreement with the Father's will, his messianic mission cannot be excluded from this agreement. This moves his death into the context of his mission. It is unlikely that in his certainty of death Jesus excluded this mission. His death means more than that of a person yielded to the will of God.

These observations also render it plausible that in keeping with the Father's will he gave his death a special meaning with salvific relevance. This interpretation obviously focuses on two factors in particular: It takes account of the disciples as those who remain, and it includes the experience of failure in Israel.

A distinctive feature of Jesus' interpretation of his death at the meal was that he linked it with proffering a gift, namely, that of bread and a cup of wine. Consuming bread and wine are indeed a matter of course in a Jewish festive meal, yet now they are shown in the light of the interpretation of his death. The distinctiveness of the giving of this gift as his interpretation of death was perceived so strongly that in the eucharistic Lord's Supper of the post-Easter community, linked with Jesus' final meal, it could become independent, and did become independent and hence removed from the meal.[39] The words of interpretation were clearly spoken by the one presiding at table, in conjunction with the customary activities at a festive meal, by the one who had to recite the accompanying prayers, in conjunction with the breaking of bread and the drinking of the cup. The former occurred at the beginning of the main meal and was associated with a prayer of praise; the latter occurred at the conclusion, associated with a prayer of thanksgiving. This was also true of Jesus' final meal, as the ancient rendering still shows: "in the same way also the cup after supper" (1 Cor 11:25; cf. Luke 22:20).[40]

The later prominence and independence of the giving of the gifts, vested with the interpretation of his death, can be considered evidence that it goes back to Jesus' Last Supper with his disciples. The words of interpretation, spoken over the gifts presented, may

---

[39] First Corinthians 11:17ff. already assumes this separation; the main meal precedes the eucharistic meal.

[40] It needs to be noted here that this practice, which adheres to tradition, departs from the Corinthian practice of the Eucharist. Cf. note 39 above. Mark 14:23 and Matt 26:27 replace "after the meal" with the simple "and" and thereby are mindful of the community's practice.

represent something new,[41] as does perhaps the common cup from which all are to drink at this festive meal. We are not sufficiently informed, however, about how this was practiced in the Passover meal or at the Jewish festive meal at the time of Jesus, whether everyone drank from his own cup or whether all drank wine from the one cup.[42] In any case the common cup soon became the hallmark of the post-Easter Lord's Supper (cf. 1 Cor 10:16).

This then was the order of this special celebration: At the beginning of the main meal Jesus took a flat loaf, spoke a prayer of blessing, broke the flat loaf and shared the pieces—signifying the gift—among the disciples. At the end, after a prayer of thanksgiving, he had the cup of wine (his own?) circulate while interpreting it as well.

Because of the special difficulties, one could forego the attempt to reconstruct the words of interpretation that Jesus spoke and, rather, speak of a farewell meal[43] with its focus on the eschatological festive meal or, even more cautiously, of a mysteriously meaningful meal.[44] One could also point to the gesture of giving, contained in the giving of the bread and cup of blessing and in this alone see the blessing signaling the salvation that Jesus offers by taking death upon himself. An act such as this is certainly focused on this intention. But since we are already considering the salvific interpretation of Jesus' death, we can go one step further.

A reconstruction has to consider the fact that the text had a liturgical function and that the liturgical use of the words of interpretation shaped them in four different forms (Mark 14:22–24; Matt 26:26–28; Luke 22:19f.; 1 Cor 11:23–25). This led to a considerable intensification and compression of the expressions. Jesus surely said much more. Thus what has been handed down to us are not words of a prayer of blessing or of thanksgiving. The text is content with the observation that he spoke a prayer of blessing and of thanksgiving.

---

[41] The interpretation of the distinctiveness of the Passover meal does not apply to the serving of it. On the words of interpretation relative to meals in the mystery cults, cf. H.-J. Klauck, *Herrenmahl und hellenistischer Kult* (2d ed.; NTA 15; Münster: Aschendorff, 1986) 92. These do not offer a genuine comparison either.

[42] Those arguing for a common cup in the Jewish festive meal regularly appeal to Dalman, *Arbeit und Sitte*, 4.393; *Jesus–Jeshua*, 148–56. The support is late, however: Maimonides and *b. Ber.* 51a. Regarding Luke 22:17, Str-B, *Kommentar*, 4.58 supports a peculiar halfway solution; accordingly the disciples shared the wine among themselves in such a way that each one filled his own cup with it.

[43] Vögtle, *Ökumenische Kirchengeschichte*, 23.

[44] H. Lessig, "Die Abendmahlsprobleme im Lichte der neutestamentlichen Forschung seit 1900" (diss., Bonn, 1953) 245.

Despite the compression of the words, a theological enrichment of content has to be reckoned with. There are essentially two interpretative categories: the concept of atonement and substitution that depicts Jesus' death as "dying on behalf of," and the idea of the covenant.

According to Mark and Matthew, both are linked with the words related to the cup ("my blood of the covenant, which is poured out for many"), without a doubt representing an overloading of the expression. According to Luke and Paul, the concept of atonement is linked with the words related to the bread: "my body which is (given) for you,"[45] though couched in a formulation of giving: "for you," rather than "for many"; the covenant is linked with the cup-related words.

In keeping with a fairly extensive consensus, the cup-related saying in the form of "This cup . . . is the new covenant in my blood" may be regarded as the older tradition. The blood as sacrificial gift and content of the cup has not yet come into view. Instead, the central feature is the circulating cup of blessing, which in the power of Jesus' blood, that is, of the impending, violent death, can convey a new relationship with God in view of the expected kingdom of God. This interpretation can also be attributed to Jesus. It should not be dismissed as secondary by arguing that it contains a scribal reflection of Jer 31:31, in which the prophet announces a new covenant for the last days. The covenant concept is typically OT, Jewish, and certainly devoid of any Hellenistic influence.[46] In an appropriate way he considers the rejection of the message by the majority of the Jewish people. Hence the singularity of its occurrence is not very crucial, especially if the new situation given in Jesus' certainty of death is considered as well. The interpretative words are not in competition, as a second cup-related saying, with the logion of renunciation ("I shall not drink again"), because the latter represents the personal imprint of an expression of great confidence.

The concept of atonement may well have been added secondarily to the Lord's Supper tradition. In this case the interpretative words about the bread would then be "This is my body," understood along the lines of the Aramaic term *guf(a)*.[47] This would mean that the bread is a sign of himself: This I am. This interpretation fits with Jesus' ministry inasmuch as it indicates the link with the fellowship

---

[45] Only Luke offers διδόμενον. Yet he also links the cup-related saying with the notion of atonement ("shed for you"), in obvious dependence upon Mark.

[46] Cf. W. Marxsen, "Der Ursprung des Abendmahls," *EvT* 12 (1952/53) 298.

[47] Cf. Dalman, *Jesus–Jeshua*, 141f.

meals that he had with people time and again. In the (brief) time until the final dawning of the kingdom this bread is his substitute. Since we do not know the detailed ambience of the evening meal, in which Jesus was more elaborate, this interpretative saying may seem difficult to us, all the more so since in the meal it was separated from the saying interpreting the cup. Yet if this suggestion is to be followed, this ambience that can no longer be reconstructed has to be taken into consideration.[48]

In this case Jesus interpreted his death symbolically and maintained his offer of salvation to Israel. To the disciples he leaves a meal in which people share in God's eschatological kingdom through the covenant with God that was opened up by virtue of his death; in this meal he remains among them in the symbol of the bread. Thus Jesus attributed salvific effectiveness to his death, though this effectiveness has to be seen in its focus on the kingdom of God. Furthermore, the link between covenant and *basileia* was plausible because in their history and formation the two terms are closely related.[49] It may also be correct to say that, in its link with the prior table fellowship with people, this special meal was meant to be repeated.

Overview

The continuing effect of the various incidents in the life of Jesus addressed in this chapter has been quite varied. In the post-Easter situation the conflict continued as the dispute between church and synagogue and became more intense. The woes against the scribes and Pharisees (Matt 23) became the prominent text of this dispute. The woes themselves have a complicated history of origin and tradition. We have already observed that they are shaped by the later dispute much more than by the conflict with Jesus. Since they later helped bring forth a negative cliché about the scribes and Pharisees, about the Jews,

---

[48] A different reconstruction is offered by Merklein, "Erwägungen," 235–38, who favors the concept of atonement as the more original one but links it with the bread-related saying in the form of ὑπὲρ πολλῶν. The only cup-related saying he acknowledges is Mark 14:25 and hence will not allow for a word of interpretation concerning the cup. This view is essentially adopted by Klauck, *Herrenmahl*, 308f., 321. Apart from the thought of whether the concept of atonement should be preferred to the conception of the covenant, the difficulty of this reconstruction is that the phrase ὑπὲρ πολλῶν is not linked with the bread-related saying in any text. In 1 Cor 11:23–25 Marxsen, "Ursprung," 303, sees the text of Jesus. For my own deduction, cf. Gnilka, *Markus*, 2.240–43, 247–49.

[49] Cf. G. Q. Quell, "διαθήκη," *TDNT*, 2.118–24; M. Weinfeld, "בְּרִית," *TDOT* 2.275–79.

linked with misunderstandings, a reconsideration at this point seems to be particularly advisable.

To some extent the pericopes of the entry into Jerusalem and of the temple protest deal with snapshots in the ministry of Jesus. As they continued to be narrated and passed on, christological and theological elements were added. The entry pericope takes on an undisguised messianic form, modeled after Zech 9:9 ("Lo, your king comes to you"). Jesus' temple protest was increasingly interpreted in terms of the destruction of the temple cult brought about by him, to the point where, in John 2:13–22, Christ, the one who died and was raised again, replaces the temple and supersedes it and thus becomes the center of the worship of the new community.

Understandably the most extensive development is found in the Lord's Supper tradition, for the Last Supper lives on in the Lord's Supper of the community. It can be mentioned only in passing here that the gifts presented in this meal are brought into even bolder relief, that they are linked with the concept of sacrifice (and atonement), and that there is reflection on the extent of the effectiveness of the eucharistic gifts. The Johannine reflection brings out the personal relationship of the individual with the exalted Christ and through him with God; here obtaining eternal life is made contingent upon partaking of the eucharistic gifts (John 6:51b–58). With Paul, the ecclesial components are more prominent. The bread, which is one, that the many are eating in the meal, makes them one in the unity of the body (of Christ), represented in the world by the community (1 Cor 10:16f.).

Select bibliography: G. Baumbach, *Jesus von Nazareth im Lichte der jüdischen Gruppenbildung* (Berlin: Evangelische Verlagsanstalt, 1971); V. Eppstein, "The Historicity of the Gospel Account of the Cleansing of the Temple," *ZNW* 65 (1964) 42–58; P. Fiedler, "Probleme der Abendmahlsforschung," *LLW* 24 (1982) 190–223; A. Finkel, *The Pharisees and the Teacher of Nazareth* (AGSU 4; Leiden: E. J. Brill, 1964); D. E. Garland, *The Intention of Matthew 23* (NTS 52; Leiden: E. J. Brill, 1979); L. Goppelt, *Christentum und Judentum im ersten und zweiten Jahrhundert* (Gütersloh: Bertelsmann, 1954); E. Haenchen, "Matthäus 23," *Gott und Mensch* (Tübingen: Mohr, 1965) 29–54; F. Hahn, "Die alttestamentlichen Motive in der urchristlichen Abendmahlsüberlieferung," *EvT* 27 (1967) 337–74; T. Huser, "Les récits de l'institution de la Cène," *Hokma* 21 (1982) 28–50; J. Jeremias, *The Eucharistic Words of Jesus* (ET; New York: Scribner's, 1966); H.-J. Klauck, *Herrenmahl und hellenistischer Kult* (2d ed.; NTA 15; Münster: Aschendorff, 1986); H. Lessig, "Die Abendmahlsprobleme im Lichte der neutestamentlichen Forschung seit 1900" (diss.; Bonn, 1953); I. H. Marshall, *Last Supper and Lord's Supper* (Exeter: Paternoster, 1980); W. Marxsen, "Der Ursprung des Abendmahls," *EvT* 12 (1952/53) 293–303; C.-P. März, *Siehe, dein König kommt zu dir . . .* (ETS 43; Leipzig: St.-Benno, 1980); H. Merkel, "Jesus und die Pharisäer," *NTS* 14 (1967/68) 194–208; H. Merklein, "Erwägungen zur Überlieferungsgeschichte der neutestamentlichen Abendmahlstraditionen," *BZ* 21 (1977) 88–101, 235–44; K. Müller, "Jesus und die Sadduzäer," 3–24, in *Biblische Randbemerkungen* (FS R. Schnackenburg; Würzburg: Echter, 1974); P. Neuenzeit, *Das Herrenmahl* (SANT 1; Munich: Kösel, 1960); H. Patsch, *Abendmahl und historischer Jesus* (CThM 1; Stuttgart: Calwer Verlag, 1972); idem, "Der Einzug in Jerusalem," *ZTK* 68 (1971) 1–26; E. Ruckstuhl, *Die Chronologie des Letzten Mahles und des Leidens Jesu* (BiBe NF 4; Einsiedeln: Benzinger, 1963); H. Schürmann, *Jesu ureigener Tod* (Freiburg/Basel/Vienna: Herder, 1975); G. Theissen, "Die Tempelweissagung Jesu," *Studien zur Soziologie des Urchristentums* (WUNT 19; Tübingen: Mohr, 1979) 142–59; A. Vögtle, 3–36 in *Ökumenische Kirchengeschichte* (ed. E. Kottje and B. Möller, Mainz-Munich, 1970); H.-F. Weiss, "Der Pharisäismus im Lichte der Überlieferung des Neuen Testament," *SSAW.PH* 110/2, Berlin, 1965, 89–132; J. Wellhausen, *Die Pharisäer und die Sadduzäer* (3d. ed.; Göttingen: Vandenhoeck & Ruprecht), 1924; P. Winter, "The Enemies of Jesus," *On the Trial of Jesus* (SJ 1, Berlin: de Gruyter, 1961) 111–35.

11

Trial and Execution

Jesus was arrested in that night, thereby triggering a chain of events that seemed to take its course logically and quickly. Before sunset the following day he was dead, killed and removed for good. The events required a certain direction as well as preparation. It is very difficult for us today to understand these events clearly. If we begin with what is most assured, it is his execution on the cross. Yet this already leads to the conclusion that in the final analysis the Romans put him to death and that the charge brought against him was political. To formulate it quite generally to begin with, he was accused of disturbing the political, public order guaranteed by the Roman state. All crucifixions known to us, from the time of the Roman procurators to the Jewish war in Palestine, came about for political reasons.[1] The situation becomes more complicated when we consider that the Jewish side was party to his trial.

In order to make it easier for the reader to follow the reconstruction of the final events, we shall be separating the individual sequences of events. In doing so, we shall attempt first of all to describe the external development of the individual events. Only then will the second step be taken, to inquire into the legal and official motives that prompted those involved to take this kind of action against Jesus. We learn little about Jesus' conduct. In the passion narratives of the Gospels he is presented as the one who was silent, accepting, suffering.

---

[1] Cf. H.-W. Kuhn, "Jesus als Gekreuzigter in der frühchristlichen Verkündigung bis zur Mitte des 2. Jahrhunderts," *ZTK* 72 (1975) 3f.

1. The arrest

"And when they had sung a hymn, they went out to the Mount of Olives" (Mark 14:26). This remark concludes the event of the Supper. Jesus' arrest took place on the Mount of Olives. It seems to be more than plausible that in a period prior to this event he prayed intensively. As far as categorizing the trial is concerned, it is important to know who gave the orders for the arrest. The information of the Gospels differs. According to Mark 14:43 the arresting squad was sent by the chief priests, scribes, and elders, that is, by the Sanhedrin. Matthew 26:47 reduces this information, by formulating it in a manner characterstic of him, to the chief priests and elders of the people. Luke 22:52 has the chief priests, officers of the temple, and elders personally take part in the arrest, while John 18:3, along with the chief priests and Pharisees as dispatchers of the squad, makes special mention of a band of soldiers (σπεῖρα—"cohort") and a captain (χιλίαρχος, 18:12) and thus involves the Romans earlier with Jesus' arrest. The rulers' personal appearance on the Mount of Olives is as unlikely as the participation by the Romans, especially given the mention of the number—a cohort has about six hundred soldiers— which is not very feasible historically. The information in Luke and John follows narrative intentions. Luke wants the rulers to be seen as those addressed in Jesus' statement, which points beyond the actual situation. In all likelihood the fourth evangelist was concerned with indicating that the trial as a whole involved both the Jewish and Roman parties, just as he lends considerable emphasis to the Roman part of the trial in his passion narrative. If the Romans had been involved in Jesus' arrest, he would have been led directly to Pilate.

From the seemingly rather anonymous group there emerges an individual who may have been the leader of the squad. He is labeled a servant of the high priest (Mark 14:47 par.). This is by no means intended to characterize him as insignificant but rather as one who enjoyed the high priest's confidence.[2] The arrest warrant was issued by the acting high priest. As the leader of the Sanhedrin, he was entitled to take steps like this. The higher Roman jurisdiction by no means removed all authority from the subordinate Jewish jurisdiction; rather, along with parts of civil jurisdiction, they were presumably also given certain preparatory tasks in particular capital matters.[3]

---

[2] In 1 Sam 29:3 David is called servant of the king, as is Naaman in 2 Kgs 5:6.

[3] Cf. H. Volkmann, *Zur Rechtsprechung im Principat des Augustus* (2d ed.; MSPAR 21; Munich: Beck, 1969) 136f. Details are difficult to obtain on whether these were

If the squad bears weapons, Jesus is considered dangerous or one reckons with possible resistance. But the latter was hardly the case, for there is no doubt at all that none of the disciples was arrested but that Jesus alone was. If one of them had offered serious resistance, his arrest would have had to be expected as well. All the disciples fled when Jesus was arrested, and deserted him. Only Simon Peter indicates an interest in seeing what will happen to his master, but perseveres for a brief period of time at best.

The episode of the disciple's blow with the sword is an added, ironic narrative feature, intended derisively about the one who led the arrest. Mark 14:47 could leave the impression that in the scene of the tumult the one who accidentally cut off the ear of the high priest's servant is from the squad. This is heightened irony. When the other evangelists attribute the blow to one of the disciples, the disciples are presumably meant to be exonerated (Matt 26:51; Luke 22:49; John 18:10).

Together with the arresting squad Judas Iscariot enters the scene as well. This information is certainly considered reliable and links what is called the Judas act with Jesus' arrest. Incidentally, this is the only historical reference point when the disciples realized that Judas made common cause with Jesus' opponents. The Gospels are silent on the issue of his motives,[4] just as the disciples had to remain in the dark regarding the agreements that preceded.[5] The most obvious answer to the question of why the services of Judas were needed is that he knew of Jesus' whereabouts at night and that Jesus certainly was not familiar to the men who arrested him. What remains conspicuous is that midnight was the time chosen for his arrest. Here too we have to depend upon assumptions: Haste was

police measures or an arrest with a written arrest warrant, whether the armed men who accompanied the high priest's servant were court attendants of the Sanhedrin or members of the temple police. The latter is more plausible. On this, cf. J. Blinzler, *Der Prozess Jesu* (4th ed.; Regensburg: F. Pustet, 1969) 126–28, who opts for the court attendants.

[4] Disappointment with Jesus may have been one motive. The suggestion of E. Stauffer, *Jesus—Gestalt und Geschichte* (DTb 332; Bern: Francke, 1957) 86, 158 n. 4, lacks credibility. On the basis of the ban from the synagogue mentioned in John 9:22, he suggests that Judas acted as a loyal son of the synagogue and thus handed Jesus over because he understood this to be his duty in keeping with the religious laws. The ban applies for the time of the formation of the Fourth Gospel but not yet for the time of Jesus.

[5] Mark 14:10f. par. is a secondary reconstruction developed from the narrative image of an opponent. On this issue, see H.-J. Klauck, *Judas—ein Jünger des Herrn* (QD 111; Freiburg: Herder, 1987).

essential. The high priest assumed that Jesus' sympathizers among the Galilean pilgrims to the festival might have obstructed his arrest.

Galilee, their home, was the place to which the disciples fled. It is very unlikely that they stayed in Jerusalem for very long. None of the Twelve appears on the way to the cross or at the cross. The return to Galilee is significant for the reconstruction of the Easter events. Jesus is led to the high priest.

2. Jesus before the Jewish court

The Sanhedrin, the highest Jewish legal authority, also called the Great Court House (*bēâ dîn ha-migdol*), was composed of seventy members, to whom the acting high priest was added as the seventy-first, if the pertinent stipulation of the Mishnah (*m. Sanh.* 1.6; *m. Seb.* 2.2) already applied at the time of Jesus. This may be assumed, however, because the number seventy takes its orientation from the model of the council of elders of the Mosaic period (Num 11:16). Whether the ruling was already in force that at least twenty-three judges were to be present for a valid resolution to be made (cf. *m. Sanh.* 4.1) remains open, of course. Without a doubt the most influential of the three groups, the chief priests, elders, and scribes, was the one mentioned first. Josephus also consistently grants the chief priests preferential status when he refers to the high court (βουλή). He describes the elders as the men of power (οἱ δυνατοί), whereas he may have construed the "chief of the Pharisees," among others, to have been the Pharisees who belonged to the group of the scribes (*War* 2.411; cf. 2.331, 316; *Life* 5). The importance of the latter should not be underestimated. On account of their major influence upon the people, the high priests and elders of the Sadducean orientation were no doubt forced time and again to take the Pharisaic viewpoint seriously. It is well known that the Sadducees and Pharisees represented different viewpoints (cf. Acts 23:1–12).[6]

The Synoptic Gospels speak of a gathering of the Sanhedrin (Mark 14:53–65 par.). Following the account of Jesus' arrest, the Fourth Gospel speaks of an interrogation before Annas, the father-in-law of Caiaphas (John 18:12–14, 19–24), concluding with Jesus being led away to Caiaphas. John does not report anything on the hearing that occurred at the latter place. For two reasons, literary and juridical, the historical value of the pericope on the hearing before

---

[6] Cf. J. Wellhausen, *Die Pharisäer und die Sadduzäer* (Hannover, 1924) 30.

the Sanhedrin has been questioned. It was taken to be a literary product of a later time that was subsequently inserted into the passion narrative by the writer of Mark or even earlier than that.[7] The juridical argument runs as follows: The legal situation in the province of Judea was such that the Romans left to the Sanhedrin, the highest Jewish court of law, the jurisdiction over capital offenses, the *potestas* or *ius gladii*. If the Sanhedrin had been involved in the trial of Jesus, they would have handled the case against Jesus entirely on their own, without Roman assistance; hence they would have sentenced him to death and executed him, presumably by stoning. Jesus, however, was sentenced and crucified by Pilate. For this reason the Jewish element would have to be ruled out.[8]

The issue of the *ius gladii*, which is frequently discussed in the context of Jesus' trial, needs to be examined more closely. Since 6 CE Judea was an imperial province, administered by a procurator *(praefectus)* taken from the equestrian ranks.[9] He actually was the one with the legal power over his province, and on the basis of a special mandate by the emperor, the comprehensive jurisdiction, including that of capital cases, was probably transferred to him, as Josephus' allusion indicates *(War* 2.117).[10] If it was the rule in the other provinces for capital jurisdiction to be left to the governor,[11] this is also to be assumed *a fortiori* for Judea, a province, situated at the periphery of the empire, that was a cauldron of instability and rebellion. The administrative structure that Rome chose for Judea is equally instructive, since it was generally only small and rebellious provinces that were entrusted to an equestrian procurator, for his office was a combination of juridical and military authority. Consequently, everything favors the *potestas gladii* being exclusively the procurator's prerogative.[12]

---

[7] Critically: S. Schulz, *Die Stunde der Botschaft* (Hamburg: Furche, 1967) 131; P. Winter, "Markus 14:53b, 55–64 ein Gebilde des Evangelisten," *ZNW* 53 (1962) 260–63; Hahn, *Titles,* 173; Linnemann, *Studien,* 109–34.

[8] More recently this theory has been argued by H. Lietzmann, *Der Prozess Jesu* (SPAW 14; Berlin, 1931) 313–22; idem, "Bemerkungen zum Prozess Jesu," *ZNW* 30 (1931) 211–15; *ZNW* 31 (1932) 78–84.

[9] Cf. Volkmann, *Rechtsprechung,* 126–50 ("The Court Organization of the Provinces").

[10] "Coponius . . . was sent as a procurator, having the power of [life and] death put into his hands by Caesar." Cf. *Ant.* 18.2.

[11] Cf. Volkmann, *Rechtsprechung,* 136f.

[12] Cf. K. Müller, "Möglichkeit und Vollzug jüdischer Kapitalgerichtsbarkeit im Prozess gegen Jesus von Nazaret," 52–58, in K. Kertelge, ed., *Der Prozess gegen Jesus,* (2d ed.; QD 112; Freiburg: Herder, 1989), for an astute argument for the unrestricted authority of the procurator of Judea.

Contradictory examples of the Jewish side executing individuals can be refuted.[13] Only two examples remain a problem: the
temple barrier and the stoning of Stephen. The Romans made the
concession to the Jews that every non-Jew entering the inner court
of the temple was subject to death.[14] This concession has to be rated
as extraordinary. We do not know, however, what would have happened if a non-Jew had indeed entered the temple sanctuary. We
have no record of an instance such as this. Would the Sanhedrin
effectively have been able to sentence a person to death without
the cooperation of the Romans? This is unlikely.[15] Commentators
agree that the stoning of Stephen represents an example of the lynch
law.[16] Stephen was stoned without a trial, outside the gates of Jerusalem, by people who were in a fit of rage. These exceptions prompt
C. Paulus,[17] a historian of jurisprudence, to make a notable distinction. He wants to distinguish between proceedings in which the
governor legally sentences a person to death with the assistance of
the Jews and those in which the Jews achieve the same *per viam facti*.
Both occurrences are equally rare. In any case, the result of this is
that the Sanhedrin did not have the *potestas gladii*.

Given these considerations, the core of information passed on
in Mark 15:1 gains historical reliability: "And as soon as it was

---

[13] Examples of the converse are the following: the execution of the apostle James
and presumably also the slaying of the daughter of a priest in the time of King
Agrippa I (41–44 CE), who briefly united Israel again and had full jurisdiction; the
execution of the Lord's brother, which probably happened during the vacancy after
the death of the procurator Porcius Festus, though it has a Roman postlude; the
stoning of Stephen; and the temple barrier. Cf. also John 8:53–9:11.

[14] Cf. Josephus, *Ant.* 15.417; *War* 5.194; 6.124–126; 4.182; Philo, *Legat.* 212. Two
of the signs have been preserved, containing the threat of death in the case indicated
above, which were affixed all around the inner temple precinct. One of them is located
in Istanbul, the other in Jerusalem. Cf. Blinzler, *Prozess,* 238–40.

[15] According to Acts 21:27–35 the crowd in the temple turns against Paul in a rage,
with the intention of killing him. Among other things, he was accused of having
brought a Greek into the temple, namely, Trophimus from Ephesus. But this is only
one charge among others. Yet the Romans step in, just as the trial of Paul is also
conducted and decided by Roman courts. According to Acts 22:25–29 Paul was a
Roman citizen.

[16] The commentaries on Acts by R. Pesch, J. Roloff, and A. Weiser concur in
aligning the indication of a trial by the Sanhedrin in Acts 6:12–7:2 with the trial against
Jesus. R. Pesch, *Die Apostelgeschichte* I (EKK 5/1; Neukirchen-Vlynn: Neukirchener,
1986) 236, reckons on the possibility that the Sanhedrin of Acts 6:15 might originally
have referred to the juridical gathering of the regional synagogue, though there were
no court proceedings there either.

[17] C. Paulus, "Einige Bemerkungen zum Prozess Jesu bei den Synoptikern,"
ZSRG 102 (1985) 439.

morning the chief priests, with the elders and scribes, and the whole council held a consultation; and they bound Jesus and led him away and delivered him to Pilate." The Sanhedrin's decision therefore is to hand Jesus over to the governor. This also preserves legality. The Jewish side, which does not possess the *ius gladii,* has to turn to the Romans for the purpose of carrying out a capital trial.

Nevertheless, the detailed account of the trial before the Sanhedrin (Mark 14:53–65 par.) cannot be dismissed so easily either. In its narrative shaping, characterized by insertions of allusions to references from the Psalms, it agrees with the passion narrative as a whole and proves to be an integral part of it.[18] The pivotal point is the high priest's question about Jesus' messianic status. While his response is shaped in the light of the Christian confession, it follows the analogous statement concerning his kingdom in the trial before Pilate.[19] This will be addressed in more detail later. Noteworthy is the temple logion, which is brought by witnesses that are branded as false but which represents a link with Jesus' protest action. It might indicate a trail leading from his temple protest, via the arrest, to the trial.

If the writer of John makes no reference to a Sanhedrin trial before Caiaphas, he does so not because of his better historical information but for narrative-theological purposes. He has presented the entire public ministry of Jesus as a single trial-like dispute with the "Jews" and hence consciously chosen to do without the Jewish trial.[20]

As far as the evaluation of the trials is concerned, it is also appropriate to observe that, while the Roman trial took place in the public eye, the Jewish judges met behind closed doors. Only with great difficulty can Simon Peter be considered as a source, he whose denial comes in the high priest's courtyard and who disappears soon afterward.[21] In a sense the narrator had even more liberty in the shaping of the pericope of the trial before the Sanhedrin, and the theological interest certainly shows through more strongly here. Nevertheless, when Jesus was led away from the Mount of Olives to the high priest and later from the high priest to Pilate, the events were public.

---

[18] At issue are references in the Psalms dealing with the suffering of the righteous. In support of this, cf. Gnilka, *Markus,* 2.279ff.

[19] The parallel structure of the account of both trials is to be noted: Inquiry of the judge—Jesus' response—his silence.

[20] Cf. J. Blank, *Krisis,* 310–15; F. Hahn, "Der Prozess Jesu nach dem Johannesevangelium," (EKK 5/2; Einsiedeln, 1970) 23–96.

[21] On the historical reconstruction of Peter's denial, cf. Gnilka, *Markus,* 2.294f.

To what place was Jesus led away? Where did the Jewish judges meet?[22] According to Mark 14:52, Matt 26:57, and John 18:24, Jesus is simply taken to Caiaphas, the high priest, whereas according to Luke 22:54 he was taken to the high priest's house. The hall where the Sanhedrin assembled at that time was probably in the Tyropoeon Valley, near the square of Xystos. Yet a gathering in the palace of Caiaphas is equally possible, if not more so. Luke 22:66 should not lead to the assumption that the Jewish judges did not come together until morning. Mark and Matthew indeed suggest nighttime, especially by interlocking the hearing and the story of Peter's denial, a significant feature of which is the fire at night. Along with Jesus' arrest at midnight, however, it is also important to note the reference made above, that he was brought to Pilate "in the morning" (Mark 15:1). This agrees with Roman court convention, according to which the Roman judges began their sessions in the early morning, at daybreak.[23]

How is the Jewish hearing to be assessed juridically? Those present at the place of Caiaphas were leading members of the Sanhedrin, to be sure. If an official death sentence was to be passed, though this is suggested only in Mark 14:64 (cf. 10:33), a gathering of the entire Sanhedrin would certainly have to be assumed. A formal death sentence is very unlikely, however. This would have made the procurator of Judea appear like the henchman of the Sanhedrin, even if he initiated proceedings of his own. In addition, it may be assumed that the Sanhedrin was not authorized to hand down the death sentence, in other words, that revoking the power of the sword also forbade imposing a verdict such as this.[24] It may be appropriate therefore to describe the Jewish trial as a preliminary hearing in which accusations worthy of death were gathered for presentation as charges against Jesus at the Roman trial. If it is also correct that they met in the house of the high priest, rather than in the official meeting place, it would be sufficient to assume that those who took the action were leading members of the Sanhedrin only and that an official meeting of the Sanhedrin did not occur.[25]

---

[22] Cf. E. Lohse, "συνέδριον," *TDNT* 7.868; Blinzler, *Prozess,* 166–70.

[23] Cf. Seneca, *De ira* 2.7.3: *ad forum prima luce properantia.*

[24] Cf. Müller, "Vollzug," 56f.

[25] Separating another investigation by the high priest from the meeting of the Sanhedrin is hardly feasible. So A. Strobel, *Die Stunde der Wahrheit* (WUNT 21; Tübingen: Mohr, 1980) 12. Cf. E. Schweizer, *The Good News according to Mark* (ET; Richmond: John Knox, 1970) 323f.

3. Jesus before the Roman court

As pointed out already, the procurator of Judea was the highest court authority in his province. He was also charged with the supreme command of the military, and his primary task was to maintain law and order. He was the bearer of imperial justice.

In his power of *coercitio* (punishment) he had almost unlimited authority concerning noncitizens, that is, those who were not Roman citizens, which also applied to Jesus.[26] This power encompassed simply the authority to punish rebellious and dangerous elements. The following dictum was considered a tacitly assumed principle: The well-being of the (Roman) people is the highest law.[27]

As a sign of his authority, he was allowed to bear a sword.[28] The preference could be assumed especially in the case of *coercitio*, though it remained outside the parameters of criminal law.[29]

From this perspective Pilate could have had the noncitizen Jesus executed without hesitation and casually, that is, he could have had him crucified summarily. Nevertheless, Jesus was given a trial, however completely or incompletely it may have been carried out. The contours of a Roman trial can certainly be recognized in the Gospels. The juridical prelude at the high priest's also suggests that a formal trial was initiated.

The determination of guilt was the goal of the Roman trial. This could be achieved in several ways. The history of Roman criminal justice is developmental. The law code of the city of Rome, about which we are best informed, was distinct from that of the procurators. W. Kunkel[30] established four principles pertaining to all forms of Roman jurisprudence: 1. The trial is public. 2. The charge is brought by private individuals. 3. There is the right of defense. 4. The verdict is handed down by a concilium. Furthermore, in the case of a confession a verdict is superfluous, in keeping with the legal dictum *Confessus est pro iudicato*. At the time of Augustus the focal point in the procurator's court was the interrogation of the accused

---

[26] Cf. T. Mommsen, *Römisches Strafrecht* (1899; reprint, Darmstadt: Wissenschaftliche Buchgesellschaft, 1961) 229–50, 37; Mitteis-Wilcken, *Grundzüge* 1.28–43; Gnilka, "Der Prozess Jesu nach den Berichten des Markus und Matthäus mit der Rekonstruktion des historischen Verlaufs," 25–28, in Kertelge, *Prozess.*

[27] Cf. H. Last, *RAC* 3.235–43, esp. 236f.

[28] Dio Cassius 53.13.7.

[29] Mommsen, *Strafrecht,* 897.

[30] W. Kunkel, *Kleine Schriften. Zum römischen Strafverfahren und zur römischen Verfassungsgeschichte,* ed. H. Niederländer (Weimar: Bohlau, 1974) 23.

by the procurator, who functioned as sole judge. This agrees with his status as the highest court authority. He may well make use of the counsel of court assistants, though without being dependent upon their opinion (cf. Acts 25:12).[31] Accusers are admitted. In the case of other provinces there is evidence that the governor also used a jury; the selection of its members was entirely left to him, however.[32] In the final analysis the determination of guilt arises from the opinion that the judge gains concerning the facts of the crime, regardless of whether he functions alone or in conjunction with others.[33]

In the trial of Jesus we hear nothing about a jury or court assistants. Trials by jury were not common in Judea and do not apply to Pilate either. Whether or not he made use of a concilium is difficult to determine. We may assume, however, that at the trial of Jesus an interpreter was used to translate the Aramaic statements.[34] The trial of Jesus essentially consisted of the charge brought by the chief priests (or their representatives?) and Pilate's interrogation. The synoptic account of the trial is shaped in keeping with this basic structure. The chief priests make the accusation, Pilate inquires, Jesus answers or remains silent (Mark 15:2–5 par.). It certainly seems credible that the chief priests tried to be at the trial personally. Regarding another case, from the time of the procurator Florus, it is said that "the high priests, and the men of power, and those of the greatest eminence in the city" came before the tribunal.[35]

When Jesus stood before Pilate, he was bound (Mark 15:1). On this particular morning the Romans were dealing not merely with the case of Jesus but also with that of two others, presumably muggers, who later on were to be executed together with him. In addition, there is the case of Barabbas. Among the places used for the trial, the discussion revolves around the temple fortress Antonia, situated in the northwestern area of the temple, or the palace of Herod near the Jaffa Gate. The discovery of a massive stone pavement of 1,900 square meters (2,272 sq. yds.) in the vicinity of the Antonia favors the former, since it was thought to have been the discovery of the *lithostroton* (The Pavement) mentioned in John

---

[31] According to Josephus, *Ant.* 20.117, Cumanus, "by the advice of his friends," had a soldier executed. This too can be taken as a reference to court assistants. On this issue, cf. Mommsen, *Strafrecht*, 139f.

[32] Supported by the first and fourth edict of Cyrene. On this, cf. Volkmann, *Rechtsprechung*, 144.

[33] Mommsen, *Strafrecht*, 435.

[34] So also Paulus, "Bemerkungen," 442 and n. 33.

[35] Josephus, *War* 2.301.

19:13.[36] The remark in Mark 15:8, "And the crowd came up," also seems to favor the Antonia because it was located at the end of the rock formation that sloped away to the north and dropped off sharply after the temple area.[37] But this stone pavement that has come to light again most probably did not yet exist at the time of Pilate and may have to be attributed to the Aelia Capitolina, the city that the Romans rebuilt after the destruction of Jerusalem in the Jewish War. "Come up" is a technical term in legal language and means the same as "going to court." It was common for the procurators to establish their residence in the palaces of earlier rulers. Concerning Florus, too, we are aware that he took up residence at the king's palace.[38] Herod's palace may be considered the place where Pilate pronounced sentence upon Jesus.[39] In front of the palace there was an open yard which was well suited as a public place of judgment.

That Pilate initiated his own proceedings against Jesus indicates that he probably was not willing merely to adopt the opinion of the Jewish rulers but was concerned with coming to grips with the matter himself. The accounts of the Gospels, with their heavy theological shaping, have given rise to the view that in the end Pilate did not hand down a formal death sentence but that the handing over of Jesus was to be construed merely as an administrative measure in the process of *coercitio*, as a writ of execution, a verdict of execution, or something similar.[40] Only John 19:13 refers to the judgment seat ($\beta\hat{\eta}\mu\alpha$) on which Pilate sat, which would presuppose a formal verdict (cf. Matt 27:19). In Luke 23:24 the verb "sentence" occurs as well; otherwise the dominant statement is, "he delivered him to be crucified" (Mark 15:15; Matt 27:26; John 19:16). Yet this has its correspondence in the theological motif of handing over ($\pi\alpha\rho\alpha\delta\iota\delta\acute{o}\nu\alpha\iota$) that pervades the entire passion of Jesus and is brought to its climax here.[41]

---

[36] The meaning of the name Gabbatha remains obscure. The term is Aramaic, but it is not the translation of *lithostroton*. Perhaps it means "hill" or "bald forehead," in which case it would refer to the regional setting. Cf. Dalman, *Words of Jesus*, 7; Str-B, *Kommentar*, 2.572.

[37] Cf. Kopp, *Stätten*, 415.

[38] Josephus, *War* 2.301.

[39] On the discussion of this, cf. Blinzler, *Prozess*, 256–59; Kopp, *Stätten*, 415–21.

[40] Cf., e.g., M. Dibelius, *Botschaft und Geschichte* (Tübingen: Mohr, 1953) 1.221–47, esp. 226f.; W. von Ammon, "Das Strafverfahren gegen Jesus von Nazareth," *Nachrichten der Evangelisch-Lutherischen Kirche in Bayern* 8 (1953), 69–72; V. Achter, *Der Prozess gegen Jesus von Nazareth* (Cologne, 1964) esp. 38f. Cf. Mommsen, *Strafrecht*, 240 n. 2.

[41] Cf. Mark 9:31; 10:33; 14:10f., 18, 21, 41f., 44; 15:1, 10, 15.

Two primary tendencies can be observed in the accounts of the Gospels, namely, to exonerate the Roman, Pilate, and to incriminate the Jewish side. Pilate thus acts almost against his will when he gives the order to have Jesus crucified. Now he surely was a political realist. The testimonial—the most thorough one about him at our disposal—given by Philo of Alexandria is hardly flattering.[42] Here the characteristics attributed to him are his being unbending, stubborn, intransigent, as well as bribable and violent. He could be put under pressure.[43] None of this should lead to sweeping conclusions, however. Thus L. Wenger argued that Pilate did not take the judgment seat until the end of the trial of Jesus, whereas his prior dealings were *de plano,* since he would have preferred to conclude the proceedings without a sentence.[44] We have already noted the Jewish participation in the trial of Jesus in the form of the charge brought by the hierarchs. The participation of the crowd is more indirect and comes into focus in connection with the so-called Passover amnesty, which we will soon address.

Some historians of law are of the opinion that the trial ended in a confession by Jesus.[45] Since the confession obviated a judgment, he could be handed over to be crucified. Here appeal is made to Jesus' response to the question by Pilate whether he was the king of the Jews (Mark 15:2 par.). But what should Jesus have confessed? Should he have admitted to the allegations made against him? Or was his silence to be construed as admission? To be sure, silence on the part of the righteous one is also one of the motifs of the Psalms (cf. Ps 38:14–16; 39:10; Isa 53:7). Incidentally the words of Mark 15:2, "You have said so," are not an explicit affirmation; instead they are a response that keeps everything in abeyance.[46]

The trial ended with a formal death sentence. This assumption is made plausible by the circumstances of the proceedings, the presence of the chief priests as prosecutors, as well as the duration of the

---

[42] Philo, *Legat.* 299–305.

[43] Cf. J. Blank, "Die Johannespassion," 148–82, in Kertelge, *Prozess,* esp. 167. A good example is found in the story of the consecrated shields, which Pilate had put up in Herod's palace but then had to have them removed on account of pressure applied by the Jews. Philo refers to it ad loc.

[44] On the first contacts of Christianity with Roman law, cf. L. Wenger, *Miscellanea G. Mercati* 5 (StT 125; Vatican City: Biblioteca Apostolica Vaticana, 1946) 569–607, esp. 578. Cf. idem, "Noch einmal zum Verfahren de plano und pro tribunali," *ZSRG* 62 (1942) 366–76.

[45] G. Thür and P. E. Pieler, *RAC* 10.36; Paulus, "Bemerkungen," 442.

[46] Cf. Gnilka, *Markus,* 2.300.

proceedings, which began in the early hours of the morning.[47] "You will go to the cross" was the sentence Jesus heard from the mouth of the Roman. That Pilate made use of the βῆμα, hence that he passed sentence from the judgment seat, can virtually be taken for granted. We have plenty of support indicating how commonplace it was for the procurators to use the βῆμα in exercising their jucidial office.[48]

Now, according to the Gospels, the trial of Jesus is interrupted by the Barabbas scene. According to Mark 15:6, Matt 27:15, and John 18:39 it is linked with a Passover amnesty regularly granted by the procurator. It is conspicuous indeed that Luke 23:18 does not mention this Passover amnesty. In his case, the release of Barabbas was achieved by acclamation by the crowd gathered at the judgment seat.[49] Which of the two versions is to be preferred? Barabbas is introduced as notorious (Matt 27:16), as a robber (John 18:40). He committed murder at an insurrection in the city (Luke 23:19; Mark 15:7). Presumably we are dealing with a ringleader of the Zealots who could count on the people's sympathies. As in the case of all the other names in the ancient Passover tradition, the mention of his name vouches for the reliability of the reported events.

A customary amnesty of a prisoner granted by the procurator at Passover is disputed. Josephus knows nothing about it. In this connection appeal is made to a reference in the Mishnah, though its dating is not certain. Furthermore, it is not unambiguously clear what situation it refers to, whether Roman or Jewish, namely, that a prisoner was indeed to be released or was granted parole so as to be able to celebrate the Passover meal.[50]

"Amnesty" (ἀμνηστία) is a Greek legal term. While the term itself does not occur in Roman criminal law, the concept is not altogether missing.[51] The Romans were familiar with forms of par-

---

[47] Cf. Strobel, *Stunde,* 135f.; A. N. Sherwin-White, *Roman Society and Roman Law in the New Testament* (Oxford: Clarendon, 1963) 47; A. Steinwenter, *Jura* 7 (1956) 263–66.

[48] Documentation from the papyri is available in Mitteis-Wilcken, *Grundzüge* II/1:36. Cf. also Josephus, *War* 2.301: "Florus . . . on the next day had his tribunal set."

[49] Luke 23:17, which introduces the Passover amnesty, is secondary. Only some text witnesses include it.

[50] *M. Pesah* 8:6 refers to one who had been promised to be released from prison. A promise by the procurator is highly unlikely. In a roundabout way the suggestion then has to be made that accomplices promised the prisoner that they would support his cause. The relationship of *b. Pesah* 91a, which clearly refers to a Roman prison, to *m. Pesah* 8:6 is problematic. In contrast to Strobel, *Stunde,* 122f., doubt is also raised by Blinzler, *Prozess,* 319.

[51] Mommsen, *Strafrecht,* 458.

don, of course. Most common among these were the *abolitio,* the legal dismissal of a criminal case, and the *venia,* the repeal of a sentence that has been issued.[52] Based on the difficulties mentioned, the Lukan version is to be preferred. People sympathetic with Barabbas achieved the release of their favorite *per acclamationem.* That something of this sort was possible can be seen from the analogous case of Phibion, which took place around 85 CE before the judgment seat of the Egyptian governor G. Septimius Vegetus.[53] It may be appropriate also to consider the procurators' susceptibility to bribes. We know of the Jewish procurator Albinus that he was willing to release prisoners for payment of a sum of money.[54] At a later time Emperor Diocletian calls on his judges not to heed the people's shouts when they want to acquit the criminal or damn the innocent.[55]

We assume that the release of Barabbas occurred the morning Jesus was condemned.[56] The association of the two events happened later. It yielded the narrative possibility of actively engaging the crowd in the sentencing of Jesus. For the Christian narrator it was incomprehensible that nobody gave Jesus support.[57]

There is very little of historical reliability that can be determined about even an indirect involvement in the trial by Herod Antipas, Jesus' Galilean ruler. We only know that he had John the Baptist executed and can assume that he also viewed Jesus with skepticism (cf. Luke 13:31). If he was in Jerusalem at the Passover, he resided in his palace. This is also where Pilate stayed. But the pericope of Luke 23:6–12 is determined by the scriptural support and is to be seen as an illustration of Ps 2:1f., "Why do the nations

---

[52] Cf. ibid., 452–56, 473–77; W. Waldstein, *Untersuchungen zum römischen Begnadigungsrecht, Abolitio—indulgentia—venia* (Innsbruck: Wagner, 1964).

[53] Cf. Gnilka, "Prozess," 35.

[54] Josephus, *Ant.* 20.215. The demand for the release of the sicarii under Albinus does not yield anything in support of a Passover amnesty. For one, the festival mentioned in this context is not specified; for another, this incident has to do with repetitive terroristic acts of blackmail. Cf. Josephus, *Ant.* 20.208–210. Strobel, *Stunde,* 125, suggests a compromise. Though he assumes a customary Passover amnesty, he argues that the release of Barabbas was achieved *per acclamationem.*

[55] Cf. R. Eisler, *Iesous basileus,* 2.464 n. 2.

[56] Bultmann, *History,* 272, argued that the acquittal of Barabbas denoted a historical incident of a later time, which the tradition of the communty then projected back onto the day of Jesus' condemnation. Yet it is only by taking the two trials as contemporaneous that the convergence of the events becomes more plausible.

[57] Whether Barabbas was freed by way of the *abolitio* or of the *venia* has to remain open. Waldstein, *Untersuchungen,* 41f., opts for the *venia.* In this case Barabbas would have been condemned already. The *abolitio* is a viable option as well.

conspire . . . ? The kings of the earth set themselves, and the rulers take counsel together, against the LORD and his anointed . . . " (cf. Acts 4:25–28).[58]

4. Causa mortis

In an attempt to determine the reason for Jesus' death, that is, the accusation made against him, the capital offense with which he was charged and on the basis of which he was sentenced to death, the most secure point of departure is the fact of his crucifixion. We have already mentioned above that in Palestine at that time all of the crucifixions were politically motivated. A charge against Jesus that could impress Pilate must fit into this broad category.

There is the inscription on the cross. The shorter rendering handed down in Mark 15:26 may be considered more original. It says, "The King of the Jews."[59] It was public. This practice is well documented for executions in the first century CE. The documents indicate its unmistakable purpose. The inscription on a plaque was intended to make known the reason for punishment to as many people as possible and thus was carried in front of the condemned one.[60] There is no evidence in support of affixing the inscription on the cross, above the head of the one crucified. But the Markan account does not presuppose that it was so affixed (cf. Mark 15:26). By presenting it in this manner, the other evangelists stylize the scene in terms of Jesus' proclamation of the kingdom (Matt 27:37; Luke 23:38; John 19:19). The inscription on the cross reliably informs us of Jesus' *causa mortis*. He was accused of claiming the kingdom for himself.[61]

---

[58] Some interpreters were on the wrong exegetical track in viewing Herod Antipas as the leading authority in the proceedings against Jesus. On this debate, cf. Blinzler, *Prozess,* 293–300.

[59] Luke 23:38—"This is the King of the Jews"; Matt 27:37—"This is Jesus, the King of the Jews"; John 19:19—"Jesus of Nazareth, the King of the Jews" (in three languages).

[60] Suetonius, *Caligula* 32: "by carrying a sign ahead of him, on which the reason for his penalty was written"; Suetonius, *Domitian* 10: "They hung a sign around the offender's neck with the inscription, 'A Thracian friend who blasphemed his Majesty' and dragged him through the arena"; Dio Cassius 54.3.7: "through the center of the Forum with an inscription giving the reason for the death penalty"; Eusebius, *Hist. eccl.* 5.1.44: "He was taken round the amphitheater with a sign announcing in Latin: This is Attalus, the Christian."

[61] The scepticism of Kuhn, "Jesus als Gekreuzigter," 6, is not justified. This practice is also documented by the Gospels, after all. It may not have happened frequently. Our information is simply too scant.

The collaboration of Caiaphas and Pilate, of both Jewish and Roman authorities in the trial of Jesus, requires our attention once more. Both authorities acted in keeping with their legal conceptions. It is not appropriate without forethought to speak of a judicial error. Even if the procurator had the entire jurisdiction at his disposal, its administration should not be understood as capricious. It simply was not the case that during Pilate's time somebody was nailed to the cross every week. Anarchic conditions occur only near the time of the Jewish War and in conjunction with insurrections leading up to it. Thus we hear of mass crucifixions under Quadratus, the legate, and the procurators Felix and Florus, and later we hear of Titus, who had many Jews crucified during the siege of Jerusalem.[62] In the pre-Christian era there were mass crucifixions under Alexander Jannaeus, the high priest, and under Quintilius Varus.

While the procurator was the representative of imperial justice, he was nevertheless accountable to the emperor, occasionally even to the Syrian governor. The Jewish side was skilled in taking advantage of this and from time to time sent a delegation to Rome to lodge a complaint. In one case Ummidius Quadratus, the Syrian governor, ordered not only the nobility of the Jews but also Cumanus, the procurator, to Rome in order for the imperial court to settle their disputes.[63] Pilate had his opposite number in Caiaphas, the high priest. Since the latter enjoyed an extraordinarily lengthy term of office and lost his post almost at the same time as Pilate, we may conclude not only that he enjoyed a certain measure of respect among the Romans but that Pilate too used his cooperation. Or would it be better to say that both knew how to benefit from their mutual cooperation? Incidentally, in the end Pilate, too, on account of misuse of his office, was recalled by the Syrian governor Vitellius.

Judicial collaboration between the Jewish and Roman authorities in the case of trials is particularly credible in the event of crimes committed against the temple. At the time of the Judean procurators, when the high priests were appointed by Rome, the superintendence of the temple was Rome's. Offerings were presented daily

---

[62] Cf. Josephus, *War* 2.241, 253, 306–308; *Ant.* 20.129, 160–166; also Schürer, *History,* Index 3.72. Mass executions occurred also in other provinces. During the time of Augustus, Volesus, the governer of the province of Asia, had three hundred people killed with axes. He is called to account for this by the Senate; cf. Seneca, *De ira* 2.5.5.

[63] On these so-called transmissions, cf. Mommsen, *Strafrecht*, 239–43. He even attributes a little shady goings-on to the procurator's criminal justice, and in this context cites the stoning of Stephen as a warning example (239 and n. 4). On the intervention by Quadratus, cf. Josephus, *Ant.* 20.129; *War* 2.241.

in the temple for the emperor and the Roman people.[64] The collaboration in the case of temple-related offenses is supported by the temple barrier already mentioned, together with its warnings of death, and by the case against a certain Jesus, the son of Ananias, which occurred shortly before the outbreak of the Jewish War. He was seized by Jews on account of blasphemous statements against the temple and then handed over to Albinus, the procurator, who had him scourged.[65] This collaboration applies even to the Jewish Diaspora.[66]

Although the Gospels contain more hints than explicit statements, we may assume that it was Jesus' temple protest, his move against the money changers and and sellers of pigeons in the court of the Gentiles, that was the reason for his arrest. Hints in this direction are derived from the temple saying of Jesus introduced by witnesses (Mark 14:58 par.) and from the remark at the end of the pericope of the temple protest, according to which the chief priests and scribes sought a way to destroy him (Mark 11:18). It is important to note that this is the first mention of the chief priests in a narrative text of the Gospel. We are familiar with the significance of the high priests in Jesus' trial.

However plausible an offense against the temple might appear as a reason for the intervention against Jesus, it is insufficient for accusing him of usurping the kingdom of the Jews. In order to fill this gap, reference has been made to a description of the conditions in Judea around the turn of the first century BCE/CE, which Josephus supplied concerning the time of unrest following the death of Herod the Great: "And now Judea was full of robberies; and, as the several companies of the seditious lighted upon anyone to head them, *he was created a king immediately,* in order to do mischief to the public. They were in some small measure indeed, and in small matters, hurtful to the Romans, but the murders they committed upon their own people lasted a long while" (*Ant.* 17.285).[67] Insurrection, disrupting order, and kingship are connected so closely that we should look upon this as a legal description of the facts of a criminal case, formulated from the Roman perspective.[68]

---

[64] Cf. Josephus, *Ag. Ap.* 2.6.

[65] Josephus, *War* 6.300–305.

[66] Augustus safeguards the transfer of the temple tax from the Jews of the Diaspora to Jerusalem. Cf. Josephus, *Ant.* 16.164, 167f., and Volkmann, *Rechsprechung,* 130f.

[67] Kuhn, "Jesus als Gekreuzigter," 5 n. 13; Müller, "Vollzug," 81.

[68] Müller, "Vollzug," 81f.

As helpful as this clue might be, some questions remain unresolved. It is correct that Pilate condemned Jesus because he saw the governmental order being threatened by him. But why did he not move against his disciples? The goal of the trial was to eliminate Jesus. The accusers must have presented Jesus to Pilate as one who threatens the order of the state. Certainly he could not be accused of killing people, as was the case with Barabbas or with the insurrectionists of the time of Quintilius Varus, to whom Josephus refers. With regard to the trial that Caiaphas and the chief priests carried out and that preceded the trial before Pilate, it is necessary, in any case, to consider the conflict that had already been brewing for some time and that culminated in Jesus' temple protest. This was the high point of it all and provided the chief priests with the (presumably welcome) legitimate possibility of taking action against him. As we have already shown, the preceding smouldering conflict was predicated upon two aspects: (1) the critique of the praxis of piety and law and (2) the claim Jesus made. The trial by the Sanhedrin was religiously motivated, although religion and the power of the state cannot be separated here. Once he was brought to Pilate, the trial could be conducted only for state-related reasons. Hence the charge "King of the Jews" is enigmatic. To cut out the religious conflict means to fall short.[69]

The Roman penal system cites two situations that were suitable for coming to grips juridically with the charge brought by the chief priests: the *perduellio* (serious hostility against the country) and the *crimen maiestatis populi Romani imminutae* (harm inflicted upon the reputation of the Roman people).[70] It is difficult to draw a boundary between them as far as the nature of the crime is concerned. The *crimen maiestatis* has wider implications, however, and is more dependent upon judicial interpretation. There were *perduellio* trials that had been dismissed and then were reopened under the charge of *crimen maiestatis*. The *perduellio* was

---

[69] Strobel, *Stunde,* 81–92, develops the argument that the Sanhedrin had charged Jesus with false prophecy and seducing the people, and derives both accusations from Deut 13. From the perspective of Deut 13, however, seduction is more precisely defined as seducing someone to turn away from Yahweh, a charge that could not be raised against Jesus. Rabbinic law likewise understands seduction as seduction of the individual to idolatry. Cf. Müller, "Vollzug," 43.

[70] On the concept of *perduellio,* cf. Brecht, *Perduellio,* 120. It is manifestly of Roman origin. The Greeks paraphrase it as follows: ἀδικεῖν τὴν πόλιν, ἀδίκημα δημόσιον. On the concept of *majestas,* cf. Mommsen, *Strafrecht,* 538f. Etymologically *perduellio* probably is derived from the old Latin *duellium,* and is synonymous with *bellum.*

more serious.[71] As one who was not a Roman citizen, Jesus could in both instances be punished by death on the cross. Which formulation of the situation Pilate may have chosen remains an open question.[72]

5. The way of the cross and the execution

Sentenced to death, Jesus was scourged by the soldiers charged with his execution. The oldest account almost ignores this torture, mentioning it merely as an afterthought (Mark 15:15). The scourging is an integral part of the crucifixion and as such began the execution process.[73] It could be inflicted only upon noncitizens. The scourging of Roman citizens had been prohibited since Cato. Caesar condemned their scourging as a serious violation.[74] For the scourging the soldiers used the *horribile flagellum*, a leather strip that was often interspersed with bone fragments or lumps of lead or had barbs attached to it. The one being scourged was stripped of his clothes and thrown to the ground or tied to a pillar. The number of blows was left to the torturers.[75]

The passion account continues with the soldiers' mocking of Jesus as the King of the Jews (Mark 15:16–20a). To be sure, this account is stylized in terms of making a travesty of the ritual of kingship. Its historical core is done justice if the interpretation of the account is not made to depend on Roman analogies; these are the result of "inappropriate erudition," which has a tendency to distort the events.[76] Its explanation arises entirely from within the

---

[71] Cf. Mommsen, *Strafrecht*, 589f. Brecht, *Perduellio*, 265, argues that a description that blurs the two concepts does justice to neither.

[72] Brecht, *Perduellio*, 301f., reports on about thirty *perduellio* proceedings. The *perduellio* encompasses such crimes as political unpopularity in the case of the victorious party of Marius and Cinna, and the attempt to reintroduce the monarchy, even if not for oneself. Among the proceedings discussed, the last point has most affinities with the trial of Jesus. Not all *perduellio* trials involve the death penalty. Brecht, *Perduellio*, 123f., guesses that *perduellio* is not to be equated with high treason.

[73] Cf. Mommsen, *Strafrecht*, 47. Contemporary documentation: Josephus, *War* 2.306, 308; 5.449; 7.200–202. Additional information is found in Blinzler, *Prozess*, 322, n. 14.

[74] Mommsen, *Strafrecht*, 47.

[75] The synagogual court was familiar with the punishment of flagellation with thirty-nine lashes (cf. 2 Cor 11:24). Josephus, *War* 6.304f., describes the scourging of Jesus, the son of Ananias: "he was whipped till his bones were laid bare."

[76] This critical expression comes from Meyer, *Ursprung* 1.187. On particular Roman festivals, such as the Sakaia, Cronia, or Saturnalia, it was customary to put a purple robe on those who were to be executed. Cf. also Philo, *Flacc.* 36–40.

situation itself.[77] Some soldiers used the interval following the sentencing, which was necessary for the preparation of the crucifixion, to express their derision of Jesus. Considering the fact that the auxiliary troops of the Jewish procurator were drafted mainly from among the Gentile Palestinians—Jews were exempt from military duty—the mocking of Jesus may also have to be viewed as an act of the general hatred of the Jews, which even then was not alien to the Palestinians.

The way from the praetorium to the place of execution led through the upper part of the city and probably out through the garden gate, which was located near the Hippicus tower.[78] In this connection we are assuming that the palace of Herod was the Praetorium, the procurator's residence in Jerusalem. Those to be executed, three of them, were accompanied by soldiers of the execution squad, which was generally under the command of a low-ranking officer; together they made their way through the streets of the city bustling with pilgrims. The inscription bearing the conviction was carried ahead of Jesus or was hung around his neck. Like the execution itself, the public procession to the place of execution was meant as a deterrent. According to Roman law, in keeping also with Jewish practice, executions were held outside the city. Those convicted had to carry the *patibulum* (the cross beam) themselves: "With outstretched arms you must . . . die outside the city gates, for you will carry the cross beam."[79] Evidently on account of Jesus' total exhaustion, a certain Simon of Cyrene is compelled to relieve him of the *patibulum* (Mark 15:21 par.). He did not carry the cross beam together with Jesus but had to relieve Jesus by carrying it alone. We are dealing with a form of forced labor that was typical for the times of an occupying power, as demanded of the Jews in general. Especially on festivals this was not uncommon.[80] Mark, that is, the old Passover account, introduces this Simon with unusual detail. He comes from Cyrene in North Africa (Cyrenaika), where there was a considerable Jewish Diaspora that even maintained a synagogue in Jerusalem (Acts 6:9). Simon either was in the city as a pilgrim for the festival or had moved from his home to Jerusalem, as

---

[77] Bultmann, *History*, 273, takes the mocking scene to be a secondary development of the scourging motif. This is not convincing. On the critique, cf. Gnilka, *Markus*, 2.308f.

[78] Hippicus, Phasael, and Mariamme were the names of the three towers situated on the northeastern corner of the Herodian palace. Cf. the city map of Jerusalem in D. H. K. Amiran et al., *Atlas of Jerusalem* (Berlin: de Gruyter, 1973) table 3.6.

[79] Plautus, *Miles glor.* 2, 6f.

[80] Cf. Flusser, *Jesus*, 133. On ἀγγαρεία cf. also Matt 5:41.

did many Diaspora Jews in their retirement years. In addition, the account describes Simon as the father of Alexander and Rufus. From this we may conclude that he was known to the earliest community—Matthew and Luke have already removed this reference—and that he became a Christian later on. Whether Rufus is the same as the one mentioned in the list of greetings in Romans (16:13) is not certain, though it certainly is possible.[81] In any case the community was able to point to an important witness of the way of the cross (and of the crucifixion?) of Jesus.

The place of execution is Golgotha. The evangelists translate the term as "the place of a skull" (Mark 15:22 par.) and thus derive it from the Hebrew *golgolta* (the second "l" was smoothed out), meaning "head" or "skull."[82] The translation is probably accurate. Most probably *golgota* is to be construed as the name of a land form, referring to a hill shaped like a head or a skull. That there were permanent places of execution has yet to be demonstrated.[83] Other interpretations, such as that Adam's skull was buried there, are legendary accretions. Golgotha is situated to the north of Jerusalem. Today its location is largely accepted as reliable, near the place where the so-called second north wall curves to the west in its southern course, hence precisely where the Church of the Holy Sepulchre preserves the memory of the site of Jesus' execution. The excavations that U. Lux-Wagner undertook between 1971 and 1974 resulted in a partially new perspective. Golgotha is to be understood as a rocky mound that rose about twelve meters (forty feet) above the base of a quarry in the vicinity.[84] This helps explain why the pilgrim of Bordeaux who visited Jerusalem in 333 CE labels Golgotha a *monticulus*.[85] Constantine, the emperor, had the mound integrated into the site of his Church of the Holy Sepulchre. Already when Aelia Capitolina was built, there probably were changes in the landscape.[86]

There is historical justification for Jesus being offered a drink as a pain reliever (Mark 15:23), if it is assumed that those offering him

---

[81] According to a widely held view the Gospel of Mark was written in Rome.
[82] Cf. J. Jeremias, *Golgotha* (Angelos 1; Leipzig, 1926) 1.
[83] Ibid., 1 n. 5.
[84] Cf. R. Riesner, "Golgota und die Archäologie," *BK* 40 (1985) 21–26.
[85] In Jeremias, *Golgotha,* 2.
[86] Aelia Capitolina encompassed approximately the northern half of the destroyed city. Golgotha was included in the territory of the town, as had already been the case, by means of the third northern wall. The forum was erected in the vicinity of Golgotha. Cf. Amiran, *Atlas,* table 3.8.

this service were women from Jerusalem. The Romans were not familiar with this practice. As far as Jerusalem is concerned, this is documented in the talmudic tradition, though there is no date associated with it. Jesus refused it.

Jesus endured the torture of crucifixion. On this point too the Gospels are extremely terse in their presentation: "And they crucified him" (Mark 15:24a). It may nevertheless be proper to recall the process of this torture. Affixed to the *patibulum* with outstretched arms either tied or nailed, the one being crucified was elevated by inserting the *patibulum* on the upright pole of the cross, either as a *crux commissa* (T-shape) or a *crux immissa* (+-shape). With regard to the crucified Jesus we may assume that he was nailed to the cross by his arms, and probably his feet as well. John 20:25 and Luke 24:39 allude to this. The nails were driven through the wrists, rather than through the palm of the hands. Thus the crucifixion was a blood-stained death. In order for the body not to be torn from the cross, a peg *(sedile)* was affixed to the upright pole. Generally the crosses were hardly taller than a man, so the legs were in a bent position. The crucified persons were stripped of all their clothes and hung on the cross naked. This description of the crucifixion has been confirmed archaeologically by the discovery of the skeleton of a crucified man in a grave on Mount Scopus, near Jerusalem, from the pre-70 CE period. The nail driven through both feet was still lodged in the skeleton.[87]

Other witnesses attest that this horrible torture enticed the tormentors to acts of sadism and orgies of hatred. Josephus describes a mass crucifixion outside the gates of Jerusalem during the city's siege under Titus: "So the soldiers out of wrath and hatred they bore the Jews, nailed those they caught, one after one way, and another after another, to the crosses, by way of jest; when their multitude was so great, that room was wanting for the crosses . . . " (*War* 5.451). Seneca seems to have seen even worse things: "There I see stakes, not all of the same kind, of course; . . . many are nailed to the cross with their head to the ground, others have a stake driven through their private parts, others stretch out their arms on the cross, I see ropes for torture, I see whips."[88] It is understandable why Cicero called crucifixion "the cruelest and most dreadful death

---

[87] N. Haas, "Anthropological Observations on the Skeletal Remains from Giv' at ha-Mivtar," *IEJ* 20 (1970) 38–59. Crucifixion is described somewhat differently by Plautus, *Mostellaria* 2.1.12f.: "Arms and legs were nailed on twice."

[88] Seneca, *Ad Marciam de consolatione* 20.3.

penalty"[89] and Josephus calls it the "most miserable death" (*War* 7.203). It was the death of slaves *(servile supplicium).*[90]

The soldiers of the execution squad were also responsible for guarding those crucified. The executioners' privilege to claim the clothing of those executed may be ancient, for the emperor Hadrian revised this law of spoils because of its abuse. Although the passion narrative speaks of the division of Jesus' garments with the words of Ps 22:18, "and [they] divided his garments among them, casting lots for them, to decide what each should take" (Mark 15:24), we may certainly assume that this did happen. Hence one may ask what the executioners got from Jesus; it can hardly have been more than a tunic and an undergarment, a belt, and perhaps a headband. Money or possessions he had none.[91]

Since Golgotha was only a few yards from the city walls, there probably were plenty of spectators. The victim got to hear the scorn of the crowd, which had always been ready—up to the medieval period and modern times—to join in executions staged by the authorities and to be entertained in this dubious manner. The mood of survivors and victors becomes apparent.

What were Jesus' final words, the manner in which he broke his silence once more, is difficult to say. Each of the evangelists shaped the scene of death in his own way. Mark and Matthew dramatized it by means of Jesus' cry of dereliction, thereby indicating his godforsakenness (Mark 15:34 par.). It is to be remembered that the cry of dereliction with which his life ends represents only the beginning of Psalm 22. According to Luke, Jesus speaks a Jewish evening prayer and prays for his executioners to be pardoned (23:34, 46). The Johannine Christ hands back to the Father the work that was given to him and that he now has accomplished (John 19:30). Were his last words merely the very human "I thirst" (John 19:28), or was it a cry without words (Mark 15:37)? A person's death is always his very personal, and finally not communicable, experience. This is also true

---

[89] Cicero, *Pro Rabirio* 5.16.

[90] Tacitus, *Hist.* 4.11. Although crucifixion had once been a common method of execution for the Romans, it was later restricted to slaves. In the time of the emperors, however, freedmen and non-citizens were increasingly included. If a Roman citizen was to be crucified, his citizenship had to be revoked first. The Esquilin was the place for the crucifixions in the ancient city of Rome. Cf. Mommsen, *Strafrecht,* 918–23, 914.

[91] Presumably the money and possessions of the one executed went into the coffers of the procurator. Besides the missionary instructions Jesus gave to the disciples, it is interesting that he asked for a coin to be shown in the dispute about paying taxes (Mark 12:15). On this, cf. Blinzler, *Prozess,* 369 n. 47.

of Jesus. We would like to assume that he died in the will of the Abba, whose will he decided to carry out obediently.

What the cause of death was in medical terms, a question which the medical profession continues to raise, can be left to rest here. It is conceivable that the weakening due to the penal scourging, the loss of blood, the hours of being in a posture of his arms stretched out and nailed fast, brought about the fatal exhaustion.[92]

The passion narrative mentions by name some of the women who were present at Jesus' crucifixion. While the names diverge (Mark 15:40 par.; cf. 15:47 par.; 16:1 par.), Mary of Magdala is always mentioned, consistently in first place; she is the disciple who comes from the town on the western shore of the Sea of Galilee, which in the Gospels is mentioned only in conjunction with the name of this woman. For primitive Christianity her importance was such that it exceeded even that of the apostles, for she was the primary witness of his crucifixion and his burial. If the men did not have the courage to accompany him on this most difficult journey, the women disciples stood the test in this hour. Even if they only watched from a distance, their attestation was irreplaceable.[93]

In the evening of the day of his execution the body of Jesus was buried by Joseph of Arimathea (Mark 15:42–47 par.). As far as the problem and the understanding of this tradition is concerned, it is important to point out the limitations of the juridical options of this process. It was Roman legal practice not to bury the bodies of those crucified but to leave to decay on the cross, to leave them to the vultures, or finally to dispose of them, for instance in a river.[94] The dishonoring of the memory of the executed *(damnatio memoriae)* could be added, though this usually had to be initiated as a proceeding of its own.[95] Those guarding at the crosses had a twofold task: to ascertain the convicts' death or even to bring it about (by breaking

---

[92] This is addressed in detail in ibid., 381–84. Much of the medical information is rather uncertain: collapse, shock. Taking the shroud of Turin into account is a dubious endeavor.

[93] Riesner, "Golgota," 24, suggests that the women might have watched from the city wall.

[94] Cf. Mommsen, *Strafrecht,* 987–90. Augustus abandons the corpses of conspirators to the vultures (Suetonius, *Aug.* 13.1f.), while Tiberius has them thrown into the Tiber (Suetonius, *Tib.* 6.19; cf. 6.29). In the context of the persecution of the Jews in Alexandria in 38 CE, the procurator Flaccus of Egypt does not allow those who died on the cross to be taken down (Philo, *Flacc.* 84).

[95] Mommsen, *Strafrecht,* 987. In the case of the *perduellio* this process was also possible after death because the punishment begins with the moment of the deed (ipso facto), according to the Roman view.

the bones), and to prevent their corpses from being taken away for burial. Thus the tradition says concerning Christian martyrs from Gaul that despite considerable efforts the believers failed to obtain their bodies from the guards.[96] It took a special act of mercy on the part of the judicial authority to release a corpse for burial. Such requests were generally made by relatives. In the case of the *perduellio* it was difficult to obtain a release.

The situation was different in the Jewish context. From the start the burial of the dead was of utmost importance in Israel. Those executed were no exception. There are very few examples in the OT that reflect the refusal of a burial, for instance, Jezebel (2 Kgs 4:10) and Jason (2 Macc 5:10).[97] The reason for a rapid burial was not respect for the dead but the deep-seated conception that those executed bring harm to the land and detract from its cultic purity: "his body shall not remain all night upon the tree, but you shall bury him the same day, for a hanged man is accursed by God; you shall not defile your land which the LORD your God gives you for an inheritance" (Deut 21:23). If the instruction in Deuteronomy 21 referred to the subsequent public exposure of the executed, in the first century CE, when crucifixion was the common death penalty, this was also applied to the crucified. With reference to Deut 21:23 Josephus says: "The Jews used to take so much care of the burial of men, that they took down those that were condemned and crucified, and buried them before the going down of the sun."[98] Deuteronomy 21 is also linked with crucifixion in the *Temple Scroll* of Qumran (64:9–11) and in Philo (*Spec.* 3.151f.). We can surely assume that the Roman procurator was familiar with this conception held sacred by the Jews. In consideration of this taboo the release of the body of a crucified one seems plausible, including the case of one condemned for *perduellio*. This release had nothing to do with respect for the dead but with avoiding the serious violation of the religious sentiments of the Jewish people. Philo too refers to the possibility of releasing the bodies of the crucified for burial.[99]

---

[96] Eusebius, *Hist. eccl.* 5.1.61. Negligent guards were severely punished, as attested by an anecdote from Ephesus reported by Petronius, *Satyricon* 111f. Cf. Mommsen, *Strafrecht,* 989 n. 1.

[97] Cf. Michel and Bauernfeind, *Flavius Josephus,* 218 n. 73.

[98] Josephus, *War* 4.317.

[99] Philo, *Flacc.* 83f. At the time of the Jewish persecution, however, the Egyptian procurator Flaccus refused the release. Such refusal also occurred at the time of the Jewish War.

When Joseph of Arimathea requests Pilate to release Jesus' body, he acts as a pious Jew who is aware of the directive in Deut 21:23. He was not a disciple of Jesus. Only in this way does it make sense that the women did not take part in the burial. It is an open question whether he became a Christian later on, as Matt 27:57 and John 19:38 state and as Mark 15:43 perhaps already hints.[100] According to Mark 15:43 he was a member of the council and according to Luke 23:50f. even a member of the Sanhedrin. The latter is doubtful. He possibly was a member of a local sanhedrin, which existed in Jewish communities.[101] A festival day was no obstacle to a burial. The prohibition of labor had limited significance here in comparison with the following Sabbath day.[102] The burial commandment superseded the commandment of rest. It is to be noted that in the Markan description the burial of Jesus is undertaken with utmost simplicity. Joseph wrapped the body in a linen shroud and placed it in a rock tomb.[103] We do not yet hear anything about it having been a new tomb or Joseph's family tomb or one in its vicinity (thus the other Gospels). Even about washing the body nothing is mentioned. Time constraints were not necessarily an issue. If the Jewish distinction, pointed out by R. E. Brown, between honorable and dishonorable burials is considered,[104] the account leaves the latter impression. If this permits us an original glimpse into the event, Jesus was buried in accordance with the dishonorable death on the cross. Nevertheless, his followers were familiar with his tomb from the start. Mary of Magdala was the first witness provided by the community. It is also to be remembered that the record of Jesus' burial is part of the Jerusalem tradition.[105] As such, it presupposed the Jerusalem community's knowledge of the tomb.

---

[100] That Joseph already was his disciple at the time of Jesus' death, as intimated by Matt 27:57 and John 19:38, is to be rejected. This characterization is intended to exonerate the disciples.

[101] According to Acts 13:29 Jesus was buried by Jews, namely, by inhabitants of Jerusalem. Cf. John 19:31 and R. E. Brown, "The Burial of Jesus," *CBQ* 50 (1988) 244f. The tradition associated with the name of Joseph of Arimathea, however, is to be preferred. Did Joseph act on behalf of the Jews? Or even of the Sanhedrin?

[102] Cf. Dalman, *Jesus–Jeshua*, 95f., and Deut 16:7.

[103] Brown, "Burial," 242, also cites the Jewish disgust with naked people.

[104] Ibid., 237, 242. In this manner Jer 22:18f. describes a burial without lament for the dead.

[105] Cf. Gnilka, *Markus*, 2.345–47. The crucified man found on Mt. Scopus was subsequently buried in the family tomb. His skeleton was found in an ossuary; in other words, he had been moved from his original tomb at some time. Evidently the family was familiar with his tomb as well.

The attempt has been made time and again to determine the precise date of Jesus' death. The divergent results, varying between the years 27 and 33, are an urgent reminder of the need to be cautious.[106] The data by means of which the calculations were made include the narrowing down of the time frame, the duration of Jesus' ministry, and astronomical considerations.

The earlier limit is the beginning of his ministry, which cannot be placed before the fifteenth year of the emperor Tiberius (October 1, 27–October 1, 28).[107] The later limit is the end of the tenure of the procurator Pilate (36). The duration of Jesus' public ministry is given as a minimum of one year and maximum of three years. But a ministry of three years is unlikely.[108] Astronomical calculations contain a number of difficulties. It is disputed whether Jesus died on the day of the Passover or on the day before, that is, on 15th or 14th Nisan (the month of spring). We prefer the day of the Passover. It was a Friday, in any case. Astronomically we could determine accurately in which years the 14th or 15th Nisan was on a Friday. What is less than certain, however, is whether the Jews yet observed the new moon with equal accuracy then. They judged by appearance. A miscalculation of at least one day is easily possible. Further, the authorities in charge of the calendar were allowed to insert a leap month prior to Nisan, in the event that the barley was not yet ready for harvesting, which was required for the sheaf-offering on 16th Nisan, or in the event that bad road conditions interfered with the Passover pilgrimage. We do not know in which years this was the case. Thus we may have to be content with the information that Jesus was executed around 30 CE, that is, the 783rd year after the founding of the city of Rome. In age, Jesus probably was just past the middle thirties.[109]

---

[106] Cf. the overview in Blinzler, *Prozess*, 101f.

[107] See above, p. 70.

[108] The three Passovers in the Gospel of John are not of much assistance because the Passover of John 2:13 was the Passover associated with the temple protest.

[109] The most up-to-date calculation by W. Hinz, "Chronologie des Lebens Jesu," *ZDMG* 139 (1989) 301–9, pinpoints it as March 30, 28 CE. In this case Tiberius's fifteenth year of office is construed differently. Hinz includes the three years of Tiberius's coregency with Augustus as part of his reign. Concerning this calculation, which is not a new one, J. Schmid, *Das Evangelium nach Lukas* (RNT 3; Regensburg: Friedrich Pustet, 1955) 94, notes that it lacks all support, both from the literature of antiquity (historians and chronographers) and from the coins of Tiberius, and that it arose merely from the desire to bring Luke 3:23 (Jesus was about thirty years old at his public appearance) more into alignment with the year of his birth.

Overview

It almost goes without saying that the passion event continued to be reflected upon and to be interpreted theologically in a very special way. Only a few trajectories will be pointed out here.

The trial before the high priest is developed into a confession scene. Before the supreme Jewish body Jesus confesses that he is the Messiah and the Son of God and thereby confirms the confession of his community. More onus is put on the Jewish side. The intention to put Jesus to death is shown to be the authorities' goal from the start (Mark 14:55). In the trial before Pilate this tendency can be noticed as well. The people are linked more intensively with the proceedings, so that Pilate is made to appear as little more than a helpless executor of the will of the crowd. The people renounce their Messiah (Mark 15:1–14). For this descriptive approach the link is, in particular, Jesus' confrontation with Barabbas. His name, the literal meaning of which is "son of the father," is a welcome opportunity to point out the cryptic style of the amnesty scene. In Matthew the people's action intensifies into the memorable call for his blood (27:25), thus pointing to the precarious relationship with Judaism. If as an evangelist he only wished to convey the turning point in the history of salvation, in which the hitherto only people of God is replaced, he also unleashed misunderstandings that have seriously encumbered the relationship between Christianity and Judaism.

Conversely, Jesus' confrontation with Barabbas provided the occasion for illustrating the sinner's acceptance through the cross, for Jesus literally took the place of the one who deserved to die. Increasingly the crucifixion and the death on the cross are presented as salvation history or cosmic events. When the temple curtain is torn at Jesus' death, the way into the holy of holies, which can bring every person into the presence of God, is opened up. When darkness spreads over the whole earth, the entire creation learns about the death of its Lord. The centurion of the execution squad, and precisely he, becomes the first one who confesses the crucified one and who perceives the dignity of the Son of God in the humiliation (Mark 15:54).

Into the tradition of the burial of Jesus sublime tones were introduced. There was an unwillingness to tolerate a burial with little honor (see John 19:39). Thus, if the glory of Easter is allowed to penetrate the burial scene in one instance, in another there are apologetic motives that can be recognized (the guard of the tomb in

Matt 27:62–66). The portraits of veneration, frequently reproduced in art, are all in place.

Select bibliography: E. Bammel, ed., *The Trial of Jesus* (FS C. F. D. Moule; SBT[2] 13; London: SCM, 1971); O. Betz, "Probleme des Prozesses Jesu," 25/1.565–647 in *Principat* (ANRW II; ed. H. Temporini and W. Haase; Berlin: de Gruyter, 1974–); J. Blinzler, *Der Prozess Jesu* (4th ed.; Regensburg: F. Pustet, 1969); C. H. Brecht, *Perduellio* (MBPAR 21; Munich: C. H. Beck, 1938); I. Broer, *Die Urgemeinde und das Grab Jesu* (SANT 31; Munich: Kösel, 1972); R. E. Brown, "The Burial of Jesus," *CBQ* 50 (1988) 233–45; D. R. Catchpole, *The Trial of Jesus* (SPB 18; Leiden: Brill, 1972); H. Cohn, *The Trial and Death of Jesus* (New York: Ktav, 1977); M. Dibelius, "Das historische Problem der Leidensgeschichte," *ZNW* 30 (1931) 193–201; D. Dormeyer, *Die Passion Jesu als Verhaltensmodell* (NTA 11; Münster: Aschendorff, 1974); J. Gnilka, "Der Prozess Jesu nach den Berichten des Markus und Matthäus mit der Rekonstruktion des historischen Verlaufs," 11–40 in *Der Prozess gegen Jesus* (QD 112; K. Kertelge, ed.; 2d ed.; Freiburg: Herder, 1989); N. Haas, "Anthropological Observations on the Skeletal Remains from Giv' at ha-Mivtar," *IEJ* 20 (1970) 38–59; M. Hengel, *Crucifixion in the Ancient World and the Folly of the Message of the Cross* (London: SCM, 1977); W. Hinz, "Chronologie des Lebens Jesu," *ZDMG* 139 (1989) 301–9; J. Jeremias, *Golgotha* (Angelos 1; Leipzig, 1926); H.-W. Kuhn, "Jesus als Gekreuzigter in der frühchristlichen Verkündigung bis zur Mitte des 2. Jahrhunderts," *ZTK* 72 (1975) 1–46; W. Kunkel, *Kleine Schriften. Zum römischen Strafverfahren und zur römischen Verfassungsgeschichte* (ed. H. Niederländer; Weimar: Bohlau, 1974); idem, *Römische Rechtsgeschichte* (5th ed.; Köln-Graz, 1967); E. Linnemann, *Studien zur Passionsgeschichte* (FRLANT 102; Göttingen: Vandenhoeck & Ruprecht, 1970); T. Mommsen, *Römisches Strafrecht* (Leipzig: Duncker & Humblot, 1899; reprint Darmstadt, 1961); K. Müller, "Möglichkeit und Vollzug jüdischer Kapitalgerichtsbarkeit im Prozess gegen Jesus von Nazaret," 41–83 in *Der Prozess gegen Jesus* (QD 112; K. Kertelge, ed.; 2d ed.; Freiburg: Herder, 1989); C. Paulus, "Einige Bemerkungen zum Prozess Jesu bei den Synoptikern," *ZSRG* 102 (1985) 437–45; R. Riesner, "Golgota und die Archäologie," *BK* 40 (1985) 21–26; A. N. Sherman-White, *Roman Society and Roman Law in the New Testament* (Oxford: Clarendon, 1963); A. Strobel, *Die Stunde der Wahrheit* (WUNT 21; Tübingen: Mohr), 1980; F. Viering, *Zur Bedeutung des Todes Jesu* (3d ed.; Gütersloh: Gütersloher, 1968); H. Volkmann, *Zur Rechtsprechung im Principat des Augustus* (2d ed.; MBPAR 21; Munich: Beck, 1969); P. Winter, *On the Trial of Jesus* (SJ 1; Berlin: de Gruyter, 1961).

12

Easter Epilogue

The story of the resurrection of the crucified one from the dead is no longer part of the earthly history of Jesus of Nazareth. Yet this is its goal, to which everything is directed and from which alone the person and work of Jesus can be fully understood. Since it does not belong to the earthly history of Jesus, it need not and cannot be addressed here.

The only thing that needs to be indicated now is how the inception of a new history came about, namely, the story of the disciples who gather afresh. It is the history of his community, the history of the church.

This new gathering came about in Galilee. What we call the Easter chapters in the Gospels are divided into two parts by regions. One part points to Galilee (Mark 16:7; Matt 28:16ff.; John 21), the other to Jerusalem (Luke 24; John 20). In scholarly research the opinion has become pervasive that Easter also began in Galilee, first of all in terms of the new gathering of the disciples.

The scattering of the disciples had been triggered by the arrest of Jesus and the subsequent events. The destination of their radical flight, as alluded to in Mark 14:50, was Galilee, their home. It is there that we meet them again. We do not know in what state of mind the disciples were when they fled and when they arrived at home, nor should we be all too concerned about it. The only thing we know is that all at once, in a new gathering, they begin to proclaim, "God has raised Jesus from the dead." For this proclamation they referred to the testimony that the crucified Jesus demonstrated that he was alive in their midst. We further know that in this new gathering Simon, who received the name Cephas, filled a leading, initiating role (cf. 1 Cor 15:5; Luke 24:34). This proclamation of the resurrection of Jesus from the dead has not fallen silent since then. The disciples of Jesus saw it and still see it as the core of their faith (cf. 1 Cor 15:14–21).

There is a woman, however, who probably preceded Simon Peter as far as the Easter faith is concerned. In the Gospels the Easter message is also linked with the tomb of Jesus and in this context also with the name of Mary of Magdala. She had waited at the cross. She knew the tomb of Jesus. Her story was embellished and in the Gospels has differing versions. John 20:11–18 tells of an appearance of the risen one to Mary that precedes the other Easter appearances. According to John 20:17f. she takes the Easter message to the apostles, which prompted Thomas Aquinas, incidentally, to call her the woman apostle of the apostles. It is not easy to evaluate this tradition. It may be the case that for juridical reasons the witness of the woman was moved into the background, since in the view of that time a woman was not competent to be a witness. The tomb, however, is not the factor that triggers the Easter faith.[1] The empty tomb was misconstrued (cf. Matt 28:13f.). It is the victor's trophy to which the Jerusalem community could point[2] and which it was not prepared to relinquish.[3]

The proclamation of Jesus was taken up afresh in the light of the Easter faith. In the light of the Easter faith the Gospels were written. In them the characteristics of the earthly Jesus are mixed with the colors of the glorified Christ. Therein lies the main reason for the difficulty of our historical reconstruction. Yet the community was convinced that the earthly and crucified one was the same as the resurrected and glorified one. The community wanted then and wants still to lead people by faith to the one who lives and who works in them.[4]

---

[1] This view is argued by H. von Campenhausen, "Der Ablauf der Osterereignisse und das leere Grab" (1958) 49–52.

[2] Cf. U. Wilckens, *Auferstehung* (ThTh 4; Stuttgart, 1970) 64.

[3] J. Kremer, *Die Osterevangelien—Geschichten um Geschichte* (Stuttgart: Katholisches Bibelwerk, 1977) 18, says quite correctly that the reference to the open, empty tomb in no wise functions as a compelling piece of evidence but functions as a sign that challenges or reinforces faith.

[4] E. Schillebeeckx coined the expression "story of one who is alive." This expression aptly characterizes our Gospels.

Appendix:
Jesus, the Christ—an Interview[1]

Those who want to learn something about Jesus are referred to the Gospels of the New Testament: texts, accounts, testimonials, surely not of the kind found in a news magazine. How would you characterize these texts?

We do indeed depend on the Gospels for knowledge of the historical Jesus, especially on the three oldest Gospels we call the Synoptics: Mark, Matthew, and Luke. These Gospels certainly have a historical interest, though a historical interest of a particular kind. They do not merely intend to recall the historical Jesus; they want to proclaim him at the same time. They want to arouse faith in him. And this means that they link the historical Jesus with the resurrected Jesus Christ. You can recognize the Gospels' particular interest in terms of what they report about him, concentrating on his public ministry, the time from his baptism by John the Baptist to his crucifixion and burial. About his upbringing, for instance, about his youth, about his childhood we learn next to nothing. Nowhere do we hear anything about what he looked like, how tall he was, what color his eyes and hair were, what he wore. All of this would have to be found in a biography. Apparently the evangelists were not interested in these questions. We might almost be tempted to harbor ill will against them for having focused on what is important for our faith, on what is significant for the Christian existence to be realized.

---

[1] This interview was broadcast on May 28, 1992, under the title "Jesus, the Christ. Anton Kentemich interviews the New Testament scholar Joachim Gnilka of Munich," in the series "Catholic World" of Bayerischer Rundfunk, the Bavarian broadcasting network.

Jesus of Nazareth: Message and History is the title of your book. This actually identifies the two components: message, history. New Testament scholarship refers to the historical Jesus and the kerygmatic Christ. What can you tell us about these two components?

Person and message, of course, are most intricately related. Concerning the message of Jesus we are informed through an ancient source that we call the logia source, which the extensive Gospels, Matthew and Luke, used and which captures especially his proclamation of the kingdom of God, as well as his message of morality. Concerning his person we are informed by the Gospels in general, and perhaps of particular interest here is the passion narrative, which represents a very ancient tradition. We are very well informed about his final days. It is the only text in the Gospels that is drawn up chronologically. This means that there we learn something about a sequence of days, beginning with his arrest in Gethsemane, through the proceedings before the Sanhedrin, then before Pilate, up to his crucifixion and burial. The rest of the tradition about Jesus comes in pericopes, as we call them, meaning that it is divided into individual texts. This is linked with the fact that what has found its way into the Gospels had for some time been handed down orally, especially the stories of his healings, but also many other things we learn about him.

Of course one can now ask, "Who was Jesus, what do we really know about him? Is not everything seen through the eyes of, in the view of, the post-Easter communities? Where do we find him?"

We find him in the Gospels. The perspective of faith is to be considered, of course. The scholarly research on the New Testament has developed criteria that enable us to reconstruct Jesus. An important criterion is "dissimilarity"; in other words, that which is original, which cannot be encountered in the environment of the New Testament, in Jewish literature or in Hellenistic literature, that can absolutely lay claim to being authentic.

We have to realize, of course, that Jesus addressed a particular time, a particular culture, and therefore also had to take up concepts and ideas that were present at the time. But from this original material we obtain a platform on which we are able to reconstruct the life and message of Jesus, or his personhood to a large extent.

Possibly there are certain parables, particular sayings, of which we are able to say, yes, this is something from him.

I have just mentioned the logia source, the source of Jesus' sayings, which is very significant as far as his proclamation is concerned, and there is the passion narrative. You have brought up the parables. These too are of considerable importance to us because we realize that these parables are consistent in a particular way, in that they cannot easily be split apart. Here we are particularly close to the message of Jesus, especially to his proclamation of the kingdom of God, for most of the parables for which we are indebted to Jesus have to do with the kingdom of God.

This actually was the central message: the kingdom of God. Is it imminent, did it come in his person, does he point to it, and what is the kingdom of God?

The kingdom of God is the center of Jesus' preaching. He surely was deliberate in taking up this concept. Contemporary Judaism was familiar with it. Of course, contemporary Judaism in part used other concepts for a similar focus, like that of the world to come, of Paradise. Oddly enough, Jesus nowhere defined or theorized about this kingdom of God; rather, he described it in parables. Perhaps it can be said that the kingdom of God means God's decision to bring about the eschatological salvation and to do so through Jesus Christ. As the eschatological salvation, the kingdom of God remains bound up with him. It is the future. It is the absolute future that is being promised to people and to the world. The kingdom of God, then, is the future but at the same time it is the present as well. It can be experienced in Jesus' ministry. It seeks to establish a new order, the order of love. It has become possible to experience this kingdom of God in Jesus, in that he talked to the people, in his healings but also in his association with people. In particular he associated with the outcasts, the sick, the wretched, those marginalized by society, and accepted them into his table fellowship and other relationships.

The blind see, the lame walk, lepers are cleansed. This also takes up texts of the Old Testament. But there are many miracle stories and many people today think that perhaps they should only be taken symbolically, only as a story intended to represent, symbolize something. Did Jesus work miracles and, if so, of what kind?

Jesus did work healings. He worked charismatic healings; this cannot be denied. With regard to this healing activity, the tradition of the Synoptic Gospels is so extensive and so varied that it cannot be brushed aside. We have accounts of healings, but we also have various statements of Jesus in which he talks about his healing activity. In addition, we have other miracle stories, such as the story of the transfiguration on the mountain, the story of him walking on the water, and many others—here we may have to take into account that the Easter perspective is having an influence. Actually these extraordinary stories can be understood only from the perspective of Easter. I would even consider the thought that, for instance, the transfiguration on the mountain or Jesus' walking on the water originally were Easter stories. In other words, they are attempts to put the Easter event into the picture.

As far as Jesus' healing activity and its distinctiveness is concerned, one has to take faith into account. The call for faith occurs in almost all the healing accounts. "Your faith has healed you," we read for instance in numerous such healing stories. In the final analysis this means that the miracle is accorded only to the believer. The unbeliever does not recognize the miracle. In Nazareth, Jesus refuses to work healings, or miracles, as the Gospels call them. And he does this because they did not believe in him. He could do no mighty work there, we are told in the sixth chapter of Mark's Gospel. Perhaps it is important as a criterion in evaluating these healings and so-called miracles of Jesus if we remember that, according to a fairly extensive Gospel tradition, the opponents of Jesus came to him to request a sign from heaven from him. This indicates quite clearly that the miracles Jesus accomplished were not sufficient. They wanted a sign that would remove any doubt and thereby dispense with faith. Jesus always rejected suggestions such as this because by means of his healings he intended to awaken faith in him and in his message.

Since it was a matter of faith, it is perhaps not proper to speak of obvious miracles, which suspend all laws of nature, but neither of deeds such as those accomplished by charismatic miracle workers and miracle healers of the time who were also around. Apparently miracles did not play a central part for Jesus.

Jesus' mighty works would certainly be misunderstood as miracles, for "miracle" would mean precisely what his opponents demanded, a sign that removes any doubt. For Jesus these mighty works need to be seen in the context of his proclamation of the kingdom of God. They are subordinate to his message. In the context of the message of the kingdom of God they also seek to make clear that Jesus' concern was to save the whole person, hence to include the person's physical existence in salvation. The salvation Jesus proclaimed does not focus on the soul only but on the person as a whole. Therefore the relationship between the proclamation of the kingdom of God and the healing activity needs to be considered, if we want to characterize his activity correctly, especially since this aspect of his ministry is perhaps no longer readily accessible to us.

Part of Jesus' message and ministry were his disciples and his special relationship to God, whom he calls Father.

Jesus was not satisfied with presenting his message merely to the people of Israel but also gathered a special group of disciples around him. There were disciples in contemporary Judaism as well. The rabbis had disciples, and so had the scribes. John the Baptist, too, gathered a band of disciples around him. That which was special and particular in Jesus' discipleship was especially the fact that, unlike the rabbis, his disciples did not choose their master but that conversely Jesus chose his disciples. Another contrast with discipleship in Judaism is that with the rabbis they learned the law. With Jesus they learned the Gospel. Of course in Judaism discipleship also meant that the disciple shared life with his master, entered life as a community with him. In the case of the rabbis this meant a limited time. In the case of Jesus discipleship was forever. Those who became his disciples remained such. For the disciple of Jesus, the long-term relationship also means sharing a common destiny, so the saying about following takes on special significance: "If any man would come after me, let him deny himself and take up his cross and follow me." Perhaps this understanding of discipleship is also important for us today because it opens up an aspect of being Christian that we may have forgotten, that as Christians we too are disciples of Jesus and remain Jesus' disciples, his pupils. This may also keep us from attributing to its origins a kind of Christianity that is perhaps too often legalistic and sometimes also rather superficial, a kind of Christianity that is too theoretical. Every genuine renewal of the church occurs in considering the source. And in my view the concept of the disciple, being a pupil of Jesus, is eminently significant.

The disciples probably also had particular expectations regarding the kingdom of God and also regarding the Messiah. Was Jesus himself convinced that he was now the Messiah or was he simply the one who made room for the revelation of God?

The disciples certainly had their biases in their conceptions and expectations. They were children of their time. That they misunderstood Jesus to the very end, at least in part, can be seen in that they denied and forsook him in the passion. Jesus did not explicitly speak of being the Messiah, but in my view his ministry can best be described by means of the category of his being the Messiah or of his ministry having messianic quality. I mentioned that the kingdom of God, the eschatological salvation, is bound up with his person. In his ethical preaching, for instance in his Sermon on the Mount, he interpreted the will of God in an ultimate way and brought it home to the people. He called disciples to follow him; he predicated the salvation of the person on faith in his message. This signals his consciousness of mission, which transcends that of the prophets, and this, I would say, is best described by means of the category of the messianic. His messianic consciousness of mission, if we may call it that, has two peculiar features, of course. The first one is that he is a Messiah who has to suffer and who is going to the cross. And for the Jewish people this was the great offense that he precipitated. The other is that as the one bringing the kingdom of God, who reveals God, he was in a very special, hitherto unprecedented, relationship with God. And in this way, I would argue, the designation of Jesus as the Son of God is able to define and describe his mission in a very characteristic and special way.

Messiah means Christ, the Anointed One. What I consider interesting is that Jesus did not just take up the truly virulent messianic expectations of the time, which were political. Apparently he stood for something else.

Apparently the political liberation of Israel was not part of his agenda. In this respect he perhaps was misunderstood quite often. Especially in exegetical scholarship, his final days were sometimes interpreted in this way. There is the zealot interpretation of Jesus, which is connected with Jesus' entry into the city of Jerusalem, where he is hailed as king by the crowds.

But Jesus rejected a political agenda; the kingdom he proclaimed was indeed a kingdom, an order, that will reach into this world, but he did not want to appear as a military Messiah who took it upon himself, for instance, to drive the Romans out of the country. His salvation was from God and focused on the ultimate aspects of the person.

And then Jesus went up to Jerusalem in order to suffer and die. What can we say today about this passion and this death, which was preceded by a trial?

To begin with, I would like to say that Jesus was surely filled with the consciousness that what awaited him in Jerusalem was a tragic destiny, namely, death. That he was surprised by his death in Jerusalem, as has occasionally been argued by hypercriticism, does not agree at all with the historical facts. Hence he was prepared to die. There was a conflict that reached way back into his ministry. It was caused by his critique of traditional piety, of those who were considered the country's models of piety. For this reason he does not arrive in Jerusalem as an unknown. It is possible that during his public ministry he appears in Jerusalem only once, namely, in conjunction with his death. Presumably he linked his appearance in Jerusalem with the intention of confronting the people of Israel with his message in this decisive location, in the holy city. And he was rejected. What finally set off the authorities, including the Roman authorities, to take action against him may have been his temple protest, that he dared to intervene in the temple enterprise. For it was not only the Jews, especially the Sadducees, the circles of the high priest, who regarded the temple as the center of Israelite piety; it was also the Romans, as the occupying power, who generally respected the deities of the nations they subjected and hence also revered Yahweh and respected the temple. In the temple, daily prayers were offered for the Romans, so that when Jesus acted in this way against the temple, they found it necessary to support the instigation of the high-priestly circles to arrest Jesus.

His death surely was a shock for the disciples. And from the Gospels we learn that they virtually scattered in all directions, that women followed him, and that they were also the first ones to be linked with the event of the resurrection. Perhaps we could address this experience of the disciples, the loss and then also the message of the resurrection a little more.

The disciples did indeed fail at the passion of Jesus. They fled; I would even argue that they returned to Galilee, their home. This means that on the whole they actually did not expect anything more of Jesus, nor did they after his crucifixion. The women stood the test. And now we are talking about Jesus having been raised from the dead on the third day, and this as the central affirmation of our faith, which goes back to the apostles. From a historical aspect we actually arrive only at the point of the disciples' faith. The apostles were the first to come to this faith and they said that they had seen Jesus. The risen one showed himself as the living one among them.

When we believe in the resurrection of Jesus from the dead, we believe the apostles' faith, we adopt their faith. In the final analysis this makes for the apostolicity of our church. One of the very important witnesses of this Easter faith, for the resurrection of Jesus from the dead, is Paul, who expresses himself in the New Testament as one who is directly involved. And so concerning this experience he says in the first chapter of the letter to the Galatians that "God was pleased to reveal his Son in me." The Easter narratives themselves, the stories of the appearances of Jesus, are now trying to express the inexpressible, to bring into the picture what has taken place here. It is an otherworldly event. But ultimately it is an event that we are able to adopt only by faith as the foundation of being Christian, in continuation with the faith of the apostles.

And the issue of the empty tomb actually aims past this message of the living Jesus Christ?

The empty tomb is not the causal element for the Easter faith. The causal element is the encounter of the risen one with his chosen witnesses. In this case the tomb of Jesus is, as it has once been formulated, joined to the resurrection faith as the victory trophy, as it were. Yet the empty tomb or the tomb of Jesus can also be misinterpreted, as we learn from the New Testament already, for instance in the hypothesis of the theft of Jesus' body that existed even then. This hypothesis continues even into our time, and recent books on Jesus are taking it up again. What is basic, then, is the attestation by chosen witnesses that the resurrected one is alive.

Luke tells of the ascension from the Mount of Olives, and from the history of religions we know of other ascension stories. I think it is interesting that the cloud is included in this Lukan narrative, since in the Old Testament it is a symbol for the glory of the Lord. What can we say about the ascension today?

The ascension is a story that we can read only in Luke and Acts in the New Testament. It represents the attempt to put a theological statement in narrative form. We may not think of the ascension as if someone had literally seen, on the Mount of Olives, how Jesus rose and was taken up into heaven. The purpose of the ascension is to express that the disciples' encounter with the risen one had come to an end. In this context Luke also refers to the forty days. If the ascension were to be understood literally, it would also have to be assumed that the resurrected Jesus came back into earthly existence. But this was not the case.

He came from eternity. "Was it not necessary that the Christ should suffer these things and enter into his glory?" This means that he becomes visible from the perspective of this glory. The Mount of Olives is the site of the "ascension" of Jesus and this then is also linked in some way with the expectation of his return. The earliest communities in part were filled with the idea that the return of Jesus was not very distant. "Men of Galilee, why do you stand looking into heaven? This Jesus . . . will come in the same way," we are told. The Mount of Olives was considered the place where the final judgment will be held. And here the cloud which you mentioned will be significant as well. The cloud is the sign of the presence of God.

Did Jesus intend the church?

This is a much debated question. There is the famous dictum of Alfred Loisy that Jesus proclaimed the kingdom of God, but what came about was the church. But things were not quite that simple. I have already mentioned that Jesus was aware of his call to the people of Israel. To begin with, his thoughts did not transcend the boundaries of the people of Israel. But neither did he only address individuals. When he addressed individuals among the people, he did so as members of this chosen people of God. It could be said, if you wish, that Israel was the church of the time of Jesus. But when it became apparent, both in the period of Jesus' ministry and later in the ministry of the apostles, that Israel refused to accept the Gospel, a new situation was given, and the apostles turned to the non-Jews, to the Gentiles. This is how the church came about. For me the continuity between the time of Jesus and the time of the church consists also of the fact that those who walked with Jesus were the same ones who in the post-Easter situation built the church, the community.

And how is it with the sacraments? Did Jesus establish the sacraments?

The most important sacrament that Jesus left is the Eucharist. Together with his disciples he celebrated a Passover meal in the final night before his death. And in this celebration he gave a special gift. He offered them bread and the cup of wine. It is not all that simple to reconstruct the words that he spoke on that occasion. But from these words, which in my opinion can be reconstructed, it follows that he understood his death as salvific and that he also wanted this meal to be observed in the future, in remembrance of his death and in anticipation of his return. In the Gospels the sacrament of baptism is attested as established by the resurrected Lord. Here we are pointed in the direction of the Easter situation. The sacraments are associated with the Holy Spirit, who was not sent until after Easter, so that the other sacraments have to be located in this post-Easter situation. The baptismal command in Matthew 28 is given by the resurrected one: "Go therefore and make disciples of all nations, baptizing them . . ." The mediation of the Spirit was linked with baptism. Therefore the linking of baptism and Spirit, that is, the giving of the Spirit as a sacrament of its own, is a later development. The essential sacraments, baptism and Eucharist, are bound up with Jesus, even if in part with the post-Easter Jesus.

Perhaps we can now return again to the initial question concerning the specific nature of the New Testament texts and witnesses. This is actually the pathway on which Jesus comes to us and the pathway on which we come to him.

Surely studying the Gospel means the possibility of coming to know Jesus, becoming his pupil. This is the concern of the Gospels, not merely to recall historical features but primarily to bring people into relationship with the living Christ; so that the reader of a Gospel such as this will think, "I am not dealing with historical, dead material of the past, but here I am encountering the one of whom I know by faith that he is alive, that he speaks to my life, and that he is at work in the church."

Bibliography

Abel, F. M. *Géographie de la Palestine.* 2 vols. 3d ed. Paris: J. Gabalda, 1967.

Bauer, W., W. F. Arndt, F. W. Gingrich, and F. W. Danker. *Greek-English Lexicon of the New Testament and Other Early Christian Literature.* ET. 2d ed. Chicago: University of Chicago, 1979.

Becker, J. *Johannes der Täufer und Jesus von Nazaret.* BibS(N) 63. Neukirchen: Neukirchener, 1972.

Berger, K. *Die Gesetzesauslegung Jesu* I. WMANT 40. Neukirchen: Neukirchner, 1972.

Billerbeck, P. and H. Strack. *Kommentar zum Neuen Testament aus Talmud und Midrasch.* 6 vols. Munich: Beck, 1926–61.

Blank, J. *Jesus von Nazaret.* Freiburg: Herder, 1972.

Blass, F., A. Debrunner, and R. W. Funk. *A Greek Grammar of the New Testament.* ET. Chicago: University of Chicago, 1961.

Bornkamm, G. *Jesus of Nazareth.* ET. 3d ed. London: Hodder & Stoughton, 1969.

Braun, H. *Jesus of Nazareth: The Man and His Time.* ET. Philadelphia: Fortress, 1979.

————. *Spätjüdisch-häretischer und frühchristlicher Radikalismus.* 2 vols. 2d ed. BHT 24. Tübingen: Mohr-Siebeck, 1969.

Bultmann, R. *Jesus and the Word.* ET. New York: Scribners, 1958.

————. *The Gospel According to John.* ET. Philadelphia: Westminster, 1971.

————. *History of the Synoptic Tradition.* ET. 1963. Reprint. Peabody, Mass.: Hendrickson, 1992.

————. *Theology of the New Testament.* ET. 2 vols. New York: Scribners, 1953.

Conzelmann, H. *An Outline of the Theology of the New Testament.* ET. London: SCM, 1969.

Dalman, G. *Arbeit und Sitte in Palästina.* 7 vols. 1928–. Reprint. 2d ed. Hildesheim, 1987.

————. *Jesus-Jeshua.* ET. London: SPCK, 1929.

————. *Orte und Wege Jesu.* 3d ed. Gütersloh: Bertelmann, 1924.

————. *The Words of Jesus.* ET. 2d ed. Edinburgh: T. & T. Clark, 1902.

Dautzenberg, G. *Sein Leben bewahren*. SANT 14. Munich: Kösel, 1966.

Dibelius, M. *From Tradition to Gospel*. ET. New York: Scribners, 1934.

————. *Jesus*. ET. Philadelphia: Westminster, 1949.

Fiedler, P. *Jesus und die Sünder*. BBET 3. Frankfurt, 1976.

Fitzmyer, J. A. *The Gospel According to Luke*. 2 vols. AB. New York: Doubleday, 1981, 1985.

Flusser, D. *Jesus in Selbstzeugnissen und Bilddokumenten*. RoMo 140. Hamburg: Rowolt, 1968.

Frankemölle, H. *Jahwe-Bund und Kirche Christi*. NTA 10. 2d ed. Münster, 1984.

Fuchs, E. *Studies of the Historical Jesus*. SBT 42. London: SCM, 1964.

Gnilka, J. *Das Evangelium nach Markus*. 2 vols. EKK. 3d ed. Zurich: Benzinger, 1989.

————. *Das Matthäusevangelium*. 2 vols. HTKNT. 2d ed. Freiburg: Herder, 1992.

Goppelt, L. *Theology of the New Testament*. 2 vols. ET. Grand Rapids: Eerdmans, 1981.

Grässer, E. *Das Problem der Parusieverzögerung in den synoptischen Evangelien und in der Apostelgeschichte*. BZNW 22. 2d ed. Berlin, 1960.

Grundmann, W. *Das Evangelium nach Lukas*. THKNT 3. Berlin: Evangelische Verlagsanstalt, n.d.

Haenchen, W. *Der Weg Jesu*. STö.H 6. Berlin: Töpelmann, 1966.

Hahn, F. *The Titles of Jesus in Christology*. ET. London: Lutterworth, 1969.

Harnisch, W. *Gleichniserzählungen Jesu*. UTB 1343. Göttingen: Vandenhoeck & Ruprecht, 1985.

Heininger, B. *Metaphorik, Erzählstruktur und szenisch-dramaturgische Gestaltung in den Sondergutgleichnissen bei Lukas*. NTA 24. Münster: Aschendorff, 1991.

Heiler, F. *Die Religionen der Menschheit*. 2d ed. Stuttgart: Kohlhammer, 1962.

Hengel, M. *Judaism and Hellenism*. ET. Philadelphia: Fortress, 1974.

————. *The Charismatic Leader and His Followers*. ET. Edinburgh: T. & T. Clark, 1981.

Hoffmann, P. *Studien zur Theologie der Logienquelle*. NTA 8. 3d ed. Münster: Aschendorff, 1982.

Hoffmann, P., and V. Eid. *Jesus von Nazareth und eine christliche Moral*. QD 66. 3d ed. Freiburg: Herder, 1979.

Jaspers, K. *Die massgebenden Menschen*. Serie Piper 126. 10th ed. Munich: R. Piper, 1988.

Jeremias, J. *The Parables of Jesus*. ET. 2d rev. ed. London: SCM, 1972.

————. *Jerusalem in the Time of Jesus*. ET. Philadelphia: Fortress, 1969.

————. *New Testament Theology I. The Proclamation of Jesus*. ET. New York: Scribners, 1971.

Jülicher, A. *Die Gleichnisreden Jesu*. 2d ed. Tübingen: Mohr, 1910.

Jüngel, E. *Paulus und Jesus*. HUT 2. 2d ed. Tübingen: Mohr, 1964.

Kee, H. C. *Jesus in History*. New York: Harcourt Brace & World, 1970.

Kierkegaard, S. *Einübung im Christentum und anderes*. Cologne: J. Hegner, 1951.

Kittel, G. and G. Friedrich, eds. *Theological Dictionary of the New Testament*. 10 vols. Trans. G. Bromiley. Grand Rapids: Eerdmans, 1964–76.

Klauck, H. J. *Allegorie und Allegorese in synoptischen Gleichnissen*. NTA 13. 2d ed. Münster: Aschendorff, 1986.

Klausner, J. *Jesus of Nazareth*. ET. New York: Macmillan, 1929.

Klostermann, F. *Das Markus-Evangelium*. HNT 3. 4th ed. Tübingen: Mohr, 1950.

Kopp, C. *Die heiligen Stätten der Evangelien*. Regensburg: F. Pustet, 1959.

Kümmel, W. G. *Promise and Fulfillment*. ET. London: SCM, 1961.

Linnemann, E. *Jesus of the Parables*. ET. New York: Harper & Row, 1966.

Lührmann, D. *Die Redaktion der Logienquelle*. WMANT 33. Neukirchen: Neukirchener, 1969.

Luz, U. *Das Evangelium nach Matthäus* I. EKK. 2d ed. Zurich: Benziger, 1989.

Merklein, H. *Die Gottesherrschaft als Handlungsprinzip*. FB 34. 2d ed. Würzburg: Echter, 1981.

Meyer, E. *Ursprung und Anfänge des Urchristentum* I/II. 3d ed. Stuttgart: J. G. Cotta, 1921.

Mitteis, L., and U. Wilcken. *Grundzüge und Chrestomathie der Papyruskunde*. 2 vols. Leipzig, 1912. Reprint. Hildesheim: Olms, 1963.

Passow, F. *Handwörterbuch der griechischen Sprache*. 2 vols. Leipzig, 1841–. Reprint. 5th ed. Darmstadt: Wissenschaftliche Buchgesellschaft, 1970.

Perrin, N. *Rediscovering the Teaching of Jesus*. London: SCM, 1967.

_____. *The Kingdom of God and the Teaching of Jesus*. London: SCM, 1963.

Pesch, R. *Das Markusevangelium*. 2 vols. HTKNT. Freiburg: Herder, 1976–77.

Preisigke, F. and E. Kiessling. *Wörterbuch der griechischen Papyruskunde*. 3 vols. Berlin: self-published, 1925–31; vol. 4, Amsterdam: A. M. Hakkert, 1969.

Reiser, M. *Die Gerichtspredigt Jesu*. NTA 23. Münster: Aschendorff, 1990.

Reumann, J. *Jesus in the Church's Gospels*. Philadelphia: Fortress, 1970.

Riesner, R. *Jesus als Lehrer*. WUNT II/7. 2d ed. Tübingen: Mohr, 1984.

Roloff, J. *Das Kerygma und der irdische Jesus*. Göttingen: Vandenhoeck & Ruprecht, 1970.

Schäfer, R. *Jesus und der Gottesglaube*. Tübingen, 1970.

Schlosser, J. *Le règne de Dieu dans les dits de Jésus*. 2 vols. EB. Paris: J. Gabalda, 1980.

Schnackenburg, R. *Gottes Herrschaft und Reich*. 3d ed. Freiburg: Herder, 1963.

_____. *Die sittliche Botschaft des Neuen Testaments* I. Freiburg: Herder, 1986.

Schmidt, K. L. *Der Rahmen der Geschichte Jesu*. Berlin: Karl Ludwig, 1919.

Schneider, G. *Das Evangelium nach Lukas*. 2 vols., 2d ed.; Gütersloh: Mohn, 1984.

Schrage, W. *Ethics of the New Testament*. ET. Philadelphia: Fortress, 1988.

Schürmann, H. "Die vorösterlichen Anfänge der Logientradition." In *Der historische und der kerygmatische Christus*. 2d ed. Ed. by H. Ristow and K. Matthiae. Pages 342–70. Berlin: Evangelische Verlagsanstalt, 1964.

_____. *Das Lukasevangelium* I. HTKNT. 2d ed. Freiburg: Herder, 1982.

Schürer, E. *History of the Jewish People in the Time of Jesus Christ*. ET. Edinburgh: T. & T. Clark, 1973–86.

Schulz, S. *Q. Die Spruchquelle der Evangelisten*. Zurich: Theologischer Verlag, 1972.

Schwarz, G. *"Und Jesus sprach." Untersuchungen zur aramäischen Urgestalt der Worte Jesus*. BWANT VI/18. Stuttgart: Kohlhammer, 1985.

Theissen, G. *Studien zur Soziologie des Urchristentums*. WUNT 19. Tübingen: Mohr, 1979.

_____. *Miracle Stories in the Early Christian Tradition*. ET. Edinburgh: T. & T. Clark, 1983.

Trautmann, M. *Zeichenhafte Handlungen Jesu*. FB 37. Würzburg: Echter, 1980.

Via, D. O. *The Parables: Their Literary and Existential Dimensions*. Philadelphia: Fortress, 1967.

Volz, P. *Die Eschatologie der jüdischen Gemeinde im neutestamentlichen Zeitalter*. 2d ed. Tübingen: Mohr, 1934.

Weder, H. *Die Gleichnisse Jesu als Metaphern*. FRLANT 120. Göttingen: Vandenhoeck & Ruprecht, 1978.

Index of Modern Authors

Scripture Index

New Testament